AF378734

Freud and Society

International Library of Group Psychotherapy
and Group Process

General Editors

Dr Malcolm Pines
Institute of Group Analysis (London) and the Tavistock Clinic,
London

Dr Earl Hopper
Institute of Group Analysis (London) and the London School
of Economics and Political Science

The International Library of Group Psychotherapy and Group
Process is published in association with the Institute of Group
Analysis (London) and is devoted to the systematic study and
exploration of group psychotherapy.

Freud and Society

Yiannis Gabriel

ROUTLEDGE & KEGAN PAUL
London, Boston, Melbourne and Henley

First published in 1983
by Routledge & Kegan Paul plc
39 Store Street, London WC1E 7DD,
9 Park Street, Boston, Mass. 02108, USA,
296 Beaconsfield Parade, Middle Park,
Melbourne, 3206, Australia, and
Broadway House, Newtown Road,
Henley-on-Thames, Oxon RG9 1EN

Printed in Great Britain by
T.J. Press (Padstow) Ltd., Padstow, Cornwall
© Yiannis Gabriel 1983
No part of this book may be reproduced in
any form without permission from the
publisher, except for the quotation of brief
passages in criticism

Library of Congress Cataloging in Publication Data

Gabriel, Yiannis, 1952–
Freud and society.
(The International library of group psychotherapy
and group process)
Bibliography: p.
Includes index.
1. Freud, Sigmund, 1856-1939 — Political and social
views. 2. Psychoanalysis — Social aspects. I. Title.
II. Series.
BF173.F85G3 1983   150.19'52   82-25061

ISBN 0-7100-9410-8

Contents

Acknowledgments

I am indebted to many friends who have helped me with ideas and critical comments; I wish to thank them all, especially Larry Rosenthal and Tim Lang. I also wish to thank Professor Blauner for his support and critical feedback. Professor Neil J. Smelser has given me the most constructive advice and constant encouragement for the past three years and it is to him that I owe the greatest thanks. I also wish to thank the editors of the present series Dr Malcolm Pines and Dr Earl Hopper for their considerable assistance. Finally, I must acknowledge the deep influence of the teaching of the late Professor Gertrude Jaeger, whose classes on Freud in 1975 were the original source of inspiration for this work.

The author and publishers are grateful to the following for permission to reprint copyright material: Beacon Press, Boston, for excerpts from 'Negations' and 'One Dimensional Man', both by H. Marcuse; Faber and Faber Ltd and Harcourt Brace Jovanovich, Inc. for extracts from 'The Cocktail Party' by T.S. Eliot; Heinemann Educational Books for extracts from 'Knowledge and Human Interests' and 'Theory and Practice', both by J. Habermas; Sigmund Freud Copyrights Ltd, the Institute of Psycho-Analysis and The Hogarth Press for quotations from the Standard Edition of the Complete Psychological Works of Sigmund Freud, translated and edited by James Strachey; Tavistock Publications Ltd for extracts from 'Madness and Civilization' and 'The Order of Things', both by M. Foucault; Weslyan University Press for extracts from 'Life against Death' by Norman O. Brown.

Introduction

Freud is one of those very few thinkers who have definitely and
irreversibly changed the way we think about the world and
about ourselves. His two major discoveries have received considerable recognition and having become part of our common
sense they appear much less shocking than when they were
first made. On the one hand, the view of sexuality as a complex
and multi-faceted motivational force, which goes far beyond
sexual intercourse; on the other, the theory of repression of
painful desires and ideas into regions of the mind which are not
accessible to memory or consciousness, the regions of the unconscious. A radically new picture of man has started to emerge
from these ideas, a view of man as desiring and yet frustrated,
as moral and yet aggressive, as rational and yet deluded, as
noble and yet base.

Freud's impact upon our age and his influence on the wider
public, however, do not stem from his ideas regarding psychic
conflict and concealed meanings in people's actions, but from the
enormous attraction of psychoanalysis and its therapeutic off-
shoots as methods of dealing with the individuals' everyday problems, anxieties and discontents. In this way, therapy appeared
to fulfil a very deep need of twentieth-century man, living in
the impersonal cities of industrial societies, for intimacy and
support. The pronounced impact of Freudian thought on Western
and especially American culture was generally due to its therapeutic promises rather than to its theoretical formulations; how
else could the land of incurable, forward-looking optimists have
embraced a deeply pessimistic doctrine of humanity, which aims
at demonstrating the stifling weight of the past over the present
and which destroys some of its most precious ideals, like
morality, altruism, religion and even the refreshing innocence
of children? The adoption of psychoanalysis by American culture,
like that of other immigrants, was accomplished only after considerable dues had been paid. Many of Freud's key ideas were
distorted beyond recognition, stripped of their disturbing
associations, to generate an optimistic and efficient clinical
psychology; concepts with a critical edge, like desire, repression
and discontent, were smoothed over or eased out to allow for
the domination of a vocabulary of authenticity.

During the same period, psychoanalysis and its therapeutic
off-shoots were becoming useful parts of an ever-expanding network of therapeutic institutions of social control based on professional power, and tended to forget the original promises in

the interest of the adjustment of the deviant.

Many of the distortions which resulted from the acculturation of psycho-analysis and the therapeutic pragmatism which accompanied its submission to the expediences of social control filtered through into the world of academia, and seriously affected its position within the modern 'human sciences'. Most of these sciences, in fact, steered clear of psychoanalysis; psychology has shown a cautious interest in Freud's theory of 'personality development' and learning, while sociology has approved of the concept of the super-ego as a measure of the internalization of social norms. Yet Freud's bold formulations on the unconscious, on repression and on symbolism as well as his detailed discussions of culture, art, religion and morality have largely been ignored. Although many social scientists may recognize Freud's discoveries as significant advances in our knowledge of man, they have remained largely uninfluenced by these discoveries. The neglect of Freud's work has been compounded by the institutionalization of psychoanalysis as a closed discipline appended to psychiatry, and by the hostile reception that it faced from philosophy. Philosophy of science has generally refused to recognize psychoanalysis as a science, on account of criteria like falsifiability, operationalization and measurement as well as a basic disapproval of the use of interpretation in dealing with 'behavioural data'. On the other hand, philosophy of mind reacted with great hostility to Freud's formulations of the unconscious, as an area of the mind whose contents and processes are not open to introspection. As Chomsky has argued, the unconscious presented both rationalist and empiricist traditions with a challenge that was easier to isolate and repress than to confront.

Yet, it is precisely through the concept of the unconscious that psychoanalysis places itself in the same theoretical space as other human sciences of today, and becomes both their guide and their servant. Without this concept, most contemporary human sciences would lack foundations, for in their efforts to unveil 'ideologies', 'social norms', 'linguistic structures' and 'psychological needs' they are constantly pursuing that implicit knowledge within which human action unfolds, and yet which does not form part of consciousness. Foucault is, therefore, not exaggerating when he argues that

> the problem of the unconscious – its possibility, status, mode of existence, the means of knowing it and bringing it to light – is not simply a problem within the human sciences which they can be thought of as encountering by chance in their steps; it is a problem that is ultimately coextensive with their very existence. . . . [An] unveiling of the non-conscious is constitutive of all the sciences of man. (1970:364)

While, however, Freud confronted the unconscious directly especially in its psychological mode, much of contemporary social science has approached it hesitantly, tangentially, almost

unwittingly. One of the aims of this work will be to confront it in
its centrality within social theory, rather than as an assumption
about homo sociologicus.

What is perhaps even more surprising is the contrast between
the general image of man which emerges from Freud and the
one presented by most human sciences of today; for there is
very little room in these sciences for the powerful sensuous
desires and the violent aggressive impulses which are not only
central in the Freudian view of man but are gradually becoming
part of our common-sense view of ourselves. By contrast, the
realms of these sciences are usually inhabited by individuals
playing their roles, performing their functions, organizing their
experiences but lacking emotions and passions, desires and
aggression, frustrations and discontents. It is almost as if the
Freudian man had been accepted as a vivid and intriguing
image, yet ultimately irrelevant to the human sciences.

There are at least two reasons which account for this neglect
of Freud's work by the human sciences and in particular the
social sciences. One reason is that Freud's theory and his concept of the unconscious in particular are seen as essentially
psychological, describing the intricacies of individual mental
processes, and therefore only peripheral to sociology. This stems
from a rather rigid distinction of individual and society along
disciplinary lines, a distinction which will be challenged, since
a close reading of Freud's views precludes not only the hypo-
statization of the individual as self, will or subject, but also
the reification of social reality as an external other, a constraint
or an object.

More generally this is a study of the possibilities opened for
social theory by psychoanalytic discourse, clarifying some of the
numerous difficulties, problems and even contradictions inherent
in Freud's work, as well as some of the standard misconceptions;
its argument is motivated by the conviction that psychoanalysis
is not only an important part of the American cultural fabric
(what some may call 'ideology'), but also a powerful instrument
for understanding society and evaluating its accomplishments
and discontents. And we come here to the second reason which
has mitigated the enthusiasm of the human sciences for psychoanalysis - its critical content. For as we shall see in Part I of
this book, psychoanalysis does not only stand squarely in the
middle of most classical and contemporary debates on man (body/
mind, social/anti-social, rational/emotive, etc.) but it also seeks
to re-introduce in the modern sciences a critical dimension
bridging the distance between the domain of 'is' and the domain
of 'ought to be' - a dimension which has tended to disappear
with the domination of positivism.

Freud's investigations led him to a view of man as a socially
repressed and self-repressing animal, an animal who represses
his innermost desires to the unconscious regions of his mind,
because he cannot tolerate the pain which would result from their
non-gratification, and an animal who seeks consolation from the

miseries of life in socially sponsored illusions. This view leads
Freud naturally to confront two related aspects of the human
predicament, discontents and illusions; according to his theory
not only is man systematically denied gratification but his consciousness is systematically distorted in his efforts to create
substitute satisfactions. Discontents and illusions are thus
locked in a vicious circle - illusions deepen the discontent which
they purport to relieve. But by emphasizing the distance on
the one hand between unconscious desires and their conscious
counterparts, and on the other between unconscious desires and
the limited possibilities of gratification, Freud's theory constantly stretches beyond the realm of description of social
reality, towards a vision of a social reality based on fulfilment
and self-understanding. Thus Freud's theory, by its very
nature, pushed him beyond the tight constraints of positivism,
which was so dear to him; as his attitude towards discontents
and illusions could not remain purely descriptive there are in
his work utopian seeds of emancipation and demystification,
which demand to be considered seriously.

This book will seek to vindicate Freud's pre-occupation with
illusions and discontents as basic concerns for all the human
sciences. Its purpose is not just to introduce psychoanalysis
in the human sciences and to examine the products of their
cross-fertilization, but to restore the quest not only for truth
but also for happiness as legitimate goals of science. To direct
this critical endeavour, I have selected six inter-related organizing themes or problematics, which not only connect psychoanalysis with other major schools of thought, but have also
been addressed by many commentators. These are six extremely
dense and rich areas in Freud's work, which frequently allow
for diametrically different interpretative possibilities. In this
way, Part I will introduce some of the central ideas and concepts
of psychoanalysis, like the instincts, the ego/id/super-ego
topography of the mind, the theories of sublimation, repression
and the unconscious, the formative process of childhood and the
relationship between individual and society, trying to preserve
the ambiguities and highlight the tensions in Freud's arguments.
It is by understanding difficulties of this kind rather than by-
passing them that the discussion of psychoanalytic ideas can
maintain the dynamism that it enjoyed during the lifetime of its
originator.

The conflict between individual desires and the requirements
of culture is examined in detail in Chapter 2, but dominates
much of the discussion in Part I. This discussion stays fairly
close to Freud's own discourse and does not address the specific
requirements of particular historical epochs, their special brands
of discontents and illusions and their special varieties of consolations. Over and above these particularities, Freud was
impressed by the universal character of the human predicament
and did not mobilize his psychoanalytic insights for a systematic
study of particular historical epochs and (with few notable excep-

tions) specific cultural phenomena. This will be the main task
in Part II, which develops a new interpretative and analytic
approach for some crucial cultural and social phenomena of the
twentieth century; fascism, the rapid expansion of bureaucratic
organizations, and the increasing popularity of psychoanalytic
and other therapies are among the phenomena which will be considered.

Of course, this is not the first attempt to develop the possibilities offered by Freudian discourse to social theory and to the
theory of contemporary societies in particular. While there has
been no paradigmatic way of 'integrating' psychoanalysis with
any of the other human sciences, there have been a series of
attempts to use some of Freud's ideas to enrich and extend existing traditions. There have also been attempts to criticize Freud
and sort out the lasting elements of his contributions from those
influenced by his 'idiosyncrasies' and the distorting lenses of
his male-dominated Viennese background. Finally, there have
been attempts to confront psychoanalysis with other systematic
doctrines in the human sciences, especially existentialism,
structural-functionalism and Marxism. Some of these attempts
will be discussed in Part II, hoping to draw from their insights
and learn from their mistakes. All these attempts will be found
to be defective in that they isolate particular aspects of
psychoanalysis, make them independent from the rest of the
Freudian discourse, and raise them conveniently to the status of
received and unproblematic truths. My approach towards these
interpretations will be very critical - my aim is in part to vindicate Freud from some of the theoretical misinterpretations and
one-sided readings which fuel the popular distortions of his
work. Chapters 12 and 13 draw from earlier discussions in
bringing together the central elements of a psychoanalytic study
of contemporary culture and develop the outline of a novel interpretation of some prominent contemporary social phenomena.
Although this outline is based on earlier arguments, it is by
necessity sketchy and speculative; its general tenor is that
although contemporary culture builds its social fabric on signifi-
cantly different psychic foundations from the ones studied by
Freud, de-sexualized love and guilt, it nevertheless generates
its own sets of discontents and illusions, which are easier neither
to bear nor to overcome.

A final comment. Although this work is undoubtedly a theoretical one and relies to a large extent on contrasting different
approaches and interpretations, it is ultimately a work 'about
the world', not a work 'about theories' - an impression which
will come across clearly as the reader gets to Part II. Nor is it
a passive contemplative description of the world, for such an
attitude would be quite incompatible with the restless activism
and persistent criticism in Freud's work, which constantly
counterposes the actual with the possible. Reading some of the
recent literature of psychoanalysis (often in conjunction with a
critical Marxist tradition), one may be struck by the degree of

detachment of the theoretical (and 'metatheoretical') from the historical discourse. Such approaches neglect the overwhelming feature of both Freudian and Marxist discourses – they are both concerned with real struggles of real people in real historical situations pointing at real historical possibilities. A 'theoretical marriage' of Marx and Freud which limits itself to the realm of ideas, without shedding light on our understanding of the world and the potential for change, is bound to remain sterile.

Part I

There are more things in heaven and earth, Horatio,
Than are dreamt of in your philosophy.

Shakespeare

Chapter 1
Body and mind

To the uninitiated, the emphasis that Freud, the 'father of depth
psychology', placed on the instincts may come as a surprise. We
usually associate instincts with the animal and biological aspects
of our nature, rather than with the deeper and darker precincts
of our souls. Time and again Freud asserts that 'instincts rule
not only mental but also vegetative life' (1933a:22:106) and that
'instincts are the ultimate cause of all activity' (1940a:23:148).
Yet, Freud's position on the mind–body problem could not be
more different than that of the 'physical monists'; unlike in
animals, instincts are not directly manifested in human behaviour
but 'represent the somatic demands upon the mind' (ibid.).[1]
Between the instinctual demand and the course of action to which
it leads, Freud interposes his psychology. Although instincts,
and especially instinctual energy, may be the primum mobile of
human life (as of animal life in general), instincts would be blind,
deaf and mute without the intervention of the mind. The mind
receives instinctual stimuli from within just as it receives sense
stimuli from outside; it decodes instinctual stimuli, it articulates
them in verbal forms, it manipulates them consciously and unconsciously, it attaches them to appropriate objects of the external
world, it tames them and civilizes them, it renders them compatible with the demands of the outer world, and, finally, it
seeks to satisfy them. Far from being the loyal and blind servant of instinctual impulses, or an automatism linking instinctual
stimuli with the organism's response, the mind shapes and transforms the stimuli and puts its own ineffaceable stamp on human
activity. Somatic and psychological factors often find themselves
in contradiction to each other, in Freud's theory – the instincts
are often opposed to and frustrated by mental agencies, and
especially by that agency known as the ego.

The relative emphasis placed by psychoanalysis on the ego
and the instincts, the mental and the somatic factor, is a matter
of considerable controversy. Is Freud to be seen ultimately as a
materialist for whom mental and social lives proceed primarily
from organic sources (Reich, Wollheim), even if frustration of
these forces has come to constitute the very essence of civilized
man (Brown, Marcuse)? Or is he primarily a symbolic or indeed
moral thinker (Rieff), for whom the somatic demands can only
be articulated through the language of desire (Lacan, Habermas),
and who sees mental and social life as conditioned by the early
confrontation between the child and social reality (Parsons,
'ego psychologists')?

Many disagreements about Freud arise from this central difference of interpretation, which has rarely been addressed explicitly.
As we shall see in the remaining chapters of Part I, the positions
taken by different commentators on all main problematics are
related to their respective positions on the problematic of body
and mind, matter and spirit. It would, therefore, appear promising to start our examination of this problematic with a consideration of Freud's views on the main concepts which dominate the
horizon – the instincts and the ego.

As we saw, the mental apparatus, in Freud's conception,
receives stimuli both from the outer world and from within the
organism itself.[2] Stimuli originating from within are said to have
an instinctual origin; unlike external stimuli which act as a
single impact and can be avoided through flight, instinctual
stimuli operate as 'a constant force' – they act as needs which
require satisfaction (1915c:14:118-19). This presents us with
the danger of improvising an infinity of ad hoc instincts, each
corresponding to every need we experience.

> People assume as many and as various instincts as they happen
> to need at the moment – a self-assertive instinct, an imitative
> instinct, an instinct of play, a gregarious instinct and many
> others like them. (1933a:22:95)

Freud realized that such ad hoc theorizing, which reduces all
mental events to as many instincts, is not only devoid of any
explanatory power, but leads to contradictory and absurd conclusions – an individual, for instance, may be said to have both
a gregarious and a privacy instinct, depending on his/her mood.
So Freud argues that various component instincts can be traced
to a few basic ones; originally, he argued that all instinctual
impulses can be seen as vicissitudes or combinations of love and
self-preservation; he later modified this view in favour of the
dualism of object-love and ego-love, and this in turn gave way
to the final dualism of Eros and Thanatos, life and death
instincts.

The question now arises of how the various component instincts
can be derived from the principal ones; how can we study the
vicissitudes of instincts? Freud's model treatment of this issue
is his discussion of sexuality in 'Three Essays on the Theory of
Sexuality'. In this work, Freud distinguishes between the object
of sexuality from which attraction emanates, its aim, i.e. the
sexual act through which it seeks satisfaction, and its source,
that is the region of the body through which the sexual excitation is experienced. Through a detailed examination of perversions (or 'sexual aberrations'), Freud tries to show that both
the object and the aim of sexuality may vary, contrary to popular
misconceptions of his time. Freud suggested that there is no
sharp distinction between normal and pathological manifestations
of sexuality, since sexuality accepted as normal comprises many
component instincts which are characteristic of perversions – all

these component instincts, present in different degrees in both
'normal' and 'perverse' sexuality, are but different manifestations
of a single psychic quantity, the libido, whose aims and objects
may vary.

> Libido is a term used in the theory of instincts for describing
> the dynamic manifestation of sexuality. (1923a:18:255)

The movements of libido, therefore, represent fluctuations of
instinctual excitations; increases of such excitations are experienced by the mental apparatus as unpleasurable, and as there
is no possibility of avoiding them through flight, the mental
apparatus must undertake to lower them. The pleasure principle
represents the programme under which the mental apparatus
seeks to lower excitations by satisfying corresponding needs.[3]
Freud's account, however, is not limited to a description of
the various guises of libido and their satisfaction under the
pleasure principle. Indeed, it could not end there, for it would
then fail to explain the wide variations in the manifestations of
sexuality. His study of sexual aberrations did not merely reveal
to him the nature and variety of libidinal transformations, but
also an underlying conflict.

> Our study of the perversions has shown us that the sexual
> instinct has to struggle against certain mental forces which
> act as resistances, and of which shame and disgust are the
> most prominent. (1905d:7:162)

The material and somatic forces of the instincts, therefore, are
opposed very frequently by mental forces; this conclusion is re-
inforced by Freud's discussion of neuroses, which immediately
follows the section on perversions, and which is encapsulated
in the famous formula that the

> neuroses are, so to say, the negative of perversions. The
> sexual instinct of psychoneurotics exhibits all the aberrations
> which we have studied as variations of the normal, and as
> manifestations of abnormal, sexual life. (165-6)

While in perversions the somatic force prevails, in neuroses it is
the mental force which prevails. The instinctual impulse is
deemed unacceptable by the mental apparatus and is not per-
mitted to enter consciousness (in most cases), while the libidinal
excitation which motivated it is dammed or allowed to find partial
discharge in substitute formations, neurotic symptoms. This is
the central theme of Freud's famous theory of repression, the
process which prevents an instinctual impulse from reaching
consciousness and restricts it to the region of the mind known
as the unconscious.
The interference of the mental apparatus in the manifestations
of sexuality cannot explain, of itself, the multiplicity of forms

assumed by the latter, unless the theme of the conflict between mental and somatic factors is placed in the context of the sexual development of the child; adult sexuality requires interpretation in terms of fixations, regressions, traumata, phantasies, anxieties and satisfactions related to libidinal organizations of childhood. This led Freud to his pioneering examination of infantile sexuality, which gained him an unwelcome notoriety and very limited recognition. His theory of the successive libidinal stages is too well known and requires no recapitulation. It suffices to make the following observations:

(i) The transition from one stage to the next has a formative impact on the mental apparatus; as Althusser puts it, it is 'the long forced march which makes mammiferous larvae into human children, *masculine and feminine subjects*' (1971:206). The major institutions of the mental organization, like the ego and the super-ego, are formed during this period, which also provides the human individual with the prototypical and momentous experiences of anxiety, love, frustration and authority.

(ii) At each stage the child's sexuality is confronted and ultimately frustrated by external reality - this creates the awareness of the self in opposition to an externality. As Mitchell has argued, 'the initiation of each stage has two characteristics: the deprivation of the self and a new awareness of the other' (1974:24). It is through frustration that the child learns to distinguish between self and external reality and it is frustration which awakens the child from its auto-erotic bliss to the struggles of the world.

(iii) At each stage, the confrontation of libido with external reality increases dramatically the child's universe of meanings. Cavities, appendages, solids and fluids acquire meanings, as do the familiar figures of the child's parental environment.

(iv) The wealth of meanings created during the first years of life is by and large repressed, with every successive frustration; it is through a string of repressions that the child triumphs over its painful introduction to the world. Infantile amnesia envelops most of these early experiences, which are forced to the unconscious, from where they will seek to burst into consciousness for the rest of life. The ego will expand, but it will continue to expend considerable amounts of energy keeping them repressed. From time to time, repressed ideas will find an outlet in highly distorted forms, as in artistic creations, dreams, slips of tongue, jokes and, of course, neurotic symptoms.

Although Freud's instinctual theory was considerably developed during the third period of his writings (starting with 'Beyond the Pleasure Principle' of 1920), he never actually provided an account of the precise vicissitudes and transformations of instincts to match his formulations on sexuality that we find in the 'Three Essays'. In his later works, sexuality becomes subsumed in Eros, a much broader motivational principle, which represents the claims of life by aiming to unite organic matter into ever-increasing entities. Eros, as a principle of unity and integration, is opposed by his 'heavenly adversary', the death instinct or Thanatos, a principle of inertia and disintegration seeking to return life to a state of inorganic peace. These new formulations opened great theoretical possibilities in our interpretation of humanity on a grand scale, its history, its culture and its alienation; yet, they shed little light on psychology per se and even less on clinical psychology. Most practising psychoanalysts remained attached to the earlier formulations of libido and sexuality, assuming that the new formulations merely extended the earlier ones in a tentative and all too uncertain way to the philosophical domain.[4] Others have argued that the later formulations completely overhaul and overtake the earlier ones, leading to a radically different understanding of the human predicament from the earlier ones.[5] These themes will be picked up again in Chapter 2, in which I will examine the implications of Freud's theory of instincts for the relation of the individual and society; what concerns us here is the degree to which mental life is dominated by instincts.

Freud frequently referred to his theory of instincts as the 'mythology' of psychoanalysis; yet, equally frequently he asserted that 'psychoanalysis [cannot] escape making some assumption about instincts' (1920g:18:51). In a rare epistemological comment, Freud suggests that the basic concepts of a new science remain indeterminate for a considerable time after the foundations have been laid. Instinct and nervous energy are for psychoanalysis much as mass and force are for (Newtonian) mechanics, much as the concept of a number is for mathematics (1940a:23:159). No science could advance without making certain assumptions about concepts which may be revised or relaxed subsequently. Now, there seem to be two contrasting interpretations of Freud's concept of instinct. The first view (embodied at its extreme in the work of Reich) attempts to account for much of mental life through an interplay of quantities of instinctual energy. This approach envisages mental or psychological conditions as the 'superstructure', so to speak, of instinctual vicissitudes, and in particular of the economics of libido.[6] Even the most ardent materialists do not deny that the programme of the instincts is modified, controlled and contained by the various psychic agencies, and especially the ego, but they stress (i) the fact that the ego can only partially modify the instincts, which 'forever press forward', and (ii) even for such partial modification it requires to use instinctual energies which it can only appropriate by making itself the object of instinctual impulses (for the ego has no energies of its own). In a well-known article, Edward Bibring has argued that as Freud moved from his earlier instinctual theories to the final dualism of Eros and Thanatos, his concept of instinct itself changed - while in the early theories, the instincts were identified in terms of their bodily origins (resulting in a certain excitation, which was dealt with in accordance to the various principles, like the pleasure and reality principles), in the

later theory the emphasis lies on the aims of instincts, i.e.
whether they direct life towards new forms of life, or whether
they direct it towards the inertia of death. Both paradigms
that Bibring outlines have a strong material character. In the
earlier paradigm,

> the instincts were regarded as tensions of energy which
> arise from the organic sphere and act in a 'disturbing' way
> like an external stimulus upon the mental apparatus, and are
> then dealt with according to the regulative principles govern-
> ing that apparatus. This is what was meant when instincts
> were defined as demands for work made upon the mental
> apparatus. (1941:125)

While in this early theory the instincts are seen as demands
which impinge on the mental apparatus from outside (from
biology, so to say) and are treated in accordance to the properties of the mental system, in the later theory

> instinct was not a tension of energy which impinged upon the
> mental sphere, which arose from an organic source and which
> aimed at removing a state of excitation in the organ from which
> it originated. It was a directive or directed 'something' which
> guided the life process in a certain direction. The accent was
> no longer upon the production of energy but only upon the
> function determining the direction. (128)

The de-emphasis of the instincts' energetic aspect may lead one
to believe that Bibring sees Freud's mature concept of instinct
as losing its materialist foundation. This, however, is not so for
Bibring emphasizes the biological arguments which led Freud to
postulate the antithesis of life and death instincts (120-2), and
in particular the need to discover the biological basis of destructiveness and self-destructiveness. Besides, Bibring states
explicitly that 'the theory of instinct has hitherto rested upon a
biological basis' (121). The latter paradigm does not dislocate
the concept of instinct from its material basis, but rather
broadens it, so as to include some of the factors which were
previously regarded as properties of the mental system. Thus,
the new concept of instinct has absorbed the 'regulating principles' (i.e. the pleasure and reality principles, the compulsion
to repeat, etc.), which now become features of instincts themselves, rather than properties of the mental apparatus in its
dealings with the instincts. So, for instance, the seeking of
pleasure becomes an integral part of Eros, rather than a way
through which the mental apparatus deals with sexual excitations.
It is therefore not surprising that Bibring concludes:

> The concepts of 'instinct', 'principle' and 'regulation', thus
> [seem] to be very much alike. Just as the instincts regulated
> the course of biological events, so, naturally, did they regu-

late the course of mental events. (ibid.)

By absorbing the different principles, the instincts' grasp over
the mental processes becomes firmer than it had been under the
earlier paradigm.

The materialist interpretation of Freud's instinctual theory
takes very seriously his neurological model of the mind expressed
in the 'Project of 1895', whose appearance in the 1950s had an
effect on psychoanalysis similar to that which the re-discovery
of the 1844 Manuscripts had on Marxism. In the Project (which
was not published during Freud's lifetime), we find rudiments
of even some of the most sophisticated later propositions on the
structure and operations of the mind, and its admirers argue
that had neurology provided Freud with the necessary analytical
tools (available today), he may never have transposed his theory
to the mental level.[7] Moreover, they argue that it is 'the neuro-
physiological model which gives conceptual anchorage to the concept [of energy]' (Solomon 1974:33). In the last instance, this
view suggests that without recognizing its biological foundations,
psychoanalysis would indeed be resting on mythology.[8]

The emphasis on the material character of instincts does not
necessarily lead to a 'reduction' of mental phenomena to neuro-
physiological processes. In fact, some of the most prominent
exponents of this materialist interpretation of instincts (and
especially sexuality) stress their biological urgency in order to
highlight the conflict between instinctual impulses and social
controls. In criticizing the 'spiritualization' of instincts' theory
by the Neo-Freudians, Marcuse sums up the claims of the
materialist interpretation:

> Only by pushing his critical regression back to the deepest
> biological layer could Freud elucidate the explosive content of
> the mystifying forms and, at the same time, the full scope of
> civilized repression. Identifying the energy of the life instincts
> as libido meant defining their gratification in contradiction to
> spiritual transcendentalism: Freud's notion of happiness and
> freedom is eminently critical in so far as it is materialistic –
> protesting against the spiritualization of want. (1955:250)

The second interpretation of Freud's concept of instinct,
which for lack of a better term I will refer to as 'mentalist',[9]
emphasizes the instincts as the somatic representatives to the
mind, and allows for a considerable autonomy of the mind in the
determination of mental events. This, in and of itself, does not
negate a materialist interpretation of Freud's view on the body-
mind problem.[10] Some writers, however, have moved to a more
extreme position, and argue that the instincts themselves are not
represented in the mind except indirectly, through their relation
to desires, wishes and needs; Habermas, for instance, argues
that, in contrast to other animals, 'at the human level we never
encounter any needs that are not already interpreted linguisti-

cally and symbolically affixed to potential actions' (1972:285).
No manifestations of instinct as pure energy, in a pre-symbolic
form, exist, according to this view. Instinctual cathexes,
neutralizations, appropriations, discharges, sublimations, etc.,
in short what Freud referred to as the 'economic point of view',
appertain to events which are never observed, and most probably, will never be observed.

> The energy-distribution model only creates the semblance that
> psycho-analytic statements are about measurable transfor-
> mations of energy. Not a single statement about quantitative
> relations derived from the conception of instinctual economics
> has ever been tested experimentally. (253)

Habermas, as well as Ricoeur, Rieff, Mannoni and Mitchell,
argues that all statements about quantitative relations and
instinctual vicissitudes are inferred from what is the real nucleus
of the Freudian discourse - the interpretation of desire, the
elucidation of double meanings, the demystification of consciousness. In short, they try to show that the economic or energetic
level of the Freudian discourse is but an inference from the
hermeneutic nucleus, which deals with verbal utterances, dreams,
articulated needs and desires, neurotic symptoms, jokes, slips
of tongue and, finally, actions - in short, our 'knowledge' of
biological instincts is purely inferred from our understanding of
psychic phenomena. Even if such quantities as libido, cathexis,
etc., do in fact 'exist', they add nothing to our knowledge of
mental events - they merely represent a form of untestable
body-mind isomorphism. Both materialist and mentalist interpretations of Freud's view of the instincts accept the centrality
of repression, but their emphases are quite distinct. The
materialist interpretations stress the economics of repression -
the blocking or damming of a pleasure-seeking force, which will
forever strive outwards, seeking expression and fulfilment. The
mentalist interpretations, on the other hand, emphasize the
dynamics of repression - the suppression of desire, i.e. of a
linguistically fixed idea, into the unconscious, and its
expression through a string of symbolically distorted ideas.[11]
Thus, while the materialist interpretation focuses on the energetic explanation of repression (without necessarily neglecting
the distortions of meanings), the mentalist interpretation
emphasizes the hermeneutic explanation of repression and
regards the energetic explanation as speculative and redundant.
   The same difference characterizes interpretation of the so-
called primary processes. The materialist view stresses the
mobility, displacements and condensations of instinctual quantities, while the mentalist view studies the displacements of some
ideas (representations) by others, their fusion in condensation
and their general ability to reform themselves into new represen-
tational wholes.
   Freud's own loyalty to the economic point of view never

faltered, as he insisted to his very last work that quantitative factors must be held responsible for the differing outcomes of different psychic conflicts (1940a:23:156, 181ff). In one of his last clinical works, he draws attention to the constitutional 'strength of the instincts' as one of the causal factors of neurosis, adding:

> for the most part our theoretical concepts have failed to give the same importance to the economic as to the dynamic and topographical aspects of the case. (1937c:23:226-7)

The strength of the instincts, Freud indicates, varies in accordance to biology, and he singles out puberty and 'menopause in women' as periods when certain instincts are powerfully reinforced. Yet he fails to provide any systematic account of the relation between instincts and the biological processes of life.[12] Rieff may, therefore, be justified in arguing that 'it is the mind - by means of its basic unit, the wish - which first defines the body's needs' (1959:73). A similar viewpoint is expressed by Mitchell, who uses the term 'desire' to express what Rieff refers to as 'wish', i.e. an impulse which is already articulated in the language of the mind and bears little resemblance to the physiological concept of instinct, as a quantity of energy:

> It is this submission of drive to desire, . . . that makes the 1914 essay 'On Narcissism' such a landmark. . . . It is from this point onwards that Freud really demonstrates how unimportant the notion of 'pure instinct' is to man, how far psychoanalysis has separated itself from biology. (1974:31)

According to this interpretation, the libidinal development of the child signifies not the different organizations of instinctual sexuality, but the process through which the child creates itself as a subject, by creating meanings for entities like penis, faeces, baby, mother, as they relate to its emerging and successively frustrated desires.

It would be fair to conclude that there is a divarication in the interpretations of the psychoanalytic concept of instinct; there is a distinctly materialist interpretation which stresses the biological character of the instincts and imparts them with an urgency and an intrinsic resistance to civilized domestication; on the other hand, there is a mentalist interpretation which argues that even if the instincts have a biological correlate, they are only accessible through their mental representatives, conscious and unconscious, and involve from their very beginning a symbolic dimension which precludes their conceptualization as pure energies. As will become apparent in my examination of the remaining five problematics outlined in the Introduction, most controversies surrounding the work of Freud hinge on this crucial bifurcation of interpretations. The debate on Freud's alleged biologism may well be the oldest one within the ranks of psychoanalysis. Both Jung and Adler took issue with the theory of libido, as did later the Neo-Freudians Fromm, Horney and Sullivan. The constant attempt of these disciples-turned-dissidents was to emphasize the importance of 'purely psychological' or cultural factors at the expense of biological and somatic factors. As most of these dissidents refused to accept Freud's concept of instinct as it had been shaped by the theory of libido, and as they sought to substitute libido by a proliferation of psychological needs and existential strivings, the area of confrontation shifted away from instinctual theory itself to the theory of the ego. It is well known that in Freud's work there is a marked shift in attention, dating from his 1914 essay 'On Narcissism', away from the unconscious and towards the ego, or, more accurately, to use Anna Freud's expressions, away from the 'contents of the id' and towards the 'processes of the ego'.

Views on the ego are nowhere as clearly bifurcated as those of the instincts. The ego seems to stand at the cross-roads of most modern psychologies, sociologies and philosophies, and has been constantly stretched by every newcomer in different directions. In some discourses the ego appears as synonymous to the 'self' or the 'personality', in others as the 'subject' or 'consciousness', in yet others as the 'feeling of self' or 'self-consciousness'; frequently we encounter the individual generally being referred to as the ego. In Chapter 5 I will study in detail the ego's position within Freud's mental anatomy, and point out some existential, culturalist and functionalist misconceptions. In this chapter, I will delineate some of the central features of Freud's concept of the ego, as it emerges from the major materialist and mentalist interpretations outlined thus far.

From its inception the ego stands in an ambiguous position. Much as the instinct stands at the interface between body and mind, the ego stands at the interface between the mental apparatus and external reality. The ego is, in the first place, the product and agent of adaptation, comprising all those mental faculties which ensure the individual's survival in a world full of dangers, threats and demands. It 'owes its origin as well as the most important of its acquired characteristics to its relation to the real external world' (1940a:23:201). The ego grows out of the id during the early years of childhood, as the child comes to experience itself through the opposition of its own desires to the realities of an external world; as the domination of the pleasure principle becomes displaced by the rise of the reality principle, the ego takes on 'the task of representing the external world to the id' (1933a:22:75). As Marcuse has suggested,

> with the establishment of the reality principle, the human being which, under the rule of the pleasure principle, has hardly been more than a bundle of animal drives, has become an organized ego. It strives for 'what is useful' and what can be obtained without damage to itself and to its vital environ-

ment. Under the reality principle, the human being develops
the function of *reason*: it learns to 'test' the reality, to distinguish between good and bad, true and false, useful and
harmful. Man acquires the faculties of attention, memory and
judgement. He becomes a conscious, thinking *subject,* geared
to a rationality imposed upon him from the outside. (1955:13f)

Most (though, as we shall see, by no means all) commentators
would argue that the ego's origins and principal characteristics
including consciousness are intimately connected to its function
of adaptation. The nature, however, of adaptation is the object
of great disagreements. The Neo-Freudian ego-psychologists
argued that Freud had underestimated the social setting within
which the child adapts itself, and proceeded to develop theories
of the ego as an agent of social adaptation; the therapeutic
implications of these views were obvious - the neurotic is a
maladapted individual in need of adjustment. Parsons takes a
similar view of the ego as an agent of social adaptation, but
finds rudiments of this view in Freud's own work; he argues
that, like super-ego which Freud saw as the precipitate of the
child's early confrontation with parental authority, the ego too
is the precipitate of the child's first 'object relations'. Although
Parsons does not limit the formation of the ego to a sequence of
adaptive responses, after the fashion of the ego-psychologists,
he emphasizes the learnt components of the ego, which emerge
from the child's interaction with the mother during the oral, anal
and phallic stages (1958:49ff).
This mentalist view comes from the important tradition in
Western thought which saw consciousness as filling the space
vacated by the instincts, as man rose above his fellow-creatures
in the animal kingdom. Durkheim, for instance, has argued:
'Truly, conscience only invades the ground which instinct has
ceased to occupy, or where instinct cannot be established.
Conscience does not make instinct recede; it only fills the space
instinct leaves free' (1960:346). Contrary to this mentalist tradition, the materialist tradition sees no general displacement of
the instincts by consciousness; Marx, for instance, in his
critique of German idealism, emphasized his argument that consciousness is not independent of the practical relations between
man and nature and between man and man. The growth of
consciousness and the attendant scientific, aesthetic and cultural
accomplishments do not signify the unfolding of reason, but
accompany the historical development of these practical relations.
Man's capacities for thought, attention, judgment, science and
so on, do not arise out of the displacement of instinct by a contemplative consciousness, but emerge in order to promote and
enhance man's practical relations with nature and with other men.
Instead of displacing the instincts, consciousness grows in a
space between the instincts and their possible satisfaction in
nature and society. Man's instinct does not recede (although it
does cease to determine behaviour) but becomes expressed

through consciousness: 'his instinct is a conscious one' (Marx 1846:122). As both Marx and the pragmatists argued, thought, attention and judgment and their institutional forms in sciences, arts, etc., aim at the satisfaction of human needs and in this sense they are profoundly practical.

Like the mentalist tradition, the materialist tradition can see the ego primarily as the product and the agent of adaptation; but instead of seeing its emergence as co-incidental with the eclipsing of the instincts, it always maintains the instincts within the picture. Instead of focusing on the social milieu in which the child will be socialized, it focuses on the instincts which have to be both satisfied and tamed through socialization. Wollheim, for instance, like Parsons, sees the ego as the product of adaptive responses and processes during the early stages of life, but, unlike Parsons, he considers these responses and processes as biological rather than social, and suggests that the ego 'breaks away from the psychic mass in accordance with biological considerations' (1975:64). In other words, Wollheim regards the child's loss of the objects of primary satisfaction and the resulting frustrations and repressions as unavoidable biological features arising from the biological peculiarities of the human species (protracted childhood dependency, upright posture, etc.) rather than by the socio-cultural specifics of different socializing agencies. Elsewhere, Wollheim argues that there is a 'hidden thesis' in Freud postulating an 'organic repression'

> derived from man's adoption of the upright posture and his consequent devaluation of olfactory stimuli and the replacement of smell by sight as the dominant sense. Anal eroticism, and later, by association with the excretory zone, genital sexuality fall victims to civilized man's increasing distaste for bodily odours. (1971:146)

Although Wollheim's argument finds support in a protracted footnote in 'Civilization and Its Discontents' (1930a:21:99–100fn), his attempts to account even for socially imposed repressions through the biological features of the species would seem to revert to the position that Freud criticized in relation to Fliess.[13] Hartmann, for one, has tried to reconcile the biological and sociological approaches, and argues that the ego, as an agent of adaptation, must be seen simultaneously from both perspectives:

> Analytic findings . . . are of great importance for sociology. At the same time when viewed from the angle of adaptation, maturation and learning, they present an essential feature in the biology of man. The relationship of the infant to his mother, the institution of reality principle, the changes in the types of instinctual gratification, may all be described 'biologically' as well as 'sociologically'. . . . As a matter of

fact, psychoanalysis is particularly interested in the psychological study of such 'social' factors which are of 'biological'
importance as well (1964:22-3)

The question as to whether the ego is the product of social or
of biological adaptation or a compromise comprising both elements
represents only one aspect of the debate on the ego. For the
ego, while an agent of adaptation, has also a very special relation
with the id, the reservoir of instinctual impulses, and, in the
view of the materialists, instinctual energies. The exponents of
the materialist view start with Freud's contention that 'the ego
is first and foremost a bodily ego' (1923b:19:26). In the first
place, the ego is itself part of the id, and developed from what
was originally a cortical layer, equipped with organs for the
reception of and shielding from stimuli (1923b:19:26, 1940a:23:
145). Secondly, they argue that whatever the formative impact
of biological or even social adaptation may have been on the ego,
it must still serve the pursuit of sensuous, bodily pleasure – the
reality principle may postpone satisfaction but cannot cancel the
pleasure principle, which continues to inform and pressurize the
ego; so Freud argues that

> the ego must on the whole carry out the id's intentions; it
> fulfils its task by finding out the circumstances in which those
> intentions can best be achieved. The ego's relation to the id
> might be compared with that of the rider to his horse. The
> horse supplies the locomotive energy, while the rider has the
> privilege of deciding on the goal and of guiding the powerful
> animal's movement. (1933a:22:77)

The last part of this extract reveals the third argument in favour
of a materialist interpretation of the ego as a bodily ego – it
must carry out its tasks with energies borrowed from the id,
because 'from a dynamic point of view it is weak' (ibid.).
 The ego, therefore, it is suggested grows out of the body,
pursues the interests of the body, and does so by using ultimately somatic energies. Of course, all three arguments are
modified or rejected by the mentalists who would see the ego as
a spiritual or even transcendental entity, closely related to the
philosopher's concept of reason. Two further arguments of some
materialists are even more controversial; first, it is suggested
that some highly intellectual processes taking place in the ego
follow what were originally somatic prototypes:

> the intellectual processes of judgement, assertion, and denial
> . . . are originally entertained under concepts that refer to,
> or include the sense of, taking something into oneself through
> the mouth, holding it in oneself, and spitting it out. And the
> significance of this account is that, in conceiving itself in an
> ineradicably corporeal way, the early ego also conceives of its
> function as (in part) corporeal functions. (Wollheim 1975:64)

Secondly, the ego conceives of itself as a corporeal ego, and in particular as a sexual ego, i.e. it is aware that intellectual activity is ultimately aimed at pleasure.

> In conceiving itself successively as (in part) a mouth, an anus, a phallus, the ego conceives of its own activity on the model of that which such an organ must engage in to secure pleasure. It assimilates mental functioning to a sexual aim, once again for better or for worse. (ibid.)

We see, therefore, that the materialist interpretation of the ego stresses its proximity to the id and approaches it, on the whole, as the product and agent of biological adaptation and the pursuit of pleasure, while the mentalist interpretation regards it as the outcome of social adaptation and stresses its intellectual, cognitive and organizing faculties. Needless to say that, barring the more extreme forms of each interpretation, Freud's writings provide ample support for both views.

Before concluding this introductory examination of the ego from the materialist and mentalist perspectives, it is worth examining two further approaches both of which challenge the view, accepted so far, that the ego gains its character from its adaptive functions, be they biological or social. Norman O. Brown, like Wollheim, begins with the notion of the ego as a 'body-ego' (1959:159). Contrary, however, to both Wollheim and Parsons who saw the ego as the precipitate of biological and social adaptations respectively, Brown argues that Freud's later work dissolves 'the naive equation of the ego and the reality-principle (and of repression and external reality)' (ibid.).[14] Instead, he suggests that the ego is the product of an incapacity to accept reality; it is formed, he argues, not by conceiving itself as a succession of pleasure-yielding bodily regions (mouth, anus, phallus), but through a succession of phantasies (and sublimations) which arise out of an inability to accept the losses of the objects of bodily pleasure. So Brown, instead of seeing the ego as the product of the early pleasure-yielding sensations, looks at it as the product of an inability to accept the losses of these sensations. He uses the formulations of Freud's short article 'Negation' to show, not like Wollheim that the ego operates after the model of early bodily satisfactions, but that the ego overcomes its frustrations by learning to accept intellectually what it rejects in practice.

> It is thus a general law of the ego not strong enough to die, and therefore not strong enough to live, that its consciousness of both its own inner world and the external world is sealed with the sign of negation; and through negation life and death are diluted to the point that we can bear them. (160)

Brown goes on to suggest that culture and its monumental edifice of symbols represent the ego's attempts to recover in phantasy objects whose real loss is intolerable.[15] Sublimation, the key process through which culture is generated from the instincts, is for Brown not a deflection of the instincts' aim but a complete renunciation of their aims; it is a negation of both the striving for pleasure, the hallmark of Eros, and the reconciliation with inorganic inertia, the central feature of the death instinct (161-5).

In spite of his unqualified emphasis on the bodily character of the instincts, Brown seeks to reconcile the materialist and symbolic threads in Freud's thought - because of the renunciation of instinct and the corresponding rise of symbolic substitutes, psychoanalysis is left with the task of interpreting double meanings, decoding symbols, phantasies, dreams and desires of the alienated ego, 'that body-ego [which] becomes a soul distinct from a body' (159). The psychoanalytic hermeneutic is the science of the *'animal sublimans,* committed to substitute symbolic gratification of instincts for real gratification, the desexualized, man' (167). On the other hand, the psychoanalytic energetic represents for Brown, as for Marcuse, the real possibility for a way out of the ego's alienated spirituality, for the need for real gratification cannot be completely eradicated, it can only be buried. Brown's major failure in reconciling the symbolic with the materialist dimension in Freud would seem to lie in his inability to identify an original cause for the ego's unwillingness to accept its predicament and its subsequent alienation in a desperate flight from both pleasure and death. To put it differently, is the ego's emergence out of an incapacity to accept reality a biological predicament, a socio-cultural event, or is it an existential failure?

The second view of the ego which moves away from seeing it as an agent of adaptation is the one offered by the Lacanian school. In a critique of the ego-psychologists who have reduced the ego to its adaptive functions, Mannoni has argued that 'as soon as Freudian analysis reached America, it was immediately absorbed into a pseudo-Darwinian ideology of social adjustment' (1971:190-1). Freud's original contribution to the theory of the ego was not through the idea of the reality principle and of adaptation, but in 'the discovery that the ego is the object of narcissism, that it belongs to the imaginary order, that it can in some way be "other" than ourselves, an image in which we can alienate ourselves' (186). Like Brown, Lacan and his followers contend that after the paper 'On Narcissism' Freud gave up the idea of the ego as an agent of adaptation, and like Brown they argue that the ego is alienated from its inception;[16] finally, like Brown, they see the ego as a symbolically endowed image, an image that becomes the object of narcissistic desires. However, unlike Brown, they do not regard the ego's self-alienation as the product of a failure to achieve instinctual gratification - as we saw earlier in our discussions of Mitchell's and Mannoni's views of sexuality, the importance of instinctual forces recedes in the work of this school of thought in favour of

symbolically mediated desires. The alienation of the ego is due to
the fact that the ego originally recognizes itself in the other,
during what Lacan calls the 'mirror-phase'. Unlike other animals,
the human child exhibits a great fascination when confronted
with his own image in a mirror - this phase represents the prototypical identification, 'the transformation which takes place in
the subject when he assumes an image' (Lacan 1968b:72). The
ego begins to emerge when the child confronts its image as a
co-ordinated gestalt for the first time - an image which he has
formed for the other (especially for the mother) earlier, but
which, in his motor incapacity and nurseling dependency, he
has never thought of applying to himself. His joy is due to his
imaginary triumph in anticipating a degree of muscular co-
ordination which he has not yet actually achieved (1953:15).

This school stresses the fact that the ego is constituted as an
image, before it is constituted as a psychic function or agency.
Correspondingly, they attach great significance to Freud's
discussion of narcissism which suggests that the ego's major
pre-occupation is to be lovable; only through taking on the
attractive characteristics of the lost objects of love and through
presenting itself as an object of desire for the id does the ego
begin to emerge; hence the constitution of the ego-ideal within
the ego.[17]

> To this ideal ego is now directed the self-love which the real
> ego enjoyed in childhood. The narcissism seems to be now
> displaced onto this new ideal ego, which like the infantile ego,
> deems itself the possessor of all perfections. (1914c:14:94)[18]

The loss of a loved object becomes a loss in the ego and may
result in the condition of melancholia, where the ego, deprived
of the perfections of the object which it has lost, becomes itself
the object of self-reproaches. This view of the ego as a lovable
image, an object of love, finds support in Freud's later formulations concerning the relation between the ego and the super-ego:

> To the ego . . . living means the same thing as being loved -
> being loved by the super-ego. (1923b:19:58)

Contrary therefore to Wollheim who argues that the ego conceives
of itself as an agency of instinctual pleasure, the Lacanian school
suggests that the ego strives to set itself up as an object of
desire.[19] In Mannoni's terms, 'the ego, which in effect succeeded
ancient reason, [is] also a figure of fantasy, an imaginary object,
a mirror of mirages - and the agent of madness at least as much
as the agent of reason' (1971:135). Mannoni, in fact, argues that
in the latest period of Freud's work the ego loses its character
of being an 'agent' (of reason, of adaptation, of self-preservation,
etc.) and becomes purely an imago, invested with imaginary
powers of objectivity, reason and control, an idol existing in
imagination. Just as the child, fascinated in front of his own

mirror-image, invests it with imaginary qualities of co-ordination and cohesion, the adult ego becomes enriched with all the qualities which will render it attractive, as an object of desire. 'The ego, which played a role in the conflict in the beginning, is not even the referee any longer, and runs the risk of becoming the stakes' (154). As a fleeing illusion, a 'representation', the ego is of secondary significance in this interpretation. Over and above the imaginary order of existence in which the ego resides towers the symbolic order, the realm which structures unconscious desires and forever constitutes and reconstitutes the human subject.

This preliminary discussion of Freud's concept of the ego begins to suggest the centrality of the problematic under consideration. Although there is a great wealth of interpretations of the ego (and although there is no sharp bifurcation of views as in the case of instincts), the following features of the ego seem to hinge on one's position on the materialist/mentalist problematic:

(i)   the ego as the product of and agent of adaptation vs the ego as an imago, a mental construction invested with imaginary qualities:

(ii) the course of adaptation as determined by a quasi-biological programme vs adaptation as dependent on cultural factors;

(iii) the ego as the psychic representative of reason vs the ego as a bodily and sexual entity, representing the interests of sensuous pleasure;

(iv) the ego as part of the id vs the ego as constitutionally opposed to the id.

The debate on mental properties and material strivings of the ego may ultimately hold the key for understanding Freud's view of man. If the emphasis is placed on the mental faculties, man emerges as a rational being, striving for meaning and identity, seeking to understand the world around him as well as himself, forever engaged in a struggle to tame the 'lower' aspects of his nature. In his effort to locate himself and his desires, man creates ever-expanding matrices of symbols and is, perhaps, above all a symbol-creating animal. If, on the other hand, the emphasis is placed on the material strivings, man emerges as a sensuous animal, constantly pursuing pleasure, seeking to unite himself with the world around him through love. To the materialist, reason is in its essence an organon for pleasure, and every departure from this principle, every insubordination of Logos to Eros, would be marking humanity's departure from its essence - humanity's alienation. As Heinz Maus argues,

the materialist is concerned not with absolute reason but with happiness (including its despised form, pleasure), and not so much with so-called inner happiness, which all too often allows itself to be complacent about outer misery, but with an objective condition, in which curtailed subjectivity comes into its own again.[20]

Both interpretations, the materialist and the mentalist, can find ample support in Freud's massive work - after all, Freud, possibly the greatest modern vindicator of Eros, was a self-professed worshipper of Logos. Like his archetypical hero, the great king of antiquity who solved with 'reason alone' the famous riddle of man, and yet whose fate was sealed from the moment he was born 'from those from whom he ought not to have been born', Freud's voluminous work seems to be affirming at the same time the fateful inevitability of Eros and the forces of the body, and also the necessary interference of Logos and the powers of an independent mind. Whether Freud asserted, in the last instance, that the essence of being is Eros, the striving for pleasure (Marcuse 1955:113), or that the affirmation of human essence can only proceed from the 'hegemony of reason' (Rieff 1959:76), can never be established conclusively. Yet it stands at the heart of all five problematics which remain to be introduced; it dominates the discussion of the relation between individual and society (Chapter 2), the question of the potential and limitations of psychoanalytic cures (Chapter 3), the nature of psychoanalytic theory and its relation to empirical considerations. Above all, perhaps, this debate dominates the discussion of the moral implications of psycho-analysis and Freud's ideal of the good life (Chapter 4), and it must ultimately decide the issue of whether Freud must be seen as mankind's conservative disillusionist or as its speculative utopist (Chapter 6).

Chapter 2
Individual and society

The discussion of the first problematic, that of body and mind,
has already introduced some of the elements of the second
problematic, that of the relation between the individual and
society (and, by implication, the relation between psychoanalysis and the social sciences). It was seen that many of
Freud's disciples who accused him of a biological bias sought to
compensate for a relaxation of the theories of instincts by
introducing a social factor. In the formulations of the Neo-
Freudians, for instance, the ego is no longer the agent of
biological adaptation but becomes the product of cultural adaptation, a process which takes place between the individual and
his/her social world. Psychoanalysis, they argue, needs to be
enriched with a sociological dimension, or at least with a sociological understanding of the world into which every child enters
on birth. The central concept through which they seek to bridge
the gap between psychoanalysis (and psychology in general)
and sociology is 'character'. This term, which Freud had
developed to denote different libidinal structures which result
from early childhood fixations and sublimations, acquires a
distinct meaning for the Neo-Freudians: a character-structure
represents a relatively stable pattern of behaviour through
which the individual relates to the world. According to this
view, character emerges from the child's 'dynamic adaptation'
to the particular cultural milieu in which he/she grows up.

> The social character results from the dynamic adaptation of
> human nature to the structure of society. Changing social
> conditions result in changes of the social character, that is,
> in new needs and anxieties. These new needs give rise to new
> ideas and, as it were, make men susceptible to them; these
> new ideas in their turn tend to stabilise and intensify the new
> social character and to determine man's actions. In other words,
> social conditions influence ideological phenomena through the
> medium of character; character on the other hand, is not the
> result of passive adaptation to social conditions but of dynamic
> adaptation on the basis of elements that are either biologically
> inherent in human nature or have become inherent as the
> result of historic evolution. (Fromm 1966:326)

The Neo-Freudians' concept of character has, of course, its
roots in the work of Reich, to whom they owe the important
argument that there is a psychic level where social ideologies

become imprinted, and through which they are reproduced.
Reich argued that socio-cultural 'considerations led to the concept of the unity of *social and character structure*. Society molds
the human character. The character, in turn, reproduces the
social ideology en masse' (1968:191). The similarity in the views
of Neo-Freudians and Reich extends to the institution in which
character structures are first formed, the family.

> The parents . . . transmit to the child what we may call the
> psychological atmosphere or the spirit of a society just by
> being as they are - namely representatives of this spirit. The
> family thus may be considered to be the psychological agent of
> society. (Fromm 1966:314-15)

Finally, both Reich and the Neo-Freudians agree that there is a
region in the personality which does not succumb to the socializing influence of the family and instead puts its own stamp on
the development of character - it is because of this 'personality
core' that adaptation is seen as dynamic rather than passive.
The underlying difference between Reich and the Neo-Freudians
concerns the nature of this personality core, which Reich saw
as composed of biological drives, whereas the Neo-Freudians
saw it, on the whole, as involving quasi-existential needs. This
difference will not concern us in the discussion of the present
problematic, since both views are in agreement that the individual and society enjoy a relative autonomy in their relation, and
neither can be reduced to an effect of the other; psychology and
sociology are seen as distinct disciplines with a common interface, personality, which links character-structure on the side of
the individual with ideological structures on the side of society.[1]
A rather similar view towards the relationship between the two
disciplines is taken by the vast majority of social scientists in the
English-speaking countries, who frequently employ the concepts
of 'personality' and 'role' as bridges between psychology and
sociology. Parsons, for instance, has argued that sociology and
psychology are interpenetrating disciplines, able of furnishing
each other with crucial starting assumptions.[2] He has suggested
that Freud's theory of the constitution of the super-ego (and
even the ego) as the 'precipitate' of successive object-relations
can serve as the basis for the study not only of the personality
system, but also of the interpenetration and interaction of the
personality and social systems. By extending Freud's discussion
of the emergence of the super-ego, Parsons has tried to show
that 'not only moral standards, but all the *components of the
common culture* are internalized as parts of the personality
structure' (1952:23). This general approach has sought to
'enrich' the Freudian theory with a sociological dimension, by
linking it to sociology through concepts like character and
cultural super-ego; although this approach has been supported
by a number of eminent psychoanalysts[3] it has been opposed by
two important groups of theorists; one originates in the French-

speaking world and continues a long tradition in arguing that
psychoanalysis and sociology exist at altogether different
theoretical spaces and that the two disciplines are essentially
incommensurable;[4] the other group, which includes Marcuse,
Rieff, Brown, Habermas and Ricoeur, argues that psychoanalysis is in itself social theory and requires no 'enrichment'
from outside. This chapter, after a brief examination of the
view of the first group, will deal primarily with the arguments
of the second group.

The argument that psychology and sociology are quite distinct
disciplines which, in spite of their thematic overlap, need not
make assumptions about each other is not as new as its current
popularity would suggest. If the theme of inter-disciplinary
overlap has dominated Anglo-Saxon academia, the theme of
disciplinary independence has been central to French academic
politics since the days of Comte, Durkheim and Saussure, all of
whom argued that a science is autonomous if it can establish the
irreducibility of its subject as well as its specificity. Durkheim,
for instance, insisted that the task of sociology was to relate
social facts to other social facts, rather than explain them by
recourse to psychology.

> On the pretext of giving the science a more solid foundation
> by establishing it upon the psychological constitution of the
> individual, it is thus robbed of the only object proper to it.
> It is not realized that there can be no sociology unless societies
> exist, and that societies cannot exist if there are only indi-
> viduals. (1951:38)

Foucault, Lacan and Althusser use similar arguments to distinguish psychoanalysis not only from sociology but also from
psychology. The object of psychoanalysis is the unconscious
and its effects, a concept which in spite of Freud's frequent
journeys into biology, psychology, physics and philosophy,
owes absolutely nothing to these disciplines. Psychoanalysis
deals with the process of humanization,

> the extraordinary adventure which from birth to the liquid-
> ation of the Oedipal phase transforms a small animal conceived
> by a man and a woman into a human child. . . . Psychology
> is lost here, and this is hardly strange for it thinks that in
> its 'object' it is dealing with some *human* 'nature' or 'non-
> nature', with the genesis of this existent, identified and
> certified by culture itself. (Althusser 1971:205, 206)

Expressing a similar point of view, Juliet Mitchell criticizes
Marcuse for 'subjecting' ideological analysis (the domain of
psychoanalysis) to the economic analysis of the performance
principle (and, presumably, the subjection of Freud to Marx),
and argues that the two constitute separate domains of investi-
gation:

> In analysing contemporary Western society we are (as else-
> where) dealing with two autonomous areas: the economic mode
> of capitalism and the ideological mode of patriarchy. . . . The
> patriarchal law speaks to and through each person in his un-
> conscious; the reproduction of the ideology of human society
> is thus assured in the acquisition of the law by each individual.
> The unconscious that Freud analysed could thus be described
> as the domain of the reproduction of culture or ideology.
> (1974:412, 413)

In Mitchell's view, neither biology nor sociology can account for
the differentiation of the sexes, but only psychoanalysis (in its
Lacanian variants) which looks at the processes of humanization,
under the law of patriarchy.[5]
Although few people with a favourable disposition towards
psychoanalysis would dispute its epistemological irreducibility,
the insistence on the complete separateness of its 'domain of
objectivity' seems to me to reflect the politics of French academy,
rather than the inner logic of Freud's discourse. While it is
undeniably true that many psychoanalytic concepts, assumptions
and methods differ extensively from those employed by other
sciences, it is equally true that its formulations cut across most
human sciences; indeed, the argument put forward by Mitchell,
Althusser and others that 'ideology is deeply unconscious' is
begging for a formulation which will link the production and
reproduction of ideologies in societies (under specific economic
and political conditions) and the production and reproduction of
ideologies in the unconscious (under specific conditions in the
process of humanization). It is precisely this link that Reich
tried to provide with his 'superficial' concept of character. It is
the same link that those theorists who believe that Freud's theory
is in itself 'sociological' have sought to establish, through a
systematic reading of Freud's writings on culture, religion and
art. The claims of this school are succinctly expressed by
Marcuse:

> In contrast to the revisionists (Fromm, Horney *et al.*), I believe
> that Freud's theory is in its very substance 'sociological', and
> that no new cultural or sociological orientation is needed to
> reveal this substance. Freud's 'biologism' is social theory in a
> depth dimension that has been consistently flattened by the
> Neo-Freudian schools. (1955:5)

This view emphasizes Freud's understanding of the individual as
uncomfortably but firmly situated between nature and culture.

> [Freud] conceives of the self not as an abstract entity, unit-
> ing experience and cognition, but as the subject of a struggle
> between two objective forces - unregenerate instincts and
> over-bearing culture. Between these two forces there may be
> compromise but no resolution. (Rieff 1959:29)[6]

The theme of the individual as being at the centre of a confrontation between nature and culture lies in the heart of Freud's
theory, from his earliest tentative formulations to his last sweeping statements on civilization and its discontents.

In order to study the claims of the view which considers
Freud's work as sociological in its very essence, it is necessary
to make a lengthy digression, in which the main threads of
Freud's social imagery will be introduced, through a historical
examination of his thoughts on culture. But before this examination is undertaken, it is necessary to dismiss a popular misconception of his work as representative of a 'methodological
individualist' perspective. According to this view, Freud has no
concept of society at all, but merely regards it as an outcome,
an aggregate of individuals. Lichtman, for instance, takes
literally Freud's statement that sociology is applied psychology
(1933a:22:179), and contends that 'Freud begins with the
individual, and views society as the sum of individual transactions' (1977:65). This atomistic interpretation would look at
social cohesion as the result of the psychological make-up of
the individual – the social whole is a happy co-incidence, with
no features or unity 'of its own'. As we shall see, it is true that
Freud's early work took social cohesion as a given; even this
early work, however, contradicts the view that he was a methodological individualist, for he never denied that individual transactions are organized within a social framework, and never
studied them as spontaneous impulses arising from the psychological make-up of the transacting parties. His underlying theme
that society demands instinctual renunciations from the individual
would be sheer nonsense, if society was seen simply as the sum
total of its parts; if the whole is not an organic whole how can it
make demands on the parts? The antagonism between individual
and society implies that they exist as partly independent entities,
whose demands clash to a certain degree.[7]

The theme of civilization as a source of instinctual constraint
is encountered in some of Freud's earliest writings. In 'Sexuality
in the Aetiology of Neuroses', he argued that civilization must
include 'the causation of neurasthenia in the list of its crimes'
(1898a:3:271), in so far as it requires renunciations of the
sexual instinct. Apart from accepting sexuality only within the
strait-jacket of institutional marriage, civilization has placed
a taboo on discussions of the 'lower instincts', and has failed to
provide adequate contraceptive measures which would be

> one of the greatest triumphs of mankind, one of the most
> tangible liberations from the bondage of nature to which we
> are subject. (277)

Having underlined the view that 'it is positively to the public
interest *that men should enter upon sexual relations with full
potency'* (278), he argued that in the twentieth century
'civilization will have to learn to become compatible with the claims

of our sexuality!' (ibid.). The failure to do so would result in
an increase of neurotic disorders and especially of neurasthenia.
   This theme of civilization as a source of instinctual constraint
is re-iterated in the 1907 essay 'Obsessive Actions and Religious
Practices':

> A progressive renunciation of inherent instincts, the satisfac-
> tion of which is capable of giving direct pleasure to the ego,
> appears to be one of the foundations of human civilization.
> (1907b:9:127)

In postulating 'neurosis as a private religious system, and
religion as a universal obsessional neurosis' (ibid.), Freud
locates instinctual renunciation at the heart of both phenomena.
In contrast, however, to the earlier article, the emphasis here
is on the taming by religion not of the sexual instinct, but of
those instincts which he describes as 'of egoistic origin'. It is
these anti-social instincts that religion seeks to silence, while
neurosis is usually the result of repression of sexual instincts;
this possibly accounts for the private character of neurosis
which contrasts with the social character of religion. In this
essay, we also encounter in one of the earliest formulations the
'sense of guilt', which will later become a central foundation of
Freud's theory of culture.[8]
   At the conclusion of his Clark lectures in 1910, Freud returned
to the earlier theme of civilization as the source of sexual
restrictions:

> the claims of our civilization make life too hard for the greater
> part of humanity, and so further the aversion to reality and
> the origin of neuroses, without producing an excess of cultural
> gain by this excess of cultural repression. We ought not to go
> so far as to fully neglect the original animal part of our nature,
> we ought not to forget that the happiness of individuals cannot
> be dispensed with as one of the aims of our culture. (1910a:
> 11:54).

Freud's insight into the cost that civilization pays for the repression of sexuality has deepened considerably, however, since his
earlier essays. The cost is not simply the misery of those inca-
pacitated by neurasthenia or obsessional disorders, but involves
the loss (one may say the waste) of instinctual energies, which
civilization could use to its advantage. It is here that we
encounter the theme of sublimation, as the instinctual vicissitude,
through which sexuality

> exchanges [its] sexual goal for one more remote and socially
> more useful. To the contributions of the energy won in such
> way for the functions of our mental life we probably owe the
> highest cultural consequences. A repression taking place at an
> early period excludes the sublimation of the repressed impulse;

after the removal of the repression the way to sublimation is
again free. (ibid.)

The importance of this formulation lies in the fact that culture is
no longer seen as a passive externality; until this point, culture
like nature had operated under the guise of the reality principle
to frustrate and suspend the pleasure principle. In this extract,
however, we find in embryo the idea that culture is itself founded
on instinctual energies; through sublimation, i.e. through the
re-direction of the aims of sexuality, culture appropriates
instinctual energies and uses them in furtherance of social ends.
    What, in fact, we have here is the rudiment of a transition
which has its direct equivalent in the developments of Freud's
individual psychology. As we saw in Chapter 1, the 1914 essay
'On Narcissism' (so crucial for the mentalist interpretations of the
ego) marked an important transition in the theory of the ego,
which was no longer seen as the product and agent of an external
reality, representing, so to speak, the external demands of
nature and culture to the mental apparatus. Instead the ego was
seen in itself as the object of desire, incapable of carrying out
its functions without first appropriating instinctual energies
from the id, by presenting itself as an attractive and lovable
image. Just as Freud was beginning to conceptualize the ego not
purely as the agent of adaptation to social and natural external-
ities in their opposition to the instincts, he was beginning to look
at culture itself as an entity not entirely outside the instincts.
Just as he was arguing that the ego can only perform its function by assimilating instinctual energies, he was beginning to
look at culture as the product of a massive re-orientation of
sexual energies. Just as the ego could make itself lovable by
appropriating the features of loved objects into an ego-ideal,
the culture can appropriate and re-direct instinctual energies
by making itself lovable through its diverse cultural accomplishments and ideals. In this sense, the cultural ego-ideal may offer
similar types of narcissistic satisfactions as the individual ego-
ideal.

   The ego-ideal is of great importance for the understanding of
   group psychology. Besides its individual side, this ideal has
   a social side; it is also the common ideal of a family, a class,
   or a nation. (1914c:14:101)

As the view of culture as an externality restricting the instincts
begins to give way to the view of culture as relying itself on a
re-direction of sexuality, the function of renunciation and
repression is complemented by the function of narcissistic compensation; by identifying with their culture's highest achievements as well as its minor idiosyncrasies, individuals re-direct
instinctual energies in socially useful directions. The highest
examples of patriotism and self-sacrifice, as well as what Freud
was later to call 'the narcissism of minor differences' (the petty

antagonism between fans of competing football clubs on adjoining grounds),[9] fulfil the same narcissistic function.

At this point, Freud's theory faced a rather obvious difficulty; in attempting to develop a theory of culture along lines suggested by his investigations on narcissism, Freud gained an invaluable understanding of the process of sublimation and its contribution in the emergence of an imago, the ego-ideal (ibid:74ff). At the same time, however, he could not account for the reasons why narcissistic libido must once again turn outwards towards the objects of the world: how is it that a narcissistic libidinal process could at the same time provide the explanation for the creation of lasting social bonds among humans? Freud made a half-hearted attempt to answer this question:

> Whence does the necessity arise that urges our mental life to pass on beyond the limits of narcissism and to attach the libido to objects? The answer which would follow from our line of thought would once more be that we are so impelled when the cathexis of the ego with libido exceeds a certain degree. A strong egoism is a protection against disease, but in the last resort we must begin to love in order that we may not fall ill, and must fall ill if, in consequence of frustration, we cannot love. (85)

Surely, Freud's argument at this point at best evades the question, at worst is circular; he fails to explain what turns the libido outwards (that libido which the ego appropriates by turning itself into an object of desire), and simply states the obvious, namely, that failure to do so would result in our falling ill; failure to do so on a general scale, we may add, would also lead to a complete social break-down. One may envisage two possibilities at least, in answering our original question of why narcissistically appropriated libido turns outwards. The first would suggest that there is something inherent in the nature of sexuality itself which forces it outwards and allows it to find no permanent fulfilment in narcissistic self-admiration. The second would lead us to look at society as having an inherent property of manipulating libido and ultimately forcing it outwards. At this point, the relevance of the first problematic is obvious; many of the materialist interpreters argue that as Freud moved from a conception of sexuality-as-quickest-possible-release to a conception of sexuality-as-Eros, the instinct, Eros, acquired an outward-looking character, aiming at integration and unification.[10] On the other hand, the mentalist approach would suggest that society and its various socializing agencies guide instinctual impulses outwards, express them and civilize them, through the intervention of the ego (and the super-ego). At this point, it is not yet possible to express a view on the merits of the two approaches, for we have only just begun examining Freud's view of society itself; besides, the difference between the two approaches may not be unbridgeable, seeing as by the

mid-1910s instinct and culture had ceased being independent
opposites in Freud's view - for by that time he was beginning
to recognize that culture, like the ego, must after all employ for
its own purposes the very instinctual energies whose unruly
behaviour it strives to suppress.

The rapprochement of instincts and culture in Freudian theory
is advanced in 'Group Psychology and the Analysis of the Ego';
it is in this work that Freud addresses explicitly the issue of
social cohesion. In order to explain various group phenomena,
like suggestion, panic, intensification of emotions, which had
pre-occupied group psychologists for many years, Freud
suggested the proposition that the bonds uniting the members
of a group are special types of love bonds or libidinal relations
(1921c:18:80ff). In this view, it is love which turns egoism into
altruism, it is love which holds social groups together.

> The libido attaches itself to the satisfaction of the great vital
> needs, and chooses as its first objects the people who have a
> share in that process. And in the development of mankind as
> a whole, just as in individuals, love alone acts as the civilizing
> factor in the sense that it brings a change from egoism to
> altruism. (103)

In this work Freud does not so much examine the functions of
culture, but rather tries to investigate the nature of social
bonds themselves; having identified them as being libidinal in
nature, he proceeds to examine in detail the transformations
which the libido must undergo in order to act as a force uniting
the members of a group. He expresses the opinion that libido
is transformed into a force of social cohesion through the
vicissitudes of identification (identification being along with
object-choice the fundamental way in which libido becomes
attached to the objects of the world); but not all identifications
lead to the formation of stable group bonds. The original identification with the father, crucial though it is for culture as the
first internalization of external prohibition, is none the less
not enough to produce lasting group bonds in itself; nor is the
form of identification which appears as a regression from an
earlier object-choice (common, for instance, in the case of homosexual identification with the parent of the opposite sex) in itself
enough. It is a third type of identification which forms the basis
of social bonds. This form of identification

> may arise with any new perception of a common quality shared
> with some other person who is not an object of sexual instinct.
> The more important this quality is, the more successful may
> this partial identification become, and it may thus represent
> the beginning of a new tie.(108)

What Freud is arguing here is more than the common-place belief
that a common quality, or a common purpose, will hold a group

together. He is rather suggesting that a common quality will
produce a libidinal bond among people, who will identify with
each other. On closer consideration, it transpires that the
common quality most conducive to stable group ties is a common
relation to a leader - a leader over whom no individual can have
any personal claims, except as a member of the group. So, for
instance, children inside a family will identify with each other
in so far as they cannot claim a special parental affection
individually. Freud proposes the following definition:

> A primary group . . . is a number of individuals who have put
> one and the same object in the place of their ego-ideal and
> have consequently identified themselves with one another in
> their ego. (116)

Three observations: First, Freud, unlike Max Weber, sees
charismatic leaders as safeguards of social cohesion (if not
social stability). Second, social stability requires that libidinal
ties within a group be sublimated, i.e. their sexual aim has
been re-directed. Not only is there no direct sexual interest
among the members of a primary group, but their primary relation
to the leader precludes the possibility of sexual satisfaction. In
practice, both types of sexual relations may occur in groups,
but Freud argues that this is detrimental for the stability of
the social bonds:

> Those sexual instincts which are inhibited in their aims have a
> great functional advantage over those which are uninhibited.
> Since they are not capable of really complete satisfaction, they
> are especially adapted to create permanent ties. (139)

So, only through the inhibition of their original aims, by keeping
the individual in a state of constant dependency, can libidinal
impulses be instrumental in the creation of permanent social
bonds. Third, Freud does not believe that there is a primary
gregarious instinct in human beings; he is careful in distinguishing his position from Trotter's view that social and group
cohesion arises from a primary herd instinct, because (i) there
is absolutely no psychological evidence to suggest that early
infancy and childhood are governed by such a social instinct,
and (ii) Trotter's view fails to account for the importance of
leaders in preserving group ties of primary groups.
   Of course, by the time Freud wrote 'Group Psychology and the
Analysis of the Ego', the earlier instinctual theories had given
way to the final dualism of life and death instincts, Eros and
Thanatos. Strangely, the concept of the death instinct hardly
figures in this work, although it was almost simultaneously
written with 'Beyond the Pleasure Principle', the work in which
the idea of a death instinct was launched. Clearly, Freud had
not yet appreciated the full implications of the death instinct
for the course of human civilization. Interestingly, his discussion

of the libidinal process which leads to the creation of social ties
through identifications owes little to the new formulations on
Eros as a life instinct uniting organic matter into larger entities;
in fact, all of his arguments concerning this socialization of
libido are extensions of the pre-1920 discussions of sexuality,
and the whole book would have qualified as a fourth essay on
the theory of sexuality. In a single fleeting reference to Eros (as
opposed to libido), however, Freud states:

> a group is clearly held together by a power of some kind: and
> to what power could this feat be better ascribed than to Eros,
> which holds together everything in the world? (92)

By subsuming libidinal economics in the category of the life
instincts, Freud's view of sexuality moved away from the compulsive automatism of the pleasure principle towards a broader
relation-building power. Eros is no longer seen simply as an
instinctual demand on the mental apparatus, dealt through the
pleasure principle. It goes beyond the pleasure principle, seeking union of the other, for only in this way can it confront the
terrifying powers of its great adversary. As Ricoeur has argued:

> What fights against death is not something internal to life,
> but the conjugation of two mortal substances. Freud calls this
> conjugation Eros; the desire of the other is directly implied in
> the emergence of Eros. (1970:291)

A similar conclusion is reached by Brown, who believes that the
eclipse of libido by Eros leaves love 'with one essential aim over
and above pleasure, which is to become one with the objects in
the world' (1959:44). Still, before concluding that all social
groupings are held together by Eros, it is important to make
three qualifications. First, Freud never saw Eros as a glorified
herd instinct leading to a spontaneous creation of group ties;
second, his discussions on the libidinal ties of groups are limited
to groups without 'too much organization' (1921c:18:16), so that
it is at least conceivable that highly organized groups are held
together by forces of a different kind;[11] third, Freud never lost
sight of the intimate relation between Eros and pleasure. The
profound irony of his theory, as we shall see in a moment, is
that, while epic battles may be raging over his head between
Eros and Thanatos, the individual never gives up his Quixotic
pursuit of pleasure. Although pleasure itself was detached from
the compulsive automatism of the pleasure principle and identified with a 'qualitative peculiarity' (1924c:19:160), it was never
compromised by Freud as a principle of individual strivings, and
some commentators, like Rieff, Brown and Himmelstein, may
have been over-eager in dissolving pleasure from Freud's mature
work. So, even if Eros provides the instinctual energy for social
types of certain kinds, it is sublimated Eros, de-sexualized Eros,
re-directed Eros which holds humans together.

In 'The Ego and the Id', as well as developing his new mental topography, involving the ego-id-super-ego triumvirate, Freud committed himself definitely to the instinctual dualism of life and death, Eros and Thanatos; the result was the momentous convergence of the death instinct and the super-ego in explaining the 'unconscious sense of guilt', the concept which Freud had first identified nearly thirty years earlier in Hamlet's utterance 'So conscience doth make cowards of us all.' 'His conscience', Freud wrote to Fliess in 1897, 'is his unconscious feeling of guilt' (1954:227) for a murder which he had never committed and yet had wished.

The super-ego grew out of the earlier concept of the ego-ideal and incorporated this earlier concept; while the ego-ideal, however, had been purely an imago against which the ego was measured, the super-ego is developed as a psychic agency, equipped with instinctual energies and carrying out psychic functions. Functionally, the super-ego became the vehicle of the ego-ideal, as well as the agent of the twin functions of self-observation and conscience (1933a:22:65-6); the super-ego idealizes, observes and criticizes. It is in this work that Freud offered an ontogenetic account of the institution of the super-ego through the child's confrontation with authority, following the institution of the ego through the confrontation with external reality. The super-ego is formed at the conclusion of the Oedipal phase, when the child masters his anxiety, by modifying his ego in a way which sets the motive of repression within itself; this is achieved through an identification with the father, who is usually seen as the original obstacle to the realization of the Oedipal desires. This identification involves both an idealized component ('You ought to be like this') and a prohibitive component ('You may not be like this'), and in this way it can be regarded as the prototypical internalization of social norms (1923b:19:34). Repression is now precipitated not by a punishing external reality, but by the super-ego - prohibition is internalized (1933a:69).

It is only through this fundamental alienation, through the institution of an agency within its own constitution to represent external authority, that the ego can master the traumatic frustration of the Oedipal episode and make the fateful leap into human culture; from this point on the conflict between the individual and society has assumed a radically different form. It is no longer the conflict between an egoistic pleasure-oriented individual and a prohibitive external law representing the interest of communal living, since the super-ego is the representative of this law within the individual him/herself. Conflict as Ricoeur has argued

> is no mere accident which [the individual] might be spared by a better social organization or a more suitable education; human beings can experience entry into culture only in the mode of conflict. Suffering accompanies the task of culture like fate,

the fate illustrated by the Oedipus tragedy. (1970:196)

As the heir of the Oedipus Complex, the super-ego inherits all the harshness with which the authority of the father was seen as threatening the desiring and phantasizing young Oedipus. This has very little to do with the actual behaviour, or indeed the existence, of the father. If the father is hard his severity will be inherited directly by the super-ego; if the father is permissive and loving, a strong super-ego will have to dictate the repression of Oedipal desires for fear of loss of love. The more permissive the parental authority, the more Oedipal desires will blossom, and the stricter the super-ego will have to be in order to carry out their eventual repression.[12]

The harshness of the super-ego never seems short of determinations in Freud's work, for both phylogenetic and ontogenetic accounts converge at this point; however, what has given Freud's concept of the super-ego its terrifying unreasonableness is not the circumstance of its genesis out of the traumatic fragments of the past, but its ever-present and unyielding association with the death instinct. It is through the position of the super-ego that the death instinct turns inwards and attacks the individual as an 'unconscious sense of guilt'. This bold hypothesis, which was to prove so central in Freud's mature theory of culture, was proposed initially to account for certain clinical conditions with pronounced masochistic elements, like obsessional neurosis and melancholia, as well as to explain a common phenomenon which inhibits the task of the therapist - the 'negative therapeutic reaction' exhibited by many patients, whereby a temporary improvement of their condition and encouraging signs of disappearance of morbid symptoms are accompanied by a 'self-inflicted' deterioration (1920g:18:12-13, 1923b:19:49, 1924c: 19:166, 1933a:22:109-10). The crucial paradox of these phenomena lies in the fact that pleasure seems to accompany neurotic misery, as if the patient's illness satisfied a need for self-punishment. By postulating an introjection of aggressive tendencies, Freud could, at long last, begin to explain the peculiar reversal of the self-preservation tendency, which had evaded his theory earlier. At the same time, he could account for the persistence of repression and the resulting morbid symptoms and suffering in cases when the repressed idea no longer presented a serious threat for the ego - in short, repression was no longer seen so much as the product of realistic fears (albeit distant) as the outcome of an effort to appease an unreasonable super-ego which handles the death instinct.

Through the arguments of 'The Ego and the Id', the super-ego emerges functionally as the faculty of idealization, self-observation and self-criticism: energetically, it emerges equipped with aggressive energies directed against the ego. As a result, the ego's position is dislocated, as we saw in the previous chapter: from an agent of adaptation, the ego comes to be seen as the victim of internalized aggression.

> To the ego, therefore, living means the same as being loved –
> being loved by the super-ego. (1923b:19:58)

It is this unequal relationship with the super-ego that determines
many of the ego's principal characteristics; thinking, reality-
testing, the 'need for synthesis', the various mechanisms of
defence and most other ego functions, as well as an unrelenting
narcissism, can no longer be seen as the requirements of adaptation, but as ploys in the ego's attempt to pacify its ruthless
master. And this is where the underlying paradox of this formulation is revealed – the ego can never be completely successful,
for its efforts are working against itself in two devious ways,
both of which are related to instinctual economics over which the
ego has no control. First, in suppressing aggressive impulses,
the ego adds to the super-ego's supplies of destructive energies
which may sooner or later be directed against itself. In its
extreme, this results in a vicious circle where the ego's kindness
fuels the super-ego's unreasonable harshness, a 'saintlihood
syndrome'. In this way,

> the more man controls his aggressiveness, the more intense
> becomes his ideal's inclination towards aggressiveness against
> his ego. (54)

The second unexpected consequence in the ego's efforts to
appease the super-ego results from the suppression of sexual
impulses; whether these impulses are repressed or sublimated,
the resulting weakening of Eros leads to a 'defusion' of aggressive instincts which are no longer controlled or neutralized.

> After sublimation the erotic component no longer has the power
> to bind the whole of destructiveness that was combined with
> it, and this is released in the form of an inclination to
> aggression and destruction. This defusion would be the source
> of the general character of harshness and cruelty exhibited by
> the ideal – its dictatorial 'Thou shalt'. (54-5)

In this way, as an agent of the weakening of Eros, the ego

> gives the death instincts in the id assistance in gaining control
> over the libido, but in so doing it runs the risk of becoming
> the object of the death instincts and of itself perishing. In
> order to be able to help in this way it has had itself to become
> filled with libido; it thus becomes the representative of Eros
> and thenceforward desires to live and to be loved. (56)

But even in 'filling itself with libido', by making itself the object
of love and wanting to be loved, the ego is indirectly assisting
the death instinct:

> The transformation [of object-libido] into ego-libido of course

involves an abandonment of sexual aims, a desexualization. In any case this throws light upon an important function of the ego in its relation to Eros. By thus getting hold of the libido from the object-cathexes, setting itself up as sole love-object, and desexualizing or sublimating the libido of the id, the ego is working in opposition to the purposes of Eros and placing itself at the service of the opposing instinctual impulses. (46)

This double vicious circle reveals the ambiguity of the ego's position when seen from an energetic point of view; whether it suppresses aggressive or libidinal impulses, in an effort to pacify the super-ego, it increases the latter's stock of aggressive energies. Trying to 'protect' itself by making itself the object of love and 'filling itself with libido' adds to its troubles for it defuses further amounts of aggression. So, while dynamically (or functionally) the ego may be the centre of all mental activity, economically (or energetically) it seems to have all mental determinations stacked against it.

By attaching the death instinct firmly onto the super-ego, Freud provided an ontogenetic explanation for why humans suffer forever from an unconscious and undeserved sense of guilt; in 'Totem and Taboo', several years earlier, he had sought to give a phylogenetic account of the same phenomenon. Whether his speculations on the primordial murder and subsequent guilt of the parricides as the foundation of civilization can be supported by anthropological research is largely immaterial, even though Freud himself seemed rather careless in regarding them as verifiable propositions. Both Marcuse and Ricoeur correctly point out that the value of these speculations is symbolic (Marcuse 1955:54, Ricoeur 1970:208ff). Freud, in the tradition of Moses, Hesiod and Hobbes, was seeking to account for the present by invoking long-forgotten primordial myths which set everything in motion. The importance of 'Totem and Taboo' lies in the fact that Freud could derive and identify the sense of guilt, upon which he saw all civilization as being founded, metaphorically, long before he could postulate the same phenomenon on a strict psychological basis.

Having established the sense of guilt firmly in the psychological make-up of the individual as it emerges from the fragments of the Oedipal episode, Freud was in a position to re-examine and, one may say, totalize his social theory in 'Civilization and Its Discontents'. Although the theme of the conflict between the individual and society which has dominated all of his earlier writings remains central, the discovery of a primary instinct working rowards dissolution and death places this conflict in an altogether different perspective. In the earlier formulations the paramount problem of civilization as well as of the ego was the taming of sexuality which was considered necessary for the survival of the individual and for social cohesion; sexuality was seen as a rebellious force, noisy, short-sighted and altogether unreliable. The creation of long-lasting

bonds among individuals necessitated its taming, domestication
and de-sexualization - in technical terms, civilized living required
sexual sublimation; to this end, civilization and the individual's
ego aligned their efforts. At the same time, however, the ego
was under constant pressure from unyielding libidinal impulses
seeking nothing short of complete satisfaction, under the dictates of the pleasure principle. This caused a conflict between
the individual and society; although the ego, on the whole,
undertook to carry out the suppression of sexuality required by
civilized living, it did so resentfully, so to speak. It also suffered the consequences of repression - morbid symptoms,
incapacitating anxieties and frequently a distortion or a loss of
the sense of reality.

In the new formulations, the relationship between the individual
and society becomes far more complex. Civilization is seen as
being constantly threatened by a force which seeks to destroy it,
by dissolving social bonds and returning all life to a state of
inorganic inertia. The awe-inspiring convergence of all mental
determinations towards an agency of internalized aggression
which Freud had studied in 'The Ego and the Id' was seen, at
once, as evidence of an inescapable instinct of death, and as
civilization's means of turning the instinct away from the bonds
which hold society together. But as the taming of the death
instinct became the over-riding problem of civilization, the
over-riding problem of the ego could no longer be the suppression of sexuality; nor could it be adaptation. Its over-riding
problem was dealing with ruthless aggression turned against
it by civilization, 'being loved by the super-ego'. At the same
time, the problems both of civilization and of the ego have
escalated drastically, for the interplay of factors which favours
survival of civilization, i.e. the sublimation of Eros and the
introjection of the death instinct, may ultimately be leading to
the demise of the individual. The survival of both has become
acutely problematic.

The central question that Freud addresses in 'Civilization and
Its Discontents' is why civilization, in spite of its technical and
cultural achievements, has failed to make individuals happy.
After re-iterating many of the earlier arguments concerning the
clash of the individual's unstoppable pursuit of pleasure and
civilization's requirements for sublimated libido, Freud introduces
the novel factor:

> Men are not gentle creatures who want to be loved, and who
> at the most can defend themselves if they are attacked; they
> are on the contrary, creatures among whose instinctual endow-
> ments is to be reckoned a powerful share of aggressiveness.
> As a result, their neighbour is for them not only a potential
> helper or sexual object, but also someone who tempts them to
> satisfy their aggressiveness on him, to exploit his capacity for
> work without compensation, to use him sexually without his
> consent, to seize his possessions, to humiliate him, to cause

him pain, to torture and kill him. Homo homini lupus. (1930a: 21:111)

It is this aggressiveness that defines the central problem of civilization.

> Civilization has to use its utmost efforts in order to set limits to man's aggressive instincts and to hold the manifestations of them in check by psychical reaction-formations. (112)

Freud's discussion of the channels available to aggressiveness is rather limited, especially when compared to the thoroughness with which he earlier examined the channels available to libido.[13] He discusses principally the turning of aggression towards an external danger (real or imaginary) and the 'narcissism of minor differences', both of which strengthen the group bonds by focusing hostility on someone or something outside the group. Two avenues for aggressiveness that Freud had hinted at earlier, mastery over the forces of nature (91-2) and the repetitive character of social routines and order (93-4), are not reconsidered. It is as though Freud was eager to examine what he considered to be the primary avenue, i.e. the ego. It is this introjection of aggression which accounts for the discontents of civilization and makes the conflict between individual and society truly tragic. As Ricoeur has argued, there is nothing tragic in the painful sacrifices that culture may impose on the enjoyment of sexuality (1970:304); but when the individual becomes victim of self-aggression, when the renunciation of pleasure and aggression simply re-inforces self-aggression, then the odds against human happiness weigh overwhelmingly against the individual.

> If civilization imposes such great sacrifices not only on man's sexuality but on his aggressivity, we can understand better why it is hard for him to be happy in that civilization. (1930a: 21:115)

The fate of the individual is forever sealed, independently of his/her own actions. Iis/her happiness is a negligible quantity from the perspective of the battle between Eros and the death instinct for the future of civilization. For the more Freud emphasized the threat posed by the death instinct, the more he appreciated the dependence of civilization on Eros for its survival.

> Civilization is a process in the service of Eros, whose purpose is to combine single human individuals, and after that families, then races, peoples and nations into one great unity, the unity of mankind. Why this has to happen, we do not know; the work of Eros is precisely this. These collections of men are to be libidinally bound to one another. Necessity alone, the advantages of work in common, will not hold them together.

> But man's natural aggressive instinct . . . opposes this
> programme of civilization. . . . And now, I think, the meaning
> of the evolution of civilization is no longer obscure to us. I
> must present the struggle between Eros and Death, between
> the instinct of life and the instinct of destruction, as it works
> itself out in the human species. This struggle is what all life
> essentially consists of, and the evolution of civilization may
> therefore simply be described as the struggle for life of the
> human species. And it is this battle of the giants that our
> nurse-maids try to appease with their lullaby about Heaven.
> (122)

Civilization must intervene in the battle of giants – it socializes
Eros by turning him outwards, and it tames Thanatos by turning
him inwards. The first task is difficult, for the individual's
commitment to unmediated pleasure is not easily surrendered;
but it is the latter which gives Freud's mature theory its tragic
pathos. Through the sense of guilt, emanating from an unyielding and tyrannical super-ego, culture turns Death against
himself; but the premium is heavy: the social individual will
suffer guilt for crimes which he/she never committed.

> Whether one has killed one's father or has abstained from
> doing so is not really the decisive thing. One is bound to feel
> guilty in either case, for the sense of guilt is an expression of
> the conflict due to ambivalence, of the eternal struggle between
> Eros and the instinct of destruction or death. This conflict is
> set going as soon as men are faced with the task of living
> together. (132)

Freud's cultural archetype is no longer Oedipus; for Oedipus,
homeless, persecuted and self-blinded, redeems himself by
mastering his remorse through reason and proclaiming his
innocence in the immortal words: 'As for my deeds, I did not act
them but rather they happened to me' ('Oed. Col.' 266). The
story of Oedipus at Colonus is the story of a man who overcomes
guilt through thought, just as what went on before 'Oedipus
Rex' is the overcoming of external coercion, the power of the
Sphinx, through 'thought alone'. Unlike Oedipus, the social
individual never redeems himself; he/she can never master a
sense of guilt and suffers for crimes which (unlike Oedipus)
he never committed; these crimes, as in the cases of Hamlet and
Mitya Karamazov, were forced on his imagination by culture
itself. From this tragic fate, the individual can find no escape,
because the only escape (as in the cases of Hamlet and Mitya)
is suffering itself – all cultural and psychic determinisms have
conspired against the happiness of the individual.

If the whole world is conspiring against him/her, it would be
fair to say that, in the whole world, he/she can only find one
ally – sensuous, object-cathected libido is the only promise of
happiness that the individual can find in the world. This is not

the Heavenly Eros who stands above civilization unifying individuals and creating social bonds, but the concrete pleasure-seeking force, present within every person. This force may frequently lead to disappointments, frustrations and illusions; yet, it is also the force which has afforded every individual some of the most valued experiences. It is, therefore, not in the slightest surprising that the individual refuses to surrender his/her allegiance to this pleasure-seeking force; as if oblivious to the battle of giants which is raging over his/her head, the individual will continue to cruise along the Quixotic adventure towards bodily pleasure, clinging to all the attendant illusions as if they were his/her most treasured possessions. The frustrations which he/she encounters on the way cannot be allowed to interfere with the objective, the course may change constantly, but the destination is the same:

> The programme of becoming happy, which the pleasure principle imposes on us, cannot be fulfilled; yet we must not - indeed, we cannot - give up our efforts to bring it nearer to fulfilment by some means or others. Very different paths may be taken in that direction, and we may give priority either to the positive aspect of the aim, that of gaining pleasure, or to its negative one, that of avoiding unpleasure. By none of these paths can we attain all that we desire. Happiness, in the reduced sense in which we recognize it as possible, is a problem of the economics of the individual's libido. There is no golden rule which applies to everyone: every man must find out for himself in what peculiar fashion he can be saved. (1930a:21:83)

Thus, the theme of an underlying conflict between the individual and society which we encountered in some of Freud's earliest works is still dominant in his last formulations. But what a dramatic transformation his view of society and culture has undergone! Originally, culture was seen as an external constraint to free instinctual gratification. The purposes and mechanisms of this constraint were unclear, or at least considered to be obvious. This rather naive sociology gives way to an increasingly rich and subtle view. First the prohibitive character of culture ceases to operate as an external constraint, as a 'reality principle', and is mediated through the super-ego. Then, the energic foundation of social bonds was studied; society was no longer seen as a given externality, outside the domain of psychoanalysis, but as the factor which requires for its own cohesion the sublimation and de-sexualization of libido, through which long-lasting social ties are formed. Freud subsequently argued that, in this task, society encounters the opposition not only of the individual, who does not easily surrender his/her quest for pleasure, but also that of the death instinct, a force which is working through the individual to dissolve social ties. In order to avert the war of all against all, culture must re-direct the

death instinct onto the individual, and use its aggressive energies in preventing outward aggression.

Economically, the central aim of culture is to sublimate Eros
outwards and to channel Thanatos inwards. Functionally, Freud
concentrates on four inter-related aspects of culture, all of
which are intimately connected to the twin economic aims. First,
culture imposes a number of moral prohibitions which become
internalized in the individual super-ego; outstanding among them
are the prohibition of incest, childhood sexuality and sexuality
outside socially sponsored arrangements, as well as prohibitions
against most types of external aggression. Second, culture offers
individuals a narcissistic satisfaction, through identification
with cultural ideals and technical and aesthetic achievements.
Third, like neurotic symptoms, culture offers a substitute
gratification - its symbolic edifices, its social rituals are not
only expressions of humanity's discontents, but also forms of
collective substitute gratification. Nowhere is this 'consolatory'
function of culture clearer than in Freud's discussions of
religion,[14] which softens man's anxieties and seeks to make life
bearable. Finally, in addition to the restrictive, narcissistic/
aesthetic and consolatory/symbolic functions, culture has an
epistemological function, upon which the first and third of the
above functions hinge. In short, it seeks to answer man's
existential questions of meaning and purposes, it offers explanations for natural and super-natural phenomena and provides
justifications for the instinctual renunciations and frustrations
which it imposes.[15] While from the economic point of view we can
study the reasons why culture causes discontents, from the
functional point of view we can identify the ways in which it
achieves its purposes and also the ways in which it expresses
humanity's discontents and tries to make them acceptable, by
offering symbolic structures which seek to flatter, to console
and to justify.

These considerations reveal an underlying concern in Freud's
mature theory of culture which is not dissimilar from Durkheim's
concern with social integration; Freud looks at social cohesion
as the product of a commitment to powerful communal symbolics,
of emotionally compelling leadership and of strong but de-
sexualized bonds. Social cohesion is deeply problematic and
requires great sacrifices from the individual; it is threatened not
by a negative condition of anomie but by the unrelenting work
of the death instinct, which dissolves what Eros has created.
But the final outcome is uncertain, and depends on quantitative
considerations. It is for this reason that Ricoeur has argued that
psychoanalysis approaches culture 'from the point of view of the
balance-sheet of cathexes and anti-cathexes of libido. All
Freudian considerations of culture are dominated by this economic
interpretation' (1970:249).

But if the success of both the individual in his strivings for
pleasure and of civilization in maintaining a cohesive society
are contingent upon economic considerations, i.e. the amounts of

libido available for different purposes, we are forced to look
more closely into the nature of Eros and the precise position
which he occupies in the relation between individual and society.
Up to this point, I have deliberately presented a dual portrayal
of Eros, which seems to characterize all of Freud's later works,
and which is undoubtedly related to the unresolved ambiguities
of the first problematic. On the one hand, there is libido as a
material force, operating through the individual and propelling
him towards pleasure; on the other hand, however, there is
Heavenly Eros, standing not only above the individual but also
above civilization, forever striving towards new unities, new
combinations, new forms of life. Preserving for a minute this
dualism we notice an interesting ambiguity in civilization's
relation to the two faces of Eros; on the one hand, civilization
manipulates sensuous libido, tames it, de-sexualizes it, sub-
limates it and turns it outwards; on the other hand, however,
civilization is seen as a process in the service of Eros, the
product of Eros, and the means through which Eros achieves
his goals. Both of these points of view are richly represented in
'Civilization and Its Discontents', where at times civilization is
presented as the superior principle using Eros for its purposes,
and at times Eros is the superior principle using civilization for
his purposes. This ambiguity is far from inconsequential, for it
ultimately decides whether the conflict between the individual
and society is to be seen as a matter of principle, central to all
civilized living, or as a matter of fact, characteristic of certain
forms of civilization, including our own. If civilization is seen as
the superior principle which manipulates the instincts in the
interest of social cohesion, then the tragic conflict between individual and society must be seen as a matter of principle and the
individual can never be fulfilled within the parameters of living
with others. If, on the other hand, Eros is the superior principle, then the conflict between the individual and society is a
historical phenomenon, specific to certain forms of civilization.
According to this line of thinking, the instincts are no longer
the objects of contradictory demands from the individual and
society, but the supreme masters. Eros, far from being a libidinal
football kicked by the individual and society in their respective
directions, becomes the source of all life. Civilization is then
seen as a process in the service of Eros, rather than as the
manipulator of Eros; it is the supreme achievement of Eros,
through which he marks his ascendancy over his great adversary.
In this view, Eros needs no domestication or socialization by
sublimation, for he is himself the source of all social things – he
is self-sublimating, to use Marcuse's expression. The individual,
far from experiencing sexuality as a pursuit of pleasure, seeks
to develop more permanent union with other human beings, in
which shared pleasure is cemented by what Freud calls
'expressions of tender feeling'. The conflict between society and
the individual is no longer inevitable, since they are both the
creations of Eros; according to this view, Freud's elaborate for-

mulations concerning this conflict are not statements of essence
but statements of fact - they reflect the condition of the present
civilization, in which arguably Thanatos has managed to infiltrate
and subvert the supreme achievements of his adversary, as
Himmelstein has argued. According always to this view, it is
perfectly possible to envisage a form of civilization in which
unrestrained Eros, in his full sexual splendour and potency,
can totally neutralize the death instinct, making the internalization of aggressive impulses totally unnecessary and relieving
the ego of the task of carrying out instinctual renunciations;
the goals of civilization and of the individual are harmonized in
a kingdom of Eros, from which his great adversary has been
banished.

Although different writers have emphasized one of the two
aspects of Eros at the expense of the other, and have often
drawn incompatible conclusions about the relationship between
individual and society, Freud preserved this ambiguity
throughout 'Civilization and Its Discontents', and near the
end he admitted that all along he had operated within a twin
paradigm of Eros - Eros as a force towards pleasure and Eros as
a force towards union with others. It is worth quoting the
relevant passage at length, for it shows Freud's unwillingness
to simplify in the interests of theoretical tidiness or polemical
expedience, two criteria which many of his followers have failed
to meet.

> Just as a planet revolves around a central body as well as
> rotating on its own axis, so the human individual takes part in
> the course of development of mankind at the same time as he
> pursues his own path in life. But to our dull eyes the play of
> forces in the heavens seems fixed in a never-changing order;
> in the field of organic life we can still see how the forces con-
> tend with one another, and how the effects of the conflict are
> continually changing. So, also, the two urges, the one towards
> personal happiness and the other towards union with other
> human beings must struggle with each other in every indivi-
> idual; and so, also, the two processes of individual and of
> cultural development must stand in hostile opposition to each
> other and mutually dispute the ground. But this struggle
> between the individual and society is not a derivative of the
> contradiction - probably an irreconcilable one - between the
> primal instincts of Eros and death. It is a dispute within the
> economics of the libido, comparable to the contest concerning
> the distribution of libido between ego and objects; and it does
> admit of an eventual accommodation in the individual, as it may
> be hoped, it will also do in the future of civilization, however
> much that civilization may oppress the life of the individual
> to-day. (1930a:21:141)

In this extract, all the ambiguities in Freud's theory of the
relations between the individual, civilization and the two faces

of Eros seem to come together. It would, perhaps, be more
accurate to talk of two paradigms of Eros, rather than two faces,
for Freud himself acknowledges his inability to bring them
together; Eros as the material force, whose unruly vicissitudes
and capricious demands determine the development of the individual, and who gives men and women the best experiences of
life, seems almost unrelated to Eros as the Heavenly power who,
through his unceasing opposition to the death instinct, determines the development of civilization and holds societies together.
The two paradigms appear to have few points of contact, and we
can well understand the confusion that prevailed among many
practising analysts, who ignored the second paradigm altogether
and proceeded to conduct their businesses on the basis of the
practical equation of Eros with libido.

Most philosophical commentators are also perplexed at this
point, and try somehow to bring about a rapprochement of the
two paradigms of Eros. The majority of them opt for a view of
Eros as inherently social, always looking for new combinations of
life, new forms of union. Ricoeur, for instance, has argued that
the second paradigm replaced the first, and concludes his discussion of Eros by arguing that 'the desire of the other is
directly implied in the emergence of Eros; it is always with
another that the living substance fights against death' (1970:291).
Likewise, Mitchell argues that 'desire is therefore always a
question of a significant inter-relationship, desire is always the
desire of the other' (1974:396). Similar arguments are offered by
Himmelstein, Marcuse and Brown, all of whom emphasize the
integrative power of Eros at the expense of the unruly,
paroxysmal character of libido. Rieff, on the other hand, in
direct opposition to this view, believes that

> Freud's image of love takes on a darker coloring than can be
> conveyed by comfortable terms like 'sociability' or 'affection'
> or, for that matter, 'love'. Eros is either greedy and sadistic
> or abjectly submissive. (1959:256)

In direct opposition to the view of an inherently 'social' Eros,
Rieff contends that 'satisfaction from an object is but a devious
means of self-love' (173). I hope that my earlier discussion has
shown how both of these contradictory interpretations have a
solid foundation in Freud's mature work, which never resolves
the ambiguity of whether sublimation and socialization ultimately
proceed from Eros (the view of most theorists) or from civilization
(the view of Rieff).

This ambiguity has a striking consequence; while both views
recognize the underlying antagonism between individual and
society, if socialization proceeds from civilization,[16] then this
antagonism assumes the forms of a 'real opposition'; if, on the
other hand, the socialization of Eros proceeds from Eros himself,
then the antagonism assumes the form of a 'dialectical contradiction'. In the first case, the individual and society confront

each other as two independent and opposed forces analogous to
two opposed forces in Newtonian mechanics; man as a pleasure-
seeking animal is opposed by a culture requiring instinctual
renunciation - man's nature embodied in his instinctual life is
opposed by culture. Seeing the individual and society as being
in a real opposition does not imply that the two are totally exclusive; it is possible for instance to incorporate within this view
the super-ego as the culture's representative within the individual, and culture's narcissistic function as the individual's gain
from culture. In principle, however, it should be possible to
establish the individual and culture as independent concepts,
whose claims bring them into opposition.[17]

In contrast to the view which sees the individual and culture
as being in a real opposition, it is possible to envisage their
antagonism as a 'dialectical contradiction'; according to this view,
neither the individual nor society can be defined independently
of the other, and the two stand in a constant and mutual definition, like two poles of a magnet. Both the individual and society
are seen as elements of an underlying unity of life, and depending on the state of this unity, the contradiction between the
individual and society may be antagonistic or non-antagonistic.
The antagonism is not an inescapable predicament of humans,
but a historical phenomenon, arising when life comes under attack
from opposing tendencies, and capable of being superseded
within a future kingdom of life.

The dialectical interpretation of the relation between individual
and society gains support if desire can be shown to be striving
towards restoring an original unity, the unity which existed
between the ego and the objects of *its* world in early infancy,
before the institution of the ego in opposition to the id (1930a:
21:66-7). This is precisely what Freud's discussion of the
'oceanic feeling' suggests, at the beginning of 'Civilization and
and Its Discontents'; this feeling is seen as a mental relic from
the auto-erotic phase of infancy, representing a primordial
desire, a longing for the restoration of this union. Rank's discussion of the birth trauma and separation anxiety would place
the original union further back in mental archaeology, to the
intra-uterine experience. 'Becoming one' with a religious community, therefore, would signify a return to a primordial oneness, the dismantling of the ego which arose out of the breach
of this original oneness, and the perfect harmonization of
individual and society within a reconstituted whole. Yet, Freud
was unwilling to accept this interpretation of the origins of
religious feelings, preferring to locate them in the child's need
for protection; infantile helplessness rather than extended
narcissism is, for Freud, the key to understanding the origin
and power of religion. Although he recognizes the possible
existence of an oceanic feeling as a relic of the auto-erotic past,
he argues that

'oneness with the universe' which constitutes [the] ideational

content [of the oceanic feeling] sounds like a first attempt at
a religious consolation as though it were another way of dis-
claiming the danger which the ego recognizes as threatening
it from the external world. (72)

In short, what Freud is arguing is that 'oneness with the
universe' is a religious illusion, aimed at consoling and placating
the individual. In order to support this argument, what he does
is to shift paradigms, to adopt once again the paradigm of 'real
opposition' between society and the individual, according to
which there can be no going back to the original unity of the
ego and the universe, once fate has broken this unity.

Norman O. Brown, on the other hand, is fully committed to
the dialectical paradigm and seeks to show that love is not just
social, not just a desire for the other, but a longing for union
with the other, after the auto-erotic experience. First, Brown
tries to show that identification and object-cathexis are not
mutually exclusive forms of love, that anaclitic and narcissistic
object-choices are not opposites but mutually re-inforcing
aspects of love, by considering the child's relations with the
mother and father. Both of these relations, he argues, involve
both possessive and identity components; love for the parents
involves being one with them, and therefore 'the collapse of
the distinction between identification and object-choice leaves
love with one essential aim over and above pleasure, which is
to become one with the objects in the world' (1959:44). The
next problem that confronts Brown is the reconciliation of Eros
as union with the other aspect of Eros, pleasure: 'How does the
desire for pleasurable activity of one's own body lead to other
bodies?' (45). Brown finds the answer to this question in the
early auto-erotic phase, which he regards not only as a phase
of union with the world, but also a phase of unmitigated pleasure.
Pleasure and union are not opposites but inseparable aspects of
a primordial experience to which the ego will always strive to
return. Neither repressions nor sublimations can eliminate this
experience which marks every human individual for life, because
both of these processes are profoundly dialectical in that they
overcome desire without eliminating it. Sublimation is a concept
inherited by Freud from Nietzsche, who had used it to denote
the psychological process through which a motivational principle
is simultaneously preserved, cancelled and 'lifted up'. Walter
Kaufmann in his engaging study of Nietzsche demonstrates how
the latter's concept of sublimation is the psychological equivalent
of Hegel's 'aufheben', both of which involve the unleashing of
an inner tension as a creative force in a process of self-
overcoming.[18] Through sublimation, a motivational principle, far
from being emasculated or negated, is transformed into a principle of creation and synthesis, without losing its essential
character. Underneath all manifestations of human creativity,
Nietzsche saw the will to power, a force which is not lost in
sublimation but rather reaches its consummation in the transfor-

mation of a desire to kill and torture an opponent into a desire
to match the opponent in a spiritual contest (Kaufmann 1956:
191ff).

Unlike Nietzsche's view of sublimation of the will to power,
Freud's theory of the sublimation of libido involves its weakening, deflection and de-sexualization - hence Brown argues that
sublimation is the negation of instincts (1959:161-5). Marcuse,
however, tries to re-discover the Nietzschean origins of libidinal
sublimation by 'aggrandizing' sexuality into Eros (1955:188);
once libido is seen not narrowly as a pleasure-seeking principle,
but as an energy of unification, the energy of Eros, then the
sublimation of libido does not necessarily involve weakening and
de-sexualization - this is what he defines as non-repressive
sublimation:

> Its fully developed form would be sublimation without desexual-
> ization. The instinct is not 'deflected' from its aim; it is grati-
> fied in activities and relations that are not sexual in the sense
> of 'organized' genital sexuality and yet are libidinal and erotic.
> (190)

Moreover, if non-repressive sublimation is the consummation of
desire, repressive sublimation itself cannot be said to eliminate
desire, but on the contrary, as Freud taught us in 'The Interpretation of Dreams', it immortalizes desire; once repressed,
desire will always strive towards expression and fulfilment. This
accounts for the fact that Brown can make two apparently contradictory statements on human essence in the space of a mere
four pages: 'The essence of society is the repression of the
individual and the essence of the individual is the repression
of himself' (1959:3), and 'the essence of man consists . . . in
desiring' (7). Only because repression far from eliminating
desire eternalizes it can the essence of mankind be simultaneously
desire and its repression.

Now, if both sublimation and repression are dialectical processes, the latter immortalizing desire, the former arguably con-
summating it, then the two paradigms of Eros, Eros as union
and Eros as pleasure, converge on the single experience of the
oceanic feeling, which signifies both the satisfaction of a
primordial desire and a union with the objects of the world. No
sublimations, no repressions can eliminate the primordial desire
for union, the hallmark of Eros, which is realized in the single
experience of the oceanic feeling.

Of course, the oceanic feeling is an exception, not a rule, and
perhaps it is a mere illusion which, like a dream, presents us
with a desire as if it were already fulfilled. But it is enough
to establish the existence of a primordial desire for union as the
quintessence of Eros, in order to present the antagonism between
the individual and society as a historical phenomenon, not as a
'real opposition'. In an alienated society, only glimpses of this
primordial desire can be observed, in a work of art, a dream or

an evasive experience of the oceanic feeling; both Marcuse and
Brown devote much of their imaginative thinking in establishing
the conditions under which the individual and civilization can
reconstitute the original union, of the individual with the objects
of the universe. Marcuse sees the possibility of this reconstitution in an overcoming of Nature as an external constraint
(Nature as Ananke), and the liberation of Eros in society, in a
way which overwhelms - one may say 'drowns' - the death
instinct; Brown, on the other hand, envisages the same reconstitution as resulting from an acceptance of Thanatos within the
kingdom of life, and a re-harmonization of the two instincts in a
dialectical unity.[19]

Compelling as the dialectic conceptualization of the individual
and society may be, does it not underestimate the power of
fate? Is it not a central theme of Freudian theory that the breach
of the original union between the individual and the world is an
irreversible and necessary step? Does the institution of the ego
not mark an immutable modification of the mental apparatus much
as the institution of the super-ego marks a further such modification? Finally, does the identification of the oceanic feeling with
the quintessence of Eros do justice to Freud's painstaking
research into sexuality, its development, manifestations and mis-
carriages, or does it sacrifice them in the interest of a purely
theoretical convergence of the two paradigms?

The view of Eros as a force trying to recreate an original
union is a plausible one, when seen from the Eros-as-union
paradigm. In 'Beyond the Pleasure Principle', when this paradigm was first introduced, Freud had argued that not only the
death instinct but Eros too goes beyond the pleasure principle,
insofar as it can be represented as 'a need to restore an earlier
state of things' (1920g:18:57). By invoking the myth of the
androgynous humans which Plato put in the mouth of Aristo-
phanes in the 'Symposium', Freud argued that the earlier state
of things that Eros seeks to restore is a primordial unity with
the other. While the paradigm of Eros which emerged from these
meta-psychological considerations may serve him well in his
speculations on civilization, it is at variance with his theory of
sexuality in ontogenesis. For how can the individual strive to
re experience a primordial unity with the world, if at the time
of this unity the individual had not emerged as an ego and the
world had not emerged as an Other? And how can this primordial unity, in its autistic self-containment, provide the prototype
of all future social ties? All of Freud's accounts of the entry of
the little child into society, far from suggesting a constant
development of Eros into unification with ever-expanding unities,
indicate a progressive manipulation, frustration and socialization
of the child's libido, so that the early polymorphous perversity
may be replaced not only with genitality, but also with post-
Oedipal respect for authority and non-sexual identification with
the social whole. From this perspective, Eros is not a power
which with the arrival of every new child into the world flowers

into stronger and more permanent bonds, but rather an unruly
newcomer who must be controlled in order that he may become
socially useful by an authority superior to his own, civilization
itself. From this perspective the quintessential erotic manifestation is not the oceanic feeling of union with the world, but the
stormy experience of bodily pleasure in a union with the loved
one; this experience, like that of the oceanic feeling, involves
unification as well as pleasure. Yet, unlike the oceanic feeling,
it does not recreate within civilization a re-harmonization of
the individual's primordial desire with society's requirement of
social cohesion. On the contrary, the state of being in love and
its consummation in the sexual union of the couple presents a
great threat to society; although society reaps the benefits of
of the sexual act, which is indispensable for the survival of
the species, it must intervene and put an end to the narcissistic
bliss of the couple, just as Zeus split the powerful androgynous
men and brought about a final end to the 'natural state of man'.
From this perspective, the breach of the original union is an
irreversible step, and the emergence of the ego seals this
breach; memories of the earlier era may still remain - this is
why Freud likens the oceanic feeling to the archaeological relics
which are scattered throughout Rome. But no return to the past
is possible, except as an illusion, a mirage, a dream. The opposition between the individual and society is a real product of
fate, not the alienation of the underlying unity of Eros.

According to the dialectical view, the individual, society and
the twin faces of Eros are all conceptually related; in Brown's
variant of this view, the death instinct is also a part of this
complex. All real tensions are the products of a tension in the
underlying unity. According to the dualistic view, all of these
entities, including the twin concepts of Eros, retain a considerable conceptual autonomy, and their conflicts arise from their
clashing requirements. Individual and society, nature and culture, union and pleasure, love and death are forever fixed by
fate in contradictory pairs, whose conflicts and compromises
make up the extraordinary adventure of life. Instincts, agencies,
principles, energies and forces, all the dominant heroes of the
Freudian doctrine are forever engaged in an epic confrontation,
like those Homeric gods, whose fights, conspiracies, treacheries,
ploys and reconciliations governed the lives of humans. Whether
human life must ultimately be seen as the tenuous outcome of the
struggle of plural forces or as a conflict-ridden commonwealth
of Eros is a dilemma which remains unresolved in Freudian doctrine and lies in the heart of the problematic of the relation
between the individual and society.

Chapter 3
Normality, neurosis and therapy

The discussion of the problematic of the individual and society
leads us to a related problematic, that of normality and pathology.
The issues which confront us here are the nature and aetiology
of neurosis, the aims, scope and limitations of therapy, the
pathogenic influence of culture and the choice of therapeutic
procedures.

There is an argument which is currently gaining considerable
support, according to which, in the last couple of hundred years,
there has been a major shift in the West's understanding of itself
away from a vision dominated by the struggle of good and evil to
one dominated by the opposition between health and sickness,
normality and pathology. This shift, highlighted by the gradual
eclipsing of priests, healers, exorcists and magicians by medical
and psychiatric experts, social workers and prison reformers,
and by the replacement of institutions of punishment and isolation
by institutions of cure and rehabilitation, co-incides with the
emergence of the social and human sciences which provide its
epistemological foundations as well as its institutional legitimation.
The human sciences developed models of order, representing the
normal state of societies, economies and souls, governed by laws
which could be isolated, articulated and studied. Major departures from these 'normal' states, like anomic break-downs of the
social order, economic crises and madness, became synonymous
to pathology, exceptions not only to the rules of the human
sciences but also to the laws governing societies, economies and
souls; such departures or irregularities were conceived as a
priori rectifiable or capable of being returned to order.

Nowhere is this shift in Western daemonology from an imagery
of the evil which has the right of existence to pathology which
does not, from Iago to Raskolnikov, clearer than in the medical
science. It may be argued that medicine was the vanguard of the
new era, since it provided this era with the central metaphor
of disease which was subsequently adopted by sociology, economics, psychology and common sense. Lepers, alcoholics and
demented people[1] were among the diverse 'deviant' groups which
were re-classified as evil disappeared from the Western world,
not through being defeated by good, but through having dissolved in the new terms of disease and health. Within the new
paradigm, all these groups, the exception, the Other, lost the
threatening quality they had possessed as incarnations of the
Evil, and became accommodated within the language of the Same,
the language of science, reason and health; they became sick,

unfortunate people, thus leaving the dark nether-worlds of evil for the white kingdoms of science and its humanistic ethic. One after another they became subjects of treatment, aimed at returning them to normality and relieving them of their suffering.

Within this general shift from a society which rejects, isolates and punishes its enemies to a society which understands, controls and rehabilitates them, Freud is credited with the dubious distinction of having extended treatment to the class of mentally sick people; psychoanalysis, in its promise of treating and curing a certain category of neurotics, those suffering from so-called transference neuroses, is seen as part of the generalized institutional attempt to rehabilitate mental disorders, through mental treatment. In this section, I will not confront directly the social function of psychoanalytic therapies and other therapeutic establishments of clinical psychology (a topic which will be addressed in Part II), but will deal with Freud's contribution to the emerging new paradigm of normality and pathology in mental states, mental health and mental sickness. Nor will I deal with the sociology of therapy, but will study therapy within the context of the Freudian discourse, as an intervention in the space of normality and pathology, its scope, aims and limitations, although I will not try to obscure the fact that in practice, as psychotherapy became entrenched in the social fabric of modern societies, its aims were deflected, its scope broadened and its limitations ignored.

It is common nowadays to think of mental health in direct analogy to physical health as the normal condition, marked by the absence of mental disease. Medical science broadly sponsors this view of physical health, by identifying disease as an abnormal condition, inflicted either from outside through contagion, or from within through genetic transmission. Health is normality and normality is the standard, while sickness is the exception. Freud's view of mental normality is quite different from this view; he never ceased to insist that normality in the mental sphere cannot exist, except as an 'ideal fiction' (1937c:23:235). Whether he was referring to the 'resolution' of the Oedipus Complex and the establishment of genitality, the dividing line between 'perversions' and normal sexuality, or the differences between neurotic, psychotic and normal behavior, he invariably stressed that psychic normality, unlike the physicians' somatic normality, can only exist as an ideal type, not as a real condition.

The sociologist must be warned at this point that, unlike Weber's ideal types, Freud's is not a theoretical construction, a heuristic device based on certain domain assumptions, against which real states can be measured. Nor is it a clinical condition, representing the absence of symptoms and pathogenic factors a virus, a chromosomic irregularity, etc.[2] On the whole, Freud adopts a purely conventional use of the term 'normality', and frequently uses it in expressions like 'what is described as normal' (1940a:23:183) or 'the majority who are assumed to be normal' (1930a:21:145). Likewise, Freud uses the term 'perver-

sion' to signify any deviation from socially accepted forms of
sexuality. Finally and more surprisingly, Freud uses the term
'neurotic' in a rather conventional fashion to denote, in the first
place, a person who appears to suffer from unusually strong
feelings of 'unpleasure, anxiety and pain' (ibid.) under circumstances which would not cause such feelings in the majority of
people, and exhibits unusual phobic, compulsive or hysterical
symptoms which inhibit, to a greater or lesser extent, his/her
social functioning. Unlike the physician who, through his
studies of diverse pathological states, their aetiology, mechanisms and symptoms, furnishes the common-sense notion of
health with scientific justifications as the absence of such
pathological phenomena, Freud appears to begin with the common-
sense notion of mental health; mental health is the general ability
to function in society as most human beings are assumed to
function. This is not, of course, the result of Freud's intellectual naiveté, but rather the consequence of his realization that
these terms can only be used in their conventional sense.

> We have seen that it is not scientifically feasible to draw a
> line of demarcation between what is psychically normal and
> abnormal; so that distinction, in spite of its practical import-
> ance, possesses only a conventional value. (1940a:23:195)

Normality, in the Freudian view, is simply a cultural product,
or what some may call an ideological element – it is neither a
logical/scientific concept nor a biological/clinical standard.
The importance of this point cannot be overestimated, and
although it usually goes unnoticed, in it lies a major contribution
of psychoanalysis; Freud's early work on hysteria as well as
earlier work on mental disorders (Breuer, Janet, etc.) had
operated broadly within the medical metaphor of health and
sickness, in trying to isolate the pathogenic factor of mental
disorders, much as Pasteur, Koch and Hansen had identified
and isolated the causes of organic disorders. In his early theory
with Breuer, Freud had attacked Janet's theory of hysteria
which regarded it as a constitutional predisposition towards
split consciousness, by arguing that its aetiology lay in the
recurrence of childhood traumata, which resulted in split consciousness. This dispute of the 1890s is almost a direct replica
of similar debates that had taken place in medicine several years
earlier between the contagionists and the geneticists – while
Janet was arguing that the splitting of consciousness is the outcome of genetic irregularity, Freud and Breuer believed that it
was the result of chance events of early childhood, especially
seductions by parents. Parallel to Breuer's view that these
memories return during what he termed 'hypnoid states', Freud
argued that the splitting of consciousness and the resulting
hysteric attacks were defence mechanisms, 'acts of will', through
which the patients sought to protect themselves from the pain
that would arise if they recognized the trauma. As will be seen

in greater detail in Chapter 5, Freud soon realized that many of
the seductions that his patients had reported to him were fictitious in nature; therefore, his hypotheses of 'splitting of consciousness' and of 'forgetting of childhood traumata' were
plainly falsified. This led Freud to the novel hypothesis of
'repression', in which the idea of defence was preserved, but
instead of having defence against actual traumata, he now
envisaged it as a defence against childhood phantasies and
desires, which had to exist in an area of the mind unable to
distinguish between truth and phantasy, the unconscious. At
the time these hypotheses seemed patently implausible, con-
tradicting not only common sense but also the whole Western
tradition of philosophy of mind, and Freud might have abandoned
them had he not decided to study dreams. The study of dreams,
like that of neurotic symptoms, revealed an unexpected wealth
of meanings, which not only supported the early tentative ideas
of the unconscious and of repression, but also demonstrated
that these mental features were not the unwelcome privilege of
neurotics; since everybody has dreams, everybody's mental life
must involve unconscious desires, inner conflicts and repressions.
Forty years later, he insisted on the same point:

> Neurotics have approximately the same innate dispositions
> as other people, they have the same experiences and they have
> the same tasks to perform. (1940a:23:183)

Far from leading him to an 'external' pathogenic factor, Freud's
investigations gradually convinced him that the underlying
mental processes of neurotics were not unlike those of normal
people - the dream was in its essence a neurotic symptom, common among normal people. Two important conclusions follow,
one theoretical and one therapeutic. Theoretically,

> we have thus established the right to arrive at an under-
> standing of the normal life of the mind from a study of dis-
> orders - which would not be admissible if these pathological
> states, neuroses and psychoses, had specific causes operating
> in the manner of foreign bodies. (195)

Contrary to medical science, Freud was arguing that in the
mental sphere normal and pathological processes were the same,
only the outcomes differed. As he never tired of repeating, the
differences between neurotic and normal have to be accounted
for by quantitative factors,[3] i.e. factors related to the availability and distribution of mental energies, both libidinal and
aggressive, which compromise his 'economic point of view'. He
did not dispute the view that quantitative factors may precipitate
what may, in fact, appear as qualitative changes under neurosis,
such as loss or distortion of reality, morbid symptoms and
incapacitating anxiety; but he was quick to point out that these
were not entirely absent even in normal conditions.

The second conclusion from Freud's view of normality has a
direct bearing on the task of the analyst; under certain conditions, the analyst may intervene in the economics of the
pathogenic processes and, by tipping the balance, so to speak,
succeed in restoring a sense of reality, dissolving the morbid
symptoms, and attenuate anxiety. Freud never argued that only
an analyst may effect such an intervention or that the intervention guarantees cure. He emphasized, on the contrary, that
'as a method of treatment [psychoanalysis] is one among many'
(1933a:22:157), that many pathological conditions, such as
psychotic and narcissistic ones, lie beyond its scope (155), and
that its effectiveness was limited:

> I do not think that our cures can compete with those of
> Lourdes. (ibid.)

He did, nevertheless, believe that psychoanalysis offered a
unique kind of therapeutic which put it in a class of its own.
  Before examining the uniqueness of the psychoanalytic intervention, it is instructive to outline the argument concerning the
aetiology of neuroses. Freud discerned two basic pathogenic
patterns, which usually occur in combination.

> The aetiology of all neuroses is indeed a mixed one; either the
> patient's instincts are excessively strong and refuse to sub-
> mit to the taming influence of his ego or else he is suffering
> from the effects of early traumas, by which I mean traumas
> which his immature ego was unable to surmount. Generally
> there is a combination of the two factors: the constitutional
> and the accidental. (1937c:23:220)

Freud pointed out that only in the latter case of neurosis may
psychoanalytic therapy be concluded successfully, with no danger
of a recurrence of the symptoms at a later stage. This is achieved
if the analyst can assist the patient's ego in replacing 'an
inadequate decision made during infancy by a correct solution'
(ibid.). Our interest, however, lies mainly with the latter and
the mixed cases, which correspond to an on-going conflict
between the id, as the representative of the instinctual forces,
and the ego as the representative of the anti-instinctual forces
(1924b:19:149). But this conflict between two psychic agencies
is influenced at every stage by the demands of external reality,
i.e. family, other people, 'culture', etc., which provides both
the raw material and the parameters of the conflict.

> Neurosis is thus the consequence of a conflict between the
> Ego and the Id, on which the ego centers because . . . it
> insists throughout on retaining its adaptability towards the
> outer world. The opposition lies between the outer world and
> the Id, and because the Ego, true to its inmost nature, takes
> sides with the outer world, it becomes involved in conflict with

its own Id. (1926e:120:204)

Nor is the super-ego absent from the pathogenic process, since 'in undertaking the repression the ego is at bottom following the dictates of the super-ego' (1924b:19:150). Thus, the pathogenic process in neurosis is rooted in repression and conflict.

Even this, however, does not exhaust the issue of the aetiology of neurosis, since not all repressions are pathogenic (1924e:19:186). If the ego is endowed with sufficient energies to invest in its anti-cathexes, it may be successful in silencing not only the original desire, whose fulfilment it cannot allow, but also the secondary manifestations that accompany repression; it may, in other words, keep out of consciousness all ideas related to the original desire (1915d). Unless the original wish becomes suddenly invested with large amounts of libido, it will only be expressed through symptoms which bear little relation to its original ideational content – phobic symptoms, little compulsions, various idées fixes and character rigidities. Once again, the strong ego can tame such manifestations provided that they do not conflict with social conventions (1926d:20:97ff). A weaker ego, however, may be unable to provide substitutive satisfactions which are capable of satisfying and silencing the original desire and at the same time do not cause social embarrassment. In such cases, the repression is said to have miscarried and becomes the nucleus of a pathogenic process. Once the ego has realized its failure to carry out a successful repression, it

> feels uneasy; it finds a limit to its power in its own house, the mind. Thoughts suddenly break in without the conscious mind knowing where they come from, nor can it do anything to drive them away. These unwelcome guests seem to be more powerful than those which are at the ego's command; they resist all the well-known measures instituted by the will, remain unmoved by logical rebuttal, and unaffected though reality refutes them; . . . [the ego] increases its vigilance, but cannot understand why it feels so strangely paralysed. (1917a:17:141-2)

So, what distinguishes in the first place the normal from the pathological ego seems to be its ability to keep repressed wishes and their vicissitudes out of consciousness. Even the normal ego, however, can never be quite sure that the repressed material will not surge back, equipped with fresh energies which may overwhelm its own defences. There is, nevertheless, a second difference between the normal and the pathological ego – the former 'chooses' socially acceptable forms to channel the substitutive satisfactions which it allows the id, while the latter 'chooses' unacceptable ones. Freud recognized that often the misery of the neurotic arises not from the compulsive or painful nature of his/her symptoms, but from the social stigma attached to them (1930a:21:108). Society, either directly or through the mediation of the super-ego, is likely to sanction aggressive symptoms among males but not among females; claustrophobia and smoking are generally accepted, while nervous twitches and agoraphobia are ridiculed and even punished. Different societies, of course, may tolerate and even encourage different symptoms, and cause different frustrations. Before looking in greater detail at why different people select different symptoms as substitutive satisfactions, it is important to mention a different strategy that the ego may adopt in dealing with an unacceptable desire; instead of repressing such a desire by opposing the original impulse with large anti-cathexes from its own supplies of libido (thus repressing it), the ego may be able to achieve a dissociation of the idea of the offensive impulse from the energy which charges it, and use this energy for a different aim. This is precisely the case of sublimation, where not only is the ego not impoverished in its fight against a painful idea, but on the contrary it manages to master the energy of this idea and channels it in novel and creative ways. It is for this reason that Freud argued that 'of many [neurotics] one can believe that they would never have fallen ill had they possessed the art of sublimating their impulse' (1912e:12:119). In his brilliant study of Leonardo, Freud discovered the seeds of artistic genius in the great artist's capacity for sublimation, his ability of turning pain into creativity, an argument which is in broad agreement with Nietzsche's view on greatness.

We must now return to the question of what causes some people to adopt socially acceptable and some people socially unacceptable forms of substitute gratification. And, even among those who possess the secret of sublimation, why do some, like Leonardo, master their neurosis, while others, like Mahler, remain its victims, by compulsively spoiling the sublime with the banal? Although Freud never addressed these issues explicitly, they can be accounted for by his increasing recognition of the role of the death instinct in the aetiology of neurosis. In his discussions between 1910 and 1920 (before the postulation of a death instinct), Freud had stressed, as we saw, the libidinal impoverishment of the ego and the strength of the offending impulses from the id. Yet, this economic point of view does not exhaust his post-1920 discussions of the aetiology problem. In 'Beyond the Pleasure Principle' (1920g), the very work which introduced the death instinct, Freud considered at length certain masochistic tendencies among neurotics, who not only seem to derive pleasure by viewing themselves as social outcasts, but also by compulsively repeating particularly painful experiences or by experiencing a strong sense of guilt as soon as they feel the first signs of recovery. He also noted the prophylactic effect that physical injuries (such as those sustained during a war) have vis-à-vis the setting-up of neuroses, and argued that one of the main resistances to cure was a 'reversal of self-preservation'. These observations led him to the belief that the neurosis may in fact represent a form of self-punishment that the patient inflicts

upon himself in order to pacify his innate 'sense of guilt', which
we discussed in Chapter 2.[4] Increasingly he came to attribute
to this factor an almost equal importance to the quantitative weaknesses of the ego. In neurosis, the ego is, therefore, not only
equipped with inadequate amounts of libido to dam the offending
impulses, but it also has become the victim of considerable
aggression from the super-ego. This last factor is subsumed, in
some of Freud's clinical writings, under what he calls the
neurotic's 'tendency to conflict',[5] which is in the last instance
responsible for the inverted relation between perversion and
neurosis – the pervert can tolerate living with his socially
unacceptable fixations, while the neurotic finds it impossible to
accept even innocuous symptoms in himself.

Having established the central features of neurosis in Freud's
theory, it is now possible to examine what effects and possibilities are available to the therapeutic intervention. And in the
first place, it must be recognized that since psychoanalysis fails
or refuses to draw a hard and fast line between health and
sickness, and since it asserts that the 'healthy man is . . .
virtually a neurotic' (1916-17:16:457), its task cannot be defined
in parallel to the task of medicine. Psychoanalysis, much like
common sense, defined neurosis in terms of the neurotic's
apparent inability to lead a 'normal and creative' life; it follows
that its task can only be defined pragmatically:

> Just as health and sickness are not qualitatively different from
> each other but are only gradually separated in an empirically
> determined way, so the aim of the treatment will never be any-
> thing else but the practical recovery of the patient, the
> restoration of his ability and capacity of enjoyment and an
> active life. (1904a:7:59)

But if the aim of the psychoanalytic treatment is defined in this
practical way, in other words as seeking to restore a broken-
down individual to a useful and enjoyable position in society,
then its successes and failures can only be judged pragmatically.[6] In psychotherapy, it is not possible for the operation to
be successful and for the patient to die. At the same time, having set the task of restoration and adjustment as the aim of the
therapeutic effort, Freud places psychoanalysis under a common
denominator with all other therapeutic methods; hence he is
candid enough to admit that

> there are many ways and means of practicing psychotherapy.
> All that lead to recovery are good. (259)[7]

Moreover, Freud was not reluctant to recommend the use of
simpler, cheaper and quicker methods where appropriate.

> I consider it quite justifiable to resort to more convenient
> methods of healing as long as there is any prospect of attain-

ing anything by their means. (262)

Within this therapeutic pantheon, where 'anything goes if it
works' (Brown 1959:155), Freud claims, nevertheless, a special
place for psychoanalysis; in spite of its inability to compete with
the cures of Lourdes, in spite of its laborious and time-consuming
nature, in spite of its limitations and inability to deal with
psychotic and autistic conditions, Freud considered psychoanalysis primus inter pares, because he believed that only in
psychoanalytic treatment the cure co-incides with self-knowledge.
Other therapies deal with the symptoms of mental disorders,
which they seek to silence by superimposing fresh impressions
through suggestion. By using Leonardo's contrast between painting, which proceeds by adding material (per via di porre), and
sculpture, which proceeds by removing it (per via di levare),
Freud argued that suggestive treatment

> superimposes something (a suggestion) and expects this to be
> strong enough to restrain the pathogenic idea from coming to
> expression. Analytic therapy, on the other hand, does not
> seek to add or to introduce something new, but to take away
> something, to bring out something. (1904a:7:260-1)

Freud had been quite familiar with suggestive treatments,
through his studies in France, where hypnotism was used to
cure mental disorders. The uniqueness of Breuer's therapeutic
success in the case of Anna O had resided in the fact that no
suggestion had been used; although Breuer had employed
hypnosis, his method had consisted of re-introducing to the
patient's ego what she had disclosed during her delirium, i.e.
the pathogenic idea, whose repression had led to the hysterical
symptoms. In contrast to the cures achieved by Bernheim and
his colleagues, Breuer's success had shown a case where
'understanding and cure almost coincide' (1933a:22:145)
   While, as we shall see, Freud abandoned Breuer's cathartic
method in favour of his own method of free association, the
principle of cure through understanding, recovery through
self-knowledge, remained cardinal in his therapeutic endeavour.
It is re-iterated in Freud's programmatic aphorisms, like 'making
the unconscious conscious' or 'where id was, ego shall be' - the
possibility of achieving these programmatic objectives, which rest
on genuine self-knowledge within the overall goal of restoring
the patient's capacity 'to enjoy life', not only established the
practical limitations of psychoanalytic therapy, but also generated a considerable tension in Freud's theory of cure.
   It is, nevertheless, important to emphasize Freud's insistence
that 'the psychoanalytic treatment is founded in truthfulness.
. . . It is dangerous to depart from this sure foundation' (1915a:
12:164), which pre-supposed that

> the relationship between analyst and patient is based on a love

of truth, that is, on the acknowledgement of reality, and that
it precludes any kind of sham or deception. (1937c:23:248)

Of course, Freud was entirely aware of the fervour with which
the neurotic clings to his/her delusions; he was also aware that
the patient may accept the 'truth' intellectually, without being
cured of the symptoms;[8] finally, he knew that premature disclosure of the 'truth' by the analyst could cause irreparable
damage to the therapeutic task and even a complete collapse of
the patient. How then did he propose to arouse a 'love of truth'
in the patient, to bring to light the repressed idea which lies
at the heart of his condition, to precipitate an emotive as well
as an intellectual acceptance and to lead him/her along the
'traversable road [which] leads from [understanding] to cure'?
In Breuer's cathartic method, understanding was forced on
the patient whose resistances were paralysed through the effects
of hypnosis; Freud found that this method was not quite satisfactory for two reasons – many patients resisted attempts to
hypnotize them and several cured patients experienced a relapse
of their symptoms, especially if they developed a negative feeling towards the therapist/hypnotist. Freud's preference for
the far more copious technique of free association was due to the
fact that, unlike hypnosis, it brought the patient's resistances
into active play during the psychoanalytic sessions. Instead of
dealing exclusively with the repressed idea, Freud began to
study the process of repression itself, and sought to reveal to
the ego not only the content of the id, but also its own mechanisms of defence.
During the analytic session, the patient agrees to reveal all
thoughts that come to him/her, irrespective of how trivial,
absurd, offensive or painful they may be. Contrary, however,
to disclosure under hypnosis, when the content of the id comes
to the surface directly, in free association the patient's resistances operate to conceal, disrupt and distort his/her thoughts.
This necessitates a process of interpretation on the part of the
analyst, who seeks to uncover the hidden meanings of the
patient's utterances, recollections and silences; these interpretations are gradually given back to the patient, as he/she
learns to overcome the resistances which kept these pathogenic
desires repressed. Freud's writings on therapy are characterized
by a subtle shift in emphasis from the original repressed desire
to the resistances, as the central factor of the pathogenic
process – the neurotic does not merely ignore truth, but actively
resists it.

The idea that a neurotic is suffering from a sort of ignorance,
and that if one removes this ignorance by telling him facts
he must recover, is an idea that has long been superseded,
and one derived from the superficial appearances. The pathological factor is not his ignorance in itself, but the root of
this ignorance in his inner resistances. . . . . In combating

these resistances lies the task of therapy. (1910k:11:225)

This extract indicates that Freud regarded Breuer's cathartic
method as one essentially based on suggestion, because it failed
to deal with the patient's resistances and 'work them through',
but merely forced the repressed through them into consciousness. His method, on the other hand, relied on revealing to the
ego not only the censored idea but also its own resistances, by
demonstrating the operation of these resistances - so to speak,
by helping the ego to catch itself in the act.[9]
   How then can the analyst prepare the ground for offering his/
her disclosures to the patient? How can the neurotic, that avowed
enemy of self-knowledge, be transformed against all his/her
resistances into a lover of truth? How does psychoanalysis
achieve its blending of understanding and cure?
   These questions cannot be answered without a careful discussion of transference, undoubtedly the single most important
factor in the patient's path towards recovery. One of the first
observations made by Freud after he had started using his free-
association technique was that some patients could 'remember
nothing of what was forgotten and repressed, but express[ed]
it in action' (1914g:12:150). These patients repeated in their
behaviour what they could not reproduce in their memory, without having any knowledge that they were re-enacting their feelings and emotions which had accompanied the pathogenic process.
Almost invariably, these feelings were transferred onto the
person of the physician, who at first was surprised finding him/
herself at the centre of the patient's turbulent passions. Freud
gradually realized that transference operated in every therapeutic relationship and that it opened unique therapeutic possibilities: through transference the disease discovers a medium of
expression within the therapeutic situation, pathogenic conflicts
can come to the surface once again, experienced as if they were
new, under conditions which made their successful resolution
possible. Transference constitutes an artificially induced illness,
'an intermediary realm between illness and real life' (154), whose
handling becomes the crucial factor towards recovery, because
it brings the patient's illness under the physician's control. By
re-living his/her disease through the relationship with the
therapist, the patient puts the therapist in a privileged position
from which he/she can influence mental events during the
session.
   As is well known, a central feature of transference is its
ambivalence; it comprises both positive and negative feelings,
although at different times the one or the other class of feelings
prevails. Under conditions of positive transference, the patient
seeks to please the analyst and many of the resistances collapse.
This situation resembles somewhat the hypnotic method of catharsis, for in both cases the analyst/therapist is placed in the
position of the super-ego (1921c:18:114-16, 1930a:21:142-3,
1940a:23:175). From this position, the analyst sides with the

ego - in lieu of the hostile super-ego, the ego has now a sympathetic listener who encourages recovery. In this way, positive transference provides the patient with a motive towards recovery, the patient's ego is libidinally re-inforced through the support he/she receives from the analyst, while the strength of the self-destructive tendencies is undermined. Positive transference is thus the first of two conditions that must be fulfilled, before the analyst can proceed with imparting his/her knowledge to the patient (1910k:11:226, 1940a:23:178). The second condition is that the patient must have overcome enough resistances, so that the repressed material is very near consciousness, i.e. many of the ideas related to the repressed material must have already come to consciousness and been accepted. Negative transference, on the other hand, appears to threaten the task accomplished whilst positive transference prevailed; the patient's

> understanding of psychoanalysis and his reliance on its efficacy suddenly vanish. He behaves like a child who has no power of judgement of his own but blindly believes whom he loves and no one who is a stranger to him. (1940a:23:180)

Yet, provided that negative transference does not reach an extreme where the analytic relationship collapses, the analyst uses it to witness the patient's resistances in operation, to understand the patient's fears and frustrations and to study the patient's conflicts, which are being re-enacted in front of his very eyes.

Transference is therefore central in the psychoanalytic treatment as it at once furnishes rich material for interpretation by the analyst and supplies the patient with the necessary supplies of energy to overcome resistances and consider the disclosures offered by the analyst. So, the handling of transference, preventing it from reaching extremes, either positive or negative, channelling it in the direction of recovery through self-knowledge, interpreting its manifestations, are all central ingredients of the art of the therapist. In short, transference represents the emotive counterpart of the intellectual agreement which the patient enters with the analyst on commencing the analytic treatment.

A rather striking but rarely commented upon feature of Freud's writings on therapy is the fact that he invariably sees the practice of the therapist as an art - an art of interpretation, an art of handling transference, an art of the timing of disclosures and so on. This contrasts with his insistence that psychoanalysis is a science, operating after the model of the natural sciences.[10] While at a theoretical level Freud was willing to articulate a set of propositions and laws after the model of the natural sciences, frequently borrowing concepts from them and employing extensive metaphors, he was unable to provide any clear rules on the practical task facing the therapist - even

the cardinal principle of honesty is qualified by the fact that
the therapist must withhold information until the time is right;
nor does Freud provide practical rules to assist the interpretation of symptoms, utterances or dreams. It is, in fact, quite
possible to read and understand the whole of 'The Interpretation
of Dreams' and yet be unable to interpret a single dream of one's
own. How can the physician be sure that his/her interpretation
of a patient's behaviour is the right one? Freud argued on
several occasions that the analyst cannot trust even a simple
'yes' or 'no' of the patient; a 'no' may well mean 'yes', 'no'
or even 'I don't know', and it is the physician's task to interpret its meaning in accordance to the circumstances of the
negation, the tone in which it was uttered, and its consequences.
But how can the physician be sure? Although Freud gives countless hints as to how one may interpret a negation or an affirmation, and how one may support one's interpretations, he never
actually provides a systematic set of rules of interpretation,
the way Jung did, for the interpretation of symbols. For Freud,
interpretation is an art, a 'techne', which can be learned
through an apprenticeship by those equipped with appropriate
sensitivities, and not a science that can be circumscribed by a
code of formal propositions. Yet, psychoanalytic theory seeks
to establish the causal links between mental events, and
operates after the fashion of the natural sciences. In this way,
psychoanalysis stands in an ambiguous position, with one leg in
the natural sciences and one leg in the hermeneutic of double
meanings. This places it in the rather awkward situation (not
shared by other hermeneutic disciplines, like literary criticism)
of having to support its interpretations and 'constructions'
with the certainty of the natural sciences, or else risk losing its
objectivity and becoming merely another form of therapy based
on suggestion. How can it be safely established that what the
analyst feeds back to the patient is indeed the truth, rather
than merely an illusion? This presents Freud with a genuine
problem which he explicitly addresses in the last work of his
life:

> The therapeutic successes that occurred under the sway of
> the positive transference are open to the suspicion of being
> of a *suggestive* nature. (1940a:23:176)

Previously, Freud has warned the psychoanalyst not to take
undue advantage of the positive transference:

> a warning must be given against misusing this new influence.
> However much the analyst may be tempted to become a
> teacher, model and ideal for other people and to create men
> in his own image, he should not forget that it is not his task
> in the analytic relationship. (175)

Freud conceded that transference, as handled by some of his

colleagues who favoured a greater intimacy and empathy with their patients, brought psychoanalysis dangerously close to suggestive treatment:

> Transference alone frequently suffices to bring about a disappearance of the symptoms of the disease, but this is merely temporary and lasts only as long as the transference itself is maintained. The treatment is nothing more than suggestion, not psychoanalysis. It deserves the latter name only when the intensity of transference has been utilized to overcome resistances; only then does illness become impossible, even though the transference is again dissolved as its function in the treatment requires. (1913c:12:143)

At this stage of his life, Freud wished to keep suggestion out of psychoanalytic treatment because he saw it as preventing the permanent success of this treatment. His argument was that suggestion could influence the intellect, not the sickness (1916–17:16:393) which re-emerges as soon as transference is resolved – it silences the symptoms temporarily without reaching the pathogenic cause. But surely this is not a very strong argument, since as Freud's optimism about the therapeutic potential of analysis declined, he accepted that some of the cures based on suggestion could be lasting, while some of his successfully cured patients experienced a relapse of their disease. Some of the cures accomplished at Lourdes influence the disease as well as the intellect, in so far as they result in 'a permanent settlement of a (pathogenic) instinctual demand' (1937c:23:224) (Freud's own criterion of success in therapy). On the other hand, Freud is candid enough to report some of the cases of his own patients, like the celebrated Wolfman (1937c:23:218), who experienced a recurrence of neurotic symptoms, some time after the successful completion of analysis. In fact, in his later work 'Analysis Terminable and Interminable', he argues that analysis can very rarely guarantee a permanent silencing of the pathogenic impulse, hence in the majority of cases it is 'interminable'. It would, therefore, be rather misleading to contrast the temporary nature of suggestive treatment with the permanent solutions provided by psychoanalytic cures, for they both have their successes and their failures.

Freud's efforts to prevent psychoanalysis from becoming a rather subtle form of suggestive treatment, his pleas against the temptation of analysts to become teachers or to develop intimate relations with their patients, his constant exhortations 'to keep the distinctions' (of what is and what is not psychoanalysis) were not due to any chauvinism on his part; although he believed that analysis was by far the strongest and most effective therapy for a narrow range of neuroses, the so-called transference neuroses, he had 'never been a therapeutic enthusiast' (1933a:22:151) and, as we saw, he freely encouraged the use of suggestive treatment where it could produce an

improvement in the patient's condition and a lessening of his/her
suffering. Freud's opposition to the mixing of analytic and
suggestive treatments was not based on any concern with therapeutic efficiency, but on a very different consideration, namely,
that his clinical experience, with its successes and failures,
was the foundation stone of his theoretical generalizations. But
if analytic sessions had not been directed towards the discovery
of truth and overcoming of resistances, and had been instead
sessions of emotional support, positive feedback and intellectual
indoctrination, if suggestion had overtaken self-education, then
any theoretical formulations based on these sessions would be
perfectly useless; the patient's 'discoveries' would be nothing
but a mirror of his/her therapist's theoretical preconceptions;
in such cases, the patient would become the mouthpiece of the
analyst's professional delusions.

It is for this reason that Freud insisted that while suggestive
treatment operates through the resistances, leaving them intact,
analysis should proceed along the far more copious path of
making the patient conscious of his/her resistances and enabling
him/her to overcome them; in this way, analysis reaches the
heart of the pathogenic process and comes face to face with the
forces involved, instead of merely white-washing the symptoms.[11]
Having faced the disease directly, psychoanalysis feels entitled
to talk about it.

In order to 'keep the distinctions', Freud never tired of
recapitulating them. Unlike suggestive treatment, the analyst
demands no blind faith from the patient (1913c:12:126) who is
encouraged to use his/her critical and investigative abilities to
their peak, nor does the analyst use emotional pressure to force
his/her interpretations on the patient. Unlike other therapists,
the analyst limits expressions of tenderness, sympathy and love
to a minimum, and tries to resolve transference at the conclusion
of the treatment, so as to restore the cured patient's independence from the source of the cure (1916-17:16:455ff). The patient
is thus encouraged to use the energies freed through transference not to develop dependency relations with the analyst,
but to conquer the forces which distorted his/her consciousness.
But, even if all these favourable conditions are fulfilled, what
guarantees can psychoanalysis offer for the truth of the interpretations which it gives the patient? The nearest that Freud
came to answering this crucial question is through a set of inter-
related propositions, which we find in the late essay 'Constructions in Analysis'. In this essay, Freud is cautious not to indicate
that the truth of the interpretation lies purely in its acceptance
by the patient or in the fact that it results in a cure; the truth
of the interpretation emerges gradually through the movement
of the analytic session, it is a process rather than a fixed state.
Single interpretations of individual mental events, like symptoms,
dreams or emotions, can only serve as departure points for more
elaborate constructions drawn by the analyst. These constructions are constantly awaiting affirmation, modification or rejection

through cross-examination, and are gradually fed back to the
patient whose reactions are in turn interpreted, so as to support
or contradict the constructions. An affirmation will only provide
support for a construction if it is followed by indirect confir-
mations, such as a surge in the patient's memories or the stubborn 'no', described in detail in the essay 'On Negation'.
Interpretations are not forced upon the patient, but if possible
the patient is led to them.

> In short, we conduct ourselves upon the model of the familiar
> figure in one of Nestroy's farces - the man-servant who has a
> single answer on his lips to every question or objection: 'All
> will become clear in the course of future developments.'
> (1937d:23:265)

Thus in the course of the analysis, interpretations of the part
must be corroborated by constructions of the whole, and vice
versa, and must 'make sense' both to the analyst, who is applying his therapeutic skills, and to the patient who gradually
develops his/her own skills of self-knowledge.

In this way, Freud tries to bridge the gap between therapy as
an art and psychoanalysis as a science. From the point of view
of epistemology his argument is not unconvincing - the therapeutic endeavour of the analyst, with interpretations, hypotheses,
researches, successes and failures, corresponds to the intuitive
part of all scientific enterprise, which, as even the most ardent
positivists would accept, involves procedures which cannot be
codified into rules of method. From the therapeutic point of
view, however, it brings out some of the weaknesses of psychoanalysis as a method of treatment. For, in the light of our
starting assumption, namely that all therapy is aimed at restoring the patient's capacity to enjoy life in a useful role in society,
is it ever possible to achieve Freud's operational goals, expressed
in the formulae 'removal of all repressions', 'making the unconscious conscious', or 'overcoming inner resistances' or even
'extending the ego's self-knowledge'? In short, is self-knowledge
a good path towards enjoyment of life? Chapter 4 will consider
Freud's philosophical position on this issue in detail, but in this
chapter I will examine rather whether self-knowledge is an
appropriate therapeutic vehicle towards recovery. In particular,
I will consider three positions, all of which can be inferred from
different readings of Freud's work; the first position is that
self-knowledge is the best if not the only vehicle towards real
recovery, and is exemplified in the work of Habermas; the second
is that recovery through self-knowledge is impossible within the
parameters of the present social system, and is represented in
the writings of thinkers with anti-therapeutic approaches, like
Brown, Marcuse and Jacoby; finally, the third position is that
there is a definite but limited scope of success of therapies
based on an education of the patient, and, in a way, is represented in the work of Philip Rieff.

Habermas regards the analytic session as a process whereby the truth about the patient's inner life comes to light through self-reflection, with the analyst acting as a catalyst. While suggestive therapies proceed by manipulating the patient's soul much as modern medicine manipulates his/her body, psychoanalysis is a movement of self-reflection, in which the patient is the agent of his own emancipation; unlike Breuer's hypnotic technique, psycho-analysis does not manipulate consciousness, but entrusts the content of the unconscious to the subject himself.

> Freud rejected Breuer's technique because analysis is not a *steered natural process* but rather, on the level of intersubjectivity in ordinary language between doctor and patient, a *movement of self-reflection.* (1972:251)

Following Freud's discussion in 'Constructions in Analysis', Habermas argues that the 'experience of reflection is the only criterion for the corroboration or failure of hypotheses' (266), and much like Nestroy's character he sees clarification in the course of 'future developments'.

> The interpretation of a case is corroborated only by the successful *continuation of a self-formative process*, that is by the completion of self-reflection, and not in any unmistakeable way by what the patient says or how he behaves. (ibid.)

In Habermas's view, the re-discovery and encouragement of this self-reflective process constitutes the unique contribution of psychoanalysis to twentieth-century knowledge; until the arrival of Freud, Habermas argues, Western science had been channelled along paths of instrumental reason (natural sciences) and hermeneutic contemplation (cultural sciences). The former sought to codify natural phenomena by postulating natural laws, and was motivated by a cognitive interest of control over nature, while the latter aimed at clarifying shared symbolics (through the study of language, art and literature), motivated by a communicative interest. The concept of cognitive interest is central in this conceptualization which approaches all scientific endeavour from the point of view of the practical interest which motivates it, rather than its object or method; this concept distinguishes sharply Habermas's position from that of the positivists, who approach science as a passive contemplation of externality; in Habermas's view 'reason inheres in interest' (287), and it is interest which guides, defines and objectifies knowledge.[12] The critiques developed by Marx and Freud are guided neither by an instrumental nor by a communicative interest, but are distinguished

> by incorporating in their consciousness an interest which directs knowledge, an interest in emancipation going beyond the technical and practical interests of knowledge. By treat-

> ing psychoanalysis as an analysis of language aiming at
> reflection about oneself. I have sought to show how the
> relations of power embodied in systematically distorted com-
> munication can be attacked directly by the process of critique,
> so that in the self-reflection, which the analytic method has
> made possible and provoked, in the end insight can coincide
> with emancipation from unrecognized dependencies – that is,
> knowledge coincides with the fulfilment of the interest in
> liberation through knowledge. (1974:9)

So, it is this emancipatory interest in self-knowledge that directs
the patient-analyst relation, and drives the process of self-
reflection forward: 'Self-reflection . . . proceeds only as long as
analytic knowledge is impelled onward against motivational
resistances by the interest in *self-knowledge*' (1972:235). What
Habermas is trying to achieve through the introduction of a
concept of an emancipatory cognitive interest is a grand reconciliation of cure and understanding.

> In the case of an objectivation whose power is based only on
> the subject not recognizing itself in it as its other, knowing it
> in the act of self-reflection is immediately identical with the
> interest in knowledge, namely in emancipation from that power.
> The analytic situation makes real the unity of intuition and
> emancipation, of insight and liberation from dogmatic depen-
> dence, and of reason and the interested employment of reason
> developed by Fichte in the concept of self-reflection. Only
> self-reflection is no longer the act of an absolute ego but takes
> place under the conditions of communication between physician
> and patient forced into being by pathology. (287)

In this extract (which incidentally contradicts some of Habermas's earlier arguments), we readily recognize the price that
Habermas pays by making the super-idealistic concept of an
emancipatory cognitive interest the vehicle of the therapeutic
process, and the bridge between self-knowledge and cure. Where
Freud had argued that the process of recovery is governed by
a multiplicity of psychological factors, some of which operate in
the direction of cure and some of which oppose it, Habermas
postulates an abstract principle which, by definition, is pressing
for emancipation through demystification, self-reflection. But
why should this principle be suspended in the plethora of cases,
such as in autistic, narcissistic and psychotic conditions, which
do not permit an analytic intervention? Why is this principle
defeated in the many cases where analysis fails? Why has mankind invariably sought emancipation and cures in doctrines which
discourage self-reflection and are based on suggestion? Habermas
is in effect substituting the whole panoply of Freudian concepts
of emotion, pain, conflict, desire and so on, with a vocabulary
of idealist philosophy in his interpretation of what goes on during
the analytic session; the key factors of transference, pay and

pain, all cardinal for understanding the analyst-patient relationship, are barely touched and throughout Habermas's discussion
the actual role of the analyst remains a mystery. Although his
analysis of the therapeutic situation remains closest to Freud's
formulae of 'shared love of truth' and 'coincidence of understanding and cure', the image of man that we get could not be
further from the one that emerges from much of Freud's work;
it is the picture of man stripped of desires, stripped of violence
and conflict and dominated by abstract 'cognitive interests'
which direct his labour, his language and his life. Instead of
Freud's fragmented and torn individual, the victim of impossible
demands and conflicting tendencies, Habermas presents us with
a picture of man as the transcendental subject, the master and
maker of his own fate. This is the price paid by Habermas for
his worthwhile but super-idealistic opposition to the positivists.
   Although Habermas presents us with the strongest case for
basing the truth and objectivity of psychoanalytic interpretations
in the analytic discourse itself (in the 'course of future developments'), his failure to connect understanding and cure, self-
knowledge and emancipation, except through the highly idealistic
and vague concept of cognitive interest, demonstrates a very
serious tension in Freud's views on the task of analysis - how
can the general therapeutic ideal of cure (capacity to enjoy life)
be reconciled with the analytic ideal of genuine self-knowledge?
Some theorists, like Brown, argue that the two are absolutely
incompatible in our society.
   Unlike Habermas, who saw truth as the outcome of a cognitive
interest in emancipation, Brown argues that 'the coming into
consciousness of the unconscious is itself a libidinal process, an
act of love directed at the real person of the physician' (1959:
146). To put it differently, where Habermas stood by Freud's
'god Logos', Brown points out that Logos is himself the child of
Eros - reason proceeds not along its own independent path
drafted by the programme of the cognitive interests, but reason
is itself shaped and directed, enhanced and inhibited, by the
dictates of Eros. Within the artificial conditions of the consultation room, under the powerful influence of transference, a
patient may catch a glimpse of his/her repressed desires and
the resistances that maintain them. The physician may encourage
him/her to develop the outward-looking alloplastic attitude which
characterizes 'normality', but no sooner has the patient got off
the couch and he/she finds it necessary to set up fresh
repressions, fresh renunciations and fresh nuclei of neurosis,
for the world does not consist of patient and sympathetic
listeners. Within an unloving world, the possibility of knowing
ourselves is precluded, as we all develop our illusions through
which we seek to protect and comfort ourselves. In spite of
his insistence on 'undoing all repressions', Freud recognized the
paradox that soon after bringing the unconscious to light, the
analyst proceeds to bury it under heavier and yet more invisible
gravestones:

> Analysis enables the mature ego . . . to review these old
> repressions, with the result that some are lifted, while others
> are accepted but reconstructed from more solid material. These
> new dams have a greater tenacity than the earlier ones; we
> may be confident that they will not so easily give way before
> the floodtide of instinct. Thus the real achievement of analytic
> therapy would be the subsequent correction of the original
> process of repression. (1937c:23:227)

In his last work, Freud does in fact admit what he had never
admitted previously - from the point of view of therapy it is
immaterial whether the mastery of the pathogenic impulse takes
place after it has become part of the patient's self-knowledge or
by merely strengthening the forces of repression. The outcome
of the struggle between the impulse which originates in the id
and the ego which strives to master it

> is a matter of indifference: whether it results in the ego
> accepting, after a fresh examination, an instinctual demand
> which it has hitherto rejected, or whether it dismisses it once
> more, this time for good and all. (1940a: 23:179)

This statement amounts to an admission that the therapeutic goal
of recovery can be achieved without the unconscious becoming
conscious, merely by strengthening the forces of repression -
the patient's ignorance has been fortified and the analytic goal
of education has been thwarted by the pragmatic demands for
recovery. It is not accidental that, following such lines of argument, eminent practising psychoanalysts have suggested that the
division between conscious and unconscious is largely irrelevant
in analysis.[13] The original therapeutic project of psychoanalysis
is deflected from emancipation through understanding to cure
and adjustment at all costs. Both Brown and Marcuse insist that
the original project was unrealizable from the very beginning:

> while psychoanalytic theory recognizes the sickness of the
> individual as ultimately caused and sustained by the sickness
> of his civilization, psychoanalytic therapy aims at curing the
> individual so that he can continue to function as part of a sick
> civilization without surrendering to it altogether. (Marcuse
> 1955:244)

In a civilization which denies individuals objects which they can
love, founded on renunciation, frustration and consolation, the
aim of personal emancipation through self-understanding can only
be an unrealizable illusion.

> In so far as psychoanalysis deflects attention from a further
> advance, to make external reality such that it can be loved,
> it can be an obstacle in the way of a final attainment of truth.
> For psychoanalysis . . . has taught that only when we can

love the world can we have true knowledge of ourselves.
(Brown 1959:151)

All that analysis can do is to give us glimpses of our desires,
which we proceed to repress afresh as soon as they have sur-
faced. But, in the light of the professionalization of psychoanalysis and its gradual assimilation in the apparatuses of social
control, even such glimpses of demystification become unlikely.
The French theorist Robert Castel has carried this thesis
further and argues that in so far as analysis succeeds in its
cures it is based not on systematic demystification but on a
systematic generation of mis-knowledge. Instead of focusing on
transference as the central feature of the analyst-patient
relationship, Castel concentrates on the contractual nature of
this relationship, which produces three distinct levels of mis-
knowledge: first, it conceals the power relations within the
analytic situation; second, it conceals the fact that the analytic
situation is built within the parameters of a professional-specialist
establishment; third, it conceals its own theoretical failures,
like its failure to come to terms with female sexuality. While
Brown had argued that the artificial situation of the couch may
encourage the patient to catch glimpses of self-knowledge
unattainable under the pressures of 'normal' life, Castel argues
that this artificial situation serves as a model upon which the
patient bases his/her subsequent experiences as a social being;
in short, Castel argues that the analytic experience induces
privatization, a-political orientations, pessimism and resignation.
Like all therapeutics, which Castel refers to under the general
term 'psychanalysm', analysis achieves its therapeutic successes
by indoctrinating individuals into accepting a passive and
resigned attitude towards life (Castel 1976, Gordon 1977). Thus,
what was seen by Habermas as a process of self-reflection, in
which understanding and emancipation co-incide, is seen by
Castel as a process of gradual mystification and adjustment,
while Marcuse and Brown believe that even if analysis were to
yield some genuine self-knowledge, this, in itself, would not
result in the patient's emancipation.

Philip Rieff, like Habermas, takes the view that Freud's therapy
does, in fact, achieve a reconciliation of understanding and cure.
Where previous therapeutics had been based on faith and commitment, the analytic therapeutic seeks to educate the patient (i)
on the futility of looking for salvation and consolation through
universal systems of meaning or through integration and 'loss
of self' in an anonymous political or religious community, and
(ii) on the possibility of attaining a genuine personal well-being
in a world which offers a 'gorgeous variety of satisfactions' to
those who are willing to consume them. Contrary to Habermas,
however, Rieff looks at cure not as an abstract state of emancipation but as a state of personal well-being in a very pragmatic
sense. Moreover, the co-incidence of understanding and cure is
seen by Rieff, not as the product of an emancipatory cognitive

interest, but as the outcome of a real historical process which
prepared Western man for an overcoming of illusions, an overcoming of the belief in salvation through faith, and for a quiet
enjoyment of what there is to be enjoyed in this world.

> Commitment therapies can be distinguished from analytic
> therapies. The latter arise in an historical period concomitant
> with the rise of democratic individualism. Commitment thera-
> pies, however, operate by returning the individual to the
> cosset of his natal community with a more effective pattern
> of symbolic integration; the therapeutic effort is transforma-
> tive; the therapist is characteristically either a sacral or an
> exemplary figure. Analytic therapies, on the other hand, are
> uniquely modern and depend largely on Freudian presupposi-
> tions. The therapeutic effort is not primarily transformative
> but informative. The assumption of analytic theory is that there
> is no positive community standing behind the therapist.
> (1966:76)

In a way, what Rieff calls 'analytic therapeutic' is highly reminiscent of Castel's psychanalysm, for it involves privatization, a-
politicism and the striving after personal well-being; the
fundamental difference, of course, between Rieff and Castel is
their evaluation of Freud's therapeutic – where Rieff sees
information, Castel sees misinformation, where Rieff sees reconciliation, Castel sees resignation, where Rieff glorifies privatization and a-politicism as signs of man's long-term emancipation,
Castel castigates them as man's permanent enslavement. The
relative merits of these views will be discussed in detail in Part
II; at the moment, it is worth noting that Rieff is one of the few
writers, outside institutional psychoanalysis, who qualifies his
optimism about the potential of analytic therapies – he is, in
other words, one of the few who recognize that analysis may
work in some cases and not in others. In this, he is closest to
Freud who insisted that unless the analyst can enter into an
alliance with the patient's ego there is no chance of therapeutic
success, through self-knowledge. In order for this alliance to
materialize, the patient's ego must be 'fairly strong', for it will
otherwise be unwilling to abandon its resistances for a second.
   This brings us to the essential irony of psychoanalytic treatment, to which Freud was referring when he admitted that

> if we want to make a compact with the patient's ego, that ego
> must be normal. (1937c:23:235)

Rieff echoes the same point more forcefully: 'Psychoanalysis is
a therapy for the healthy, not a solution for the sick' (1959:xiii).
The educational function of analysis, therefore, requires that
the ego has already acquired a certain strength and is willing to
engage in a process of self-observation with the physician's help;
yet, it is the weakness of the ego which usually stands at the

heart of the pathogenic condition. So, psychotic and autistic
conditions, as well as serious neurotic disturbances, are unavailable to analytic treatment, and the educational potential of
psychoanalysis is only open to those who are already nearly
normal. In short, self-knowledge is available to those who
least need it.

This discussion of various interpretations of Freudian therapy
highlights the point that the co-incidence of understanding and
cure, that corner-stone of Freudian therapy, is if not impossible
highly unlikely, within the parameters of our civilization. Even
when genuine self-knowledge is gained, it frequently has to be
repressed afresh to prevent new frustrations, new conflicts and
new suffering. Towards the end of his life, Freud had come to
the conclusion that

> the expectation that every neurotic phenomenon can be cured
> may . . . be derived from the layman's belief that neuroses
> are something quite unnecessary which have no right to
> exist. (1933a:22:153)

It would seem that as Freud grew increasingly pessimistic about
the scope and potential of analytic treatment (as well as of other
therapeutics), he gradually came to the view that the final
inhibition to the reconciliation of understanding and cure
originated in repressive civilization itself.[14] At the same time,
it seems that in retrospect he realized that the cures at which
he had aimed all along involved something qualitatively different
from the cures offered by other therapeutics; he had not been
trying merely to restore the broken-down individual to society
at any cost, but to liberate the individual from a life of delusions,
governed by fear, guilt and ignorance. This, for a variety of
reasons, had proved impossible in the majority of cases, so that
Freud had to accept as the therapeutic aim of analysis the aim of
all therapies, where success and failure are judged entirely by
pragmatic criteria. Therapy moved steadily in the pragmatic
direction - hence Freud's capitulation discussed earlier - where
self-understanding is sacrificed in the interest of strengthened
resistances. Theory, on the other hand, as formulated in Freud's
later writings moved in a different and increasingly critical
direction from therapy. As a result, a gulf developed between
Freudian theory and Freudian therapy, between the art of
analysis and the science of psychoanalysis. While therapy proceeded from the cultural given of normality to treat deviance
as pathology, Freud's late work engages in a systematic critique
of normality and points to the conclusion that what is considered
normal may in a strict sense be neurotic. Normal people are
those who can best cope with their neurosis and manage to
express it in socially acceptable ways. The statement that
'analysis achieves for neurotics what normal people accomplish
for themselves without it' (1937c:23:225) can be seen, in this
light, as a profoundly pessimistic comment on the impossibility

of analysis achieving anything beyond adjustment and coping.
Even if, in the course of therapy, one disentangles one's Oedipal
complications and comes face to face with one's secret desires
and wish-fulfilling phantasies, one proceeds to repress the newly
acquired knowledge, like the millions of 'normals' who achieve
the same result never having come in contact with this type of
self-knowledge.

Many of Freud's disciples sought to extend the scope, efficiency
and economy of therapeutic treatment, in the interest of the goal
of recovery, by introducing a variety of novel elements to the
analytic relationship, and gradually the entire therapeutic establishment (and this includes most practising psychoanalysts)
shifted away from 'making conscious the unconscious' towards
ever more elaborate techniques of pampering the ego, culminating in interpersonal intimacy and 'unconditional positive regard'.
As the sympathetic loving machine replaced the often ruthless
surgeon, the unconscious was forgotten, behind a barrage of
humanist ethics and the quest for 'authenticity'.

While Freud continued treating patients until the last months
of his life, he rarely refers to cases he treated after the First
World War. As the schism between increasing therapeutic pragmatism and increasing theoretical criticism deepened, the bond
that had united the art of the therapist with the science of the
theorist weakened; as the proceedings of psychoanalytic sessions
became governed by the expediency of recovery at the expense
of the search for truth, the couch became a rather unreliable
field in which to conduct research.

On the other hand, many theoretical contributions in the
Freudian discourse, and in particular those exploring its
critical potential, have been made by theorists with no direct
therapeutic experience. In a way it may be thought idiosyncratic
to choose accounts of the analytic session and cures, offered by
non-therapists, as I did earlier; yet all these interpretations,
in spite of their differences, point in a direction which would be
quite unacceptable to a practising Freudian analyst of today,
namely, that in seeking to reconcile understanding and cure,
Freud was attempting the near-impossible, for the cures he was
aiming at constantly overflowed the usual therapeutic aim of
adjustment. Yet, Freud's therapeutic efforts, with their unexpected successes and frequent disappointments, and his confrontation with the near-insurmountable obstacles present in the
paths of his treatments, provided much of the raw material for
the development and testing of his theories and left him with a
sound appreciation of the factors inhibiting therapeutic success,
as he had wanted it to be.

The therapeutic impasse to which Freud had been led made the
reconsideration of what is culturally defined as normal all the
more urgent. Instead of examining the neurotic from the
Archimedean point of normality, it is essential to investigate
normality, the culture's given, from Freud's experience of
neurosis, its causes, its symptoms, its consequences and the

obstacles which stand in the way of its successful resolution.
At this point, it becomes necessary to examine what conclusions
can be drawn about the normal individual living in our society,
on the basis of Freud's clinical experience with neurotics.

Chapter 4
Culture, normality and morality

We must clarify at the outset of this chapter that we will not deal
here with Freud's theory of moral behaviour and the various
cultural and psychic institutions which govern such behaviour,
examined in Chapter 2. Instead, we will look at the moral
significance of the Freudian discourse itself, i.e. we will not
look at psychoanalysis as a science of morality but as moral
philosophy. Of course, we must be aware that this is a dangerous area since, as Hartmann has stressed, Freud was unequivocally against attempts to deduce moral positions from his
scientific propositions (1960:20). Yet, this is precisely the path
which the therapeutic dilemma which we faced in the previous
chapter is forcing us to take. If psychoanalysis, in its therapeutic aim of cure through understanding, finds itself in
opposition to the social system in which it operates, it expands
de facto into social critique. And it must be beyond doubt that
psycho-analysis is a social critique and not merely a description
of social reality. Every major commentator of Freud has had to
confront the moral aspects of his theory, one of them,
Philip Rieff, entitled his important book 'The Mind of the
Moralist', and has argued that Freud is the moral thinker of the
twentieth century par excellence. Of course, there have been
many epistemological objections to scientific theories which entail
normative statements, but these objections will be examined in
greater detail later.

Elements of social critique can be found in some of Freud's
very earliest works. In his 1898 essay Sexuality in the Aetiology
of Neuroses, he points out that in so far as civilization inhibits
sexual fulfilment, it may be responsible for neurasthenia and
other neurotic disorders; in failing to provide adequate contraceptive measures and, more importantly, in failing to recognize
the importance of sexual fulfilment which is inhibited through a
variety of moral inhibitions, civilization creates what Freud
regards as unnecessary and possibly dangerous discontent and
frustration. He stresses that

> it is positively to the public interest *that men should enter
> upon sexual relations with full potency,* (1898a:3:278)

and warns

> in the next century . . . civilization will have to learn to
> become compatible with the claims of sexuality. (ibid.)

Twelve years later, Freud concluded his series of lectures at
Clark University with the same theme:

> A certain part of the suppressed libidinous excitation has a
> right to direct satisfaction and ought to find it in life. The
> claims of civilization make life too hard for the greater part of
> humanity, and so further the aversion to reality and the origin
> of neuroses, without producing an excess of cultural gain by
> this excess of sexual repression. We ought not to go so far as
> to forget the original animal part of our nature, we ought not
> to forget that the happiness of individuals cannot be dispensed
> with as one of the aims of our culture. (1910a:11:54)

We notice immediately that the range of the victims of sexual
repression imposed by civilization has broadened the majority
of humanity is now seen as victim of unnecessary restrictions on
sexuality. In his major indictment of civilization, late in his life,
we find an amplified echo of the same theme:

> There is no longer any place in present day civilized life for
> a simple natural love between two human beings. (1930a:21:
> 105fn)

Of course, immersed in a positivist ideology of science, Freud
was fairly reluctant to make overt moral statements and
evaluations, much like Max Weber. At the conclusion of 'Civilization and Its Discontents', that harshest indictment not only
of the outrages of the twentieth century but also of what most
people would regard as its supreme achievements, Freud asserts
that

> for a wide variety of reasons, it is very far from my intention
> to express an opinion upon the value of human civilization.
> (1930a:21:144)

In spite of such disclaimers, moral evaluations and social critique
are central to Freud's work; not only do these critical passages
draw some of Freud's most passionately imaginative writing, but
they form an integral part of his discourse:

> We are not reformers, it is true; we are merely observers;
> but we cannot avoid observing with critical eyes, and we have
> found it impossible to give our support to conventional morality
> or to approve highly of the means by which society attempts to
> arrange the practical problems of sexuality in life. We can
> demonstrate with ease that what the world calls its code of
> morals demands more sacrifices than it is worth. (1916-17:16:
> 434)

It is to these critical aspects of psychoanalysis that we turn our
attention in this chapter; how does Freud assess culture? What

are the criteria on the basis of which he evaluates whether the
cultural given of normality is indeed a desirable state of affairs
or not?

The first three quotes in this chapter, aimed at demonstrating
the critical flavour in Freud's writings, may have created the
false impression that his criticism was based on the unqualified
value of unrestricted sexual pleasure; this in fact is not the case,
for, as Rieff has argued, Freud was no naive advocate of the
senses; nor was Freud unaware that a certain degree of sexual
restriction may be unavoidable, as the premium required for
civilized life. He even suspected that 'our possibilities of
happiness are already restricted by our own constitution'
(1930a:21:76-7). Still, in Freud's work we discover a considerable area of tension between his analysis of what human reality
is and what it ought to be, and the question arises of where he
finds his imagery of what human reality ought to be. The great
moralists of the past have drawn their social critiques either
from philosophical ruminations on the nature of virtue or from
a god-given ethical principle; ethical intuitionists and ethical
rationalists have proceeded in their critiques of society by
measuring it against the ideals of a holy community and a repub-
lic respectively. In the last one hundred and fifty years, however, a different tradition of social criticism has emerged - one
where the emphasis lies not so much on the ethical ideal as on
humanity itself, its strivings and alienation, its potential and its
actuality. It would not be misleading to suggest that the social
critique of this tradition is scientific rather than moral, for it is
motivated neither by an abstract conception of a paradise lost
nor by chimeric visions of a future utopia, but by deep concern
and a review of humanity's actual struggles, its frustrated
strivings and the depth of its discontents. This is not to deny
that this tradition has developed its own utopias and its own
myths of the fall, but these have been based as much as possible
on the study of the actual situation.

The theme of discontent and frustration recurs endlessly in
the writings of the main exponents of this tradition; Marx and
Freud never tired of contrasting the unequalled technical achievements of the bourgeois era with the persistence or indeed the
escalation of misery, destructiveness, frustration and sickness.
Like all masters of the forgotten art of rhetoric, both Marx and
Freud launch their monumental social critiques, in 'The Communist Manifesto' and 'Civilization and Its Discontents', only
after they have completed eloquent encomiums of their adversary,
so that the contrast between technical triumphs and cultural
miseries becomes all the more telling.

Yet, the heart of Marxist and Freudian discourses is not
occupied by this contrast, but rather by the key concept of
struggle. For Marx, estranged labour (the key, in his view, to
the general alienation of mankind) is the consequence of the
capitalist phase in the struggle of classes, just as for Freud,
neurotic misery is but an unsuccessful attempt at resolving

mental conflict. It is not accidental that both Marx and Freud sought to answer the riddle of 'history's motive force' through the concept of conflict. Marx opens 'The Communist Manifesto' with the statement: 'The history of all hitherto existing society is the history of class struggles.' While Freud sees history in drastically different ways, it is struggle which propels it forward:

> instinctual repression upon which is based everything that is most precious in human civilization. The repressed instinct never ceases to strive for complete satisfaction . . . and it is the difference in amount between the pleasure of satisfaction which is *demanded* and that which is actually *achieved* that provides the driving factor which will permit no halting. (1920g:18:42)

Of course, the type of conflict that Marx and Freud place at the centre of their theories as the driving force of history, class struggle and the return of the repressed instinct, places them miles apart, and attempts to 'integrate' Marxism with psychoanalysis have invariably stumbled on this point. Yet, it is crucial that for both Marx and Freud struggle is as much a feature of our civilization (and all civilization) as is misery. It is precisely in the strivings of the present that all hope for an overcoming of misery lies, and it is through these strivings that we can occasionally catch sudden glimpses of what may be entailed in human emancipation. At this juncture, Marx and Freud are joined by the third great summit of the critical tradition which we are presently discussing, Nietzsche.

'*I teach you the overman.* Man is something that shall be overcome. What have you done to overcome him?' are Zarathustra's first utterances to the world. The common theme of overcoming humanity's alienation must not be obscured by sterile classifications of Marx as a dialectical materialist, Nietzsche as a dialectical monist and Freud as a metaphysical dualist; nor must these labels obscure their common concern with the systematic distortion of humanity's consciousness, for they all three put the mind's contents under the closest scrutiny in order to show that the mind is neither the empiricists' blank sheet, nor the seat of the rationalists' reason. Unlike the great moralists of the past, they see the distortion of consciousness neither as the product of an evil force nor as a simple state of ignorance, but as the systematic consequence of social oppression and psychological weakness; in a society torn by conflict, contradiction, frustration and misery, intimidated, fragmented and insecure souls are doomed to systematic mystifications, illusions and distortions. It is not accidental that Marx, Nietzsche and Freud reserved some of their most caustic critiques for religion, which they all held responsible for a major distortion of consciousness; nor is it accidental that they saw their task not as one of education, but rather of demystification - not only of exposing

humanity's illusions but revealing the causes of these illusions
in the social and psychological spheres and fighting against the
·forces of mystification.

Our discussion of the previous problematic has provided two
valuable starting points from which to embark on our study
of Freud's social criticism. First, the distance between health
and disease is nowhere as drastic and clear cut in the mental
field as it is in the organic field. The underlying processes of
neurotics are the same as those of normal people. Normal people
exhibit de facto neurotic elements in their mental constitution,
even if these are infrequently noticed; the conflicts experienced
by neurotics are the same as those experienced by normal
people, only the outcomes vary, and the degree to which they
inhibit social functioning. Unlike normals, neurotics appear
incapable of leading their lives in an acceptable way, they undergo acute crises of anxiety, morbid symptoms and pain, and
finally they are afflicted by an obviously distorted sense of
reality - innocuous things become invested with daemonic
powers, dead persons are resurrected in imagination, fears are
magnified out of all proportion, and there is a general impair-
ment of judgment.

Second, in seeking to relieve patients from their pain, restore
their sense of judgment and appreciation of external reality and
re-establish them in a creative role in society, psychoanalysis
as a mode of therapy finds itself in substantial concord with the
social function of adjustment. Yet, as we saw earlier, in spite of
his final capitulation to the demands of practical expedience,
Freud had in fact been trying all along to achieve something
more than mere adjustment - a positive reconciliation through the
cure of a genuine self-knowledge with a capacity for enjoyment
and creativity. Knowledge was not merely restricted to the
restoration of the patient's common sense and conventional
judgment - it was not restricted to teaching the patient not to
be afraid of mice - but aimed at opening a whole new horizon of
self-knowledge which scanned both inner and outer worlds, and
would enable the patient to understand and master the origins
of his/her fear of mice. So, the knowledge aimed at by psychoanalysis had expanded considerably beyond the requirements of
other therapies. Likewise, Freud did not aim to make life merely
tolerable for his patients, but through investigations of sexuality in its manifold expressions, he tried to open new avenues
of enjoyment, creativity and fulfilment for his patients.

Thus psychoanalysis discovers new meanings for the values
of pleasure and truth, enjoyment and understanding, quite
distinct from the meanings they possess within the cultural
standards of normality; and it is from a perspective which
involves the twin values of pleasure and truth, the combined
claims of Eros and Logos, that Freud undertakes his cultural
evaluation. Of course, he was not the first great moral thinker
to base his critique of the present on a alchemy of pleasure and
truth, nor was he the first to recognize the formidable obstacles

in the path of a reconciliation of Eros and Logos, both for the
moral individual and for the moral thinker. What is rather novel
is that he based his understanding of pleasure and truth on
empirical investigations into the nature of their opposites, misery
and delusion. Freud's investigations into sexuality, its perversions, vicissitudes and frustrations, holds the key to his understanding of pleasure, while his investigations of the unconscious
extended this understanding and shaped his view on the factors
distorting human consciousness. Although the two investigations
proceeded simultaneously, I will first examine the new meanings
that Freud discovered for the value of pleasure and then look
at his conception of truth.

Pleasure is, in the first place, the result of the satisfaction
of sexual desires, in their infinite variety. It is especially the
fulfilment of unmediated, untamed and often perverse desires
that brings about pleasure.

> The feeling of happiness derived from the satisfaction of a wild
> instinctual impulse untamed by the ego is incomparably more
> intense than that derived from sating an instinct that has been
> tamed. The irresistibility of perverse instincts, and perhaps
> the attraction in general of forbidden things finds an economic
> explanation here. (1930a:21:79)

Clearly, in Freud's view, pleasure is not an abstract ethical
principle, but rather a lived experience associated with the fulfilment of the individual's most basic strivings.

> In the developmental process of the individual, the programme
> of the pleasure principle, which consists in finding the satis-
> faction of happiness, is retained as the main aim. (140)

The pleasure principle sets in motion and controls mental
events.

> In the theory of psychoanalysis we have no hesitation in
> assuming that the course taken by mental events is automat-
> ically regulated by the pleasure principle. (1920g:18:7)

Yet, the programme of the pleasure principle is

> at loggerheads with the whole world, with the macrocosm as
> much as with the microcosm. There is no possibility at all of
> its being carried through; all regulations of the universe run
> counter to it. (1930a:21:76)

In spite of all these regulations, however,

> we must not – indeed cannot – give up our efforts to bring
> [the pleasure principle] nearer to fulfilment by some means
> or other. Very different paths may be taken in that direction.

> . . . By none of these paths can we attain all that we desire.
> Happiness in the reduced sense we recognize as possible is a
> problem of the individual's libido. There is no golden rule
> which applies to everyone: every man must find out for him-
> self in what particular fashion he can be saved. (83)[1]

It is clear, I think, that Freud's ethical pluralism concerns the
means used towards the attainment of pleasure, not the origin
of pleasure itself. His evaluation of culture and its main institutions is based, in the first place, on whether they permit
adequate instinctual satisfactions and on whether their standard
of normality involves more restrictions than are strictly necessary
for civilized living.

However, Freud's hedonism is not limited to the satisfaction
of primary instinctual impulses; pleasure takes two additional
meanings, which while subordinate to the first cannot be reduced
to it – the first is the minimization of socially inflicted unpleasure,
and the second is the satisfaction of mediated desires. The first
one is clear in Freud's negative evaluation of religion – religion
is criticized not only for imposing prohibitions which are not
necessary for the maintenance of social cohesion, not only for
perpetuating a variety of illusions, but also for creating an
unnecessary amount of suffering through the introjection of
aggression and the accentuation of the sense of guilt in every
individual. Only through an unyielding and 'authoritarian' super-
ego can religion ensure the observance of unnecessary curbs on
sexuality and enjoyment in general. Unlike sport and art which
seek to provide socially acceptable outlets for aggression in
various symbolic forms, religion turns aggression inwards in
the form of a sense of guilt, which adds to the misery imposed
on the individual through the different prohibitions. These two
functions of religion, although instrumental for the maintenance
of social bonds, far outweigh in Freud's evaluation its positive
contribution to the happiness of the individual – that of consoling him/her for the unhappiness of life. Religion, through its
restrictive morality based on self-sacrifice, renunciation and
non-fulfilment, through its deprecation of present, lived enjoyment in the interest of future rewards, and through the culti-
vation of a sense of guilt and weakness, is a major source of the
unhappiness for which it seeks to console the individual.

The third aspect of Freud's understanding of pleasure is the
satisfaction of impulses and desires which have been mediated
by the ego. Chapter 2 of 'Civilization and Its Discontents' is
devoted to an enumeration of the various methods of mediated
satisfaction, through which each individual may attempt to fulfil
the programme of the pleasure principle. The methods are
mediated because, with the exception of love, they do not represent satisfactions of primary instinctual impulses pressing
through the id and requiring gratification; rather, these impulses
have become tamed by the ego, under the civilizing influence of
culture, and satisfaction usually comes in symbolic forms, as in

the case of art. Freud examines in turn intoxication, yoga, art, science, work, love and beauty and finds that with the exception of love,

> such satisfactions seem 'finer and higher'. But their intensity is mild as compared with that derived from the sating of crude and primary instinctual impulses; it does not convulse our physical being. (1930a: 21: 79-80)

Failure to attain pleasure through these mediated methods may precipitate frustration but seldom triggers off repressions, which are reserved mainly for the frustrations of primary impulses. In spite of their lower intensity, these satisfactions are not discounted by Freud, especially when they do not violate the second major value, that of truth. On the contrary, these satisfactions represent culture's contribution to the individual's well-being. Cultures which provide a wide selection of such options and encourage the individual to channel his/her libido along paths that maximise pleasure have Freud's whole-hearted support, while those which are symbolically impoverished or proclaim a single road to salvation are criticized. This, once again, is the case of religion, which somehow contrives to fail on all of Freud's evaluative criteria:

> Religion restricts this play of choice and adaptation, since it imposes equally on everyone its own path to the acquisition of happiness. (84)

In Freud's view, our culture has failed to make such mediated and symbolic satisfactions available to all its members to equal extent. Work, the major form of mediated pleasure, perhaps, is a necessary evil for the majority of people. Cultures like ours, whose benefits, both material and symbolic, accrue to a privileged minority of people, are likely to require more severe instinctual restrictions and more intense internalization of aggression in order to achieve social cohesion. This democratic-egalitarian thread runs through many of Freud's mature writ-ings.[2]

There can be little doubt that Freud, through his investigations into the different expressions of sexuality, its fulfilment and its suppression, revealed new and unexpected facets of the pleasure criterion. Sexual desires considered until his time as perverse, unacceptable and sick were shown to be quite normal components of sexuality, making quite legitimate claims to gratification. Although these investigations have a scientific character, there can be little doubt that they are not devoid of a normative content. Freud's attempts to define pleasure 'scientifically' through the pleasure principle and the diverse manifestations of libido cannot overshadow the underlying assumption that pleasure is also desirable, both for the individual, who 'must not give up the goal of the pleasure principle', and for culture, which 'cannot

dispense with the happiness of individuals as one of its aims'.
Thus, pleasure must be seen as both a central analytical concept
in psychoanalysis and a normative concept of outstanding significance.

Yet, as we saw in Chapter 1, the theory of instincts is one
of the least developed areas of psychoanalysis and it encounters
severe difficulties in distinguishing between primary and
derived impulses, basic and sublimated instincts, spontaneous
and acquired instinctual components. How then are we to compare different kinds and degrees of satisfaction and decide
which ones are primary and which ones substitutive or symbolic?
Two particular types of satisfaction seem to pose special problems; first, those components of sexuality which we recognize
as early childhood fixations, and, second, those which result
from the sating of aggressive instincts. The former are products
of early fixations and yet re-appear later in life with the intensity of primary instincts; as for the latter, it is questionable
whether their satisfaction affords any pleasure at all, or merely
a lowering of mental tension, since in his 1924 essay The
Economic Problem of Masochism, Freud restricted the pleasure
principle to the claims of libido and introduced the 'nirvana
principle' to express the claims of the death instinct.

Attempts to clarify Freud's hedonism will take us along two
competing paths; the first argues that Freud provided us with
an attitude and a method of self-knowledge which allows each
one of us to obtain maximum pleasure, in accordance with our
personal psychological make-up and life history. De Sousa and
Rieff, who both take this view, stress Freud's ethical pluralism,
and each proposes an archetype of a moral person, who is in a
position to invest his/her libido along channels of maximum
satisfaction - in this respect de Sousa's 'analysed man' and
Rieff's 'psychological man' amount to the same concept. The
second path, taken by Brown and Marcuse, stresses the universal
character of bodily pleasure as the predominant value in
Freudian ethics, and views the problem of libidinal choices
merely as the problem of sexually frustrated humans - it is a
question of discovering the second best when the best has been
made unavailable. Both paths draw heavily from the therapeutic
task of psychoanalysis: the former generalized Freud's therapeutic task into a cultural project and argues that analytic
activity, whether it takes place in the consultation room, at the
cocktail party or in the intimacy of inter-personal relations,
is a genuine avenue towards well-being. The limitations of
Freudian therapy were due to the fact that Freud sought to
emancipate those who were least amenable to it - the neurotics;
its successes are promised to those who are amenable to it, the
healthy ones. Brown and Marcuse, on the other hand, argue
that instead of infusing every aspect of culture with a psychoanalytic self-consciousness, Freud's therapeutic experience
points inexorably in the direction of a radical overthrow of the
present culture and its institutional and moral infra-structures.

Instead of generalizing the therapeutic task into a cultural project, Brown and Marcuse propose its transformation into a
project of changing culture.

In order to appreciate the differences between the two views,
and the evaluation of culture which they each attribute to Freud,
it is necessary to introduce the second evaluative criterion,
truth.[3] This criterion, as de Sousa points out, is an epistemic
criterion, representing true knowledge of reality, both inner
and outer (1974:212). Surely, no aspect of Freud's critique of
religion is so persistent, so unyielding and so severe as his
critique of the illusory nature of its doctrines, its systematic
distortion of reality and its 'patently infantile' claims.

> Its technique consists in depressing the value of life and
> distorting the picture of the real world in a delusional manner
> – which presupposes an intimidation of intelligence. (1930a:
> 21:84)[4]

Freud's commitment to truthfulness is unqualified – it informs
his practice as a therapist and his investigations as a scientist.
This commitment, as he sees it, derives from the fact that
psychoanalysis is above all else a science and must accept the
scientific Weltanschauung. Yet, what is more interesting is that
for Freud the value of truth is not restricted to those for whom
science is a vocation. For Freud, as for Socrates, life without
knowledge is not worth living, and every effort to stifle independent thinking is unequivocally renounced. The advocacy
of his 'god Logos' draws from Freud, in the last part of 'The
Future of an Illusion', such impassioned writing that the
Socrates of 'Apologia' comes immediately to mind. While psychoanalysis was put forward by Freud as the method for acquiring
true knowledge of the inner world,[5] he did not regard self-
knowledge as a privilege reserved for the psychoanalytic and
psychoanalysed élite; given favourable social circumstances and
the availability of the right method, every individual can and
must strive towards knowing him/herself and the world within
which he/she lives.

Just as the investigations of sexuality brought out the value
of sensuous pleasure, Freud's study of the functions, development and disorders of the ego led to an elucidation of the value
of truth. The ego is that mental agency which has been differentiated from the rest of the mental apparatus through its
contact with the external world and, among its functions, it
includes reality-testing, i.e. it determines whether a given
perception corresponds to the external world or whether it is
purely hallucinatory or phantastic. Chief among the characteristics of mental disorders is a weakening or a loss of this
sense of reality – in psychotic conditions, a whole new reality
is fabricated possessing the status of external reality (1924b:
19), while in most neuroses reality becomes ignored or distorted,
as the objects of the real world become invested with extra-

ordinary meanings and powers (1924e:19). The same distortions
of the sense of reality characterize the quasi-pathological conditions of dreams or being in love (1930a:21:66), as well as
culturally induced pathological conditions, like religious faith.
Freud, being no philosopher of knowledge, does not seek to
differentiate between truth and illusion through any philosophical
discussion into the nature of truth; his underlying assumption of
knowledge is a positivist one, as we shall see in the next chapter
– true knowledge reflects the real world. His key distinction
between true knowledge and illusion is a psychological one –
illusions can be shown to constitute wish-fulfilments, convenient
lies aimed at making life more tolerable, which resist falsification
and contradiction. Much as Durkheim studied religion from the viewpoint of its social function, Freud studied it in terms of the way
it becomes entrenched in the individual soul – once this has been
done, the falseness of its doctrines becomes transparent. Once
again, the criterion of truth is not for Freud purely a descriptive one – a 'demarcation criterion' defining the line between true
and false knowledge. Like the pleasure criterion, it too involves
a normative component: illusions are not just errors, but
neurotic symptoms which re-inforce man's alienation. Freud does
not criticize religion for being false, but for causing and re-
inforcing humanity's alienation. So, both pleasure in a sensuous
sense and truth in the sense of self-understanding are also
normative points, and indeed, emancipatory points with a utopian
potential, which will be studied in Chapter 6.

At this point we run into a serious difficulty; for if illusions
and other distortions of reality are precipitated by the fact that
reality is too painful to bear, i.e. that truth runs contrary to
pleasure, if what distinguishes them from true knowledge is the
fact that they remain loyal to the criterion of pleasure, then
Freud's two values are at least in partial contradiction to each
other. But if the two independent values, truth and pleasure,
cannot be met through a common programme of action, how are
we to decide which one of the two constitutes the superior moral
principle? How can we assess a culture which thwarts the one
in the interest of the other?

In order to confront this difficulty it is necessary to take
again the two competing lines of interpretation, for they both
attempt to answer our original question – Freud's evaluation of
culture – from a perspective which harmonizes the two basic
values, through radically different interpretations of their
meanings.

In concert with Rieff's interpretations of the instincts as
mediated by the mind,[6] his emphasis on primary sensuous satisfaction as a component of the pleasure criterion is minimal.

Freud was no celebrant of the senses; there is no trace of
the lyrical in his analysis of the sexual instinct and its
satisfactions. He hardly claimed or – from what we know of
his life – himself desired to be rid of the civilizing aversions.

While urging, for the sake of our mental health, that we dispense with such childish fantasies of purity as epitomized in the belief that Mother (or Father) was too nice to have done those nasty things, Freud at the same time comes to the tacit understanding that sex really is nasty, as an ignoble slavery to nature. (1959:170)

Rieff stresses the hardness and even the brutality of sexuality as exemplified in childhood discoveries, and concludes that bodily pleasure is far from being Freud's underlying value; although the claims of sexuality must be respected[7] and, within reason, satisfied, they are neither the major nor the only avenue to pleasure.

[Sexual] pleasure is defined, after the manner of Schopenhauer, as a negative phenomenon, the struggle to release oneself from unpleasure, or tension. . . . To understand [sexual] pleasure as its own abrogation is hardly a form of hedonism; such a concept serves better as a critique of it. (171)

Although Rieff recognizes the diversity of sexual manifestations, he sees the economic formulae of libido, expressed in 'Three Essays on the Theory of Sexuality', not so much as expressing man's potential and demands for sensuous satisfaction, but rather as emphasizing the constitutional limitations in the attainment of pleasure. The libido cannot be directed towards the other in substantial quantities because the ego will remain without adequate supplies to carry out its own functions; hence, concludes Rieff, somewhat arbitrarily, 'satisfaction from an object is but a devious means of self-love' (171).

Sexuality can become a genuine source of pleasure if it can be made to serve the ego, rather than overwhelm it, as part of a package of 'normal love', a notion developed by Rieff through a consideration of three rather neglected little essays by Freud, dating from 1910, 1912 and 1918. In these essays, Freud suggests that love consists of a harmonious blending of two currents, sensuality and affection; affection, or 'higher love' is not merely a sublimated form of sexuality but derives from the encounter between the child and parental authority. In the 1912 essay, Freud had argued that the affectionate current is the older of the two (1912d:11:180), and saw it as a constituent of what he considered at that time to be the second primary instinct, self-preservation.[8]

Having postulated the fusion of sensuous love and affection as the criterion of 'normal love'. Rieff argues that 'there exists a strong tendency for the two currents, affection and sensuality, to become "divided". This dualism in the capacity to love is characteristic of most neuroses' (1959:177). The neurotic's failure to effect the fusion of the two currents is due to the fact that 'nature and culture both conspire against the merger. Culture does so by its notorious tendency to repress sexual

pleasure. But Freud rightly viewed this as a less serious threat
to normal sexuality than the one offered by nature' (175). Any
dissociation of the two components of love, including adultery,
frigidity, impotence, orgiastic as well as ascetic religions, is
seen as a symptom of neurotic disorders. The 'achievement of
love' is seen by Rieff as an ethical problem.

To summarize: While sexuality may contribute to pleasure if,
contrary to the pressures of both nature and culture, the
individual can achieve a harmonious blending of sensuousness
and affection, Freud is far from painting it couleur-de-rose.
'His dictum that neurosis can always be traced to a disturbed
sexual life hardly indicates a joyful interpretation of sexuality.
. . . Freud argued far more strongly that sexuality is vulner-
ability than that it constitutes strength' (181). Thus Rieff
emphasizes that while sexuality is a constant source of unhappiness, neurosis, tension and frustration, its potential for pleasure
is limited. Once again, it is as a negative principle that it
affects people's lives and becomes 'a problem in the mechanics
of satisfaction' (ibid.).

At this point we can introduce Rieff's archetype of a normal
person - he is the person who does not engage in futile rebellion
against the frustrations he experiences, for this is the neurotic's
rebellion out of weakness, but instead

> is active and outgoing. Expedient normal attitudes lead to some
> achievement in the outer world. The brisk managerial ego of
> the normal personality devotes itself to aggression against the
> environment, to the practical use of objects; it does not fixate
> upon them. . . . Again, the economic metaphor discloses
> Freud's ideal of health as well: a fully employed libido. (388)

The reason why the normal person is able to tolerate and master
frustrations accompanying sexual life, and enjoy the pleasures
which accrue from a libido carefully invested upon objects
guaranteeing maximum returns, is, according to Rieff, his/her
knowledge of him/herself as well as of the world in which he/she
operates, a world conceived as a vast libidinal stock exchange.
It is in this way that truth, the second underlying ethical
principle, enters Rieff's discussion. The model of man who
corresponds to this ideal of normality is given by Rieff the
archetypical name 'psychological man', who, having absorbed
the Freudian message, 'takes on the attitude of a scientist with
himself as the ultimate object of his science' (1963:13). For the
psychological man 'a sense of well-being has become the end,
rather than a by-product of striving after some superior communal end' (1966:261).

For the psychological man, culture has ceased being a constant
source of frustrations; having reconciled himself with his inner
conflicts, he is able to attain well-being through the 'gorgeous
variety of satisfactions' (241) that culture, in its technological,
economic, artistic and other achievements, offers him.

A fairly similar view is taken by de Sousa, who sees Freud's
moral ideal as the 'analysed man', by which he refers to a
similar characterological prototype as Rieff.

> To measure the relative worth of the frustration and the result-
> ing achievements, we need to evaluate *ends*. The 'economic'
> point of view affords definite standards only if it is grounded
> on meaningful calculations of utility. But such calculations
> make clear sense only if the pleasure principle makes clear
> sense. The difference between satisfactions of different *kinds*
> has always caused trouble for systems akin to Utilitarianism.
> The usual solution offered, from Plato to Mill, is to appeal to
> the experienced judge: he who has experienced both can make
> the real distinction between real and illusory wants, and
> higher and lower pleasures. This device has its Freudian
> counterpart in the *analysed man*. (1974:217)

De Sousa's treatment of Freud (and Plato!) as a utilitarian and
the appeal to experience (rather than episteme) as the ultimate
judge need not trouble us in this extract. What concerns us is
that the analysed man, like Rieff's psychological man, is able to
reconcile knowledge of truth with the attainment of pleasure;
he is the man who knows how to invest his libido and never
aspires for higher returns than he can reasonably expect. Both
de Sousa and Rieff see Freud as postulating a moral ideal,
equivalent, say, to Plato's virtuous man, in terms of which both
individuals and cultures may be evaluated.

Now, as we saw at the beginning of Chapter 3, Freud's concept
of normality which informs his practice as a therapist and his
investigations as a scientist is that in the mental sphere normality can only have a conventional meaning - only culture can
define what is normal and what is abnormal. As a therapist he
had tried to 'transform . . . hysterical misery into everyday
unhappiness' (1895d:2:232), hysterical misery being seen as an
abnormal condition, everyday unhappiness as a normal one.
Yet, we now emerge with a new view of normality, no longer as
the cultural product and guideline of psychotherapy, but a moral
concept, which is the outcome of the inner logic of Freudian
thought itself. Living a life of 'everyday unhappiness' immersed
in frustration, illusion and deprived of all creativity, joy and
self-knowledge may meet the cultural criterion of normality but
do not meet the moral criterion. The two views of normality
are equally important in the Freudian discourse, the former as a
corner-stone of both clinical practice and scientific generalizations, the latter as the launching platform of Freud's social
critique. Freud's awareness of the twin concept of normality,
which he employed, is hinted in the following extract in which
conventional morality is criticized:

> We say to ourselves that anyone who has successfully under-
> gone the training of learning and recognizing the truth about

> himself is henceforth strengthened against the dangers of
> immorality, even if his standard of morality should in some
> respects deviate from the common one. (1916–17:16:434)

The cultural and moral standards of normality define two
distinct conditions of neurosis – all therapeutics seek to alleviate
the former, but only psychoanalysis contributes in the dissolution of the latter.[9] The two standards may approach or even
co-incide with each other, and the nearer the cultural standard
gets to the moral one, the more favourable the evaluation of the
culture at hand; in such a culture, the ones who fail to organize
their life in a way that would be governed by a harmonious
coexistence of pleasure and truth are, in fact, the ones classified
as sick.

Rieff's psychological man appears to be at one and the same
time Freud's ideal of normality, and a cultural standard of
normality, increasingly prevalent in industrialized countries of
the West; such societies, it is argued, enhance the individual's
endeavour towards self-knowledge, by not forcing religious and
political ideologies upon him; moreover, they enhance the individual's strivings towards personal well-being by not forcing him
to live by the ethics of asceticism, self-denial and altruism;
finally they provide the individual with investment opportunities
for his libido.

In the light of this positive evaluation of contemporary Western
cultures and of those individuals who have adopted the character-
structure of the psychological man, Rieff's belief that 'in
America today, Freud's intellectual influence is greater than that
of any modern thinker', and his judgment that 'it is a good omen
that [Freud] is treated as a cultural hero' come as no surprise.
Freud taught the twentieth-century man to adopt the 'analytic
attitude', through which he can rationalize his frustrations and
maximize his pleasures; Freud thus emerges as the scientific
interpreter of our era, its leading ideologue, its prophet and its
outstanding moralist.[10]

It is clear that in Rieff's presentation, Freud's ideal of normality represents a reconciliation of man with his conflicts. In
this reconciliation, the role of culture is a negative one; culture
is praised for not inhibiting the individual's path towards
emancipation, and its own contribution to his well-being is
limited to providing avenues for sublimations. If Freud is the
leading moralist of contemporary America, it is because he
emerges from Rieff's reading as the major advocate of individualism. Freud vindicated the strivings of the twentieth-century
man towards fulfilment and well-being through the pleasures
offered by a permissive, consumer-oriented society. He postulated an ideal of a normal man who, instead of pursuing pleasure
blindly, chooses his satisfactions carefully. Unlike the neurotic,
who becomes fixated to unattainable or imaginary goods, the
normal man looks for pleasure where it can be found, always
aware that the 'possibilities of happiness are restricted by our

constitution' (1930a:21:76), and capable of relinquishing some of his desires. It would be fair to conclude that, in Rieff's interpretation of Freud, pleasure is a value which must ultimately be subordinated to truth, if it is to be fulfilled at all; in normality, the intellect must learn to tame desire.

The second line of interpretation which we will now examine, that of Brown and Marcuse, also involves the two levels of normality, which I have just postulated. It too stresses the twin values of truth and pleasure as central in Freud's view of normality; but, unlike Rieff, Brown and Marcuse are not willing to compromise pleasure in the slightest bit. While Rieff sees therapeutic successes and failures as evidence of our constitutional need to accept the taming of desire, Brown and Marcuse see them as evidence of the need to change civilization itself; while Rieff stresses the aspect of Freudian doctrine which seeks to reconcile man with himself and with a given world, Brown and Marcuse place their emphasis on Freud's revelations on the strength of human desire:

> It is a Freudian axiom that the essence of man consists, not, as Descartes maintained, in thinking, but in desiring. (Brown 1959:7)

> [Freud's] metapsychology, attempting to define the essence of being, defines it as Eros - in contrast to its traditional definition as Logos. (Marcuse 1955:113)

Yet, desire, the striving towards fulfilment through love, is constantly frustrated. If desire were automatically satisfied, if the pleasure principle had the stage all to itself, then desire would no longer define the essence of man, for there would be no striving towards fulfilment - fulfilment would come automatically. As we saw earlier,[11] it is repressed desire, forever moving forward, always seeking satisfaction, which is the driving force in Freud's view of history. So, repression is the key to understanding Freud's view of history, and it provides the starting point of both 'Eros and Civilization' and 'Life Against Death':

> According to Freud, the history of man is the history of his repression. (Marcuse 1955:11)

> In the new Freudian perspective, the essence of society is repression of the individual, and the essence of the individual is repression of himself. (Brown 1959:3)

Instead of subordinating pleasure to truth, Brown and Marcuse argue that Freud saw every renunciation of desire as ultimately pathological, whether guided by rational consideration or by irrational anxieties, whether it is carried out successfully or whether it backfires in a firework of neurotic symptoms. For Brown and Marcuse, in the final analysis, there can be no successful repression – all repressions are the sign of 'the disease called man'.[12] In their interpretations of Freud, we are all unfulfilled, repressed, neurotic; the difference between those labelled 'neurotic' and the 'normals' is that the latter have a socially usual and useful form of neurosis[13] and that they have accepted with a greater degree of resignation socially imposed repressions.

Unlike Rieff, who saw Freud's therapy and theory as components of the same task of educating humanity, Brown and Marcuse see an underlying disharmony between Freud's metapsychology, with its emphasis on universal discontent, frustration and neurosis, and his therapeutic task of returning neurotics to normality. As a therapy, psychoanalysis can simply not live up to its own standards as a theory; it merely substitutes new repressions for old ones, softer symptoms for more severe ones, hidden conflicts for manifest ones. As Marcuse puts it:

> While psychoanalytic theory recognizes that the sickness of the individual is ultimately caused by the sickness of his civilization, psychoanalytic therapy aims at curing the individual so that he can continue to function as part of a sick civilization without surrendering to it altogether. (1955:224)[14]

A question arises at this point. Why do Brown and Marcuse insist that we are all neurotic and that our civilization is neurotic, rather than simply say that we are frustrated, alienated or plainly unhappy? This would allow for the term 'neurosis' to be used in the therapeutic sense – i.e. a deviation from what culture defines as normal. Their reasons are partly polemical – they try to vindicate the term 'neurosis' from the meaning it has acquired in the hands of those who have reduced psychoanalysis to a mechanism of social control. More important than the polemical reasons, however, are the theoretical reasons; as we saw in Chapter 3, the mental processes of 'normals' are nearly identical to those of 'neurotics'; the differences between the two are quantitative – the price they pay for their repressions. The sense of reality of normals is affected by many of the distortions, illusions, false ideals, irrational fears and memory lapses that are common among neurotics. Both normals and neurotics are frustrated by society which forces them to renounce their most precious desires; they both experience a sense of guilt as their super-egos interlock with the cultural super-ego (1930a:21:42); they both partake in civilization and its discontents. Under Marcuse's and Brown's critiques, the social distinction between neurotic and normal loses its significance, it simply dissolves. Society is the underlying cause of neurosis, and is, therefore, denied the right to define it – everyone is neurotic, society is sick. Freud himself in the famous passage towards the end of 'Civilization and Its Discontents' writes:

> But there is a question which I can hardly evade. If the

> development of civilization has such a far-reaching similarity
> to the development of the individual and if it employs the same
> methods, may we not be justified in reaching the diagnosis
> that, under the influence of cultural urges, some civilizations,
> or some epochs of civilization - possibly the whole of mankind
> - have become 'neurotic'? (1930a:21:144)

In this passage, the use of the word 'neurosis' in quotation
marks suggests that Freud reached the conclusion himself that
psychoanalysis is inextricably tied to two distinct but inseparable
meanings of neurosis and two distinct but inseparable meanings
of normality, a moral one and a culturally-given one. Yet, the
size of this discovery seems to embarrass him, for he continues:

> The diagnosis of communal neuroses is faced with a special
> difficulty. In an individual neurosis we take as our starting-
> point the contrast that distinguishes the patient from his
> environment, which is assumed to be 'normal'. For a group all
> of whose members are affected by one and the same disorder
> no such background could exist; it would have to be found
> else-where. And as regards the therapeutic application of our
> knowledge, what would be the use of the most correct analysis
> of social neuroses, since no one possesses authority to impose
> such a therapy upon a group? But in spite of all these diffi-
> culties, we may expect that one day someone will venture to
> embark upon a pathology of cultural communities. . . . For a
> wide variety of reasons, it is very far from my intention to
> express an opinion on the value of human civilization. (ibid.)

By placing their emphasis on the value of pleasure in its
generalized form, Brown and Marcuse reach the conclusion that
Freud was hesitating to express in the above passage - namely,
that the attainment of normality in the moral sense requires a
complete re-organization of society ('social therapeutic'), along
lines which permit instinctual gratification and which, somehow,
eliminate the need for turning the individual's aggression against
him/herself. Nothing short of a society whose essence is no
longer the repression of the individual, nothing short of an
individual whose essence is not the repression of him/herself,
can take humanity out of its sickness. It is from this point that
Brown and Marcuse attempt to evaluate culture, and especially
our culture, on Freud's behalf.

A new problem arises, however, with this kind of critical
line. If all cultures are sick, if all individuals are neurotic, are
Brown's and Marcuse's critical evaluations of our culture not
devoid of any moral implications? Does their critique not proceed,
like those of the great religious moralists, from an Archimedean
point outside this world, from an ideal which is unattainable in
this life? Had Brown and Marcuse opted for such an interpretation
of Freud's thought and his higher ideal of normality, they might
have joined Rieff in recommending a second best solution, such

as reconciliation through rationalization. What distinguishes
their approaches from theological ones (quite apart from the
cardinal point that their critique proceeds from a scientifically-
derived perspective, rather than a god-given or an intuitive
one) is that they each envisage a possibility of a real society
meeting their ideal of normality; they both see neurosis,
contrary to theological views of the alienation of man from God,
as a historical, not an existential condition. The primordial fall
was not a tumble from heaven but a real historical event; neurosis
set in under concrete historical conditions, and its abolition will
occur within the realm of the history of civilization.

The success or failure of both Brown's and Marcuse's arguments rests on this single point – can they convince us of the
possibility of a non-repressive civilization? At least one Freudian
critic before them engaged on the same enterprise; Reich,
contrary to the spirit of his Neo-Freudian contemporaries, saw
that the only way out of neurosis was not a reconciliation with
instinctual controls, for the strength, persistence and very
essence of desire makes such reconciliation impossible, but rather
the lifting of these controls. Where Marcuse and Brown differ
from Reich is that in their eagerness to show the possibility of
a non-repressive civilization they do not overlook the formidable
obstacles presented to such a possibility. The fulfilment of
desire cannot be reduced to the achievement of high orgastic
potency in monogamous heterosexual intercouse, nor can the
death instinct be reduced to a manifestation of the frustration-
aggression automatism. Above all, Brown and especially Marcuse
are well aware that in order for society to function as an integrated whole certain crucial conditions need to be met, and any
ideal of normality must fulfil these conditions, if it is not to be
a fresh idealist artifact, propelled by 'a fresh idealistic misconception of human nature' (1930a:21:143); there could be no
greater violation of the spirit and substance of Freudian discourse than such a conclusion. In the chapter devoted to Brown
and Marcuse, in Part II, I will examine and assess their different ideals of normal society and normal individual carefully, for
if they are shown to be purely utopian, then their critiques
of culture lose their vigour, and become merely academic exercises
in the building of wish-fulfilling illusions.

The differences between Brown's and Marcuse's reading of
Freud and that of Rieff are surely remarkable. All three are
perceptive, scholarly and profound interpreters; yet, Freud
emerges from the first two as a major critic of the twentieth
century and a visionary of a radically different future while Rieff
presents him as a great apologist and moralist of the twentieth
century, whose critical endeavour is aimed at the illusions of the
past. Few of history's great thinkers have offered themselves to
such contrasting interpretations, and yet there can be little
doubt that Freud's writings, with their delicate ambiguities and
unending ambivalence, offer ample justification for both readings.
The source of this may be found in the lasting tension between

pleasure and truth as evaluative criteria of our culture. Not
only Freud's psychology but also his social critique appear to
be based on the philosophical dualism of reason and passions
at loggerheads with each other - the fulfilment of the passions
inhibits the pursuits of the intellect, while the strengthening
of the intellect necessitates the taming of the passions. This
Platonic tension between truth and pleasure would appear to
add to a twin conception of normality and a twin conception of
neurosis (cultural and moral ones) a twin conception of history.
When seen from the perspective of the intellect, as in 'Totem
and Taboo' and 'The Future of an Illusion', history is presented
by Freud as a slow process of maturation, a steady growth of
humanity out of the painful illusions and grandiose aspirations
of childhood. According to this view, reason gradually tames
instinct, civilizes it and channels it. On the other hand, works
like 'Civilization and Its Discontents' present a rather different
picture of history; far from representing maturation, the
growth of instinctual controls and repressions deepens humanity's
discontents, compounds its illusions and sustains its alienation.
Pleasure becomes more evasive, more difficult to envisage and
even more difficult to attain; according to this view civilization
does not grow wiser but sicker.

Founded on the dualism between truth and pleasure, Freud's
final evaluation of culture is appropriately ambivalent:

> Of the psychological characteristics of culture two appear to
> be the most important: a strengthening of the intellect, which
> is beginning to govern instinctual life, and an internalization
> of the aggressive impulses, with all their consequent advant-
> ages and perils. (1933b:22:214)

Yet, this ambivalent assessment of history raises as many
questions as it answers. Is it true for instance that the intellect
has tamed desire or aggression, in what has been described as
the most violent century in history? Moreover, does such a
taming necessarily indicate the increasing sovereignty of Logos?
Might it not be itself the result of emotional forces (like religion)
which immerse humanity in deeper illusions? Part II will suggest
that our age is no freer from illusions and ideals than previous
ages, even if they lack the sweeping and universal character of
religious ones.

An even more important difficulty with Freud's assessment of
history, however, arises from the fact that the dualism between
passions and intellect, which is central to the argument, is not a
metaphysical dualism according to Freud's own psychology. Like
Nietzsche, Freud refused to accept Logos as a super-natural
principle; while Nietzsche, however, saw both passions and
reason as expressions of a superior principle, the will to power,
Freud approached the intellect as first and foremost a servant
of desire. In this Freud agrees entirely with Marx - that the
development of man's intellectual powers comes in response to

the expedience of social life, of needs and desires. In this way,
the pursuit of truth cannot ultimately be seen as a separate and
contrary principle from the fulfilment of desire and the pursuit
of pleasure; the Faustian frustration is for Freud the archetype
of the impotence of reason when divorced from practical considerations. On the contrary, for Freud the pursuit of truth is
ultimately connected with the fulfilment of human needs and the
gratification of human desires. The relation between Eros and
Logos in Freud's work is complex but unambiguous. The gratification of desire can only proceed from an accurate knowledge of
desire rather than from its repression; the intellect must therefore dissolve socially sponsored illusions which inhibit man's
self-understanding and help each individual gain a clear and
accurate idea of him/herself, his/her desires, fixations, loves
and hates. With Freud pleasure becomes not only a legitimate
but an ultimate aim of man's self-knowledge; his science dissolved that old science of sexuality, which throughout the second
half of the nineteenth century stubbornly defended bourgeois
morality. Instead of seeking to legitimate the repression of
unorthodox pleasures by classifying them as abnormal and
relating them to all sorts of bodily and spiritual evils, Freud
vindicated the abnormal as constitutive of and indispensable
in what was regarded as normal. Sexual aberrations, far from
being the predicament of evil minds and sick bodies, resulted
from desires common to most people and yet unknown to them.
With Freud, the science of sexuality breaks its compact with the
institutions of morality and control and places itself unreservedly
on the side of pleasure; and it is through being explored
scientifically that pleasure itself is vindicated morally.

But in the Freudian scheme, pleasure is not just the aim of
the pursuit of truth about oneself; the bringing to light of this
truth, which Victorian morality assisted by the institutions of
social and intellectual control had successfully concealed, cannot
be accomplished through the adoption of a passive contemplative
atttitude; neither the discovery nor the acceptance of truth can
arise from direct introspection. On the contrary, it is transference which provides the emotional foundations on which the
pursuit of truth is built. So, as Brown has aptly argued, 'the
coming into consciousness of the unconscious is itself a libidinal
process, an act of love directed at the real person of the
physician' (1959:146). In the undoing of repressions which stand
in the way of fulfilment and self-knowledge, the Freudian
criteria of pleasure and truth meet in perfect harmony, complementing each other and enhancing their mutual realization.

Now, if desire, once identified, were promptly satisfied, the
split between pleasure and truth would not arise. But, as we
have seen time and again, culture in general, and our culture in
particular, is not well-disposed towards such gratification; it can
permit neither the free fulfilment of sexual desires nor the
uncontrolled satisfaction of aggressive impulses. Logos then
assumes a second function, that of taming the instincts, trans-

forming their aims, attenuating their intensity. But this second function is no longer in the service of pleasure; on the contrary, the intellect is now asked to break its compact with pleasure and proceed against its original purpose. Instead of being a servant of desire, the intellect becomes the instrument of culture. It is at this point that the Logos of gratification becomes a Logos of self-control, and it is here that Freud's two ethical criteria of pleasure and truth become antagonistic.

What is ironic is that in its new capacity, the intellect is carrying out an almost identical function to that of the original illusions and repressions it helped to dissolve: it consoles the individual with substitutive satisfactions and offers justifications and rationalizations for abandoning the pursuit of pleasure. It is little wonder that the individual feels cheated; his self-knowledge far from leading to pleasure and fulfilment is demanding the renunciation and frustration of desire. Psychoanalysis may have strengthened his powers of reasoning, helping him to bring to light a host of hidden desires, hidden passions, hidden loves and hidden traumata; and yet, it is these same powers of reasoning which now dictate the acceptance of a second best.

It is here that Freud once again confronts the tragic quality of human fate. Self-knowledge, that sine qua non of the fulfilment of desire, leads man to a realization that his desires cannot be fulfilled, either because they are too monstrous and society cannot permit them or because their fulfilment would bring about intolerable amounts of pain, or simply because the conditions for their fulfilment do not exist. The question then arises of what is the value of truth as an evaluative criterion. Would Oedipus not have been better off had he followed Jokasta's sensible advice 'never to find out who he is'? In the myth of Oedipus we are faced with the archetype of the tragic quality of self-knowledge; the intellect, the powerful instrument of redemption from the arbitrary powers of the Sphinx, is also the medium which reveals the superior powers to which man, in spite of all his struggles, must remain subordinated. Yet, the intellect cannot find peace in accepting these superior powers; if it did, the tragic quality would be entirely lost. On the contrary, when the full dimensions of the human tragedy have been revealed, we arc left to contemplate the distance between what has happened and what should have happened; we are forced to be critical. Oedipus himself is the archetype of this unwillingness to accept fate through the indignant arrogance which he displays when, as an old, blind and persecuted man, he continues to proclaim his innocence and refuses to be broken.

For similar reasons, Freud's confrontation with the tragic fate of mankind cannot lead to a passive pessimism; fate must be challenged and questioned at every opportunity; his investigations into unconscious desires are accompanied by a constant search for the possibilities of their fulfilment, under a different system of constraints. His theory, by offering a radically new understanding of both pleasure and truth, confronts social reality with a critical and questioning attitude, which at times assumes utopian dimensions. Discontents and illusions, the double burden of every culture, are not just brought to light but undermined and subverted by lines of argument and imagination in which culture is no longer the enemy of pleasure and truth, but the commonwealth in which the claims of both Eros and Logos can find their final fulfilment.

Chapter 5
Science and philosophy

The most common issue discussed in relation to psychoanalysis
by non-psychoanalysts may well be whether Freud's theory is
scientific or not; this issue has acquired a notoriety which justifies a brief historical introduction. Twentieth-century philosophers
of science, self-appointed safekeepers of the sanctum sanctorum
of episteme, were quick to realize that psychoanalysis appeared
to violate some of their most precious canons, above all those of
testability and falsifiability/verifiability; in their eyes, Freud
could claim neither the rigour nor the objectivity of a 'real
scientist'. Thus, some of the most prominent among these philosophers, like Wittgenstein and Popper, addressed caustic pole-
mics against psychoanalysis, sparking off a 'debate', whose
vigour is accounted for by the youth and insecurity of both
disciplines, the aggressor and the potential victim, yet, whose
sterility may be unparalleled in the field of academic discourse.
Philosophers of science, having failed dismally to influence
research in the natural sciences through their methodological
formulae (except insofar as the ideology of science they generated could be used to legitimate state-financed and state-directed
research projects), found in psychoanalysis an easy target
against which to direct their ample rhetorical talents. A few,
with a more intimate knowledge of Freud's thought, tried to show
that psychoanalysis is in fact a science (at an early stage, of
course), not by challenging the rules of positivist methodologies,
but by performing elaborate mental gymnastics to show that
psychoanalysis conformed (or could be made to conform) with
these rules.

As the debate grew, philosophers of science became increasingly
aphoristic, their attacks on psychoanalysis taking the shape of
a ritual of scattered sarcasms, which abound in the epistemo
logical scriptures (from Popper to Lakatos). The friends of
psychoanalysis, on the other hand, bulldozed through Freud's
texts 'proving' their conformity with the latest criterion of objectivity or the latest rule of method, whether this was falsifiability,
observational language, operationalization of concepts, predictive prowess or indeed reduction to flow diagrams and computer
programming models.[1]

Of course, positivism is gradually but inevitably getting out of
vogue; it is becoming increasingly apparent that it is not merely
a method ('the scientific method') of looking at and learning
about the world, but a complex mesh of assumptions about how
the world can be known, indeed about the world itself. Briefly,

the world is too complex to be contained within the logical
categories of positivism and science (yes, even great hard
science) is too sloppy and ingenious to follow the rational
methods of positivism.[2] The plausibility of the positivist
critique of psychoanalysis has been seriously undermined by
these developments, and the popularity of Freud's work has
been on the increase in recent years. Equally importantly, as
psychoanalysis is no longer under constant attack and pressure
to defend itself against epistemological pharisaism, it may
undertake a critical self-examination without being driven to
the arid lands of the scientificity debate. A large number of
issues are awaiting elucidation through self-examination and
self-reflection – the relation of theoretical formulations to
empirical data, the scope and historical specificity of psychoanalytic generalizations, the possibilities of prediction, the loci
of theoretical tensions, contradictions, lacunae and question-
marks in psychoanalytic discourse, the relation between theory
and therapy and the interests served by the psychoanalytic
establishments are some such issues. If we are willing to lay to
rest our old epistemological formulae, discussion of these issues
seems quite promising for several reasons. During Freud's
lifetime, psychoanalysis was a dynamic discipline, whose central
formulations were reconsidered, re-assessed, modified and even
rejected on many occasions. A chronological reading of Freud
reveals the expanding brilliance of a mind always willing to take
theoretical risks and never satisfied with the safe rewards of
'normal science'. Yet, while Freud never hesitated to make the
most provocative speculations into new areas of knowledge, he
also showed an eagerness to submit them to the strictest critical
tests, modify them and even relinquish them temporarily until
on later occasions he could pick them up again, in new and
sharper articulations.

At the same time, however, Freud like most innovative
scientists often had to make ad hoc assumptions about areas of
knowledge not yet investigated, occasionally ignored or re-
interpreted empirical evidence, and sometimes relied on the
common sense of his day. Finally, propaganda, conscious and
unconscious, abounds in his writings; the ridicule which he
stoically accepted for several years left a deep mark on him,
and he constantly worried about the status, reception and future
of psychoanalysis. Far from representing theoretical pollution,
all of these features were indispensable for the development and
advance of psychoanalysis. Kuhn and Feyerabend have argued
convincingly that these features (ad hoc assumptions, re-interpretation of evidence, propaganda, etc.) figure prominently in
all great scientific innovations of the past (although never recognized by traditional philosophers of science), without detracting
from their scientific value; without them scientific discovery is
impossible, both on socio-historical and on logical grounds.

What then could be more exciting than looking at Freud's own
criticisms of his work at each stage of his theoretical develop-

ment, the reasons which forced him to alter his formulations, and the methods which he employed to test them? Although philosophers of science have quarrelled for years about the nature of the 'method' involved in the Copernican revolution, it is fair to say that only recently have they started looking into the actual work of scientists themselves, like Galileo and Copernicus, and studying how they actually reached their theoretical conclusions, rather than projecting their own assumptions about how these scientists must have proceeded to reach the conclusions they did. A similar approach to the work of Freud is now overdue; in this essay, I will introduce four features of psychoanalysis which complicate its gnosological self-reflection - Freud's unabated and unqualified positivism, the complexities of his causal imagery, the strangeness of some of his fundamental concepts (in particular the concept of the unconscious) and the value component of his writings (which we encountered in the previous chapter).

Freud's positivism was fervent and unqualified; science is the only reliable route to knowledge, and the scientific Weltanschauung has Freud's whole-hearted support as the only way of dissolving humanity's illusions. Psychoanalysis,

> as a specialist science, a branch of psychology - a depth psychology of the unconscious - is quite unfit to construct a Weltanschauung of its own: it must accept the scientific one. (1933a:22:158)

Freud scornfully rejected suggestions that psychoanalysis is an artistic or philosophical form, and insisted that it 'is a natural science - what else could it be?' In response to a letter from Einstein, he wrote:

> Of course I know that you 'admired' me out of politeness and believed very little of any of my doctrines, although I have often asked myself what indeed there is to be admired in them if they are not true, i.e. if they do not contain a large measure of truth. (Quoted in Jones 1963:494)

Freud's positivism is founded on three pillars - emphasis on observation, insistence on psychic determinism, and isomorphism between central postulates of psychoanalysis and corresponding postulates in physics. Like most great scientists, from Aristotle through Newton to Einstein, Freud is at pains to argue that science is the child of observation:

> [The scientific Weltanschauung] asserts that there are no sources of knowledge of the universe other than the intellectual working-over of carefully scrutinized observations - in other words, what we call research - and alongside it no knowledge derived from intuition, revelation or divination. (1933a:22:159)

Emphasis on observation is what distinguishes science from philosophy; although Freud admitted that philosophers had frequently anticipated his formulations, he saw himself as the first one to submit them to critical tests in a systematic way.[3] He believed that the main accomplishment of psychoanalysis was the extension of the scientific method to the study of the internal universe, thus complementing the physical sciences.[4] He was quite aware that such an extension is not without its problems:

> Every science is based on observations and experiences arrived at through the medium of our psychical apparatus. But since *our* science has as its subject that apparatus itself, the analogy ends here. We make our observations through the medium of the same perceptual apparatus, precisely with the help of the breaks in the sequence of 'psychical' events: we fill in what is omitted by making plausible inferences and translating it into conscious material. (1940a:23:159)

So, unlike other sciences, psychoanalysis needs to face perception and consciousness with scepticism, for one of its aims is to uncover the distortions present in perception and consciousness. Observations do not 'speak for themselves', as Freud pretends that they do in natural science, but need to be translated, or to use the more fashionable term, interpreted – only then can they be used as empirical data. Example: dreams, slips of tongue, phobic symptoms, hallucinations and even straightforward types of action can only be used to corroborate theoretical constructions after they have first been interpreted. Yet, interpretation involves its own theoretical assumptions, without which most mental events remain insignificant phenomena, ignored by scientific common sense (who after all had studied dreams, jokes or slips seriously before Freud?) or classified by the behaviourists. In psychoanalysis, therefore, it becomes quite apparent that passive observation, 'free from preconceptions', etc., is simply impossible.

What then guarantees that 'plausible inferences' can be drawn from most events of the mind, what justifies the task of interpretation? Freud's attempt to 'extend research to the mental field' would be utterly implausible if the mental events, which provide the starting point of interpretation, were random or highly subjective and idiosyncratic. If the determinism apparent in the physical phenomena were eclipsed in the mental field by some transcendental human quality, not only Freud's positivist convictions but his entire project would crumble. Yet, Freud was absolutely convinced that all these phenomena that had previously defied explanation, jokes, dreams, parapraxes, slips, phantasies, accidents and even feelings, are determined no less firmly than physical events, and large parts of his research were devoted to establishing this point. All these events are not shown to be merely determined but overdetermined down to their minuscule and 'secondary' details, i.e. it is usually possible to

identify more than one concurring determination bringing about
a certain mental effect.

Mental determinism does not merely mean that mental events
are not random or transcendental, but also that the underlying
causes can be found in the psychological sphere; in this way
they can be studied as outcomes of psychic processes - hence
they belong to the realm of depth psychology. Of course, as is
well known, Freud believed that, underlying mental events,
there are neuro-chemical processes, our knowledge of which is
still inadequate. It is also well known that even in his last work
he did not discount the possibility of psycho-pharmacology taking over the therapeutic task from analysis.[5] As, however, he
came to appreciate the complexity of psychical phenomena, he
recanted his pre-1900 belief that one day explanation (not just
therapy) may be reduced to the neurological or indeed to the
chemical and physical levels, and tried to establish the theoretical
autonomy of the unconscious and its effects. Reductionism still
fascinates philosophers and scientists, as shown by the renewed
interest in bio-sociology and bio-psychology, though I must confess that I cannot quite understand why one would feel compelled
to 'explain' the allegory of the cave, Hamlet, or the theory of
relativity in terms of their creators' neuro-biological peculiarities.

Freud does not merely assume that psychical phenomena are
concurrent with neuro-biological processes, but that there is
an isomorphism between psychological and neurological processes.
The model introduced in 1895 as A Project for a Scientific Psychology suggests that psychological processes reflect neurological
ones, much as in Homer the Trojan War tilted one way or another
depending on the state of the parallel on-going war amongst the
gods. Freud retained many of these neurological formulations
after translating them into a psychological language, so that,
for instance, the quantity Q of the 'Project' (nervous energy)
is recuperated as libido (psychic energy), the constancy principle becomes the pleasure-pain principle and so on. Although
isomorphism is limited to one domain of psychoanalysis alone, the
economic one, and does not extend to mental topology or mental
dynamics, it re-inforced Freud's positivism - if neuro-biological
processes are merely expressions of scientific laws, psychological processes are too, by implication. If the transformations
of psychic energies are underlined by transformations of nervous energies and the latter are subject to natural laws, then
the former too are subject to natural laws.

It is possible that Freud's positivism was honest, the result of
the intellectual climate of his time and of his limited interest in
philosophy; it is equally possible that it was a propagandist
element, for he dreaded the possibility of psychoanalysis being
branded as quackery and discarded. The ridicule and contempt
with which some of his early ideas were received taught him the
importance of propaganda in scientific writing and many of his
later works are masterpieces of rhetorical style. Whether his
commitment to positivism was genuine or not, Freud must have

been aware that his theory constantly expanded beyond the
boundaries of positivism, as did his methods of discovery and
testing. In this respect, he was like Durkheim, an arch-positivist,
whose theories have a depth that constantly defies the narrow-
ness of his method. As we saw, in spite of his stress on observation, Freud's use of empirical data requires a process of
interpretation, which is contrary to most positivist postulates;
the establishment of psychic determinism is effected through the
use of this method and, therefore, unacceptable to a positivist.
Finally, his isomorphism is rather naive, given that he never
established the correspondence between a single mental event
and its underlying neuro-biological process. But the most obvious
way in which Freud's theories outpace his positivism lies in his
causal imagery. While as Jones has suggested 'Freud never
abandoned determinism for teleology' (as Jung was to do), his
causal imagery is far from the simple cause-effect automatism
of the behaviourists. More importantly, Freud seems to make use
of different models of causation in different places, and it is
worth taking a closer look at this point. Freud's scientific
universe involves a variety of discourse, or as he preferred to
call them 'points of view'. The same psychic phenomenon can
and indeed must be examined from a variety of points of view;
for example, repression can be examined dynamically, as the
process through which the ego determines that a certain idea
is dangerous, takes action to drive it out of consciousness and
suffers certain consequences; repression can also be studied
economically, as the process through which the energy cathected
upon a 'dangerous' idea is neutralized by an opposed amount of
energy made available by the ego; finally, it can be studied
topographically as a process through which an idea is constric-
ted to an area of the mind inaccessible to consciousness, and
substituted in consciousness by an apparently unrelated idea.

   This way of looking at the same situation from different view-
points tends to puzzle the abstract scientist, who likes to tackle
his problems head-on, but it is quite familiar to engineers.
Example - the flight of an aeroplane can be examined from a
dynamic point of view, in terms of the forces of propulsion,
weight, lift, drag, etc. which are in operation; the same flight
can be studied from the thermodynamics point of view, in terms
of the features of combustion at high altitudes, using different
fuels, different turbine parameters and so on; it can equally
be studied from the points of view of structure and material
strength, cybernetics, electrical and electronics, fluid dynamics,
ergonomics and cost-accountancy to name but a few. An engineer
studying the flight from one vantage point need not possess all
the information available to studies from other vantage points,
and yet he is able to proceed with his study in a relatively
autonomous fashion. Thus, the dynamic engineer studies the
equilibrium of the plane in flight, relying on the thermodynamics
engineer to furnish adequate propulsion for a minimum engine
weight, on the material strength engineer to provide alloys that

are both light and can withstand the stresses and strains of flight, the cybernetic engineer to provide control systems which guarantee the right aerofoil angle at every moment of the flight; he also relies on a whole host of other people to carry out their part of the design and flight programmes, not least on the pilot, who is assumed to be numerated and to have no obvious compulsion for exciting dives.

Psychoanalysis proceeds in its study and practice in a somewhat similar fashion, along partly independent programmes. The three levels of the theoretical discourse, topographic, economic and dynamic, have common interfaces and frequently draw assumptions from each other; yet, they are constantly kept separate in Freudian discourse, not in response to practical and institutional considerations of division of labour (as in the engineering example above), but because they each have a distinct character, which does not permit an easy integration with the others. Although the explanatory accounts of a mental event offered from the three points of view are seldom incompatible, they can rarely be unified into a single explanatory principle, for the three involve different starting assumptions, different concepts and different causal imageries. The topographic point of view seems to have no causal imagery whatever – it is merely descriptive, and its key concepts are descriptive of certain mental properties that ideas have; ideas are allocated to different areas of the mental apparatus in accordance with these properties. For example, topographic study may locate the idea 'I want to become a great engineer' in my conscious, the idea 'I hate my analyst' in my repressed unconscious, the idea 'I like cigars' in my ego-ideal and the idea 'four times seven equals twenty-eight' in my preconscious; likewise, it may locate the mental process of attention in consciousness, and that of repression in the unconscious. Being merely descriptive, the topographic point of view may appear somewhat inconsequential and some eminent analysts, like Arlow and Brenner, have suggested that in Freud's mature theory it is transcended in a general structural point of view, according to which the importance of the quality of being conscious or unconscious is de-emphasized. This is not a view shared by this essay, which pays the utmost attention to the quality of consciousness, 'our one beacon-light in the darkness of depth psychology', in Freud's words. The topographic point of view, after the fashion of a mental map, does not only highlight the existence of a new mental territory discovered by Freud, the unconscious, but also makes a further important contribution, analogous to the contribution of a geographical map. A map of Europe does not merely designate areas where inhabitants speak a particular language or belong to a specific administrative or political system; it also informs us that in order to travel from London to Paris it will be necessary to devise means of staying dry while crossing considerable aquatic masses. In an analogous way, the topographic point of view gives us valuable information about the itinerary of

different ideas as they travel into different mental locations, as
well as their properties at each stage of their journey. The
topographic point of view has nothing to say about where the
idea will find the energy (means of transport) to cross boundaries, about why it makes the crossings or what forces oppose
its path; these are the tasks of the economic and dynamic points
of view.

The economic point of view, centring on the principles of
constancy and transformation of energy, has still memories of its
infancy as a biological model in the 1895 Project. This is a world
of mechanistic determinations, where transformations of energy,
binding and unbinding, cathecting, discharging, abreacting,
catharizing, sublimating, etc. determine mental events and
especially mental regularities - as Ricoeur, Habermas and
Solomon have argued, there is no doubt that the economic point
of view represents a mechanistic model of the mind. Some writers
have more or less reduced the whole psychoanalytic discourse to
this model; the most perceptive among them, like Fingarette and
Wollheim,[6] are disappointed because they discover that this
model fails them at the most crucial point: why does the ego
repress? Given that the theory of repression is the central pillar
of psychoanalysis, if, as Fingarette suggests, psychoanalysis is
unable to answer this crucial question, then its entire edifice
collapses.

Yet, consultation of the most obvious text, Freud's essay
'Repression', reveals a direct answer:

> the motive and purpose of repression [is] nothing else than
> the avoidance of unpleasure. (1915d:14:153)

A direct answer, undoubtedly. But also an answer which moves
into a different universe - a universe where mechanistic causation
is lost amidst the company of motives and purposes, strategies
and conflicts, agencies and actions. In contrast to the mechanistic model of mental economics, mental dynamics rely on a much
more complex causal imagery, where events are seen no longer
as 'outcomes' but as 'functions'. Ricoeur observes that many of
the 'mechanisms' of Freud's neuro-biological period were gradually
replaced by the concept of 'psychic work', like dream-work and
mourning-work (1970:85), while Jahoda suggests that even the
defence mechanisms, a term to which Freud stuck until the end
of his life, are in fact functions of the ego: 'The term "mechanism" is unfortunate here; they clearly are purposeful strategies,
consciously or unconsciously designed to make life easier and
more manageable, not mechanical routines with causes but no
purposes' (1977:66). Jahoda develops her argument and suggests
that the causal imagery in Freud's discussions of the entire
psychic system is essentially a functionalist one. Functionalist
interpretations of Freud tend to subordinate mental economics
to mental dynamics, and in some cases they reach at equally
distorted images of the mental apparatus as those which sub-

ordinate dynamics to economics. According to the functionalist
tradition in sociology and psychology, functionalist interpreters
of Freud conceptualize the mind as a system with various functional components, ego, id and super-ego, operating in a
changing environment. Within this system, the ego, with its
'need for synthesis' and its 'essential property of organization',[7]
is the structure in dominance assuming both integrative and
adaptive functions, and gives the system its unmistakable
identity. It is the ego which receives the often conflicting
demands of the other sub-systems (which for reasons of mental
topography cannot communicate with each other), and constantly
devises compromises which ensure the survival of the individual
as a whole. In spite of its apparent plausibility, this functionalist approach does not work; although it cannot be denied that
there are strong functional elements in Freud's dynamic point of
view, this approach, by subordinating economics to dynamics,
energetics to hermeneutics, and determinism to teleology, loses
sight of the most important feature of Freud's psychology - conflict. In Freud's view, conflict is not the concomitant of adaptation, but the very basis of his view of the individual and the
world in which he/she operates. Instead of a conflict between
nature and society, conflict between society and the individual
and conflict between the individual and him/herself, functionalist readings of Freud usually end up with a harmonious picture
of nature and culture, and an individual nicely integrated in
society and even better integrated within him/herself.
  In conclusion, it must be clear that both extremes in emphasis,
i.e. the subordination of one point of view to the other and vice
versa, lead to positions which are absolutely untenable within
the Freudian discourse; the one tends to eliminate or neglect
conflict while the other fails to explain it. In this way, we
begin to understand Freud's insistence on the maintenance of
the theoretical autonomy of the three levels of his discourse.
All three levels have an important contribution to make in a
complete psychoanalytic explanation of a mental phenomenon,
and their accounts must support and corroborate each other,
without eclipsing them. But the contrasting causal imageries
involved in these accounts are a lasting source of theoretical
tension and a major complication in the gnosological self-
reflection of psychoanalysis.[8]
  The failure of the functionalist interpretation of the three
'agencies' of the mental apparatus introduces us to the third
such complication - his central concepts. Three groups of concepts have come under particularly severe criticism - the
instincts, the ego/id/super-ego triumvirate and the unconscious.
These concepts have generally been dismissed by positivist
philosophers as obscurantist, ungrammatical, self-contradictory,
non-operational and ultimately nonsensical. Freud's candidness
in referring to instincts as 'mythical entities', 'indeterminate'
and so on may have fuelled those attacks which originated in a
'pictorial' theory of language; most of the central concepts of

psychoanalysis, including those suggesting a mental map, were bound to be seen as nonsensical to the numerous enthusiasts of early Wittgenstein. Now, Freud, like most practising scientists, believed that if a concept is necessary in articulating theoretical propositions, one need not worry too much about establishing a pictorial correspondence between the concept and 'a fact of the world' - he believed that as theory progresses, concepts are gradually elucidated, refined and specified, or alternatively discarded. Explanation of mental phenomena, he argued,

> cannot be effected without framing fresh hypotheses and creating fresh concepts; but these are not to be despised as evidence of embarrassment on our part but deserve on the contrary to be appreciated as an enrichment of science. They can claim to the same value as approximations that belongs to the corresponding intellectual scaffolding found in other natural sciences, and we look forward to their being modified, corrected and more precisely determined as further experience is accumulated and sifted. So too it will be entirely in accordance with our expectations if the basic concepts and principles of the new science (instinct, nervous energy, etc.) remain for a considerable time no less indeterminate than those of the older sciences (force, mass, attraction, etc.). (1940a:23:159)

This argument, which clearly clashes completely with Freud's positivist pretences, is exactly the conclusion that many distinguished philosophers of science *circa* 1980 have reached. Feyerabend argues that not only 'empirical' sciences but also analytic ones develop without precise definitions of their central concepts, so that even arithmetic 'developed without any clear understanding of the concept of a number' (1975:257), and reaches the obvious conclusion, which is anathema to the pictorialists and most twentieth-century philosophy: 'We see . . . how essential it is to learn talking in riddles, and how disastrous an effect the drive for instant clarity must have on our understanding' (ibid.). It is only through gradual working-through that concepts become sharpened in the hands of practising scientists, not through the methodologist's demand for precise definitions.

In Chapter 1, we examined the difficulties inherent in Freud's theory of instincts; many of these difficulties stem from the instincts' ambiguous position at the interface of biology and psychology, combining as it were a materialist and a symbolic dimension. In this chapter, I will limit myself to the other two sources of conceptual difficulties, the ego/id/super-ego triumvirate and the unconscious.

Freud's idea of splitting the 'self' into three agencies, 'minipersons' or homunculi (as different authors have seen them) was the target of early criticism from the ego-psychologists, who gradually buried the id and the super-ego in order to develop theories of (integrated) personalities. Freud's anthropomorphism has been criticized most succinctly by Thalberg,

in a provocative article entitled 'Freud's Anatomies of the Self'.
Thalberg begins his attack on what he sees as Freud's partition-
ing of the mind by asking the question 'Is our ego awake or
asleep when we sleep?' (1974:158). He then parades nine quotes
from 'The Interpretation of Dreams' involving the concept of the
ego in different capacities, now asleep, now a vigilant watch-
man, now semi-asleep or drowsy, now a guardian of sleep, now
a censor and so on. So what is the ego up to while we sleep,
after all? Conceptual confusion, concludes Thalberg. But this
is not the end of his story, for he goes on to raise a number
of 'who' questions which provide the coup de grâce. 'Whose sleep
is the ego trying to protect?' 'Whom does the super-ego watch
when it engages in self-observation?' 'Whose pleasure are the
instincts striving for?' 'Whose interests is the ego trying to protect in its repressions?' 'Why should my ego seek my advantage?'
and so on. His arguments have a strength that will force many of
the uninitiated to accept Wittgenstein's verdict that psychoanalysis is a 'powerful mythology', or Popper's view that the ego,
the id and the super-ego are as scientific as Homeric gods.

It is beyond doubt that in 1899, when Freud published his
'Interpretation of Dreams', many of his central concepts had not
crystallized, especially the concept of the ego which at times
he tended to identify with consciousness or with the person as
a whole. It would seem totally unreasonable, in view of what
I argued earlier, to expect complete conceptual clarity in a
work which pioneered a totally novel domain of theoretical discourse - even so, however, Freud is much more cautious than
Thalberg suggests. An examination of the nine propositions,
quoted by Thalberg, reveals, first of all, that Freud does not
use the term 'ego' in all of them, but also uses the terms
'censor', 'consciousness' and 'normal ego' which are not necessarily synonymous with the ego. As Freud developed his theory,
several functions of the ego came to the forefront in a more or
less systematic way, like flight from external dangers, reality-
testing, perception, critical and moral attitude, repression,
narcissism, thinking, synthesis, etc. It is, therefore, perfectly
possible to go back to the Traumdeutung and investigate which
of the ego functions are suspended during sleep (motility,
reality-testing, external perception, etc.) and which ego functions persist (internal perception, repression in a reduced way,
etc.), removing in this way the question of whether the ego
(as a mini-person) is asleep or awake. Of course, Freud carries
considerable responsibility, because his rhetorical metaphors of
the 'poor ego' and its 'three harsh masters', the 'censor', the
'rider and the horse', etc., have re-inforced the charges of
anthropomorphism - but, as soon as we study the ego as a complex of functions, the anthropomorphism dissolves.

Thalberg's 'who' questions appear to be driving us to the conclusion that Freud is operating within an implicit notion of self,
which is never directly mentioned but is always indispensable
in his arguments. The ego strives for the safety of the self, the

instincts are sources of pleasure for the self, the super-ego
is observing the self, the environment threatens the continuity
of the self and so on. This is indeed the position taken by
many functionalist readings of Freud; yet, at closer study, it
seems to me that the idea of 'self' or pure subjectivity, just like
the idea of God, only enters Freud's discussions as an illusion
in the technical sense, never as a concept. The ego, in its constant and frustrated efforts to keep things under control within
its own organization, compensates for its desperate troubles by
imagining itself all-powerful, well organized, independent, the
seat of a free will, a mini-god. There is a variety of psychoanalytic accounts of how this illusion comes about, through
identification with imaginary gods and fathers, narcissism, projection, sublimation, etc., but it is nevertheless an illusion. It
now becomes transparent why Freud put himself on the same rank
as Copernicus and Darwin, as a great destroyer of man's illusions
about himself. Copernicus's heliocentric system smashed man's
illusion that he was the centre of the universe, while Darwin's
theory of natural selection dented irreparably his felt superiority
over his fellow creatures in the animal kingdom. Freud's contribution was probably 'the most wounding' for man's narcissism,
for it showed that 'the ego is not master in its own house' (1917a:
17:189). The self, with its powers of subjectivity, transcendence,
will and wholeness, is itself nothing but a mental artifact, an
illusion created by the ego, which cannot be taken seriously as
a concept of the scientific discourse; in Freud's analysis man
and his mental apparatus figure only as a fragmented and diversi-
fied structure, never as a whole personality or self.

Althusser expands this critique of man's illusion about himself:

> Since Marx, we have known that the human subject, the
> economic, political or philosophical ego is not the 'centre' of
> history - and even in opposition to the Philosophers of the
> Enlightenment and to Hegel, that history has no 'centre' but
> possesses a structure which has no necessary 'centre' except
> in ideological misrecognition. In turn, Freud has discovered
> for us that the real subject, the individual in his unique
> essence, has not the form of an ego, centered on the 'ego',
> on 'consciousness' or on 'existence' - whether this is the exist-
> ence of the for-itself, of the body-proper or of 'behaviour' -
> that the human subject is decentered, constituted by a struc-
> ture which has no center either, except in the imaginary
> misrecognition of the 'ego', i.e. in the ideological formations
> in which it 'recognizes' itself. (1971:218-19)

Conclusion: while it is essential to study the ego as a complex
of diverse functions ('structure' in Althusser's terminology),
we must resist the temptation of seeing these functions as contributing to the integration, welfare, adaptation, etc. of the
self or of a unified human essence, for, as we saw, there is no
self in Freud's vocabulary, except as an illusion, just as there
is no God, except as an illusion.

I suggested earlier that Freud's rhetorical metaphors have
fuelled charges of anthropomorphism, a feature totally absent
from his thought. The positive contribution of these metaphors
is that they serve as a constant reminder that mental functions
are in partial contradiction - in short, the mental apparatus
operates as if it were made up of several mini-persons, each
with his own task to fulfil, a task which brought him in regular
conflict with other mini-persons. Even those functions which
pertain wholly to the ego are not fully integrated, but involve
contradictions; one of them in particular, the self-critical one,
stands in such strong contradiction with most other ego-functions
that Freud split it from the ego and called it super-ego. Freud's
view of the mind is that of a split, complex, self-deluded and fragmented entity, and nothing could be further from truth than seeing
what he calls the 'mental apparatus' as synonymous to the self of the
interactionists or the personality of psychologists; nor should the
different mental agencies or functions be seen as effects of a central
essence, whether it be called personality, self or 'man'.

It would, therefore, be perfectly possible to re-write much of
the Freudian 'dynamic point of view' purging it of all anthropomorphism, and using a functional vocabulary; so, for instance,
the famous metaphor of the ego and its three harsh masters
would be translated into a complex of functions (the ego-
functions) within structural limits (negative determinations)
posed by the id and super-ego functions and from external
reality - should these limits be violated, then the complex of
ego-functions collapses. Although such translation is perfectly
possible, it robs the Freudian discourse of its liveliness, elegance
and charm for the sake of a dubious conceptual clarity; in addition, it would subject Freud's arguments to the misunderstand-
ings, noted earlier which arise from established functionalist
traditions, notably a dangerous de-emphasis of conflict. It is
far from certain that functionalist jargon, with its un-Freudian
assumptions of integration and co-ordination, would serve
Freud's discourse better than his string of imaginative and provocative metaphors.

Freud's mental trichotomy was not only an ingenious scheme
for explaining the causes and manifestations of mental conflict.
It was also a monumental step towards articulating the relationship between the individual and the social whole from a new
perspective, which transcended the old views of man as 'by
nature' social (Aristotle) or as 'by nature' anti-social (Hobbes).
Each of the three protagonists, ego, id and super-ego,
represents one distinct aspect of the individual's ambivalent
relationship with culture - the id with its blind defiance of all
external considerations, the super-ego with its slavish and
uncritical subordination to external law, and the ego with its
compulsive urge towards mastery and control of externality. It
is through his stubborn refusal to look at the individual as an
integrated personality, character or self that Freud avoided the
shortcomings of most theorists who discussed the relationship

between the individual and society. Man is both a social animal
and an anti-social one, a moral and an amoral one; culture both
develops man's potential and thwarts it, man both submits to
culture and rebels against it. In brief, Freud's mental trichotomy
enables him to assess not only the relationship between individual
and society but also the costs of culture to the individual, the
renunciations, conflicts and discontents it creates.

This new vision of the relationship between individual and
society which emerges from Freud's mental trichotomy would
not have been reached had Freud limited his analysis to visible,
conscious phenomena. We must not forget that Freud was not the
first thinker to 'divide' the individual into different agencies,
and that many philosophers since Plato had engaged in similar
projects. What differentiates Freud's theories from these as well
as from more recent psychological theories of 'split' selves and
elevates them way above them was his ability to open the gates
of the unconscious to us, so that the underlying meanings of
mental events as well as of cultural artifacts (religious ideas,
works of art, myths, etc.) were made accessible to systematic
study. It is the study of this unconscious dimension of all three
mental agencies, id, ego and super-ego, that reveals that the
neat dovetailing of individual and institutional super-ego, individual and institutional motivation, personal and social needs is
problematic and entails contradiction as well as concord; in
short, that culture is not only internalized but also resisted by
the individual. It is in this respect that Freud's theory enabled
him to move way beyond Durkheim in the study of religion, by
showing the cost at which religion contributes to social cohesion.
Freud agreed with Durkheim's argument that religion cements
the social bond. Yet, through an appreciation of the unconscious
desires fulfilled by religion, Freud was able to move further
and argue that religion was a substitute gratification and that it
aggravated the disease from which it sought to console the
individual. In this chapter, I will not seek to assess Freud's
theory of religion, but it must be appreciated that his effort to
discover unconscious desires behind it gave his analysis a depth
and a critical edge which Durkheim's theory, brilliant though it
is, lacks.

But if it is the unconscious dimensions of the ego, the id and
the super-ego which add unforeseen riches to our analysis and
introduce this important critical dimension to our study of culture,
we must now turn our attention to the unconscious, that most
brilliant and controversial of Freud's discoveries. As Juliet
Mitchell has argued, most critiques against Freud can be seen
ultimately as critiques of the unconscious, most departures from
Freud must be seen as breaks from the unconscious. Yet, as I
will try to show, the concept of the unconscious marks the best-
hidden and most secret assumptions of most contemporary human
sciences, an assumption without which it would be impossible for
them to pursue their manifold and apparently unrelated goals.

The unconscious has attracted the attention of most twentieth-century philosophers, including Wittgenstein, Sartre, Lacan, Popper and Chomsky; some, like Lacan and Chomsky, believe that in the unconscious lies a genuine revolution in Western thought, a breach from the central assumption of both rational- ist and empiricist philosophies that the contents of our minds are available to us through simple introspection. Others, like Popper and Sartre (strange bedfellows!), have argued that the concept can be refuted on logical grounds alone. In this dis- cussion, I will focus on Freud's mature theory of the unconscious, that is, the form taken by his theory after the instinctual division between Eros and the death instinct, after the id had become an entity in its own right, and after the theory of the ego and super-ego had taken its final shape.

Freud was by no means the first theorist to argue that certain mental processes are unconscious. In a well-researched book, Lancelot L. Whyte traces the idea of such processes at least as far back as the seventeenth century in the work of Cudworth, Norris and Leibniz: these ideas kept intriguing philosophers and poets through the eighteenth century and by the middle of the nineteenth there was a considerable all-round interest in uncon- scious mental processes. The issue was addressed directly by the German physician C.G. Carus (1789–1860) in his work 'Psyche' (1846) and by the philosopher E. von Hartmann in 'The Philosophy of the Unconscious' (1869), and between 1870 and 1880 at least six books were published with the term 'unconscious' in their title, in Western Europe. All these books were toying with the idea that the mind is structured in such a way that not all of its contents are available to consciousness at will. Although Freud was familiar with the work of Carus, what affected his early formulations to a greater extent was the clinical idea of a split consciousness, as the central phenomenon in hysteric attacks, which he learnt from Charcot. In his early theory, developed jointly with Breuer, Freud regarded hysteric attacks as cases of splitting of consciousness precipitated by the recurrence of a traumatic memory; Freud's first original contribution was to suggest that the reason why traumatic memories resulted in the splitting of memory is defence, as opposed to the theory of 'hypnoid states' (Breuer) or constitutional predisposition (Janet). Freud argued that the recurrence of childhood traumata (e.g. seduction by parents) can be so painful that the patient tries to isolate it and all related experiences, through a split in consciousness, which is thus seen as 'an act of will' (1894a: 3:50). In this way, it is ensured that the trauma is kept separate from normal consciousness (which contains feelings of love and respect for the parents), that its strength is weakened and that its energy is converted into an unrelated form, that of hysteric body symptoms.

At the age of forty-one, Freud may have felt that this theory of neurosis as defence was his one original contribution to science; but, as is well known, he was in for a nasty surprise, as it became increasingly evident that not all of his patients

could have been victims of 'pervert fathers'. In fact Freud was
soon to realize that many of the reported seductions were purely
fictitious,[9] and was forced to acknowledge that his early theory
had collapsed; he felt, however, that 'in the general collapse
only the psychology has retained its value. The dreams still
stand secure, and my beginnings in metapsychology have gone
up in my estimation. It is a pity one cannot live on dream-
interpretation for instance' (Letter to Fliess 1954:221). This
was the first of several instances where Freud had the courage
to abandon what he could not defend on empirical grounds, and
his courage paid off more than he could have dreamed. Having
repudiated the aetiology of hysteric attacks, Freud turned to
the dreams and his 'beginnings in metapsychology'. Dreams,
which Freud later called the 'royal road to the unconscious',
were seen as 'normal pathological phenomena', i.e. as phenomena
demonstrating the operation of certain neurotic mechanisms among
'normal' people – it was the study of dreams which led him to
study the unconscious, not as an exceptional case, the predicament of those who had suffered a split consciousness, but as a
normal part of the mind. Much of 'The Interpretation of Dreams'
is devoted to the study of the properties of unconscious ideas
and desires, their constant tendency to burst into consciousness,
the frequent distortions they undergo when they do reach consciousness and the reasons which prevent them generally from
reaching consciousness. During sleep, Freud argued, the forces
which prevent 'dangerous' desires from reaching consciousness
are weakened, and dreams provide an outlet for many of these
desires to reach consciousness, and find satisfaction, albeit in
highly distorted forms. Dream interpretation proceeds in the
opposite direction from that of the dreamer's dream-work –
instead of masquerading desires, interpretation leads us back to
them, providing us with the key to the unconscious.

Contrary to public misconception which has tended to regard
the unconscious as a messy jumble of ideas and impulses arising
from the depths of the human soul, Freud's unconscious represented, in the first place, the state of ideas and desires which
have undergone repression. Unconscious and repression are
linked in Freudian theory like Siamese twins; there is nothing
in the unconscious, as Mannoni, has pointed out, to suggest the
Platonic depths, where the world of pure forms seeks expression
through language (1971:55). Nor does the unconscious bear
any resemblance to the virgin and unpolluted personality core
which has become the trademark of 'humanistic' psychology.
There is nothing mysterious, mystic or mystifying about Freud's
concept of the unconscious – although unconscious ideas and
desires do not share the properties of conscious ones, they are
nevertheless, normal, structured and knowable.

Through 'The Interpretation of Dreams' and his subsequent
research of other mental phenomena, like slips of tongue, jokes,
parapraxes, neurotic symptoms, Freud developed a fairly comprehensive picture of the properties of the unconscious. First

of all, unconscious ideas are exempt from contradiction, so that,
for instance, love and hate for the same person may happily coexist.[10] Second, ideas in the unconscious are not temporally
structured, nor are they altered by the passage of time; ideas
that have been relegated to the unconscious recently have no
greater vividness than early childhood repressions. Third,
unconscious ideas are absolutely invulnerable to reality-testing;
for example, the belief that someone loves me may persist in the
unconscious, irrespective of countless experiences of the contrary. These freedoms, however, do not imply that unconscious
ideas defy order - the order which they obey is articulated in
Freud's theory of the primary process (conscious processes
being termed 'secondary'). The essence of primary process is
motility of cathexis, which involves two inter-connected properties of unconscious processes; first, when unconscious ideas
become cathected with definite amounts of mental energy they
display an overwhelming tendency towards discharge, irrespective of moral or reality considerations. Unconscious ideas thus
charged are usually referred to as 'desires', 'impulses' or
'wishes' (or at times even 'instincts') and their discharge
would result in pleasure. So,

> the sovereign tendency obeyed by these primary processes is
> easy of recognition; it is called the pleasure-pain principle,
> or more shortly the pleasure-principle. (1911b:12:219)

The pleasure principle defines the programme of unconscious
desires: discharge through any means (including, when everything else fails, hallucination) and at any cost. The second
feature of motility concerns the relative ease with which cathectic charges can move from one unconscious idea to another
(displacement) or can join several ideas together and form a new
and often self-contradictory unity (condensation). It is precisely
these twin properties of unconscious ideas that the ego exploits,
when it allows a dangerous desire to reach consciousness after
making sure that the original desire has been rendered unrecognizable - condensation and displacement are at work in most
dreams, puns, lapses and neurotic symptoms, as well as in much
of every-day behaviour, when anger, fear, love, etc. find
inappropriate and often 'irrational' objects upon which they
become attached.

Before going on to examine how the unconscious can become
known to us and studied, it is necessary to provide some clarification over an issue which has led some philosophers to reject
the unconscious on logical grounds alone - if their argument is
correct, surely there is no point in examining whether the unconscious is knowable at all, for there is no unconscious at
all, except as a fallacious hypothesis.

The unconscious, as we have seen, contains, in the first place,
repressed ideas, which, when cathected, seek discharge. The
unconscious and repression are thus conceptually linked. Yet,

as Freud's understanding of the complexities of mental conflict
deepened, the early topography which identified the unconscious
with repressed instinctual desires and the pre-conscious with
the anti-instinctual forces required considerable modification.
In brief, it became apparent that repressed desires were not the
only psychic elements possessing the quality of being unconscious; quite frequently the anti-instinctual forces as well as
the generalized sense of guilt and the 'need for self-punishment'
were shown to have an unconscious existence. This precipitated
the 'second topicality' of psychoanalytic theory, according to
which the major criterion of different psychic systems was not
accessibility to consciousness, but rather the functions of the
systems in psychic conflict.

In the context of the present discussion, it is not necessary to
take a position on the current debate in psychoanalytic theory
as to whether the second topicality superseded the first (Arlow
and Brenner) or whether it merely provided a more convenient
vocabulary for the same theoretical positions (Lacan and followers).
It suffices to say that following Freud's elucidations in 'The Ego
and the Id', many of the functions of the ego, including several
(but not all) mechanisms of defence, were shown to be unconscious themselves. As Anna Freud has argued, 'the defensive
measures of the ego against the id are carried out silently and
invisibly. The most we can ever do is to reconstruct them in
retrospect: we can never really witness them in operation'
(1966:8).

Thus, in Freud's later theory, not only repressed ideas and
desires (now identified with the id) but also many defensive
functions of the ego (including the process of repression itself)
possess the quality of being unconscious. In Freud's words:

> We recognize that the *Ucs.* does not coincide with the repressed;
> it is still true that all that is repressed is *Ucs.*, but not all
> that is *Ucs.* is repressed. A part of the ego too – and Heaven
> knows how important a part – may be *Ucs.*, undoubtedly is
> *Ucs.* (1923b:19:18)

Although different groups of analysts differ on the importance
they attribute to the quality of being unconscious, there is
little disagreement on this general point, since in their daily
efforts they do not merely seek to reveal to the ego the repressed
desires but also to overcome the ego's resistances and reveal to
the ego its own defensive mechanisms.

Yet, this obvious point, endlessly re-iterated by Freud,[11]
seems to have escaped quite a large number of philosophical
commentators, who restrict the unconscious to repressed
instinctual forces, and identify the ego with consciousness or
subjectivity, according to the philosophical tradition. This is
precisely Sartre's premise in a syllogism that leads him to
reject the concept of the unconscious. For Sartre, the ego is
'the psychic totality of the facts of consciousness', while repres-

sion is a typical case of 'mauvaise foi' or self-deception, since
the ego is both concealing something from itself and unaware of
doing so. But if the ego is indeed lying to itself, it must, like
every liar, (i) know the idea which it seeks to conceal or distort,
and (ii) know that it is lying (for a liar cannot lie unwittingly);
this double reductio ad absurdum leads Sartre to dismiss much
of psychoanalytic theory and especially the concept of the unconscious as 'mere verbal terminology' (1956:47:54). His syllogism,
however, involves both misconceptions described earlier: (i)
it ignores the fact that the ego is itself to a considerable extent
unconscious (hence, Sartre cannot accept that it is possible for
it to conceal something and at the same time to be unaware of
it, since the entire process of concealment takes place unconsciously), and (ii) it identifies the ego with a consistent 'subject'
or 'self' who is aware of his actions (anthropomorphism). Conclusion: Insofar as the ego is unconscious, it too may involve
contradictions in its organization (just like the id), it too may
have idealized pictures of itself which do not stand up to reality-
testing - so the ego may at the same time narcissistically over-
value itself and masochistically demean it. Moreover, the ego,
by possessing unconscious elements, may delude itself in ways
which are much more subtle than lying; it may, for example,
avoid testing some of its beliefs empirically ('I could be a great
athlete, if I really wanted', 'X loves me', 'I am a Don Juan',
etc.), it may forget all unfavourable evidence or it may seek to
counter it through sophisms and rationalizations. This is crucial
for an argument which will be developed in Chapter 13, namely
that contemporary man is sailing in a sea of narcissistic delusions,
which amount to a number of convenient and often contradictory
'half-truths' about himself and the world within which he operates. These half-truths are invoked regularly not as moral
justifications for action, but as embellishments of the narcissist's
self-image.

Having clarified the issue of the unconscious components of
the ego, it is now necessary to look much closer at the unconscious itself and examine how Freud sought to demonstrate its
existence and bring its contents to light. Freud was, of course,
aware that the unconscious, with its timelessness, its internal
contradictions, its resistance to education, its stubborn disregard for reality and above all its inaccessibility to consciousness, would be a red rag for contemporary philosophy.

> To most people who have been educated in philosophy the idea
> of anything psychical which is not also conscious is so incon-
> ceivable that it seems to them absurd and refutable simply by
> logic. (1923b:19:13)

So, all his major discussions of the unconscious begin with an
almost ritual presentation of the philosophical argument against
the unconscious, and, then, an examination of the reasons which
have led psychoanalysis inexorably towards it - the explanation

of those phenomena that had previously defied rational explanation. After all, the contribution of philosophy to the discussion
of the passions since the days of Plato has been overshadowed
by its concern for reason.

But if the unconscious is by definition inaccessible to consciousness how can we be sure of its existence, and how can we ever
hope to know its contents, whether these contents are ideas or
processes? Freud's answers to these questions proceed from
three aspects of the unconscious: (a) the pre-conscious, (b)
unconscious/repressed ideas and desires and (c) the unconscious
as a mental system. At the first and simplest level, there can be
little doubt about the existence of pre-conscious ideas and
thoughts, which although not constantly in consciousness may be
recalled at will - people's names, the various principles of
mathematics, past events and so on may all belong to the pre-
conscious, in so far as they have left a permanent trace in our
memories. At the second level, Freud seeks to demonstrate the
existence of unconscious ideas and desires. The first evidence
he invokes is provided by Bernheim's experiments in hypnosis;
while a person is under hypnosis, he/she is asked to execute a
certain action at a fixed time after his/her awakening. After the
person has regained consciousness and although he/she has no
recollection of what occurred during the hypnotic session, he/
she proceeds to carry out the required act at the prescribed
moment (1912g:12:261). Even after the act, the patient is unable
to offer an explanation as to the reasons for the act, which
leads Freud to conclude that the command was at all times unconscious, and that at the required moment it became active. On
this principle of re-activation of unconscious ideas, Freud based
his theory of hysteric attacks; as we saw, originally he believed
that these attacks were triggered by the recurrence of a traumatic memory, but in the light of the fictitious nature of many
of these traumatic memories (after he developed his theory of
the unconscious through the study of dreams), Freud was to
argue that repressed desires and phantasies can operate just
like repressed memories, for the unconscious does not recognize
the difference between fact and phantasy. What is common in
both early and later theories of transference neuroses is the
element of defence in their aetiology, and while Bernheim's
hypnotic experiments offer useful corroborating evidence for the
existence of the unconscious, Freud insisted that

> we obtain our concept of the unconscious from the theory of
> repression. The repressed is the prototype of the unconscious
> for us. (1923b:19:15)

From this point on, the proof of the unconscious rests on the
proof of repression, knowing of the unconscious rests on unveiling repressions. Here Freud invoked considerable theoretical
support for his theory of repression from the experiences he had
accumulated through his therapeutic practice, and his study of

mental life as mental conflict. This support has been challenged
by those who argue that the analysand's utterances and behaviour during the analytic session are so burdened by the effects
of suggestion that they are completely unreliable as scientific
evidence. Just as religious individuals may receive regular
communications through mysterious voices, it is argued that
psychoanalysed neurotics learn to speak through the language
of the unconscious. On the other hand, some friends of psychoanalysis, like Habermas, have made the dangerous suggestion
that the scientificity of psychoanalysis lies in the emancipation
of the patient - surely the failure of psychoanalysis to cure a
neurotic symptom would then have to be seen as evidence of its
non-scientificity, something which would have horrified Freud,
who as we saw earlier conceded that psychoanalytic cures cannot
compete with the faith-healing at Lourdes. Whether or not the
analytic session furnishes psychoanalysis with valid empirical
evidence and whether or not the patient's recognition of an unconscious desire after the lifting of the resistances is proof of
the unconscious desire (rather than of brain-washing), one
thing is clear: the patient's utterances, his gestures and his
silences, his resistances and recognitions, his passions and his
indifferences, his negations and his affirmations cannot be
fitted directly into any explanatory scheme - unlike the observations of natural sciences, psychoanalytic observations require
interpretation before they can be used to corroborate theoretical hypotheses. Before the signs issued by the analysand can
be fitted into an explanation, their meaning must first be
deciphered and clarified.

Philosophy of science is, of course, becoming aware that in
natural sciences, too, observations are not direct impressions
of nature on our senses, nor are most natural quantities, fields,
forces, masses and so on, observable quantities. The appro-
priation of nature by the observer requires a host of assumptions
including assumptions about the observation medium, measurement, and the sensory apparatus of the observer. The healthy
scepticism of Galileo's religious opponents when first exposed to
the telescope and their plausible suspicion that the impressions
of 'stars' 'seen through' the instrument may have been hidden
inside it should alarm us to the fact that even straightforward
observations are inferences based on diverse assumptions. Nor
are observations ever conclusive, so that even if nature kept
furnishing us with white swans and black ravens we would be
wise to proceed with caution in our generalizations. As Lakatos
has argued 'it is not that we suppose a theory and Nature may
shout NO; rather, we propose a maze of theories, and Nature
may shout INCONSISTENT' (1970:130).

Nature, however, does not communicate meanings, while psychoanalytic patients and human beings in general do; psychoanalysis
proceeds initially from the interpretation of these meanings and
the discovery of unexpected meanings, behind apparently mean-
ingless phenomena. Freud's theory of repression was corrobor-

ated by countless instances of dreams, symptoms, slips of tongue and other such phenomena, which, upon psychoanalytic interpretation, revealed desires and ideas which clashed with the patient's values, beliefs, etc., i.e. desires and ideas which the patient had good reasons to conceal from himself. Now, psychoanalysis can neither interpret every dream (1933a:22:13) and every symptom, nor can it be absolutely certain that a single interpretation is correct. It is possible not only to misinterpret a dream, but also for an experienced analyst to impose his/her erroneous interpretation on a dreamer. So, just as a single observation in the natural sciences cannot be expected to prove or disprove a theory, we can hardly expect a single interpretation to lead us to the unconscious idea behind it – interpretations of dreams, symptoms and other mental events of an individual must be set against each other until a coherent pattern of unconscious desires begins to emerge; in this way, we move from individual interpretations to constructions.[12]

This brings us to the third level at which Freud tried to validate his concept of the unconscious – the unconscious as a system. Until now, I examined unconscious ideas and the distortions they undergo in reaching consciousness; but as we saw earlier the unconscious is not the sum-total of repressed ideas, or in Brown's words 'a reality of which we are unconscious' (1966:216). More than being a property of certain ideas, the unconscious is a mental structure dominating the human mind, and ideas belonging to it behave in accordance to its laws.

> Unconsciousness seemed to us at first only an enigmatical characteristic of a definite mental act. Now it means much more to us. It is a sign that the act partakes of the nature of a certain mental category known to us by other and more important features, and that it belongs to a system of mental activity which is deserving our fullest attention. The index value of the unconscious has far outgrown its importance as a property. The system revealed by the sign that single acts forming parts of it are unconscious we designate by the name 'The Unconscious'. (1912g:12:266)

The study of the unconscious as a system, beyond revealing the laws in accordance to which repressed ideas behave, reveals an important secret of these ideas, by anchoring them to certain crucial but neglected childhood experiences. These are the experiences linked to the complex known after the name of the great riddle-solver of antiquity who failed to solve the riddle of his own origin and fate until it was too late. The deeds of King Oedipus, in Freud's interpretation, gain their tragic pathos by reflecting the accomplishment of what generations of young Oedipodes, at an early stage in their lives, phantasized and desired, by bringing to light what generations of humans have kept secret from themselves. It is these early childhood desires, overwhelming love as well as violent hate, that threatened every

young human with annihilation and which set in motion the prototypical anxiety and the prototypical repression. In future, the
re-activation of these desires is confronted with fresh repressions, no longer triggered by the fear of annihilation from the
outside (by an all-powerful and fearful father) but from within.
'As a rule the ego carries out repressions in the service and at
the behest of the super-ego' (1923b:19:52), itself the precipitate
of the resolution of the Oedipus Complex, and the seat of the
terrible heritage of guilt.

I will not dwell on these well-discussed themes at any greater
length. The relevance of the Oedipus Complex to my argument
is that it lies squarely in Freud's view of the unconscious as a
structured system, with its own laws and its own core content.
This makes it possible now to validate specific interpretations
and constructions in terms of the contents and the laws of the
unconscious as a whole; for while the laws of the unconscious
are universal, the contents of particular individuals' unconscious
may vary and do vary in a systematic way - the underlying structure of the Oedipus Complex may be shared by every social
individual, even if the specific Oedipal desires of different
individuals vary. So, we would not be surprised, for instance,
if the dream of a homosexual revealed an identification with
the parent of the opposite sex, or if a symptom of a phobic boy
revealed a fear of parental authority. In a way, this procedure
is not unlike that of the natural scientists' use of observation
in general - both situations engender the possibility that the
scientist's expectation may influence his/her observation or
interpretation. Psychoanalysis, however, faces another major
difficulty here. It was argued earlier that the unconscious can
accept contradictions, so that it may be argued that any inference that we make from the interpretation of mental phenomena
can be fitted into the unconscious mental structure - so, for
instance, we may find that a homosexual's dream reveals identification with the parent of the same sex, and a phobic child's
symptom reveals defiance of authority without this causing us
any theoretical embarrassment; the flexibility of the unconscious,
and especially the possible transformation of an idea into its
opposite, enables us to account easily for such irregularities.
In 'The Interpretation of Dreams', for example, Freud states
repeatedly that dream-work can transform a dream-thought into
its opposite. The question then is this: given that the unconscious can contain contradictory ideas and desires, how can we
check inferences about unconscious mental life against each other
and against the unconscious system as a whole? Are there any
inferences which cannot be fitted into the unconscious? Are there
any constructions or interpretations which can be proved false?

Psychoanalysis has often been attacked on this point. Yet, it
seems to me that it stems from a misconception - although the
unconscious admits contradictory ideas, it does not admit all
ideas, for as we saw, its core is made up of the ideas and desires
of the Oedipus Complex in their different masquerades. These

ideas and desires are not arbitrary, nor are their transformations arbitrary. Equally importantly, not all unconscious ideas are active at all times, i.e. they do not function as desires seeking discharge constantly. In validating interpretations we do not ask merely whether a particular desire was part of the unconscious, but also what could have made it active at a particular time. Interpretations and constructions which fail to establish the underlying motives, desires and ideas as parts of the unconscious structure or fail to indicate how these were activated immediately lose their plausibility.

In addition, the *distortions* undergone by these ideas and desires in becoming conscious can be submitted to further interpretations in terms of the ego's defensive activities, which like the instinctual forces are on the whole unconscious but structured and knowable. Thus each interpretation is doubly validated and articulated – in terms of the content of the id, which entails the original instinctual element, and in terms of the defensive operations of the ego which precipitated the distortion. If an interpretation fails either of these checks (as so many do), it loses its plausibility and is rejected.

To recapitulate: Freud is led to the hypothesis of the unconscious and of an unconscious process of repression through his interpretation of countless phenomena that had previously defied scientific explanation; specific interpretations are tested against each other and at the same time reveal the properties, contents and laws of the mental system from which these desires emanate, the id, and of the system which distorts them, the ego. Then having gained an understanding of the organization of the unconscious, it is possible to validate specific interpretations of mental events and assess their plausibility. What started as a speculative hypothesis about the properties of certain ideas, which are too painful to be allowed free access to consciousness, developed into a formidable theory of the mind, whose explanatory potential must have surprised Freud as much as anyone else. Through the concept of the unconscious, Freud explained how the long-forgotten past is preserved in the present, forgotten and yet active. The unconscious is the unknown but knowable present in which the past is buried and through which it is resurrected; its effects are ever-present in mental life, and while their logic is strict and unmistakable they puzzle and confuse the ego. For the unconscious is ultimately a vast realm which the ego, in its constant misrecognition of itself as a dominant will, subjectivity or self, fails to recognize as its property and its master.

Freud's brilliant new conception of the mind as a structure dominated by three mental agencies, all of which involve unconscious components, did not merely stretch our understanding of mental phenomena to a depth never attained before, but also opened new horizons for other disciplines in the human sciences. Both the sociological concept of norm and the Marxist concept of ideology would lose their bearings without the implicit or explicit assumption of an unconscious dimension along which they become internalized. The unconscious is equally indispensable for linguistics, where it is argued that people can use a language without knowing its grammatical rules in a conscious way. The unconscious is 'a way of explaining how [the system of rules of language] can be simultaneously unknown and yet effectively present' (Culler 1976:76). In all of these views, cultural elements (like norms, moral constraints, 'ideologies' and linguistic structures) become constitutive of the individual by being engraved in unconscious areas of his/her mind (principally in parts of the ego and of the super-ego), from where they can regulate his/her behaviour and shape his/her conscious perception and understanding.

But it is not only this descriptive aspect of the unconscious which cuts across the human sciences. Equally, the systematic aspect, encapsulated in the concept of the id, permits us to look at cultural and social phenomena from an original and transparent viewpoint. As Freud's paradigmatic discussion of religion reveals, cultural artifacts can be approached from the same interpretative standpoint as mental phenomena; in short, cultural phenomena can be interpreted as collective expressions of repressed desires and also as culture's attempts to provide her own collective substitutive satisfactions. In this way, psychoanalytic hermeneutics can be extended to cultural hermeneutics in studies of religious beliefs and practices, rituals, artistic creations, myths, beliefs and ideologies, and even some aspects of social and political behaviour. These interpretative possibilities will be examined in the conclusions to Part I (Chapter 7).

This brief analysis suggests that the human sciences encounter the unconscious not only as the psychic level in which culture becomes constitutive of the individual but also as the source of fundamental needs and desires which cultural institutions may seek alternately to frustrate, modify, tame or gratify. Nor should it be thought that the unconscious is a concept occasionally invoked by these sciences on disparate occasions; rather it is a theoretical rock on which many of their theoretical concepts are anchored, without which their claims would appear totally absurd. We can now see why Foucault insists that

> the problem of the unconscious - its possibility, status, mode of existence, the means of knowing it and bringing it to light - is not simply a problem within the human sciences which they can be thought of as encountering by chance in their steps; it is a problem that is ultimately coextensive with their very existence. . . . [An] unveiling of the non-conscious is constitutive of all the sciences of man. (1970:364)

Before the unconscious, the study of man did not exist, man had not entered the space of Western episteme - he was the given, the forever absent spectator of Las Meninas, the invisible king,

whose presence was only glimpsed in the distant reflection of a
mirror.

> In classical thought, the personage for whom the representation
> exists, and who represents himself within it . . . is never
> to be found in that table (or picture of representation) himself.
> Before the end of the eighteenth century, *man* did not exist.
> (308)

Psychoanalysis occupies a privileged position in the human
sciences, because

> whereas all human sciences advance towards the unconscious
> only with their back to it, waiting for it to unveil itself as fast
> as consciousness is analysed, as it were backwards, psycho-
> analysis, on the other hand, points directly towards it, with a
> deliberate purpose - not towards that which must be rendered
> gradually more explicit by the progressive illumination of the
> implicit, but towards what is there and yet is hidden. (374)

Psychoanalysis has paved the way for the human sciences to
pursue their 'project of bringing man's consciousness back to its
real conditions, of restoring it to the contents and forms that
brought it into being, and elude us within it' (364). But also,
by making this process of unveiling and restoring possible,
psychoanalysis functions as a 'perpetual principle of dissatisfac-
tion', a critical agency within the human sciences, constantly
undermining and subverting their final claim of having uncovered
'what is'.
It is at this point that psychoanalysis parts company with the
other human sciences, leaving the white, germ-free, value-free
realm of contemporary science, where 'what is is and what is not
is not', for the murkier grounds of thought, which some call
utopia, where 'what is' reveals constantly interesting possibilities
about what might be. Having revealed the depth of humanity's
discontents, delusions, renunciations, repressions and alienation,
as well as the strength of humanity's wishes, desires and
instincts, the Freudian discourse opens up a distinct possibility
of a different reality based on self-knowledge and fulfilment.
It is only in this way that we can understand how psychoanalysis,
that pessimistic doctrine of man, that constant reminder of fate,
could have become the launching pad of so many twentieth-
century utopias. The other human sciences are shocked and
torn - some try to dissociate themselves from Freudian 'mythology', neglecting that their central assumption of the unconscious is its fruit; the more perceptive ones, as so often happens,
are confused, intrigued by psychoanalysis and are forever
struggling to guide it along the path of reason.
But the divide is a deep one; for while the other human
sciences remain firmly within the realm of the 'representable',
directing their elaborate cameras at the colourful pictures of the
world, at social norms, at linguistic rules, at dominant ideologies,
etc.,

psychoanalysis advances and leaps over representation, overflows it on the side of finitude, and thus reveals, where one
had expected functions bearing norms, conflicts burdened
with rules, and significations forming a system, the simple
fact that it is possible for there to be system (therefore signi-
fication), rule (therefore conflict), norm (therefore function).
(374)

What it also does, however, is to fuel a nagging suspicion that
there can be norm outside ideology, rule outside the law, and
system outside the system, or to move outside Foucault's terminology, that there can be (moral) normality outside (cultural)
normality, in the sense that these concepts were introduced in
the previous chapter. This is the fourth complication that I
mentioned at the outset of this chapter - the constant criticism
and the nascent possibility of a different reality from the one
currently embodied in the unconscious leads to an intermeshing
in the Freudian discourse of 'descriptive' and 'normative' statements, which although a key ingredient of ancient thought, has
become anathema since Hume's famous dichotomy. Freud's discussion of the unconscious, however, like Marx's discussion of
capital, due to the nature of the object under scrutiny, cannot
remain purely descriptive; neither Freud's theory of repression
nor Marx's theory of exploitation could be articulated in a discourse of purely descriptive statements, for they both under-
mine the system whose existence they have just established. To
the extent that these systems entail alienated consciousness in
their very make-up, any theory seeking to demystify consciousness is at once an attempt to subvert.
Through the concept of the unconscious and his efforts to
demystify consciousness and reveal humanity's discontents, Freud
joins a great critical tradition in Western thought, the tradition
which the dogmatic separation of 'is' and 'ought' sought to
liquidate. As Leo Strauss has argued in his critique of Weber's
insistence on value neutrality, the opposition between 'is' and
'ought' is not a logical one, but rests on a defeatist belief that
there is no possibility of a genuine knowledge of the 'ought', so
we might as well preserve the purity of our knowledge of the
'is' (1953:41). In contrast to this conservative approach, the
critical tradition has endeavoured to discover bridges between
what 'is' and what 'ought to be', striving to make knowledge
an active force in life and not merely a passive instrument to be
used in accordance with the interests and values of the strong.
Plato had short-circuited the two types of statements through
the Socratic theory of virtue - where nobody errs knowingly, or
in our words he/she who knows what virtue is, acts as he/she
ought - proving that there is no logical contradiction between
the two; Freud's discussion of the unconscious suggests that
the connection is indeed a theoretical necessity.[13]

Chapter 6
Utopia and illusion

Freud's pessimism is well known. Equally well known is his
reluctance to suggest large-scale solutions for the problems of
humanity. In spite of his persistent criticism of some of humanity's most precious ideals, he stubbornly refused to provide
blueprints for the future. Although on many occasions he
suggested that some of the discontents of civilization could be
mitigated through a more equitable distribution of its rewards,
he was generally hostile to those philosophies which entertained
'idealistic views of human nature', to messianic messages and to
'socialist experiments'. His own theory not only did away with
the traditional and convenient distinction of the higher and the
lower sides of our nature, but also highlighted those aspects of
our nature which had been repressed for generations – those
aspects of our nature which Mannoni aptly characterizes as
'colonized', which include murderous and cannibalistic desires,
incestuous and castrating impulses, egoistic and savage wishes,
frequently directed towards those we most love. Most of these
Freudian discoveries were received with the same mixture of
horror and indignation and also a strange fascination that the
European colonizers showed towards the 'primitive' people,
whose savage habits shocked but also fascinated their civilized
sensitivities. At the same time, Freud tried to show that what
the civilized West regarded as its supreme cultural accomplishments were in fact either devious means of satisfying primitive
desires, or half-hearted attempts at compensating for the non-
satisfaction of such desires. Through his studies of substitutive
satisfactions sought by neurotics, Freud developed a model of
the ulterior motives of religious, artistic and cultural pursuits.
Idealist doctrines and utopian visions are not simply mistakes,
but illusions, collective day-dreaming, which affords a narcissistic satisfaction as well as a consolation for the real miseries of
life. It is the profound unhappiness of life, the painful discontents of civilization, which account for the fact that humans
can cling tight to views that are

> so patently infantile, so foreign to reality, that to anyone with
> a friendly attitude to humanity it is painful to think that the
> great majority of mortals will never be able to rise above them.
> (1930a:21:74)

It is because they console and flatter, or to use Rieff's expression
because they function as therapeutics, that illusions have never

lost their grip over mankind - yet, in Freud's view, far from
removing the miseries of life or cancelling the discontents of
civilization, illusions are a symptom of what they purport to
cure.

Given the unequivocalness of Freud's critique of religious and
political utopias and his rather dark view of human nature, it
may be strange to suggest that utopia is a problematic featuring
prominently in the Freudian discourse. Yet, our discussion of
the previous five problematics has revealed several junctures in
which a utopian thread seems to be woven into his argument;
moreover, it is quite interesting to note the influence of Freud's
work on most twentieth-century utopian ideals. It is as though
Freud, by revealing the breadth and power of sexuality and the
depth of its social repression, by articulating human discontents
which had previously remained muted, unleashed torrents of
utopian imagination. As Marx had articulated in the nineteenth
century the discontents arising from economic exploitation and
political oppression, Freud seemed to provide an explanation,
a theory and indeed a vocabulary through which the anxieties
of twentieth-century man could be voiced and comprehended. As
a result, some of the earlier utopian threads based on ideas of
deprivation, inequality and exploitation were expanded in the
direction of sexual frustration and alienation.[1]

Put simply, the paradox which confronts us here is that
psychoanalysis, while claiming to be the ultimate critique of all
utopias, has become a launching platform of utopian inspiration.
Is this due purely to a corruption of Freudian thought, or does
this latter contain itself a utopian seed?

Two features of Freudian doctrine have stimulated massive
utopian speculations, his mental geography and his emphasis on
sexuality as a source of life and pleasure. Many of Freud's
humanist heirs, unwilling to look at the unconscious as a colonized land, inferred from his mental geography the existence
within our souls of a terra incognita, a virgin territory, a
personality core, which aeons of cultural development had neither
discovered nor polluted. These humanist heirs developed a
psychology of authenticity and a utopia of authenticity, according
to which man's very final salvation and emancipation lie in the
rediscovery of this virgin land inside us. This requires the
stripping away of layer after layer of cultural residues, role-
playing and social conditioning and the gradual demolition of
the defences which make up a 'character armour' around this
personality core. This utopia of authenticity (which perhaps is
a psychological re-working of Rousseau) tries to reveal man's
essential humanity underneath an alienated superstructure
created by culture; its motivation lies not only in the theories
but also in the therapeutic practices of the first generation of
psychoanalytic 'radicals', including both Reich and Fromm.
Although authenticity lies in the heart of most therapeutic
developments since then, it is totally alien to Freud's own views
as a theorist and to his practice as an analyst. Freud never

entertained an image of the human being as being composed of a
good inner core and an alienated superstructure - indeed, if
Freud had any image of an inner core at all it certainly comprised
hate as well as love, murder as well as affection, envy as well as
altruism, egoism as well as sociability, possessiveness as well as
generosity. And in his practice as a therapist, Freud never
sought to peel off the unpleasant sides of our inner world and
have them dispossessed as an 'armour', but, as we saw in
Chapter 3, he sought to help his patients recognize and understand in themselves what would otherwise be too painful to
accept. In this respect, the Neo-Freudians' therapeutics bear a
closer resemblance to the pre-analytic therapeutics of suggestion
and catharsis than to Freud's.

If the 'utopia of authenticity' totally contradicts our reading
of Freud in the previous five chapters, sensuous and aesthetic
utopian images, fuelled by his investigations into sexuality,
have been suggested in several points of our earlier discussion.
In spite of the different paradigms of Eros which we encountered
in Chapters 1 and 2, there can be little doubt that Freud was
not puzzled by questions like 'What does man want in life?' or
'What makes man happy?' Eros, in his diverse guises, provides
the answers to such questions. Eros 'forever pressing for satisfaction' defines the final end of all human endeavour, the end
which even if we cannot attain we can never give up; for Freud,
the problem is not knowing what man really wants, but understanding how to achieve it - in short, libidinal economics.
Although Freud 'suspects' that we are prevented from achieving
pleasure by a 'piece of our own psychical constitution' (1930a:
21:86), the pursuit of pleasure through the different channels
of libido is the unquestioned centre-piece of his psychology. We
may only be able to experience or witness happiness in imperfect,
short-lived and relative forms, yet absolute, perfect and permanent pleasure haunts Freud's theory much as the concept of
perfect rest haunted that of Aristotle. The ultimate goal, in both
cases, eludes the real world and yet cannot be evaded - although
it is a profoundly practical goal, it can only be grasped in
thought.

As we saw in Chapter 4, Marcuse and Brown developed utopian
visions by starting precisely from this crucial point of Freudian
discourse. Both Marcuse and Brown start their long speculative
journeys from the same point - a culture founded on the repression of the individual is a sick culture and a soul founded on the
renunciation of pleasure is a sick soul. But what was for Freud
a point of critical evaluation of the present, becomes for Marcuse
and Brown a point of projection of utopian visions: Marcuse
builds a fully-blown utopia, a state of perfect fulfilment within a
kingdom of Eros, while Brown develops a utopia in which the
supreme ruler is a reconstituted unity of Eros and the death
instinct. Both of these utopias emanate from the material character of bodily pleasure, and both Marcuse and Brown, like Reich,
emphasize the material and indeed biological inevitability of Eros,

but they also expand Eros along lines suggested in Freud's later
works. The two paradigms of Eros, identified in Chapter 2, are
reconciled – Eros as the unique source of pleasure and Eros as
a principle of union merge into a single utopian vision, a 'Utopia
of Eros'. This is not to reduce the utopias of Marcuse and Brown
to naive pansexualist visions, in which sex is presented as the
universal panacea – they both draw their lessons from Freud's
insights into complexities of human sexuality as well as from his
investigations into the manifestations of the death instinct; nor
do they disregard the anti-social implications of the sexual bliss
of the couple. Within their utopias of Eros, the pleasure of the
individual, the cohesion of society and the survival of civilization
instead of being antagonistic become mutually re-inforcing. As a
source of pleasure, Eros is detached from the compulsive, mani-
pulative and individualistic automatism of 'mature genitality' and
its attendant violence, and becomes fully active through a total
resexualization and resensitization of the body in a reconstituted
state of polymorphous perversity. The body ceases to function
as an instrument and especially as an instrument of labour to
become a total object of cathexis, an instrument of pleasure
(Marcuse 1955:184). The Utopia of Eros resurrects the body
(Brown 1959:307f), and yet, in the restoration of the early childhood supremacy of the pleasure principle, the autism of early
auto-erotism is transcended through a new sensuous union with
the objects of the world, animate and inanimate. It is through
this sensuous union of man with other men, with the objects of
nature and with his own creations that Eros accomplishes his
supreme achievement, both as a unique source of pleasure and
as a supreme principle of union.

But the Utopia of Eros is not the only utopia suggested by
Freud's work. Just as the Utopia of Eros emerges from the
emancipatory point of pleasure, a Utopia of Logos can be derived
from the emancipatory point of self-understanding, a point as
seminal as pleasure, lying in the centre of Freud's therapeutic
practice.[2] Unlike with the Utopia of Eros, Freud himself, in his
uncharacteristically optimistic little book 'The Future of an
Illusion', suggested a variant of the Utopia of Logos (and I will
argue later that this utopia has all the features of the classical
utopias), which was subsequently developed in the work of
Philip Rieff.[3] Freud's Utopia of Logos precludes the Utopia of
Eros, since it starts from the premise that self-understanding
must begin with the recognition that painful conflicts and
renunciations of pleasure are part of the human predicament,
they are man's fate. All man can do is to understand them, accept
them, learn to live with them and enjoy those qualified forms of
pleasure that are available to him.

This utopia, although far less optimistic than the previous one,
seeks nevertheless to alleviate the suffering caused by inability
to cope with instinctual restrictions and by miscarried rebellions
against fate, which result in private and public illusions. It is
ultimately a pragmatic utopia as well as a critique of all other

utopias, and especially religion. In his burning indictment of
religion, Freud argued that it is far preferable for man to control
his instinctual nature through reason than to suffer the surplus
frustration of forced repressions and the surplus misery of
miscarried rebellions. In proclaiming his 'god Logos', Freud
stressed that

> men cannot remain children for ever; they must in the end go
> out into 'hostile life'. We may call this 'education to reality'.
> Need I confess to you that the sole purpose of [this book] is
> to point out the necessity for this forward step. (1927c:21:49)

But in 'Why War?' Freud exhibits his far more characteristic
scepticism as to the power of his god:

> the ideal condition of things would of course be a community of
> men who had subordinated their instinctual life to the dictator-
> ship of reason. Nothing else could unite men so completely
> and so tenaciously, even if there were no emotional ties between
> them. But in all probability that is a Utopian expectation.
> (1933b:22:213)

It is Philip Rieff who has given us the clearest picture of the
Utopia of Logos (although, like Freud, he would never refer to
it as a utopia), by contrasting Freud's informative therapeutic
with all other therapeutics, which aim at re-integrating the individual by submerging him/her in a collective illusion. Psychoanalysis is not a cure of souls, certainly not a consolation for the
sick, but a gradual and continuous process of self-criticism,
self-education and self-understanding for those strong enough
to surrender some of their most precious illusions (1959:xiii).

> Commitment therapies can be distinguished from analytic
> therapies. These latter arise in an historical period concomit-
> ant with the rise of democratic individualism. Commitment
> therapies, however, operate by returning the individual to the
> cosset of his natal community or by retraining him for member-
> ship in a new community with a more effective pattern of
> symbolic integration; the therapeutic effort is transformative;
> the therapist is characteristically either a sacral or an
> exemplary figure. Analytic therapies, on the other hand, are
> uniquely modern and depend largely on Freudian presupposi-
> tions. The therapeutic effort is not primarily transformative
> but informative. The assumption of analytic theory is that
> there is no positive community standing behind the therapist.
> (1966:76)

The Utopia of Logos, in Rieff's formulation, liberates the individual from the ancient compulsions of seeking consolation through
universalistic illusions which seek to infuse lives with meaning,
and enables him/her to select and enjoy those satisfactions which

are available to him/her. Like the successful business executive,
man learns the limits of his powers and makes those decisions
which will optimize the returns on his investment. Thus in contrast to the sensuous ego which inhabits the Utopia of Eros,
Rieff proclaims the managerial ego as the inhabitant of the
Utopia of Logos.

Now, in Chapter 2 we examined the obstacles standing in the
way of a reconciliation of the two paradigms of Eros, just as in
Chapter 3 we examined the obstacles to the success of a therapy
based on understanding. There are countless theoretical threads
in Freud which would appear to converge in condemning both
the kingdom of Eros and the kingdom of Logos to the imaginary
domain of utopias, and none more so than a critique of false
consciousness which he shares with Marx. Yet, before introducing Freud's criticism of illusion (and by implication utopias), it
is important to recognize that the starting points of both utopias
are firmly located in his discourse, since both pleasure and
understanding are indispensable not only to his psychology but
also to his social critique. The reading of Freud as a social critic
which emerges from his twin conception of normality,[4] must in
itself involve the possibility of emancipation. If neurosis is the
universal sickness of humanity, one must, at least, be able to
visualize a healthy society, even if there are strong factors
preventing its realization. A problem is not a problem unless one
can, at least in principle, envisage a solution even if there are
no ways of reaching this solution. In breaking this positivist
barrier between what is and what ought to be, Freud willingly or
unwillingly enters a land populated by utopian ghosts; and there
can be little doubt that there is a nascent imagery in his thought.
encompassing sexual fulfilment, overcoming of exploitation, the
resolution of some painful conflicts and the dissolution of all fatal
illusions, all of which belong to the 'ought to' domain. And it is
by constantly keeping these ghosts in the background of his
discourse, and occasionally inviting them to come forward, that
Freud stimulates the utopian imagery of even his most sober-
minded readers. For, as Gouldner has argued, 'the utopian, like
the tragic, thus accents the distance between "what is" and what
should be' (1976:89).

There can be little doubt, therefore, that psychoanalysis is
constantly being pulled from two emancipatory standpoints,
sensuous pleasure and self-understanding, which account for
Freud's great discoveries and for his 'critical eyes' (1916-17:16:
434). Yet, while his enthusiastic epigoni departed from these two
emancipatory standpoints to build large-scale utopias, Freud's
steadfast reluctance to do so himself appears to have weakened
once, in the frequently quoted last ten pages of 'The Future of
an Illusion'. The optimism displayed by Freud in these pages is
so untypical of his theory and attitude that it requires a careful
examination; first however it is essential to recapitulate his
critique of utopias and illusions in general, since it is in comparison to this critique that his utopian proclamation of his 'god

Logos' reveals its paradoxical nature.

As we saw in Chapter 4 and 5, Freud's critique of society does not proceed from a preconceived or god-given moral perspective. It is a critique coming from within society itself, through a careful consideration of its mechanisms, discontents, illusions and, indeed, alienation. His entire theoretical endeavour did not aim simply at exposing and articulating the discontents of civilization, but also at showing how deeply these discontents are rooted in a psycho-social system. Civilization's discontents, both conscious and unconscious, are parts of an alienated system, and can neither be wished away, nor eliminated simply by educating humanity. Why? Because an integral part of the alienated psycho-system is humanity's resistance to reason and passionate clinging to illusions, which provide a substitutive satisfaction and a consolation for the miseries of life. Illusion is for Freud a structural component of the alienated psycho-social system, just as false consciousness is a structural component of the alienated system studied by Marx. Both Freud and Marx regarded the distortion of man's self-knowledge not as a negative condition of ignorance (Socrates, but not Plato for whom emotions may systematically distort the functions of the intellect), but as a positive condition of 'mis-knowledge', precipitated by social, psychological and economic conditions of different determinate systems - in short, consciousness is systematically distorted.

It is for this reason that neither Marx nor Freud regarded utopias merely as errors, but Marx saw them as signs of alienated consciousness while Freud saw them as illusions. Utopias are both worse and better than errors - errors can be rectified through reason, while reason alone is insufficient to dissolve utopias, but at the same time utopias give us important clues concerning the alienation of the system with which they are systematically related and indicate a potential for transcending alienation. So, Freud can reach the real desires through the substitutive satisfactions afforded by utopias, and in particular he can study the way in which utopias provide consolation. It is not accidental that Marx and Freud were two of the most merciless critics of religion, for they both saw religion as the quintessence of distorted consciousness. Nor is it accidental that they both looked carefully but with profound scepticism at utopian projects of emancipation. Such projects (i) entertained a cheerfully optimistic view of human nature and a naive view of human society, and (ii) appealed to reason for their implementation, in the belief that their social desirability would bring them into being. In this way, they underestimated or completely neglected the systematic causes of the alienation of consciousness, i.e. in the case of Marx, the exploitation and oppression inherent in the capitalist system of production and the fetishism of commodity-exchange, in the case of Freud, the need for consolation which stems from the suppression of sexuality and introjection of aggression. Marx, like Freud, did not actually paint a utopian picture, for this would repeat the central shortcoming of utopian socialists, who had held 'a picture of society designed as though there were no other factors at work than conscious human will' (Buber 1950:8).

It may be argued that this discussion overlooks what is the most important difference concerning Marx's and Freud's views on the future - contrary to Freud, Marx appears to have left us with a legacy, a socialist vision of the future, which has undoubtedly been the most powerful, universal and inspiring revolutionary utopia during the last two centuries. It may be argued, in other words, that Marx advanced much further than Freud, and articulated his utopian imagery into a fully-blown ideal of a communist society. This argument, however, is rather misleading, for Marx would abhor the equation of communist society with a utopian vision, an equation which was largely espoused by Mannheim's sociological heirs. Marx himself categorically denied the equation:

> Communism is not for us a *state of affairs* which is to be established, an ideal to which reality will have to adjust itself. We call communism the *real* movement which abolishes the present state of things. The conditions of this movement result from the premises now in existence. (1846:126)

So, while both Marx and Freud analysed what they saw as an alienated system, they both objected to utopian visions of human emancipation with equal forcefulness. Utopias express an emancipatory longing, but permit this longing to influence their understanding of alienation, thus concealing the causes and pervasiveness of alienation; they represent a rebellion against alienation, and yet are at the same time symptoms of alienation, and frequently re-inforce and perpetuate it.

However, both Marxism and psychoanalysis, as we saw in the previous chapter, are critical analyses and not mere descriptions of alienation, for every aspect of alienation departs from the domain of the actual and crosses into the domain of the possible - it becomes a critique. Thus, Marx did not merely describe a system of economic exploitation and political oppression, nor did Freud merely describe a system of instinctual repression and renunciation, but inevitably they developed powerful critiques of this system. They analysed critically the causes of exploitation and repression and were able to stipulate, with greater or lesser clarity, the preconditions and possibilities of emancipation - Marx reached the conclusion that the abolition of bourgeois property and the dismantling of the capitalist state apparatus were central and indispensable elements in an emancipatory transformation of society, while Freud, more implicitly, regarded the overcoming of guilt and the lifting of instinctual repressions as directly analogous elements. Where, however, Marx differs from Freud is in his argument that the emancipatory transformation is not merely possible but that there is a real and unstoppable historical movement towards emancipation (as is indicated by the last quote).

It is precisely Marx's life-long, painstaking and detailed investigations of the 'laws of motion' of capitalist society that set him apart from the utopian socialists he so persistently criticized. By comparison to these analyses, Freud's theory appears strikingly static, and it is often argued that Freud mistook historical phenomena pertaining to the Victorian era for elements of human nature. Thus Lichtman: 'Freud not only *reified* bourgeois human nature; he reified *bourgeois* human nature' (1977:4-5). Although it may be true that Freud took certain features of Victorian man and especially woman for universals, these charges are not entirely fair – as we saw in Chapter 4, Freud did have a view of history, albeit an ambivalent and an ambiguous one. What, however, is undoubtedly lacking from his argument is a theory of demystification – although he showed that illusions represented a systematic distortion of consciousness, he was unwilling to specify the historical conditions of demystification. Unlike Marx and Lukacs, who saw praxis, active participation in the class struggle, as the historical precondition of demystification, Freud at times intimated that no such condition existed (hence the tragic fate of mankind to learn the truth when it is too late), and at times implied that reason alone can dissolve illusions of itself. What is rather striking is that in his therapeutic practice Freud did offer a model of demystification; as was seen earlier, the emancipation of the neurotic from his/her delusions is accomplished by the intellect, not in a passive contemplation but in the turbulent process dominated by transference, by displaced feeling. Only when libido is mobilized for the pursuit of truth, only then can the intellect dissolve those consolatory illusions which had earlier been so dear to it. The lifting of repression and its symptoms is thus the outcome of a compact between Eros and Logos. Yet, in his social discourse Freud seemed to adopt the Platonist position that the intellect alone can bring the dissolution of cultural illusions. In this sense he never managed to offer a convincing social analogue to the concept of transference as the support of social demystification. Freud's Platonist position in 'The Future of an Illusion' is the result of a serious failure on his part to appreciate that the lifting of repressions and the ending of illusions at the social level require not just the expanding powers of the intellect but also a radical reorganization in the distribution of power – of that power which has been established and feeds on repression and mystification. At the individual level, the lifting of repressions required the transference of emotional energies to different imagos of meaning and authority; at the social level, it required a fundamental challenge to the power structure of society which benefits from repression and illusion.

It is interesting that unlike Marx and Nietzsche, the other two summits in the critical tradition, Freud aimed his cultural critique against untruthfulness (illusion) and non-gratification (discontent) but did not attack directly the power structures. Although he was frequently critical of the unequal distribution of social resources, he tended to regard oppressive power relations as an additional burden on the individual rather than as a central feature of his/her alienation. And yet, his own discussion of the child's early confrontation with power during the Oedipal phase as well as his experience with transference should have highlighted the intimate connection between knowledge and pleasure (his two ethical standards) and power. For what else is transference than the shift of emotional energies which corresponds to a new authority relation between the analysand and the analyst's benevolent dictatorship? In short, although Freud established the relation between repression and culture he neglected the relation between repression and power. Illusions are not just wish-fulfilling consolations contributing to social integration, but they are also 'ideologies' contributing to the maintenance of specific power relations.

As a result of this inability to extend his discussion to power relations (a step that had to wait for Reich and Marcuse) Freud never managed to formulate a theory of transition. The important question which arises is: If Freud failed to provide a systematic connection between his emancipatory standpoints of truth and pleasure and a historical theory of transition, are these stand-points not subject to the criticism that they represent themselves illusions, wish-fulfilling inventions of the mind? If neither pleasure nor self-understanding represents historical phenomena, past, actual or possible, are they to be seen as mere 'ideals types', abstractions, whose value is heuristic, but certainly not moral? It is these questions which I will try to answer in the rest of this chapter.

First of all, we must recognize that two of the three writers who stretch these emancipatory standpoints to large-scale utopias, Marcuse and Rieff, do provide socio-psychoanalytic theories of transition; whether these theories are satisfactory or not will be examined in Part II, but it must be clear that their utopias emerge from a critical evaluation of the possible entailed in the actual. In this way, their utopias, unlike those of the utopian socialists, are not mere fancies emanating from an alchemy of wit and indig nation, reason and desire. Perhaps, the kingdoms of Eros and Logos (as they are described in the studies of Marcuse and Rieff respectively) do not deserve the title of utopia at all, since they are proclaimed neither because of their desirability nor because of their reason, but because, according to their authors, they are entailed within the present system. Brown's utopia, on the other hand, is a 'way out', indeed a blueprint for survival, and lacks a theory of transition which makes it more shocking, more desperate, more radical and more utopian.

In understanding Freud's position on this issue, it is instruc-tive to begin with some of the arguments he put forward in 'The Future of an Illusion'. I have already indicated that this work is uncharacteristically optimistic; I will now suggest that in this work, we can in fact discern a utopian paradigm, which although seriously qualified, has a lot of the attributes of pre-Marxist utopias. Freud's central question in this book is

> whether and to what extent it is possible to lessen the burden
> of the instinctual sacrifices imposed on men, to reconcile men
> to those which must necessarily remain and to provide a com-
> pensation for them. (1927c:21:7)

The question is an unashamedly moral one, as so many of Freud's
questions. But in answering it, Freud develops a Utopia of Logos,
which is totally uncharacteristic of his style and temperament.
After criticizing religious answers to the question along lines
presented earlier, Freud suggests that reason alone can mitigate
suffering and yield the greatest possible happiness:

> Our God, Logos, will fulfil whichever of [our] wishes nature
> outside us allows, but he will do it very gradually, only in
> the unforeseeable future, and for a new generation of men. (54)

Freud's utopia proclaims not only the desirability of Logos, but
also its supreme power: 'In the long run nothing can withstand
reason' (ibid.).

Although Freud invokes the achievements of modern science in
a lukewarm, uncharacteristic and hardly-convincing attempt to
provide independent evidence for the supremacy of reason, the
gist of his argument is that Logos must prevail and will prevail
because it is desirable – but is this statement not the quintessence of a utopian illusion? The way in which he brushes aside
his earlier arguments that reason is, for the vast majority of
people, no match for the 'passions'[5], is characteristically utopian:

> Since men are so little accessible to reasonable arguments and
> are so entirely governed by their instinctual wishes, why
> should one set out to deprive them of an instinctual satisfaction
> and replace it by reasonable arguments? It is true that men
> are like this; but have you asked yourself whether they *must*
> be like this, whether their innermost nature necessitates it? (47)

Yet, a few pages later, the supremacy of Logos is presented as
a real historical possibility, without any discussion of the transition.

> We may insist as often as we like that man's intellect is power-
> less in comparison with instinctual life, and we may be right in
> this. Nevertheless, there is something peculiar about this
> weakness. The voice of the intellect is a soft one, but it does
> not rest till it has gained a hearing. Finally, after a countless
> succession of rebuffs, it succeeds. This is one of the few
> points on which one may be optimistic about the future of man-
> kind, but it is in itself a point of no small importance. And
> from it one can derive yet other hopes. The primacy of the
> intellect lies, it is true, in a distant, distant future, but prob-

ably not in an *infinitely* distant one.(53)

Thus while Marx tries to establish the emancipation of consciousness on a material historical development, spearheaded by
class struggle, Freud, like Enlightenment thinkers, takes the
dissolution of illusions under the power of reason as self-evident.
His optimism concerning the emancipatory potential of reason in
these extracts brings to mind the optimism of the utopian socialists, while the unqualified confidence in the power of reason to
impose itself 'in the long run' reveals an attitude similar to that
of sociologists who have seen the recent history of mankind as
a process of 'rationalization'. His arguments in the last pages of
'The Future of an Illusion', coming with a modicum of theoretical
support, seem so alien to the discourse of a man who had 're-
discovered' the irrational, emotive and darker sides of our
nature, that they beg for an explanation outside the terms of
his theoretical formulations. His optimism concerning the power
of reason to demystify human consciousness and bring about a
limited emancipation of mankind becomes even more surprising
when his arguments on the removal of social illusions are set
against his qualified analysis of the process of personal demystification which takes place during the therapeutic session. First,
the patient's gradual self-discovery, self-acceptance and self-
understanding are brought about not through the powers of
reason, but through the careful handling of transference by the
physician. The interpretations offered by the analyst are not
accepted on the basis of their plausibility – in fact, psychoanalytic interpretations of neurotic and other phenomena are
not only shocking but also eminently unreasonable on first
acquaintance. On the contrary, assuming that the cure is
successfully accomplished through self-understanding (rather
than through the internalization of novel illusions), reason
prevails because affective factors are brought to its support.
Thus, the analyst is not an educator, but one whose position
enables him/her to manipulate the patient's emotions and re-
direct them in support of the latter's intellect. But Freud's
theory of social demystification, as was seen earlier, lacks a
social agent who will accomplish a similar task on a massive
social scale.[6] Reason triumphs through its own power. Equally
surprising, however, is Freud's optimism in these passages
when it is set against the serious reservations which he was
developing at about the same time over the therapeutic potential
of psychoanalysis as a cure based on understanding – since,
as Freud was coming to realize, transference-assisted intellect
may be incapable of dissolving the neurotic delusions and distortions of large numbers of patients, it was unreasonable to
argue that reason alone would dissolve social illusions pertaining
to 'collective neuroses' through its own devices.

Had Freud concluded his powerful critique of religion by
examining the preconditions and possibilities of demystification
of consciousness on a social scale, there could be no obvious

objection to his arguments. But in moving from the emancipatory point of self-understanding to the theocracy of Logos without an adequate theory of transition, he replicated the shortcomings of those who advocated utopian solutions to humanity's sickness - he projected a utopia of self-understanding from the emancipatory point of self-understanding. Of course, Freud was aware that he could not defend his utopia against his own theory of illusion; he was honest enough to admit that

> I know how difficult it is to avoid illusions; perhaps the hopes
> I have confessed to are of an illusory nature too. (1927c:21:53)

Nevertheless, Freud was willing to vindicate and defend his Utopia of Logos even qua illusion; he continued:

> But I hold fast to one distinction. Apart from the fact that no
> penalty is imposed for not sharing them, my illusions are not,
> like religious ones, incapable of correction. They have not the
> character of a delusion. If experience should show - not to
> me, but to others after me, who think as I do - that we have
> been mistaken, we will give up our expectations. Take my
> attempt for what it is. (ibid.)

I am not interested in discussing Freud's utopia *qua* utopia here, since in Part II I will assess the merits of Rieff's more developed version of the same utopia. I will only point out that the Utopia of Logos is a profoundly contemplative and conservative utopia, in which the break from the present consists in an understanding and acceptance of the present founded on resignation (an attitude Freud was to evaluate negatively as characteristic of Yoga in his next major work). It is positively surprising that the emancipatory point of self-understanding should have led Freud to what can fairly be described as a utopia of the status quo; nearly thirty years earlier, he had selected as his motto on the title-page of 'The Interpretation of Dreams' a quote from the 'Aeneid':

> Flectere si nequeo Superos, Acheronta movebo
> (If I cannot bend the gods above, I will shake the infernal
> depths).

And yet, near the end of his life, he seemed to side with the gods!

It is perhaps fortunate that Freud lived a further twelve creative years after the publication of 'The Future of an Illusion', for had this book been his last one, it would no doubt have supported the view that at the end of his life Freud abandoned his tragic view of the human condition for a utopia which combines a naive optimism with an uncritical acceptance of the status quo. But in the works which followed, and above all in 'Civilization and Its Discontents', the tragic view returns to

crown Freud's supreme achievement, in revealing the secrets
of man's desires, and the forces that conspire in concealing
them from him and keeping them in endless suspension. Although
a few echoes of the god Logos reverberate in these later works,
the Utopia of Logos moves to its twilight phase. The controlling
of instinctual life by the intellect is no longer a universal road
to salvation, but one of many different ways in which each
individual may choose to pursue the end of happiness:

> Happiness, in the reduced sense in which we recognize it as
> possible, is a problem of the economics of the individual's
> libido. There is no golden rule which applies to everyone:
> every man must find out for himself in what particular fashion
> he can be saved. (1930a:21:83)

Although it is possible that intellectual control over the instincts
may have been Freud's own way to salvation, his theoretical
assessment is only slightly more favourable than his assessment
of Yoga:

> One may therefore hope to be freed from a part of one's suffer-
> ings by influencing the instinctual impulses. . . . The extreme
> form of this is brought about by killing off the instincts, as it
> is prescribed by the worldly wisdom of the East and practised
> by Yoga. If it succeeds, then the subject has, it is true, given
> up all other activities as well - he has sacrificed his life; and,
> by another path, he has once more achieved the happiness of
> quietness. We follow the same path when our aims are less
> extreme and we merely attempt to *control* our instinctual life.
> In that case, the controlling elements are the higher psychical
> agencies, which have subjected themselves to the reality prin-
> ciple. Here the aim of satisfaction is not by any means relin-
> quished; but a certain amount of protection against suffering
> is secured, in that non-satisfaction is not so painfully felt in
> the case of instincts kept in dependence as in the case of unin-
> hibited ones. As against this, there is an undeniable diminution
> in the potentialities of enjoyment. (79)

But the intellectual control of the instincts is only one of the
ways in which an individual may solve the 'problem of the
economics of libido'; nor is it one which occurs in isolation,
except, perhaps, in Yoga, as conceived by Freud. Control over
one's instincts is usually accompanied with control over or even
manipulation of the social reality:

> One can try to re-create the world, to build up in its stead
> another world in which its most unbearable features are elimin-
> ated and replaced by others that are in conformity with one's
> own wishes. (81)

Although this may lead to psychotic disorders (as Freud empha-

sized in the lines which follow), it also represents an attitude
shared, to a greater or lesser extent, by normal people, who,
in their daily lives, seek to alter social situations to suit their
interests and needs.

> A reaction which combines features of both these [i.e. neurotic
> and psychotic reactions to reality] is the one we call normal or
> 'healthy'; it denies reality as little as neurosis, but then, like
> a psychosis, is concerned with effecting a change in it. This
> expedient attitude leads naturally to some active achievement
> in the outer world and is not content, like a psychosis, with
> establishing the alteration within itself; it is no longer *auto-
> plastic* but *alloplastic*. (1924e:19:185)

Yet, Freud's Utopia of Logos, with its resigned moderation
allows little room for alloplasis - for an attempt to bring about
changes in a world outside. The Utopia of Logos begins in the
mind and ends in the mind.

I hope that it is now clear that the last pages of 'The Future of
an Illusion' must not be regarded as the logical conclusion of
the Freudian discourse; it is the building of one particular
utopian vision out of a thread in his arguments which starts off
at the emancipatory point of self-understanding. Yet, as soon
as a utopia of quiescent moderation has emerged it comes into
contradiction with the main elements and momentum of Freud's
argument, for it overestimates both the potential of reason to
lead to happiness and its power to impose itself over other factors
in human history. I am not denying that it is possible to identify
what I referred to as a nascent utopian imagery in psychoanalysis, involving ideas like sensuous pleasure, resolution of
painful conflicts, dissolution of illusions, since all of these ideas
are linked to the two emancipatory points of pleasure and self-
understanding, which lie at the heart of his discourse. That
Freud succumbed to the temptation of projecting a large-scale
solution to the sickness of humanity in 'The Future of An Illusion'
is surprising, and his attempt to proclaim Logos as the supreme
principle of emancipation was a failure. That Freud's epigoni
succumbed to the same temptation is not so surprising - as a
brilliant scientific discovery, opening up new and unsuspected
continents of human knowledge, psychoanalysis excited immensely
the imagination of many twentieth-century social and cultural
scientists, who proceeded to experiment with it as an analytical
tool in diverse areas of study. Most great scientific discoveries
of the past since Copernicus, Darwin and Einstein have had
massive reverberations in the whole configuration of knowledge
of their time. But their influence did not stop at the level of
'what is'; it extended into the realm of 'what ought to be': by
shedding a different light on what is, most great theoretical
advances opened new possibilities not only in the domain of theory
but also in that of practical living. In the same way, psycho-

analysis, by (i) revealing in the unconscious an entire part of
ourselves which had previously remained unknown, and (ii)
demonstrating the strength of sensuous desires as the primary
sources of human happiness, did not merely reverberate in other
human sciences, but opened up new practical possibilities for
mankind. In the intellectual world, the large number of utopias
of Logos, Eros and authenticity (some of which will be discussed
in Part II) inspired by the work of Freud bear testimony to test
possibilities.

Our final impression from our discussion so far may well be
the lasting tension in Freud's works between the utopian and
the tragic elements. The utopian, forever reaching towards the
overcoming of frustration and delusion, and the tragic, which
looks at unhappiness and self-deception as humanity's final fate
and regards utopian projects as pathetic and doomed attempts by
humanity to escape from this fate, are never far behind Freud's
arguments, even in their greatest technical detail. It is perhaps
this lasting tension which infuses Freud's writings with their
passion and accounts for their exceptional power.[7]

Thus, in spite of its tragic outlook on human life, psychoanalysis undoubtedly opened new utopian possibilities, some of
which were explored by subsequent theorists. But these possibilities were not limited to the world of social thinkers and
intellectuals. Psychoanalysis was not only a scientific advance,
but also a cultural event (as great advances in science are),
which re-oriented our cultural sensitivities, influenced our ways
of thinking and acting, and introduced a new vocabulary in our
language. Many of its concepts and ideas filtered into common
sense; they were frequently distorted beyond recognition, but
so were the main ideas of many other scientific innovators. In
order to understand these distortions as well as in order to
develop the interpretative and critical potential of psychoanalysis
as cultural theory, it is necessary to study it also as a cultural
event, a task which will be undertaken in Part II. Like Marx,
Freud may not have changed the world in the way he would have
liked, but he certainly did change it; he did not merely interpret
it.

Chapter 7

Psychoanalysis and culture

The six problematics which we have examined reveal Freud's
thought as complex, ambivalent and at times contradictory. It is
not surprising therefore that it allows of as many different
interpretations as that of few major thinkers. The temptation to
simplify in presenting a coherent intellectual portrait, by weed-
ing out uncomfortable and unresolved tensions, is great; it
is also one for which some of his admirers have fallen as readily
as his critics. It is for this reason that Freud has emerged from
some accounts as an apostle of sensuousness and from others as
an apologist of reason, from some as the biologist of the mind
and from others as the psychologist of the body, from some as
the pessimistic moralist and cynic and from others as the hidden
optimist and even potential revolutionary. What is strange is that
Freud's work shows him to be many of these things at once, and
more importantly it shows him to be a far more consistent thinker
than what emerges from the accounts of his admirers and critics.
Freud's consistency, far from being in conflict with the existence
of unresolved problematics in his work, lies precisely in his
unwillingness to simplify, to harmonize and to force theoretical
solutions. Throughout his life he was uniquely able to tolerate
and accept imperfections, lacunae and riddles as well as a large
terra incognita in his discourse, until solutions and clarifications
emerged naturally 'in the course of future developments'. At no
stage did he feel compelled to provide a grand synthesis or a
final account of his work, something that so many of his followers
tried to do on his behalf. Even his final work 'An Outline of
Psychoanalysis' is full of his customary conditional statements
and admissions of ignorance. In a frequently quoted extract from
a letter to Lou Andreas Salome, he says:

> I so rarely feel the need for synthesis. In short, I am evidently
> an analyst and believe that synthesis offers no obstacles once
> analysis has been achieved. (Letter dated 30 July 1915)

By contrast, the portraits painted by most of his admirers and
critics tend to be monochromatic, revealing their authors' constant pre-occupation with synthesis, an inability to tolerate
theoretical tensions and a determination to iron out ambiguities
and contradictions. In addition, such accounts lack the dramatic
quality of Freud's work; contrary to his analytic method which
generates fragments in all directions, breaking up entities into
their constituents, breaking up façades as well as theories, the

followers' synthetic method resembles the piecing together of
select fragments which do not always fit together, the building
of elaborate and intricate structures which threaten to collapse
under the first blow of a critical wind. No such danger exists
for Freud's own work, which admits contradictions without
forcing them into ready-made solutions. Rieff is doubly right in
the statement that Freud 'accepts contradiction and builds his
psychology on it' (1959:xx). What Rieff, like other commentators,
is unwilling to live with is the idea that contradiction is as much
part of the subject-matter of Freud's psychology as the psychology itself, for as we have seen, there are no straight-
forward answers to the ambiguities of the central problematics.
As soon as we force a solution in the terms of one problematic,
we create total chaos in the terms of some of the others. Reich
and Fromm, for instance, force a solution to the problematic of
therapy and normality and instantly find themselves in serious
difficulties in other areas; similar difficulties are experienced by
the other authors we discussed. It is as if the strength of the
Freudian discourse lay in the harmony of its ambiguities; these
seem to be spread unevenly in the six main areas in a way which
propels the discourse forward. At the same time, the unevenness
does not threaten the discourse with total collapse, as is the
case with some of the authors who will be discussed in Part II.

It may be argued that a discourse comprising so many speculative hypotheses, ambiguities and contradictions as Freud's
cannot claim to be scientific, but this view rests on a simplistic
positivist conception of science. A more realistic assessment
recognizes that natural sciences, like the human sciences, also
contain a plethora of anomalies, puzzles and paradoxes, which
provide them with an impetus for change. Nor are their basic concepts more accurately defined than Freud's definitions of some
of his fundamental concepts.[1] Finally, the 'accurate' sciences
seem to have received serious setbacks in respect of their claims
to 'predictability', on which so often in the past they based
their claims to primacy. Psychoanalysis, especially in some of
its applications in marketing and prediction of consumer
behaviour, does not fare so badly in terms of its predictive
power, when compared with some of the off-shoots of physics,
chemistry and biology, like meteorology, seismology and vol-
canology as well as some more traditional areas, like the study
of turbulence by fluid mechanics.

One issue that our earlier discussions have tended to emphasize is the critical position occupied by psychoanalysis in the
human sciences. Far from studying the individual in isolation,
Freud approaches him/her as social from the outset; he/she is
not just constrained by social factors, but is the bearer of social
prohibitions, social norms, social symbols, social artifacts.
In addition, psychoanalysis, through its central concepts of
desire, repression, unconscious and so on, elucidates certain
crucial assumptions shared by the human sciences. Finally,
through its study of symbolism, it can initiate a new study and

interpretation of cultural phenomena, such as myths, works of
art and religious beliefs. In these conclusions, we will bring
together these psychoanalytic contributions to the study of
culture, without losing sight of the ambiguities inherent in them.

In the first place, psychoanalysis approaches cultural phenomena
not in terms of their causes or their function, but in terms of
their meaning. Just as the first breakthrough in the area of
psychology came from the interpretation of symptoms and dreams,
Freud, in the first place, approaches cultural phenomena from
the point of view of interpretation. His initial reflex was to look
at them as collective counterparts to individual neurotic symptoms,
expressing collective desires or at least shared desires – in this
way, he discerned some striking similarities between religious
rituals and the symptoms of obsessive neurotics (1907b). Shortly
after his first speculations into the genesis of culture in 'Totem
and Taboo', Freud wrote:

> The neuroses themselves have turned out to be attempts to
> *individual* solutions for the problems of compensating for
> unsatisfied wishes, while the (social) institutions seek to
> provide *social* solutions for these same problems. The recession
> of the social factor and the predominance of the sexual one
> turn these neurotic solutions of the psychological problem
> into caricatures which are of no service except to help us in
> explaining such important questions. (1913j:13:186-7)

Social and cultural phenomena can be interpreted after the model
of interpretation of dreams and neurotic symptoms. Myths,
religious beliefs, artistic achievements, cultural artifacts of all
kinds, political and social behaviour itself, can all be interpreted
as manifest symptoms of underlying unconscious structures,
indeed the same underlying structures that we discover through
the interpretation of dreams, symptoms, slips of tongue, etc.
In this way, Freud's investigations into religion add a new
dimension to the classical formulations of Weber and Durkheim –
religion is not merely a source of meaning in people's actions,
it is not merely a force of social cohesion and identity, but it is
also a symptom representing the solution offered by society to
a psychic problem and reflecting the underlying structure of the
problem.
  Although Freud never engaged in a systematic interpretation of
the cultures of particular periods, his interpretations of specific
cultural phenomena such as religious beliefs, myths, artistic
creations and war-time destruction reveal an unexpected wealth
of insights and possibilities. Yet, there are several unresolved
issues in this cultural hermeneutic, which arise from the fact
that interpretation of cultural phenomena cannot and should not
be seen as a special case of psychoanalytic hermeneutics. As
Ricoeur has recognized, in the first place, psychoanalysis' knows
cultural phenomena only as analogues of the wish-fulfilment

illustrated by dreams' (1970:155). But, it does not stop there.
As the earlier quote suggests, Freud was fully aware that
neurotic solutions isolate individuals and personalize the problem
while social solutions bind individuals together into stable and
cohesive groups. The zoophobia of little Hans and Sophocles'
Oedipus Rex may have been built on the same psychic foundations
which come to light through the work of interpretation; yet,
the two cannot be identified as identical symptoms, not even for
a strict psychoanalytic purpose. While the former isolated the
little boy, caused intense anxiety and inhibition and distorted
his sense of reality, the latter has united audiences, like all
great works of art do, through the centuries and provided
communal channels of emotional release.[2] Unlike the dream or the
neurotic symptom, the work of art, like the religious idea, seeks,
to a greater or lesser extent, to communicate something to a
public; it is not only a symptom, but also an instrument of
expression and communication. The technical terms, the work of
art, the religious idea and indeed the philosophical theory usually
undergo far more extensive 'secondary elaboration' by the ego
than does the dream or the neurotic symptom: their 'regard for
representability' is far greater than that of more private means
of expression. Unlike the neurotic who develops his/her own
symbolic language, the artist and the philosopher must submit
to the communal symbolic. Of course, both the artist and the
philosopher stretch their symbolics to their extreme, forever
discovering new and unexpected possibilities of beauty and
truth. The content constantly overflows the form without destroy-
ing it, and in doing so it reaches outwards towards a public.
Dreams and neurosis can hardly claim to represent beauty or
truth - although they may indeed lead towards the paths of
beauty and truth, once they have been mastered; and they lack
a public.

The psychoanalytic study of culture cannot, therefore, limit
itself to cultural hermeneutics, just as the psychoanalytic study
of neuroses and dreams cannot end with the task of interpretation. The oneiric hermeneutics of 'The Interpretation of Dreams'
point inexorably towards the 'metapsychological' last chapter,
i.e. towards the discussion of the underlying mental process,
mental energies and mental institutions. In short, the interpretation of dreams is not an exercise in literary criticism, as
many of Freud's contemporaries thought, but a via regia to the
unconscious, the unique path towards the secrets of the psyche.
Having discussed and interpreted many dozens of dreams,
having identified the primary processes as found in the dream-
work, Freud devotes the last chapter of his book to a meta-
psychological discussion, which represents the theoretical yield
of his painstaking labours of interpretation.[3]

Freud's metapsychological discussions are organized around
three general 'points of view', which were examined in Chapter
5: the economic, which focuses on the vicissitudes of mental
energies, the dynamic, which analyses the qualitative aspects

of mental conflict, and the topographic, which articulates the
properties and spatial inter-relations of mental institutions.
These same points of view dominate the psychoanalytic discussion
of culture, which proceeds from the interpretation of cultural
phenomena. The dynamic discussion of culture centres on the
contradictory demands of the individual and the social whole; in
particular, it examines the extent to which civilization restricts
individual pleasure, the ways in which it protects the individual
from unpleasure, and also the mechanisms through which it
becomes itself a source of unpleasure and guilt. Thus the interpretation of cultural phenomena, their translation from one
language to another language, the discovery of their underlying
meaning, is inextricably related to the study of the relationship
between individual and society. Just as the interpretation of
dreams ties in with their psychic functions, the interpretation
of religious ideas ties in with the different socio-psychic functions of religion, such as control, rationalization and consolation.

The dynamic discussion of culture is complemented by the
economic discussion, which deals with the mechanisms through
which psychic energies are re-directed by culture along paths
which promote social cohesion and minimize social destructiveness.
It is this economic discussion which elucidates the nature of
social bonds, the obstacles to the formation of such bonds as
well as the cost of these bonds to each individual. The greater
the amounts of libido invested in social bonds, the smaller the
amounts of libido available for individual pleasure, the smaller
the amounts available for narcissistic satisfactions, the smaller
the amounts available for the binding and 'fusing' of destructive
impulses. The greater the amounts of 'de-fused' destructive
energies, the greater the harshness of the super-ego, the
greater the experience of frustration and discomfort. Such
economic considerations loom always in the background of Freud's
cultural discussions and frequently come to the forefront. It is
they which are ultimately responsible for what Freud regards as
the tragic fate of mankind.

> Every renunciation of instinct now becomes a dynamic source
> of conscience and every fresh renunciation increases the
> latter's severity and intolerance. (1930a:21:128)

> The more man controls his aggressiveness, the more intense
> his ideal's inclination towards aggressiveness against his ego.
> (1923b:19:54)

All Freudian discussions of culture are, therefore, not only dominated by the 'balance-sheet' of cathexes and anti-cathexes of
libido (Ricoeur 1970:249), but also of destructive energies. It is
often argued that Freud never complemented his pioneering
researches in the 'Three Essays on the Theory of Sexuality'
with an equally comprehensive study of the death instinct, its
development, vicissitudes and aberrations.[4] This, of course, is

quite true, but we are fortunate that in his investigations of
cultural phenomena he devoted his attention to the vicissitudes
of both instinctual forces, although, once again, his cultural
erotics are more advanced than his cultural thanatotics. Both
the tragic and the critical aspects of Freud's cultural discussions
hinge on these economic considerations, for it is they which
reveal both the hopelessness of man's quest for happiness and
the complete failure of our culture to support this quest.

Finally, the dynamic and economic discussions of culture are
grounded in the topographic discussion, which studies the
social 'input' in the various mental institutions; it is this discussion, for instance, which reveals the secret of the super-
ego, that mental institution which originates in the identification
with parental authority at the resolution of the Oedipus Complex,
and subsequently becomes the seat of social norms and rules.
Although Parsons' view that all three protagonists of the second
topography, the ego, the id and the super-ego, are all constituted socially represents a rather rash generalization, it is
quite true that they each represent one aspect of each individual's ambivalent relationship with culture – the id with its
blind defiance of all external considerations, the super-ego with
its slavish and uncritical subordination to external law, and the
ego with its compulsive urge towards mastery and control of
externality.[5] It is through this stubborn refusal to look at the
individual as an integrated personality or character and through
his insistence that each person is a fragmented complex of
different and often contradictory functions, that Freud avoids
the shortcomings of most theorists who try to articulate the
relationship between individual and society. Man is both a social
animal and an anti-social one, culture both develops man's potentials and thwarts these potentials, man both submits to culture
and rebels against it. Of course, it would be much more convenient to build one's theory on one or other assumption (Hobbes
and Aristotle), but reality has little regard for our convenience.

It may be thought that as Freud refers to the dynamic,
economic and topographic discussions as 'meta-psychological', he
somehow abstracts the individual from his/her social milieu and
looks at the psyche as an autonomous entity. This does indeed
apply to some of his epigoni and to some of contemporary psychology which looks at culture as an external influence on a
psychic given. I hope, however, that our discussion has indicated that there is no such danger with Freud, for his metapsychology is social on every level.

It is now possible to suggest an almost exact epistemological
analogue in Freud's discussions of personal phenomena (dreams,
neuroses, etc.) and cultural phenomena (art, religion, etc.).
There is an underlying movement in 'The Interpretation of
Dreams' from a hermeneutic discussion (from manifest conscious
dream-content to latent unconscious dream-thought) to an
examination of processes (dynamic and economic) and then to an
articulation of mental structures (topographic). In the first

place, Freud interprets the manifest content of dreams in an attempt to reveal the latent unconscious dream-thought. The manifest content is the product of a process which distorts the dream-thought, what Freud called 'the dream-work'. Through the work of interpretation, Freud proceeds in the opposite direction from that of the dream-work. In this operation he resembles the archaeologist who extrapolates latent structures from manifest ones, by undoing the work of time. Yet, what Freud soon realized, like good archaeologists sometimes do, was that the material he was starting off with had not just deteriorated as a result of the passage of time, but, in the majority of cases, had been deliberately tampered with. The material had been deliberately distorted, in order to frustrate and mislead attempts at interpretation. It is this realization which led Freud to postulate the existence of a censor - a malicious but ingenious agent, who not only erases what he finds objectionable, but, through omissions, changes in emphasis, careful substitutions and other subtle tactics, distorts the text's meaning. This made the work of interpretation both harder and easier; it made it harder, because, unlike religious and literary hermeneutics, psychoanalysis was facing an enemy determined to mislead and confuse, an enemy who operated in the mind of the patient as much as in the mind of the analyst. At the same time, however, it made it easier, once the purposes of this evil daemon, its character and its methods of operation became known to the analyst. Freud was thus forced to make a 'bold hypothesis', namely that dreams represent fulfilments of unconscious desires, and that they are censored to the extent that they might contradict the contents of consciousness. Having made this assumption, Freud could proceed as though he knew the purposes of the censor, and his interpretations based on this assumption bore considerable fruit, (a) because the unconscious desires he discovered underneath the manifest content of the dream could receive independent verification, and (b) because he gradually discovered that the censor was using the same four methods in his task - the primary processes.

Thus, Freud's hermeneutic, by looking at the distortion of meanings as a systematic process and not as a mere accident, led him to a discussion of psychic processes, at two distinct levels. First, the processes through which certain ideas (representations) are replaced in consciousness by others, apparently unrelated ones.[6] Second, the processes through which energies originally attached to some ideas (representations) are displaced and channelled along different paths.[7] In short, what we have is a discussion of psychic processes from our two familiar points of view, the dynamic and the economic.

So, the first movement in 'The Interpretation of Dreams' takes Freud from his interpretation of meanings to the study of psychic processes responsible for the distortions of meaning, their functions, energies and mechanisms. But this movement is complemented by a second movement, a movement which takes him from psychic processes to psychic structures from which the psychic processes proceed. Thus, in the last chapter, Freud entered a long series of speculations into the different areas of the mind, their interrelationships and properties, which was to last for the rest of his life. His early speculations into mental topography were tentative and at times unclear; so, for instance, his first postulation of the unconscious did not distinguish between the dynamic and the descriptive aspects of the concept or between the unconscious as the reservoir of mental energies and the unconscious as the reservoir of repressed ideas. Yet, the pattern of the Freudian discourse has already been established – from meaning to processes and from processes to structures.

I believe that the same pattern can be discerned in Freud's cultural discussions. First, cultural phenomena are analysed symptomatically, in an effort to reveal meanings behind symbols, desires behind social institutions and so on. The discussion then moves on to the processes (repression, identification, sublimation, etc.) through which cultural phenomena acquire their specific meanings, the distortions undergone by these meanings and so on. Finally, the discussion moves to the underlying structures responsible for cultural phenomena. Freud's discussion of religion, for instance, springs from an examination of religious ideas (totemism (1939a:23:82ff), the Credo Apostolicum, the belief in a single God, etc.) and religious practices (circumcision (1939a:23:26ff and passim), the Christian holy communion, (1939a:23:84, 87), religious 'ceremonials' (1907b), etc.); these lead him to a variety of unconscious desires, such as desires for paternal protection, for consolation and for the self-infliction of punishment. From the level of interpretation the Freudian discourse moves to the study of processes through which the unconscious desires are translated into religious phenomena; these processes underlie religious life much as the processes of the dream-work underlie the mental transformations during sleep, and include processes like introjection of aggression, sublimation of sexuality, identification with religious leaders. Finally, from the study of such processes, both in a dynamic and an economic sense, the discourse moves to the structures represented by religious collectivities; in 'Group Psychology and the Analysis of the Ego', Freud provides us with the archetypical discussion of religious bonds in the Christian Church. Needless to say that no single work encapsulates all steps of the discourse, nor did Freud pursue his investigations along the different paths in a chronological order. Yet, the underlying logic of his investigations into cultural phenomena is much the same as the one which we encounter in Traumdeutung.

Several qualifications are needed at this point. First of all, it should not be thought that Freud in any sense tries to reduce cultural phenomena to psychological ones; although the underlying logic may be the same, both the assumptions entering the two discourses and the nature of the processes and structures

analysed are different. The assumption that sleep must be preserved at all costs, which underlies much of the oneiric discourse, is substituted in the cultural discourse by other
assumptions, such as that social cohesion must be preserved.
Thus while the process of repression (in the weakened form we
encounter it in dreams), in the context of a discussion of dreams,
is articulated in terms of its mental function the same process,
in the context of a discussion of religion, is articulated in terms
of its social function. While the dominant theme in the oneiric
discourse is the mental conflict whose outcome is the manifest
content of dreams, the dominant theme of the cultural discourse
is invariably the conflict between individual and society. Put
more generally, we may be justified in arguing that the fundamental difference between the individual and the cultural discourse is that in the former transformations of meanings, mental
processes and mental structures are analysed in terms of their
mental functions and the emphasis lies on mental conflict, while
in the latter, transformations, processes and structures of a
very similar character are analysed in terms of their social
functions and the emphasis lies on the conflict between the
individual and the social whole.

At this point, it is absolutely necessary to distinguish this
position from the frequent arguments of those who suggest that
Freud can only approach cultural and social phenomena by
'reducing' them to their psychological analogues. Although, as
we shall see, Freud was on occasions guilty of such reductions,
it is crucial to emphasize that there is no direct isomorphism
between his social and his individual discourses, a point that
is directly reflected in his steadfast rejection of the concept of
'collective unconscious'. As we shall see very shortly, this concept is absolutely indispensable if the process of individual
repression is seen as possessing a direct social analogue, for
where else could the ideas and desires repressed collectively
go, but to a monumental collective unconscious?

Freud's faith in the nineteenth-century formula 'ontogeny
recapitulates phylogeny' is well known and it is sometimes
presented as evidence of his alleged reductionism. His arguments
in 'Totem and Taboo' and 'Moses and Monotheism' do indeed draw
various apparent parallels between infantile conditions and those
of 'primitive' people; what Freud seems to be doing is placing
the Oedipal drama (or, at least, one variant of this drama)
at the root of civilization, just as the Oedipus Complex was
identified as the mark of the individual's entry into culture.
As a result, just as many neurotic conditions may be traced back
to the resolution of the Oedipus Complex, it is argued, Freud
seeks to trace social and political behaviour to those archaic
events associated with the alleged murder of the primal father.
It is, therefore, necessary to look into these phylogenetic arguments, assess their significance and examine whether they do,
in fact, represent attempts to reduce social phenomena to psychological ones through the assertion of direct isomorphism.

Exponents as well as critics of the isomorphic interpretation of
Freud seem to concentrate on revolutionary conflict as typical
of this psychological reductionism.[8] Briefly, it is argued that
Freud regarded all revolutionary conflict as a simple 're-enactment' of the sons' rebellion against the tyrannical primal father
of the horde. The murders of Christ and Moses as well as all
political revolutions are thus but repetitions of the primal murder.
This account dismisses all economic, social and political factors
as the real causes of revolutionary rupture, in favour of psychological ones: the alleged relics or primal memories which
propel mankind to engage in an occasional purging of its leaders.
Moreover, this argument dismisses all revolutionary behaviour
as ineffective, irrational or, more precisely, neurotic (Rieff
1959:267); for the moral of the primal murder is that the hated
father returns after the murder to dominate his sons with even
greater ruthlessness – they end up by restoring his prohibition
in the form of a moral law – the incest taboo ensures the rule of
the tyrant in absentia. Hence, all revolutionaries are doomed to
restore the rule whose downfall they instigated, history as 'Animal
Farm' writ large. This argument, as we would expect, enjoys a
great popularity with conservative admirers of Freud as well as
with some of his radical critics. The truth, however, is that it
contradicts the mainstream of the Freudian discourse on so
many points that it can hardly be seen as anything more than a
wishful reconstruction.

In the first place, Freud never dismissed 'rational' social and
economic factors as causal of revolutionary uprisings. On the
contrary, he explicitly viewed hostility and rebelliousness as a
rational response to sexual, economic or political domination:

> If we turn to those restrictions that apply only to certain
> classes of society, we meet with a state of things which is
> flagrant and which has always been recognized. It is to be
> expected that these underprivileged classes will envy the
> favoured ones their privileges and will do all they can to free
> themselves from their own surplus of privation. Where this is
> not possible, a permanent measure of discontent will persist
> within the culture concerned and this can lead to dangerous
> revolts. (1927c:21:12)

Moreover, in spite of his frequently expressed scepticism towards
the Russian Revolution, he did not dismiss it a priori, nor did
he dismiss the revolutionary leaders as neurotic:

> [They] are men of action, unshakable in their convictions,
> inaccessible to doubt, without feeling for the sufferings of
> others if they stand in the way of their intentions. We have
> to thank men of this kind for the fact that the tremendous
> experiment of producing a new order of this kind is now
> actually being carried out in Russia. At a time when the great
> nations announce that they expect salvation only from the

> maintenance of Christian piety, the revolution in Russia – in
> spite of its disagreeable details – seems none the less like the
> message for a better future. (1933a:22:181)

Secondly, a careful reading of Freud's work reveals that his
intention is very far from 'reducing' all social, political and
cultural phenomena to psychological analogues, notwithstanding
his rash and often misunderstood statement that sociology,

> dealing as it does with the behaviour of people in society,
> cannot be anything but applied psychology. (179)

The two earlier extracts show that Freud was quite willing to
employ the concept of class in determining the attachments that
different groups of people develop in their society and their
propensity to rebel against it. But, as Freud recognizes, class
is a category of political economy, not of psychology, since it
emerges from an analysis of the production and distribution of
wealth. Only after class has been articulated in terms of socio-
economic relations can Freud identify differences in the psychological make-up of individuals belonging to different classes.
Thus psychoanalysis can complement without eclipsing explanations of social phenomena undertaken from different levels of
analysis. As is apparent from his own discourse, Freud was
never reluctant to approach the same phenomenon from a number
of 'points of view' simultaneously, without reducing one point
of view to the terms of the others; it would be totally inconsistent on his part to suggest that the theoretical approaches of
other disciplines should be absorbed in a single psychological
or psychoanalytic perspective.
Perhaps the most important argument against the reductionist
interpretation of Freud's work is that the isomorphism on which
it is based is contrary to the main lines of his own discourse.
First of all, the analogue of the primal murder and the Oedipus
Complex is not nearly as straight-forward as it is sometimes
suggested. As we have seen already, the infantile Oedipus
Complex unfolds entirely in the realm of the child's imagination,
where the technicalities of both murder and intercourse are
totally absent, as Freud repeatedly reminds us, and go far
beyond the cognitive competence of three- or four-year-olds.[9]
In contrast, Freud's account of the primal murder, the totem
meal, the incest taboo, etc. presents the episodes of the Oedipal
situation not only in their full technical detail, but indeed as
facts: the Oedipus Complex has become an Oedipal drama,
phantasy has been replaced by action. But are we to take these
events literally? Is it necessary to wait for the anthropologists
to tell us that such events are unlikely to have happened? And
does this mark the end of Freud's cultural discourse? The
answers to all these questions, as we shall see, must be firm
negations. Let us first try to understand the phenomena, whose
explanation led Freud to regard each individual as the bearer of

an 'archaic heritage', a complex of memories of primeval events
associated with the murder of the primal father. These phenomena
were both cultural and psychic and seemed to admit of no alternative psychoanalytic or other explanation; they included, in the
first place, the relationship between civilization and an overwhelming sense of guilt, which could not be explained in terms
of any individual's actual deeds. Of course, Freud's ontogenetic
account of the Oedipus Complex has provided a firm foundation
for the sense of guilt, both in a dynamic and an energic sense;
the phylogenetic account simply re-inforced this foundation, or,
more accurately, it fulfilled the function of this foundation
before the latter had been fully articulated. But the ontogenetic
argument needs no re-inforcement to account for the strength
of man's moral sense, it is fully capable of doing so on its own.
Second, the hypothesis of the archaic heritage seeks to provide
a phylogenetic explanation of repression and of distorted consciousness. It proposes that distorted consciousness, in its twin
forms of ideals and illusions, grows out of guilty conscience:
not only are the desires of the sons (kept alive during the rule
of the tyrannical father) properly repressed for good, but the
murdered father himself returns to dominate his sons, and yet
is perceived as benevolent; he is idealized after his death,
even though this idealization leads to a new and subtler form
of oppression: repression. The sons no longer know their
desires which have been exiled to the unconscious. Once again,
the phylogenetic account re-inforces other arguments, without
in any way being indispensable.
  Yet, there is a third group of phenomena which would appear
to require the assumption of an archaic heritage if they are to
be explained at all. These are essentially psychic phenomena,
accessible through analysis, which consist mainly of symbolic
structures which seem to recur endlessly in the dreams of many
people and seem to permit no alternative explanation.

> Dreams bring to light material which cannot have originated
> either from the dreamer's adult life or from his forgotten
> childhood. We are obliged to regard it as part of the *archaic
> heritage* which a child brings with him into the world, before
> any experience of his own, influenced by the experience of
> his ancestors. (1940a:23:167)[10]

By invoking a common archaic heritage, Freud tries to account
for 'fixed symbolism' in dreams and symptoms, the uncanny
propensity of standardized symbols to occur in dreams of
different individuals and myths of different peoples. Freud
asserts that

> though we may admit that for the memory traces in our archaic
> inheritance we have so far no stronger proof than those
> remnants of memory evoked by analytic work, which call for a
> derivation from phylogenesis, yet this proof seems to me con-

vincing enough to postulate such a state of affairs. If things
are different we are unable to advance one step further on our
way, either in psychoanalysis or in mass psychology. It is
bold, but inevitable. (1939a:23:100)

Once the archaic heritage has been accepted

> then we have bridged the gap between individual and mass
> psychology and can treat peoples as we do the individual
> neurotic. (ibid.)

This would suggest that we can talk of social repression, social
symptoms and social delusions in a fashion directly analogous to
individual neurosis. Above all, we could talk of a collective
unconscious as the great depository of humanity's collective
repressed experiences. Freud, contrary to our arguments,
seems to be well on his way towards isomorphism and reduction.

However, the entire argument seems to be founded on extremely
weak bases. In the first place, the assumption that memory
relics are intergenerationally transmitted seems to rest on a
psychological variant of the hypothesis of the inheritance of
acquired characteristics – an eminently plausible hypothesis
related to Lamarckism, which unfortunately has been consistently
discredited by twentieth-century biology, even during Freud's
own lifetime.[11] Freud was well aware that his variant of Lamarckism was untenable in terms of the biological evidence (128), but
saw it as such an indispensable part of his theory that he
remained committed to it. This is rather surprising, since the
hypothesis of the archaic heritage seems to be in such contradiction with Freud's account of the child's cognitive development
and his studies of memory, that one may feel that he had become
so enamoured with phylogenetic speculations that he simply
refused to relinquish them in the light of overwhelming factors
pointing in the opposite direction. How else could he ever hope
to reconcile his childhood psychology with the statement that

> the archaic heritage of mankind includes not only dispositions,
> but also ideational contents, memory traces of the experiences
> of former generations. (99)

Would it not be absurd to suggest that the child in its primary
autism is also a depository of ideational contents and memory
traces? At a stage when the distinctions between ego and *alter*,
real and imaginary, good and bad and so on have not yet been
learned, would it not be absurd to expect the child to have
'memories' of deeds allegedly committed by his ancient fore-
fathers?

There can be little doubt that the hypothesis of the archaic
heritage is highly problematic not only in terms of independent
support and empirical validation from anthropologists[12] and in
terms of contemporary biological science, but in terms of other

features of the Freudian discourse itself. Yet, this hypothesis
intervenes countless times as an ex machina deus in Freud's
arguments, either to explain phenomena which cannot be explained
otherwise, or to lend its support to ontogenetic arguments.
As such it would seem to fill an important gap in Freudian theory
and yet it seems to create infinitely more problems than it
resolves. In addition, it creates the dangerous appearance of
isomorphism which encourages reductionist interpretations.

Fortunately, towards the end of 'Moses and Monotheism', Freud
moves to a slightly different position from the one represented
above – a position which can be supported by references to the
'archaic heritage' in 'Totem and Taboo' as well as in some other
writings, especially those concerned with psychotherapy, like
'Analysis Terminable and Interminable'. The essence of this
position lies in the realization that it makes little sense to talk
of repression, symptom-formation, anxiety, etc. as collective
processes, but rather that they should be viewed as processes
experienced collectively by individuals living in a society and
being the bearers of the society. In other words, mankind does
not possess one collective unconscious, but the underlying
unconscious structures are shared by all individuals, and they
are structures which cannot be explained by individual psychology alone. (We shall return to this point shortly.)

> It is not easy to translate the concepts of individual psychology
> into mass psychology, and I do not think that much is gained
> by introducing the concept of a 'collective' unconscious – the
> content of the unconscious is collective anyhow, a general
> possession of mankind. (132)

But if the contents of this 'archaic heritage' are seen as structures shared by many individuals, rather than as a trace in one
mass collective unconscious, then they need not be memory
traces at all, let alone memory traces of real events, nor need
they, properly speaking, be intergenerationally transmitted. In
fact, the section which follows the above extract gives us an
extremely perceptive parallel between archaic residues and
language.

> We must conclude that the mental residue of those primeval
> times has become a heritage which, with each new generation,
> needs only to be awakened, not to be reacquired. We may think
> here of the example of speech-symbolism, which certainly
> seems to be inborn. It originates in the time of speech-
> development, and it is familiar to all children without their
> having been specially instructed. It is the same in all people
> in spite of the differences in language. What we may still lack
> in certainty we may acquire from other results of psycho-
> analytic investigations. We learn that our children in a number
> of significant relationships do not react as their own experi-
> ences would lead us to expect, but instinctively, like animals;

> this is explicable only by phylogenetic inheritance. (132-3)

Just as Chomsky's argument on linguistic structures rests on a denial of their being 'residues' of primeval experiences or inter-generationally transmitted (through a learning process) but regards them as mental structures, characteristic of the human mind, Freud's hypothesis of the archaic heritage can be salvaged by simply regarding these archaic 'residues' as unconscious mental structures. Just as every child's mind can be said to be pre-programmed by linguistic structures without actually assuming that it contains verbal elements (of particular languages) at birth, we can suggest that the child's mind is also pre-programmed by the Oedipal structures of love for another, hate of brutal power, guilt, etc., without assuming that the unformed ego contains memory traces, or ideational components whatsoever at birth. The circumstances of ontogenesis will determine how these Oedipal structures will be 'awakened' or activated and to what use they will be put, in a way similar to the development of the linguistic faculty. And these circumstances are to a large extent dictated by the specifics of the culture through which the child will become an individual man or woman. In this way, both the sexual permissiveness of the Trobrianders and the oppressiveness of fin-de-siècle Vienna can be seen as derivatives of the same basic Oedipal structures, involving the sensuous element and the element of fear for authority.

In itself, the hypothesis of an archaic heritage adds about as little to our understanding of the Oedipal structures and their activation as does the Tower of Babel to our understanding of linguistic structures and the diversification of linguistic idioms. But in this case, the entire primeval drama, outlined by Freud in his diverse 'anthropological' writings, can be seen as a gigantic metaphor, or indeed as a myth. It is for these reasons that we fundamentally agree with writers as different as Ricoeur (1970:208), Mitchell (1974:315), Marcuse (1955:54), Mannoni (1971:132) and Brown (1966:3), all of whom regard Freud's phylogenetic accounts as 'scientific myths'. With his speculations into man's mythical past, or more accurately with his postulation of such a past, Freud joins the long tradition of cosmogonical thinkers from Moses to Hesiod, from Hobbes to Rousseau, who sought to elucidate humanity's present by invoking distant events. Whether Freud's myth can claim to be scientific depends on whether the interpretation of the present to which it leads can receive consistent and independent validation - in short, whether the unconscious structures extrapolated from the myth of the primeval murder can be established independently.

Why then did Freud invent this myth? What is the use of the myth? Is it merely an attempt by Freud to outdo Jung at his own game? How far can the metaphor be stretched? Is all mankind the bearer of the archaic heritage or only some cultures? To one with no personal experience in psychotherapy, Freud's discussions of the archaic heritage have a peculiarly hollow, if not redundant, character. It is true that in his interpretations of dreams and neurotic symptoms, Freud seems to encounter a narrow range of symbols with uncanny regularity. Yet, on the whole, the hypothesis of the archaic heritage re-inforces onto-genetic explanations rather than leads towards them; and it certainly does not replace them. Likewise, Freud's cultural discourse gains relatively little from this hypothesis which cannot be accounted for through the analyses of relations within the social collectivity. It seems to me that the outstanding contribution of this hypothesis lies in illustrating graphically the significance of our culture as the root of two phenomena. These phenomena do, in fact, receive independent validation in a variety of ways, yet their profoundly social aetiology may have escaped us without the metaphor of culture being founded on murder and desire. These phenomena are the repression of sexuality and the self-inflicted and unjustified sense of guilt (to which some may add the fear of death); all of these phenomena have been mistaken by many thinkers as existential or biological in their aetiology; Freud's metaphor reminds us what his theory has been telling us all along - their causes lie in the nature of society itself.

Now, had Freud's major pre-occupation been to account for fixed symbolism in dreams, would it not have been simpler to postulate universal symbolic archetypes or a 'biological sense of guilt' (Rank) from which such archetypes may derive, instead of fabricating a confusing, if brilliant, mythology, worthy of the Hebrews and the Greeks? In answering this question we are forced to look at the deeply socio-historical character of Freud's discourse; for the myth of the primeval murder represents nothing if not an effort to link the fate of the individual to that of the species, and, more importantly, to link that fate not to biology or to a quasi-mystical collective unconscious, but to human history. Both Mitchell and Marcuse have articulated this eloquently:

The unconscious is everyman's heritage of how mankind lives. As Freud says, each separate individual cannot start the process of human history anew, on his own; he must acquire it. . . . Freud and de Beauvoir agree that it is shared history that makes for shared perceptions and common symbols. (Mitchell 1974: 315, 316)

[Freud's] psychology does not focus on the concrete and complete personality as it exists in its private and public environment, because this existence conceals rather than reveals the essence and nature of personality. It is the end result of long historical processes which are congealed in the network of human and institutional entities making up society, and these processes define the personality and its relationships. Consequently, to understand them for what they really are, psychology must unfreeze them by tracing their hidden origins. (Marcuse 1955:52)

Far from reducing social to individual 'development', the hypothesis of the archaic heritage seeks to ground the individual in
human history - without this grounding, the individual becomes
a reified abstraction, missing its essential ingredient, the inescapable bearing of the fate of the species. Freud's hypothesis
of the primeval murder reveals man as a species-being, in the
tradition of Feuerbach and Marx, and therefore an inescapably
social being - that is each individual can only be seen as
representative of humanity as a whole. The origin of those
phenomena which establish the relation between the life of the
individual and the society in which he/she lives is society itself
- the repression of sexuality, the self-inflicted and unjustified
sense of guilt and even the incapacitating fear of death are all
social in their origins. It is for this reason that 'individual
psychology is this *in itself* group psychology in so far as the
individual itself still is in archaic identity with the species'
(Marcuse 1955:51). We can now claim, without any risk of being
reductionists, that we agree with Freud's assertion that

> sociology too, dealing as it does with the behaviour of people
> in society, cannot be anything but applied psychology.
> (1933a:23:179)

But while arguing for the significant interconnections among
human sciences, Freud never threatens to simplify these interconnections into an all-embracing psychological commonwealth.

> Freud is trying to establish that the individual's psychology
> cannot be transferred in a complete or simple way to a collective/
> social situation, nor vice versa, but the two must share
> common features, and these can be analysed and the mode of
> their inter-relationship considered. (Mitchell 1974:316)

Thus, while Freud is allowing an infinite variety of individual
character-structures, depending on the circumstances of each
person's upbringing as well as 'constitutional' factors, he does
not regard it as accidental that each individual is confronted,
upon arrival to this world, by the same underlying problems,
from whose formative impact it is impossible to escape. Just as
biology has dictated that during his/her protracted incapacity
the child must depend on some other for nourishment and support,
the history of the species has dictated that the child can only
be accepted as a member of human society after he/she has
experienced a traumatic frustration of desire and a traumatic
confrontation with authority. These experiences will leave the
child with deep scars, since they represent battles which the
child cannot possibly hope to win, no matter what the circumstances of rearing. These scars, including an underlying distortion of consciousness in the shape of a non-ending sequence of

illusions and ideals, and an unyielding sense of guilt, are the
inevitable trademark of history, and arise as if our ancient
ancestors had been ill-treated by their father and had subsequently murdered him, and as if both the resentment of the
father and the responsibility for their deed had been stamped
on every new arrival in human culture.

Once we have appreciated the metaphorical character of Freud's
phylogenetic speculations, we are in no danger of reduction or
isomorphism; for the metaphor of the archaic heritage can reduce
neither the social to the psychological nor vice versa - properly
speaking a metaphor can explain nothing at all (unless people
end up by taking it for granted, in which case it is no longer
a metaphor); a metaphor can only illustrate, and I have sought
to show how the metaphor of the archaic heritage illustrates the
interconnections between individual and society. At best, a
metaphor can serve again and again in supporting theoretical
explanations, so that it eventually becomes concretized into a
theory or replaced by a theory which subsumes it. Both of these
phenomena are common enough in Freud's work, as in the work
of every other major scientific innovator, where, for instance,
the early metaphors of the censor, the split consciousness or
indeed the hypothetical seductions (which, of course, Freud
originally mistook for real) were transcended by the theory of
repression. Instead of saying that a person behaved as if an
internal censor had withheld information from him (or as if he
had been seduced by his parent), Freud was then able to say
that this information (or this desire) had been repressed.

A perennial difficulty in Freud's discussions is the distinction
between metaphor (or heuristic artifact) and theory; this is
compounded by the fact that some of his theories - including the
original formulation of the unconscious - started life as metaphors, while others were later relegated to being metaphors.
This, however, must not discourage us from preserving the
distinctions, without which there results considerable theoretical
and epistemological confusion, as the misconceptions arising in
relation to the 'archaic heritage' amply demonstrate.

Having argued that the archaic metaphor cannot explain anything, it must be perfectly clear that it does not, contrary to
Freud's claims, explain fixed symbolism, it does not explain
contemporary social phenomena, and above all it does not explain
the tragic fate of mankind - it can explain neither guilt nor
distorted consciousness. The reverse is true - that this metaphor
has been drawn from all these phenomena without adding anything
to our knowledge of them. It merely illustrates some of the
central features of these phenomena, without, however, enabling
us to draw conclusions or inferences. As Ricoeur has pointed out,

> one does psychoanalysis a service, not by defending its
> scientific myth as science, but by interpreting it as myth. At
> the end of *Totem and Taboo*, Freud thinks he can derive Greek
> tragedy from the historic totem meal. The truth of the matter

is the reverse: the Freudian myth is the positive transposition,
in terms of the ethnography of the beginning of the twentieth
century, of the tragic myth itself. (1970:208)

What then *is* the value of the metaphor of the archaic heritage
qua metaphor? Quite apart from demonstrating Freud's sensitive
handling of the relationship between the individual and society,
I find relatively little of value in this particular myth, in terms
of either the individual or the cultural discourse. Fixed symbolism is illustrated but not explained – the myth simply suggests
that individuals share certain symbolic representations as if they
had been the bearers of an archaic heritage, which they patently
cannot be in the literal sense. Equally, although it provides a
powerful illustration of what may be called the tragic fate of
mankind, it adds nothing to our understanding of the repression
of sexuality, the operation of guilt or the setting up of illusions
and ideals, whether individually or collectively. It is through the
detailed arguments of his other works that guilt and distorted
consciousness as well as the restrictions on sexuality are articulated in terms of the functions of society, the demands of
biology and the structures of the mental apparatus. The hypothesis or myth of the archaic heritage adds nothing to these
arguments.
Moreover, by creating a cosmogonical myth, Freud established
a rather dangerous tradition, whereby each of his followers
felt entitled to modify the myth or simply 're-interpret' it to suit
his/her own purposes and to 'support' his/her theoretical and
political views. Thus, for instance, Rieff interprets the myth as
an illustration of the futility of political action, Marcuse as an
illustration of the guilt which arises from the betrayal of the
revolution, Fromm as an illustration of the eternal rebellion
against patriarchal authority, and so on. These disagreements,
compounded by disagreements over the interpretation of the
other towering myth of psychoanalysis, the myth of Oedipus
Rex, have opened the way for accusations that psychoanalysis
seeks to explain the fate of mankind by reducing it to a few
myths. I hope that my discussion has shown that such accusations are entirely without foundations, when we look at the
Freudian discourse as a whole; I will concede, however, that
these powerful myths exercise such a grip on Freud as well as
on other psychoanalytically oriented theorists that their fictional
character is ignored.[13]

In conclusion, we can argue that the underlying movement of
Freud's individual and cultural discourse is one, from meaning
to process to structure; yet, there is no direct isomorphism
between the two. In developing both discourses, Freud not only
interpreted dreams, symptoms, cultural artifacts, etc., but,
at times, also invented metaphors and myths, consciously or
unconsciously. For instance, he argued that some children were
behaving as if they had been victims of parental seductions,

and that most boys experienced feelings of anxiety, expressed
in dreams, symptoms, etc., as if they had been threatened at
some stage with castration. Likewise, he argued that the whole
human species, in its cultural and social creations, in the
symbols that recur endlessly in personal and social life, and in
ideas through which it seeks comforting and consolation, seems
to be such as might have been if the entire species had been
the victim of ill-treatment by a tyrannical father and subsequently
murdered that father. Freud himself rarely made it clear whether
his hypotheses were to be taken literally or metaphorically. In a
revealing passage from 'Totem and Taboo', he writes:

> No one can have failed to observe . . . that I have taken as
> the basis of my whole position the existence of a collective
> mind, in which mental processes occur just as they do in the
> mind of an individual. In particular, I have supposed that the
> sense of guilt for an action has persisted for many thousands
> of years and has remained operative in generations which have
> no knowledge of that action. I have supposed that an emotional
> process, such as might have developed in generations of sons
> who were ill-treated by their father, has extended to new
> generations which were exempt from such treatment for the
> very reason that the father had been eliminated. (1912-13:8:
> 157-8)

In this extract, the essentialist flavour of the first sentence
(highlighted by the use of the word 'existence') is qualified by
the hypothetical and indeed metaphorical character of subsequent
sentences.

Some of Freud's metaphors were later replaced by theoretical
arguments, while others survived throughout the discourse on a
precarious and ill-defined line of existence. Nevertheless, many
of Freud's metaphors operated as indispensable instruments in
his discussions, until greater clarification in the shape of a
theoretical proposition arrived at a later stage.

One significant area opened by Freud's work which will be
explored in Part II concerns the contribution of psychoanalysis
to an understanding and a possible critique of particular cultures
and more especially our present one. This is a rather undevel-
oped area of Freud's own work which, while differentiating
carefully between alternative courses of individual development,
'behind all the differences among the historical forms of society
saw the basic inhumanity common to all of them' (Marcuse 1955:
235). In talking about the individual, Freud examines in detail
the various neurotic and 'non-neurotic' 'roads towards salvation',
the different possibilities offered by the economics of instinctual
energies, etc., while in talking about societies and cultures he
seems satisfied in analysing the common demands made by all
of them. In his cultural investigations he isolated different types
of neurotic delusions and idealizations, while his cultural discussions address all types of religious illusions and ideals. In

Part II we will mobilize psychoanalytic insights for an analysis
of particular social structures, we will study their illusions,
discontents and consolations and will attempt to judge whether
Freud's diagnosis can still be valid - that underneath cultural
idiosyncrasies looms the same fundamental disease.

Part II

They were predictable people, predictable because they worked for the robot. What the robot said they would also say, what the robot did they would do and what the robot believed was what they believed. . . . There was no *originating passion* in them.

Paul Scott, 'The Raj Quartet'

Introduction

Part I has shown conclusively that Freud's theory is profoundly
social. Although in his early work he seemed to regard society
as a source of external constraints on the sexual and personal
lives of individuals, he later became increasingly concerned with
the question of social cohesion which appeared to him highly
problematic. Unless the civilization succeeds in the task of taming the death instinct, through a re-orientation of the life
instincts, its very survival must come into question. Moreover,
through the concept of the super-ego, Freud overcame the early
dualism of individual and society, and came to regard the individual both as socially constituted and as the bearer of society.
Of course, Freud never succumbed to the opposite temptation of
dissolving the individual in society and attributing the latter an
existence sui generis, whose features and effects have nothing
to do with the properties of the units which constitute it. Both
society and the individual are concepts, and neither can be
taken as an independent given; they stand in constant and
mutual definition through a relationship which involves both
concordance and contradiction. In this way, Freud pursues a
road which is quite distinct from that of liberalism, philosophical
rationalism since Descartes and healthy commonsense, which
move from the point of the individual as something naturally
given, an economic agent, a transcendental subject or the
inhabitant of a visible body. Freud's road is also quite distinct
from that of sociology, which has developed instruments enabling
its practitioners to see societies, groups, organizations, institutions, etc. without seeing individual men, women and children.
For Freud individuals cannot be studied except as social individuals and society cannot be studied except as a society
composed of individuals.

While it is true that Freud's theory is social at all points, it
is also true that Freud did not mobilize his psychoanalytic
insights for a systematic study of particular cultural periods or
particular cultural phenomena. This does not mean that Freud
was uninterested in or uninfluenced by the social events taking
place during his lifetime; on the contrary, he was shocked by
the unprecedented violence released by the First World War and
by the suffering that mankind was capable of inflicting upon
itself; he was very interested in the 'great experiment that is
now [1927] in progress in the vast country that stretches
between Europe and Asia' (1927c:21:9). These as well as other
social phenomena (the persecution of Jews, the gradual decline

of religion, the Young Turks, etc.) not only interested him but exerted a considerable influence on his theories. Yet, there can be little doubt that the underlying logic of Freud's discourse is not historical. To be sure this discourse involves an ambiguous view of history, but his emphasis lies on the conflict between all forms of civilization known to him and the individual, a conflict which assumed different forms but whose aetiology was uniform. Although different cultures may differ in the extent to which they frustrate instinctual forces and in the kinds of gratifications that they permit, they all share the characteristic of manipulating and suppressing human desires and thus creating discontent; likewise, although different cultures may offer different consolatory ideals to individuals, they all generate illusions which ultimately re-inforce the discontents which they purport to mitigate and rationalize. Discontents and illusions are both central social concepts in the Freudian discourse and not incidental ideas; they affect all cultures and define the contours of the human predicament. Yet, as critical concepts, they also underline the distance between 'is' and 'ought to' and emphasize the need for change.

For these reasons, our discussion of the central problematics in Part I did not attempt to offer an interpretation of modern culture or of the cultural movements of the twentieth century. Nor did we study the impact of psychoanalysis itself, its doctrines, therapeutic efforts and general attitude on contemporary culture. Both of these tasks will be undertaken in Part II, in which we will examine the theories of those thinkers whose cultural studies and evaluations were informed by psychoanalytic insights. For this discussion my choice of authors may appear eclectic - there is not a special discussion of some of Freud's outstanding commentators, like Ricoeur, Lacan or Wollheim, since their formulations do not address directly the interpretation and evaluation of culture, while I introduce the work of Ernest Becker, who can hardly be thought of as a Freudian, because his arguments link with the psychoanalytic study of culture.

The first two commentators to be studied are Reich and Fromm, both of whom mobilized psychoanalytic insights, concepts and theories (in forms often distant from Freudian ones) to understand the central social phenomenon that dominated Europe during the 1920s and 1930s before culminating in one of the most horrendous episodes of human history. In spite of the serious theoretical weaknesses of their endeavours, I will argue that their contributions in understanding fascism as a social phenomenon, rather than as a narrow political event, are outstanding. The remaining theorists whose work will be addressed in Part II used psychoanalysis to elucidate the nature of Western societies as they emerged after the Second World War; their studies encompass a wide variety of social and cultural phenomena which are sometimes said to define a 'mass society', a 'post-industrial society' or an advanced capitalist society. The increasing dominance of large-scale bureaucratic organizations (including the mass media and the state), the weakening of traditional religious and political values and social bonds, the advance of a 'welfare state', the social and political movements of the past twenty years, 'consumerism', the crisis of the family, the new orientation towards love, sexuality and interpersonal relations and the increasing popularity of psychoanalysis and other methods of therapeutic treatment are among the phenomena which occupy prominent places in the discussions of these theorists.

All of the theorists whose work will be discussed do not simply describe or interpret social phenomena, but faithful to the spirit of Freud, they constantly broaden their discussions in the direction of social critique; their central pre-occupation, like that of Freud in his social writings, is the articulation and analysis of the discontents and the illusions of twentieth-century man, the causes of these discontents and the factors that prevent human fulfilment and self-understanding. It is not surprising therefore that most of them are inexorably compelled to provide a utopian alternative, a vision of society which has finally superseded the anxieties, oppression, guilt and ignorance of contemporary man. As we shall see in the chapters which follow, most of these theorists pay heavy dues as a result of their utopian tendencies; for in their eagerness to establish the possibility of their utopian ideals, they both underestimate the depth of discontents and their systematic foundations and they also tend to simplify theoretically in ways which reduce the validity of some of their arguments. For these reasons my discussion will be very critical, trying to discern the insights into social phenomena offered by these analyses from some wish-fulfilling speculations.

A very important result of our discussion in Part I is the location of certain crucial contradictions or points of theoretical tension in Freud's discourse. These contradictions are frequently expressed in alternative paradigms which coexist without being strictly compatible within each of the six problematics. We found, for instance, competing paradigms for the concepts of instinct, ego, Eros, normality, neurosis, Logos, therapy and illusion. As we shall see in Part II, most commentators seek to simplify the situation, by opting for some paradigms at the expense of others; this hardly does justice to Freud's discourse, which while perhaps becoming more internally consistent (through these simplifications) loses some of its interpretative and analytic power. In their eagerness to support utopian arguments or merely to establish theoretical consistency, many of these commentators have simply ignored entire areas of psychoanalysis, or have neglected inconvenient analytic facts. In Freud's work, on the other hand, conflicting paradigms were never subjected to forced synthesis, but became the sources of further study, further elucidation and indeed further analysis; they were creative contradictions, which instead of prompt resolution, waited, often for years, for higher levels of theoretical articulation. It is for this reason that all these contradictions and ambiguities must be kept alive rather than concealed and repressed, in the hope that they will be transcended through their constant confrontation with reality.

Chapters 12 and 13 conclude earlier arguments by presenting a novel interpretation of contemporary culture which overcomes some of the difficulties encountered by other authors. As I mentioned earlier, this interpretation is by necessity brief and focuses on a limited number of selected phenomena of which bureaucratization and narcissism are the outstanding ones; although the discussion is more speculative than the rest of this work, I believe that there is considerable support for its general theme, that although our culture has softened the discontents of earlier culture arising from guilt and sexual frustration, it nevertheless generates a new complex of discontents and illusions which, as in previous eras, reinforce each other.

Chapter 8
The first radicalization of Freud: Reich and Fromm, the optimistic utopians

Reich and Fromm belong to the last generation of psychoanalysts
to emerge during Freud's lifetime. In their different ways, they
were both impressed by the new horizons in human self-knowledge
opened by psychoanalysis, and they both mobilized psychoanalytic insights in their interpretations of contemporary social
phenomena, outstanding among which was the rise of fascism,
not only as a political system but as a social phenomenon and a
mass movement. Fascism did not merely shock and horrify Reich
and Fromm – it brought to light new and previously unsuspected
manifestations of the human psyche, new adventures in communal
violence and the emergence of an ideology which combined a novel
glorification of racial and masculine virility with an unqualified
acceptance of an authoritarian ethos. Both Reich and Fromm felt
that psychoanalysis could be brought in to elucidate these
phenomena; but neither stopped at this point, for they both
took very seriously Marx's final thesis on Feuerbach, according
to which philosophers have sought to interpret the world when
the point is to change it. Reich and Fromm sought, therefore,
to stretch psychoanalysis into a strategy for changing the world,
and in the case in hand, into a strategy for combating the rise
of fascism. In so doing, Reich and Fromm undertook two of the
earliest attempts at bridging the gap between Marx and Freud.
In their view, dialectical materialism and psychoanalysis were
ideally suited for each other – the former lacked a psychology,
while the latter lacked a sociology and a politic. Marx's analyses
of economic exploitation and social oppression had failed to
recognize the extent to which these phenomena had shaped and
become entrenched in human souls. Alienation under capitalism
did not stop at feelings of powerlessness, meaninglessness and
lack of fulfilment; nor did alienation merely distort an otherwise
sound consciousness. Alienation totally moulded human beings
into accepting and indeed liking their oppression, it paralysed
all resistances, it dissolved all criticism and it eliminated all
visions and desires pointing to a future of freedom, fulfilment
and happiness. A social revolution could not lead to a genuine
revolutionary emancipation of mankind, as long as it aimed
purely at the destruction and overcoming of capitalist institutions.
Even if successful, such a revolution would leave the deformed
crippled capitalist souls intact, and sooner or later would be
doomed to resurrect the capitalist institutions in new guises with
new rhetorics. It is at this point that both Reich and Fromm
sought to introduce psychoanalysis as the radical complement to

Marxism in understanding the world and drawing a revolutionary programme for changing it.

In order for psychoanalysis to fulfil this role it had to undergo a thorough purge. While both Reich and Fromm were impressed by Freud's clinical theories (in spite of their diametrically different understanding of them), they were troubled by what they saw as Freud's insensitivity towards cultural factors and their effect on the formation of personality, by his resigned acceptance of the inevitability of repression and renunciation, and by his postulation of the death instinct as a feature of man's biological constitution. Contrary to the conclusions reached in Part I of this study, Reich and Fromm believed that Freud had abstracted the individual not only from the interactive context of the family where 'early socialization' takes place, but also from the broader cultural and historical conditions. For these reasons, they criticized Freud's metapsychology (i) for generalizing from a limited range of clinical observations, drawn mostly from middle-class, fin-de-siècle, Viennese neurotics from authoritarian families, and (ii) for allowing his own personality, and especially his well-known pessimism, to influence his arguments.[1] In this way they made it their task to cleanse psychoanalysis from Freud's idiosyncrasies and to provide it with a sociological backbone by linking it with the edifice of historical materialism.

As we saw in Chapter 2, the concept through which both Reich and Fromm try to bridge Marxism and psychoanalysis is that of 'character-structure'. The notion of psychic character had first been used by Abraham and Freud to denote the organization of libido, which is composed of 'instincts that have been fixed since childhood, of constructions achieved by means of sublimation, and of other constructions, employed for effectively holding in check perverse impulses' (1905d:7:238).[2] By contrast, Reich and Fromm use character in a different way, to denote relatively stable patterns of observable behaviour traits, which, in their view, develop out of the process of early socialization.[3] In spite of their very different understanding of the psychological nature of character-structures, both Reich and Fromm see them as the psychical level in which ideologies become embedded; they both agree that because ideologies become engraved in this way in the constitution of individuals, they cannot correspond on a one-to-one basis to the conditions of the 'material basis' of society; the economic conditions prevailing in a social system may change without bringing about an automatic change in the dominant ideologies. Moreover, the transformations and modifications of character-structures follow certain rules of a psychological nature and do not merely echo the laws of historical development. Thus not only do ideas lag behind the developments of social relations, but they enjoy a relative autonomy. It follows that a political revolution cannot succeed in emancipating humanity, unless there is an independent effort to undo and modify pre-revolutionary character-structures.

But why revolution? it may be asked. Apart from their conviction in the revolutionary message of Marx, both men were deeply influenced by Freud's view of the psyche as an arena of painful conflicts, compromises and renunciations; at the same time, they pursued the utopian implications of psychoanalysis (examined in Chapter 6) with far greater fervour than Freud, and argued with unqualified optimism that the restrictive and repressive nature of our society is a historical characteristic, not a theoretical necessity; in their view, all of Freud's statements on the relation between the individual and society are statements of fact, not statements of essence, and they envisaged not only a possibility of harmony between man and man, but also between the individual and society and between the individual and him/herself. Harmony, or at least the potential for harmony, can be seen as the idée fixe of both Reich and Fromm and this may be a strange fixation in thinkers fascinated by Marx and Freud; in order to establish this potential for harmony as an objective possibility, Reich and Fromm devoted extensive parts of their works to showing that there is no ultimate antinomy between individual and society, man and man, culture and nature. In this way, both Reich and Fromm emerge with imageries of human nature capable of fulfilment, pleasure and self-realization through participation in a social whole; this human nature is, at present, concealed behind the oppressive armour of character-structures, which, as we saw, reflect the social relations of oppression and exploitation. Thus, in the work of both of these theorists we have the nucleus of the now fashionable theories of 'authenticity', according to which there exists an unpolluted human core, a noble savage, underneath the oppressive layers of socialization in every individual. In spite of the atrocities that they were witnessing, Fromm and Reich were prepared to argue that human nature is fundamentally noble and altruistic, trying desperately to break through the oppressive shell of character in order to achieve fulfilment through a harmonious coexistence in society. The twin preconditions for this liberation of the human essence are the dissolution of oppressive social relationships and of oppressive character-structures. The former is the task of political revolution, the second is the task of therapy, and note how both tasks are tasks of undoing. It is interesting that both Reich and Fromm gradually shifted their emphasis from the first to the second of these preconditions, and developed therapeutics whose scope and ambition went far beyond those of psychoanalysis.[4]

But if human essence is good, how could Reich and Fromm explain the persistence of the oppressive political structures and character-structures and the suffering to which they led? And how, in the first place, could good human nature have created a cruel, inhumane and oppressive social and psychic world for itself? It is interesting that both writers searched for the answers to these questions in the notion of fear, which they regarded as the lever through which human nature is

repressed, fear of instinct according to Reich and fear of freedom according to Fromm.[5] Moreover, both Reich and Fromm saw
the family as the institution which uses the leverage of fear
during childhood, i.e. when the individual is most dependent
and vulnerable, to repress the child's human nature and to establish within him/her the oppressive forms of social relations
in the shape of oppressive character-structures.

> Parents – unconsciously at the behest of authoritarian, mech-
> anized society – repress the sexuality of infants and ado-
> lescents. Since the children find their way to vital activity
> blocked by ascetism . . . they develop a sticky kind of
> parent fixation characterized by helplessness and guilt
> feelings. This in turn prevents their growing out of the
> infantile situation with all its sexual anxieties and inhibitions.
> Children thus brought up become character-neurotic adults
> and re-create their illness in their own children. And so it
> goes on from generation to generation. In this way, conser-
> vative tradition, a tradition which is afraid of life, is per-
> petuated. (Reich 1968:200)

> The parents . . . transmit to the child what may be called
> the psychological spirit or atmosphere of a society just by
> being as they are – namely representatives of this spirit.
> *The family thus may be considered to be the psychological*
> *agent of society.* (Fromm 1966:314–15)

Reich's and Fromm's view concerning the socializing and tension-
relieving functions of the family as a social agent owes nothing
to Freud's formulations of the traumatic drama of the Oedipal
confrontation – the child carries neither incestuous desires nor
murderous rivalries but is a confused and frightened innocent
who is going to be moulded through the visible interaction which
takes place within the family embrace. Although Reich's and
Fromm's views on early socialization through the family interaction had a considerable influence on later sociologists, they
were stripped of their undeniable pathos which looked at the
child both as the innocent victim of socializing manipulation and
as the innocent fool who carries the promise of redemption without knowing it. It is this doubly dramatic quality which is
undoubtedly lost in later theories of socialization, since for
Reich and Fromm this process involves not merely the induction
of the infant into culture's rules and norms but also into culture's
pathologies. Yet, contrary to the conclusions reached by recent
advocates of 'anti-psychiatry', neither Reich nor Fromm advocated the abolition of the family as a means towards the dissolution
of repressive character-structures; they both insisted that these
functions of the family are historically specific to patriarchal
nuclear families of capitalist societies, and advocated the
matriarchal family as a unit which would promote the individual's
potential instead of instilling authoritarian and renunciatory

traits. Malinowski's anthropological research was a strong influence on both writers, even though the messages they each derived from his encounter with the Trobrianders were quite different.

The similarities in the works of Fromm and Reich are striking; however, they are even more striking when we consider their diametrically opposed psychologies. While they broadly agree on the functions of character, their views of human nature looming underneath the character-structures could not be more different - where Reich discovers a biological human essence glorified in genitality, Fromm discovers a highly symbolic human essence striving for identity, meaning and freedom. While Reich found his paradigm of human happiness and fulfilment in uninhibited orgasms, Fromm found it in free self-realization through creative work and love. Thus the two writers represent opposed trends in the first of the six problematics examined in Part I (body-mind), they represent similar positions in the second, third and fourth problematics (individual-society, therapy and morality), they have limited interest in the fifth (science-philosophy), and although both investigate and extend the utopian potential of psycho-analysis they end up with rather different utopian imageries. In order to assess their views and the plausibility of their common departure from Freud we will now have to look at their general theories separately. Of course, the sections which follow should not be seen as exhaustive studies of the thought of the theorists concerned - there are already dozens of volumes dealing with the thought of Reich alone, its development, peaks and absurdities. My concern here is to highlight the departures of these two thinkers from the Freudian discourse and their relevance for an interpretation of contemporary social and cultural phenomena.

WILHELM REICH

Reich's interest in sexology came before his acquaintance with the work of Freud.[6] What attracted him to Freud's views of sexuality were two interconnected ideas - first, that sexuality goes far beyond procreation and becomes manifested in diverse symptoms, some of which are of a non-sexual character; second, that for Freud, unlike for earlier writers on sex, libido did not mean 'a conscious desire for sexual activity' (1968:51) but was an instinctual energy underlying all the manifestations of sexuality. From these two points, it immediately becomes apparent why the orgasm emerged as Reich's principal preoccupation, a kind of monomania, and why he fundamentally misunderstood the nature of the unconscious, which he saw merely as the reservoir of energy. The orgasm was, in Reich's view, the only healthy and natural way of discharging libidinal energies; while Freud had seen anal eroticism, sublimation in work and art, oral fixations, feelings of 'tender love', identifi-

cations and even narcissism as legitimate and 'normal' manifestations of sexuality, Reich regarded them as profoundly abnormal
manifestations of an inability to derive satisfaction through
genital sexuality. Moreover, he believed that erective and
ejaculatory potential did not coincide with normality, unless it
led to 'full orgastic potency', a concept which is central to his
theory:

> Orgastic potency is the capacity for surrender to the flow of
> biological energy without any inhibition, the capacity for
> complete discharge of all dammed-up sexual excitation through
> involuntary pleasurable contractions of the body. (114)

Failure to achieve orgastic potency meant that the accumulated
libido was not totally released through the sexual climax, thus
making itself available for pathological manifestations, which
stand further in the way of successful release. This is what
Reich defined as neurosis, and insisted that 'not a single neurotic
individual possesses orgastic potency' (ibid.).

Reich saw the libidinal discharge which takes place during the
orgasm as a purely biological phenomenon, centred on the
genital region, and he regarded phantasies both as an indication
of the failure to reach orgastic potency and as an obstacle of
libidinal discharge - at the moment of the orgasm, the world,
including the awareness of one's sexual partner and even of one's
own body, must sink into oblivion, and all attention, all sensa-
tion, all feeling and all experience must be concentrated to the
genital. The orgasm is the moment of truth, the moment to which
everything that went on before has been leading, the moment
that sentences all that has gone on before to oblivion. The orgasm
both justifies and annihilates the foreplay, just as the moment of
truth in the corrida both justifies the teasing game of the
picadors and reveals its hollowness - at the moment of truth, the
arena, the spectators, the music disappear, indeed the man and
the bull disappear, and the whole world is reduced to the experience of death delivered by a sword.

It is in genital sexuality, consummated in uninhibited orgasms,
that Reich discovers the essential goodness in human nature -
everything else is pathological. As we can imagine, Reich's theory
of neurosis owes its origin to Freud's theory of the actual
neuroses, such as neurasthenia, anxiety-neurosis and hypochondria, whose aetiology was linked to the amounts of uncath-
ected libido being converted to anxiety or symptoms. What,
however, distinguishes Reich's view is his constant insistence
that the only avenue for full sexual gratification and complete
discharge is monogamous, heterosexual intercourse. By shifting
attention from transference neuroses to the actual neuroses,
renaming them stasis neuroses, and ultimately dissolving all
neurotic conditions to this category, Reich did not merely emphasize the economic factor in the aetiology of neuroses, but in
fact loses sight of psychic conflict altogether. Neurosis repre-

sents an irregularity in libidinal economics which manifests itself
in the form of a moral inhibition, whose function is obscure and
unnecessary. It is not altogether surprising, therefore, that
Reich gradually abandoned psychoanalysis for bio-energetics,
concentrating exclusively on the economic mechanisms of neurosis
- repression, anxiety, inhibition, symptoms gradually recede in
his analysis. The unconscious becomes merely the reservoir of
biological energy, the virgin human core in which unpolluted
genitality resides.[7]
   Reich's pre-occupation with sexual economics has two consequences, a negative and a positive one. The negative one is the
enormous and often naive simplification of large areas of Freud's
thought, especially in what concerns psychic conflict, processes
involving phantasies and polymorphous perversity, the relation
between symptoms and inhibition. For these failures Reich has
been criticized ad nauseam, and it is not my intention to re-
iterate these criticisms, which should be obvious to most readers
of his work.[8] The question now arises of how Reich, having bulldozed the subtleties of Freud's mental dynamics, can account for
neurosis and the failure of orgastic potency. Reich's answer lies,
of course, in his theory of character-structure, and it is in his
tentative and incomplete attempt to relate oppressive psychic
structures to exploitative social relations that the positive consequence of his pre-occupation with sexual economics lies. His
theory of character-structure not only earned him a considerable
reputation among psychoanalysts but is still part of Neo-Freudian
orthodoxy.[9]
   Reich was led to his theory of character by the observation
that his patients' resistances seemed to be organized around
specific traits, which they found particularly hard to overcome.
He observed a considerable range of such traits, including
politeness, orderliness, muscular contractions and rigidities,
nervous twitches. Unlike Freud and others who had seen such
behavioural traits as symptomatic of certain organizations and
sublimations of libido (what Freud understood by the term
'character'), Reich reached the conclusion that they co-incided
with the resistance themselves. The sum-total of a person's
character traits formed a protective armour around the person,
an armour which prevented him, among other things, from reaching orgastic potency. The aim of Reich's therapy was, therefore,
to confront the patient's armour in a head-on collision, undo the
character-traits which make it up, and make their energy
available for orgastic discharge. In this way, in 'Character
Analysis', Reich challenged the central Freudian doctrine in
psychotherapy, that confronting the symptoms directly does not
lead to the lifting of the resistances, nor to the dissolution of
the repressions, but, at best, may replace old symptoms with
new (more innocuous) ones. Reich argued that repression is
nothing but the channelling of genitality to character resistances
which inhibit genital fulfilment, and if these resistances could
be broken down then the neurotic condition was automatically

lifted. It can be seen quite clearly, I think, that the question of
what function was fulfilled by the character-armour within the
context of the individual did not bother Reich, and he never
sought to explain what this armour was intended to protect the
individual from. As far as he was concerned, this armour was
a quite redundant structure (talking always from the point of
view of the individual) which could be removed through appropriate therapeutic manipulation. Freud's critique may almost
have been addressed at Reich personally:

> The expectation that every neurotic phenomenon can be cured
> may, I suspect, be derived from the layman's belief that the
> neuroses are something quite unnecessary which have no right
> whatever to exist. (1933a:22:153)

While this is a cardinal omission in Reich's theory and it led
him to a naive optimism concerning the potential of psychotherapy, it had a rather fortunate theoretical consequence. While
character-structures were regarded as quite redundant in terms
of the individual, Reich insisted that they were central for the
existence and reproduction of a social system based on exploitative and authoritarian relationships. The character-structures,
so to speak, were both the outcomes of exploitative and authoritarian social relationships and, at the same time, they re-
inforced and cemented these relationships, by engraving them in
the individuals' psychological make-ups and reproducing them
intergenerationally. This was perhaps Reich's supreme and
undeniably genial discovery: the authoritarian, exploitative
and exploited individual is the sexually frustrated individual,
and vice versa. The meaning Reich attached to sexual frustration
was too narrow in its attachment to genitality, but otherwise his
discovery was of supreme importance, and it remains supremely
important today long after the 'decline' of fascism.
It is by becoming engraved in character-structures that
ideologies become, in Reich's view, material forces, insofar as
they inhibit the natural flow of biological energies towards discharge, and re-channel them along socially expedient but
pathological paths. It is unclear whether Reich envisaged any
ideology capable of promoting sexual fulfilment and social
emancipation, but almost invariably he referred to them, as well
as to phantasies and, eventually, all symbolic functions, as
obstacles to sexual discharge. It is in this way that the whole
symbolic edifice of society, what one feels tempted to call
'culture', becomes a material force opposing what is good in man
- his capacity for uninhibited sexual enjoyment. 'Sexual inhibition changes the structure of economically suppressed man in
such a way that he acts, feels, and thinks contrary to his own
material interests' (1970:66).
Reich saw the family as the principal agent of suppression of
the child's 'vital life-impulses'; yet, he did not think that all
forms of family carried out this brutal function, which was a

'relatively late' development associated with the rise of 'authoritarian patriarchy'. Nor did Reich think that the family suppressed the child's sexuality in its own interests, for he was firmly convinced that the authoritarian-patriarchal family was an agent of the capitalist economic system. In what way, then, did Reich see the suppression of sexuality as functional to capitalism? The suppression of the child's natural sexual impulses

> makes the child afraid, shy, fearful of authority, obedient, 'good', and 'docile' in the authoritarian sense of the words. It has a crippling effect on man's rebellious forces because every vital life-impulse is now burdened with severe fear; and since sex is a forbidden subject, thought in general and man's critical faculty also become inhibited. In short, morality's aim is to produce acquiescent subjects who, despite distress and humiliation, are adjusted to the authoritarian order. Thus, the family is the authoritarian state in miniature, to which the child must learn to adapt himself as a preparation for the general social adjustment required of him later. *Man's authoritarian structure* - this must clearly be established - *is basically produced by the embedding of sexual inhibitions and fear in the living substance of sexual impulses.* (1970:64)

In this outstanding passage, Reich demonstrates the enormous critical potential of Freud's concept of the super-ego as the psychic basis of fascistic and authoritarian individuals, in a way which could not have displeased Freud himself. Where Reich goes beyond Freud is in that his critique of bourgeois morality is linked to the social requirements of authoritarian cultures - once again, an extension that Freud, no great admirer of the super-ego himself, would not have disapproved of.[10] But Reich's extension of his argument did displease Freud: if authoritarian traits and their expression in aggressive, insecure, submissive, uncritical, rigid and sadistic behaviour are instilled in the earliest years of childhood by the patriarchal family in the interest of the capitalist system of social and economic oppression, the postulation of a primary death instinct becomes unfounded and redundant. For these reasons, Reich rejected Freud's argument that aggression in its diverse manifestations has an instinctual basis - for Reich, it is the outcome of the suppression of sexuality by family and civilization. The death instinct is a historical phenomenon with no foundation in the biological constitution of human beings - this, as we saw earlier, contains nothing but genitality. It was this disagreement over the death instinct that precipitated Reich's split from Freud.

Reich's optimism, expressed in his conviction that human nature is 'biologically' good, may appear paradoxical given that Reich was developing his theories during the years of the rise of fascism in Europe - he personally suffered great persecution, before he finally was forced to settle in the United States. Yet,

it is precisely in his studies of fascism that he showed his
brilliance as a practical thinker of concrete social situations. In
'The Mass Psychology of Fascism' (still one of the best works on
the subject), he demonstrated how authoritarian character-
structures are mass-produced by the families of intermediate and
displaced social classes; the father's economic insecurities, being
trapped between the ideologies of big business and a class-
conscious proletariat, result in an 'identification with state
power' (1970:80), as embodied in the Fuehrer, and replicate
this relation within his own family. He becomes a little Fuehrer,
expecting obedience, respect and admiration. It is in this way
that the family, by suppressing genitality, provides the psychic
infra-structure of the fascist movement, reproduces authoritarian
ideologies and prepares individuals for unquestioning submission
to authority, even if this implies the execution of atrocious
acts.

Reich's discussion of fascism tries to establish fascism as a
political movement with mass support and not as a mere political
manoeuvre of the ruling class. Nor did fascism represent merely
'false consciousness' - its success was due to its emotional appeal
to the masses and its ability to establish itself on a massive re-
orientation of instinctual energies; this was something that most
of Reich's contemporary Marxists, with their mechanistic theories
of fascism, refused to accept, thus being taken by one surprise
after another. At the same time, Reich's analysis of fascism
sought to deny any connection between authoritarian violence
and any innate instinct of destruction; the fuel for fascism was
seen as suppressed genitality alone. These arguments tend to
support a view which has frequently been expressed apropos of
Reich - that he gradually moved to a Manichean position, according to which everything related to the id, the instincts, the
body and biology was good and everything related to the ego,
the character, the mind and sociology/psychology was bad. And
yet, Reich's Manicheism seems to lack the vital ingredient, the
struggle between good and evil, and it is here that the crucial
weakness in his argument lies. In his eagerness to demonstrate
the non-instinctual character of aggression and the possibility
of harmony within the individual and between the individual and
society, Reich falls victim to his own harmonistic views, for he
was left without a vehicle for social change. In order to prove
that sexual repression serves capitalist society and especially
fascism rather than that it is inherent to all societies (Freud),
in order to establish the possibility of sexual fulfilment in
society as an objective possibility, Reich developed such neat
and convincing correlations between psychological and ideological
structures that he emerged with a picture of complete socio-
psychological integration, the only tension coming from biology.
It was the ironic predicament of the first theorist bold enough
to attempt to synthesize Marx and Freud that he should end up
without the one common ingredient of the two original theories,
conflict; he thus emerged with a Marxism without politics and

a psychology without psyche.

In Reich's Manichean world, the evil has already gained total supremacy, and it is left to the activist visionary spirits of Marx and Freud to remind us of the old adversary. It is equally ironic that Reich's theory, starting from an optimistic view of human nature as libido, leads to a far more hopeless conclusion than Freud's far darker and dualistic view of human nature. It is truly remarkable that in spite of these implications of his theories and in spite of the vicious persecution which he faced throughout his life Reich retained both his optimistic attitude towards human nature and his fighting spirit.

Both his optimism and his fighting spirit must have been motivated by a belief that in his theory of the orgasm he had discovered, at last, the long-awaited solution to the problem of human suffering. His zeal was quite literally a missionary zeal, for he was preaching not merely to a world of unenlightened, but to a world content in its alienation. Had it not been for this brilliant insight, that the sexually repressed fascist may actually enjoy his alienation, I would have suggested that the twentieth century is unlikely to produce an intellectual Quixote quite like Reich – his nobility of feeling and extraordinary flashes of genius were only matched by his disarming inability to justify his own position in the world.

ERICH FROMM

Like Reich, Erich Fromm was in the first place impressed by what he saw as Freud's discovery of a hidden self.

> *Freud* discovered a new method which enabled him to study
> the total personality and to understand what makes man act
> as he does. This method, the analysis of free associations,
> dreams, errors, transference, is an approach by which hither-
> to 'private' data, open to self-knowledge and introspection,
> are made 'public' and demonstrable in the communication
> between subject and analyst. The psychoanalytic method has
> gained access to phenomena which do not otherwise lend
> themselves to observation. At the same time it uncovered
> many emotional experiences which could not be recognized
> even by introspection because they were repressed, divorced
> from consciousness. (1947:40-1)

While, however, Reich believed that Freud's method had revealed man as a sensuous being frustrated by cultural forces, Fromm rejected out of hand Freud's theories of instincts, which he regarded as a remnant of nineteenth-century biologism.[11] The image of man that Fromm receives from Freud's interpretative method is that of an irrational, confused, emotional being deeply frustrated by his present conditions of social existence; yet, the needs which are presently frustrated have little to do with the

desires that arise from Freud's theory of instincts and are more
reminiscent of Mayo's 'social man'. In place of the Freudian theory
of instinctual vicissitudes, Fromm, at the outset of his work,
postulates three a priori inter-related needs: self-preservation,
work and sociability (1966:32ff). Given Freud's extreme caution
and his painstaking research into instinctual theory, Fromm's
way of establishing these primary needs on a quasi-existential
basis appears positively flimsy, and involves no discussion of
clinical data whatever. Having shifted the motivational parameters
to this quasi-existential basis, Fromm establishes what he regards
as the main problem in psychology, the problem of 'relatedness'
between the individual and his/her world as they historically
develop, and proposes that

> man, the more he gains freedom in the sense of emerging from
> the original oneness with man and nature and the more he
> becomes an 'individual', has no choice but to unite himself with
> the world in the spontaneous activities of love and productive
> work or also seek a kind of security by such ties with the
> world as destroy his freedom and the integrity of his individual
> self. (37)

In shifting psychoanalysis in this direction, Fromm was not only
influenced by the theories of Horney and Sullivan, but also by
Marx's newly-discovered early theory of alienation and Weber's
account of the Protestant ethic; at a deeper level, he was
influenced by the attempts of his colleagues of the Frankfurt
School to provide an explanation for the phenomenon of Nazism,
its terror and authoritarianism as well as its frightening appeal
to the masses.

Like Reich (and probably influenced by Reich's work on
fascism), Fromm developed a theory of character to account for
the archetypical fascist traits. But unlike Reich, Fromm did not
regard the authoritarian character-structure as the product of
sexual frustration (since he rejected sexuality as a primary
motivational principle), but as the result of an existential fear
- a fear of transcending the negative condition of freedom from
the bonds and constraints of primitive unindividuated life
through the positive freedom to engage in the spontaneous
activities of love and productive work. Having emerged as an
individual free from the constraints of nature and of overbearing
collectivist culture, the individual must seek to infuse his/her
life with meaning and to develop his/her creative energies in a
free relationship with other individuals. This, in Fromm's view,
is a fearful prospect, and failure to rise to the challenge leads
to a deep sense of aloneness and anxiety. The next step is for
the individual to take recourse in one of the escape mechanisms,
seeking consolation and comfort (155). The premium is heavy:
the individual has lost his/her freedom. Enter character.

Fromm identifies three mechanisms of escape: authoritarianism
(sadism and masochism), destructiveness and automaton conform-

ity. These along with love constitute Fromm's four orientations towards socialization, which is one of the two aspects of the original problem, the relationship between individual and society (relatedness).[12] The authoritarian character corresponds to the individual whose escape from freedom is achieved through sado-masochistic relations with his fellow humans, although it may also comprise traits from the other two escape mechanisms, destructiveness and automaton conformity. Thus, like Reich, Fromm approaches character as a representative of visible patterns of behaviour, through which men and women interact with the world. But while Reich sees character (and especially authoritarian character) as the product of sexual repression (not only through childhood but during the entire life of an individual) based upon fear of the instincts, Fromm regards character as the product of an escape from freedom necessitated by the individual's inability to cope with his existential condition.

Fromm elaborated this theme in 'Man for Himself', in which he distinguished between historical and existential dichotomies. The former can be overcome through courage and knowledge, even though those who benefit from them will seek to present them as an inherent part of the human condition. Existential dichotomies, on the other hand, are parts of the human condition and cannot be avoided - death and the necessity of living in the historical era in which one is born are such dichotomies.

Reading Fromm's postulation of the existential needs, we are once again struck by the total absence of empirical and clinical date and the rather superficial nature of his theoretical discussion. Just as the fixed needs were introduced in 'Escape from Freedom', the existential dichotomies are invoked on an almost ad hoc basis; it is never quite clear in Fromm's work why needs like self-preservation, work and sociability, and constraints like death and the historical period in which each individual happens to be born, are part of human nature and human condition. Moreover, it is not quite clear why these needs, even assuming that they exist, have a primary character. Freud, for instance, had argued that there is no primary self-preservation instinct but that a need for survival may arise out of the complex vicissitudes of sexuality; likewise, individualist philosophers since Hobbes had sought to demonstrate that sociability is not a 'natural' characteristic of mankind; nor should work be seen as a primary need or as a derivative of the need to live, for, even if such need existed, it could equally be satisfied by the subordination and work of other human beings - no ancient Greek philosopher ever even considered work as a worthy activity for a free individual. Similar questions can be raised against Fromm's postulation of existential constraints like death or one's social environment; death, for instance, is only experienced as a constraint when individuals develop a fear of death during their lifetime. It is possible, for example, to argue that the fear of death is simply the product of a life deprived of fulfilment and satisfaction; as Brown has suggested:

> Anxiety about death does not have an ontological status, as
> existentialist theologicians claim. It has a historical status
> only, and is relative to the repression of the human body; the
> horror of death is the horror of dying with what Rilke called
> unlived lives in our bodies. (1959:108)[13]

Now, one need not necessarily agree with Brown's account of
how death comes to be experienced as a terrifying constraint
(and Wagner's ecstatic vision of the Liebestod suggests precisely
the opposite - death as the final transcendence of unlived lives).
Nor does one have to agree with the individualist philosophers'
arguments that man is not naturally sociable, or with Freud's
(and Nietzsche's) arguments that there are many things dearer
to life than life itself. Yet, all these arguments raise serious
doubts about Fromm's existential needs and dichotomies, postulated in the brief space of a dozen pages or so of 'Man for Himself' (47-58), in which Freud's meticulous investigations into
instinctual vicissitudes are dismissed.

On the basis of his speculations on the existential condition of
man, Fromm develops an imagery of man's essential nature, just
as Reich had developed an equivalent imagery through his theory
of the orgasm. And just like Reich, Fromm sought to use this
imagery to fill what he saw as the 'missing link' in Marxism. In
Jay's words:

> [Fromm] argued that Marx's psychological premises were few -
> fewer than Fromm was later to assert himself. Man to Marx
> has certain basic drives (hunger, love, and so forth), which
> seek gratification; acquisitiveness was merely a product of
> specific social conditions. Marxism was, however, in need of
> additional psychological insights, which such Marxists as
> Kautsky and Bernstein, with their naive, idealistic belief in
> inborn moral instincts, had failed to provide. Psychoanalysis
> could provide the missing link between ideological super-
> structure and socio-economic base. In short, it could flesh
> out materialism's notion of man's essential nature. (1973:92)

Now Reich's image of 'man's essential nature', based on the
theory of the orgasm, may not have provided the missing link
satisfactorily, but it was certainly rooted in one tradition of
psychoanalysis; the same cannot be said of Fromm's image,
which shares more common features with the theological traditions
referred to by Brown, than with Freud's. All that Fromm's
theory seems to have in common with Freud's is the view that
the individual is deeply frustrated and fails to realize his/her
potential.

It is now quite instructive to turn to Fromm's precise image
of human nature in greater detail, for his persistent use of
this term - in a period when Marxists and Freudians alike, with
the single exception of Reich, rejected it out of hand - singles
him out.[14] Perhaps the most compelling feature of his image of

human nature as far as Marxists were concerned was his emphasis
on man as a social animal; after all, it was Marx himself who had
said that 'man is in the most literal sense of the word a zoon
politicon, not only a social animal, but an animal which develops
into an individual only in society' (1904:268). Although Marx
refrains from using the word 'nature' in this passage, the relevant passage of his source is liberally sprinkled with the word:

> what each thing is when fully developed, we call its nature,
> whether we are speaking of a man, a horse or a family.
> Besides, the final cause and end of a thing is the best, and
> to be self-sufficing is the end and the best. Hence it is evident
> that the state is a creation of nature, and that man is by nature
> a political animal. . . . The proof that the state is a creation
> of nature and prior to the individual is that the individual,
> when isolated, is not self-sufficing; and therefore he is like
> a part in relation to the whole. But he who is unable to live
> in society, or who has no need because he is sufficient for
> himself, must be either a beast or a god: he is no part of a
> state. A social instinct is implanted in all men by nature.
> ('Ethnics', Book 1, Ch. 2)

Aristotle's characteristically dynamic (and teleological) use of
the concept of nature may be thought of as providing the basis
for Fromm's conceptualization (and perhaps Marx's?). Jay, for
instance, has argued that 'at all times Fromm affirmed the reality
of human nature. It was, however, not a fixed concept like the
Roman *natura*, but rather an idea of man's potential nature
similar to the Greek *physis*' (1973:89). Now, it is quite true that
Fromm's diverse needs have a transcendental character - work
unleashes new and unsuspected creative energies and creates
new and unsuspected needs, love affords new and unsuspected
emotional and sensuous experiences, sociability reveals new and
unsuspected ways of realizing one's potential through participation in a social group. It is for such reasons that Fromm consistently refers to life as an art, since art is par excellence the
human activity which brings out new potentials, unknown to the
artist before he/she embarked on a creative project. Yet, this
potential is a fixed potential in Fromm's formulations; this is not
the case either for Marx or for Aristotle, both of whom realized
the inaccessibility of the realm of freedom, the realm of the
unmoved mover or the transcending subject, to the powers of
our sciences. Not so for Fromm - just as Reich articulated his
utopian vision in the 'science' of bio-energetics, Fromm articulated his utopian vision in his 'humanistic ethics: the applied
science of the art of living'. This rather tenuous concept reveals
a central ambiguity in Fromm's thought, which arises from the
fact that he both wishes to see life as a transcendental process,
as an art, and at the same time to articulate the norms of this
art as a science, i.e. he wishes to see life both as the application
of a scientific system of ethical norms and as a transcendental

art form. This contradiction is, I think, irreconcilable since art, after all, constantly transcends the stylistic criteria of aestheticians and discovers new and unsuspected forms of beauty; looking at life as an art, when he seeks to define moral behaviour scientifically, Fromm is doing as much injustice to life as he does to art.

The contradiction in Fromm's conceptualization of human nature and human life is not accidental, but seems to stem from his efforts to remain both a social critic and a psychotherapist. As a social critic he held a transcendental view of mankind, striving collectively to realize an unknown potential; yet, as a psychotherapist, he was concerned with the concrete problems, anxieties and delusions of individuals, and ended up by seeing neurotic conditions as indicative of 'moral failure' (1947:v). I understand this to mean that the neurotic's suffering is the result of his having made an incorrect 'value judgment' or having failed to resolve a 'moral problem', through ignorance of the good life. Fromm's humanistic ethics aim at enabling the neurotic to correct his error by providing him with 'scientific' information of the good life. Contrary to Freud, Fromm believes that he can conclusively cure neurosis by educating the patient, by helping him understand his moral problem and solve it in accordance with the knowledge he has received. But is the solution of the neurotic's problem possible and if so how can the solution be assessed? Of course, one way of assessing the solution would be to see whether it has enabled the patient to re-adjust himself successfully in society, and lead a 'normal' life. Yet, Fromm explicitly denounces adjustment as a criterion of therapeutic success - adjustment may signify nothing more than what he had defined as 'automaton conformity' (1966:208ff), an orientation which is motivated by fear of freedom not by striving towards freedom.

But if mental health (and ipso facto moral virtue) is not equivalent to adjustment, it can only correspond to the realization of man's thwarted potential, which Fromm has identified rightly or wrongly with spontaneous activities, such as love, productive work and play; and it is here, of course, that the contradiction re-appears, for Fromm (like Reich), speaking as a therapist, envisages the possibility of individual self-realization within the present social context; speaking as a social critic he insists that the present civilization thwarts human potential and that only collectively can mankind transcend its present condition of alienation; as a therapist he looks at human suffering not as an integral part of the social system, but as the result of individual moral failure (and ignorance). As a social critic he indicts present society for permitting precious few avenues for self-realization; as a therapist he expresses surprise at how many people are healthy. What he does not seem to realize is that the meaning of the word 'healthy' changes every time he changes hats.

Fromm the therapist:

It might seem that the psychoanalyst, who is in the position
of observing the tenacity and stubbornness of irrational
strivings, would take a pessimistic view with regard to man's
ability to govern himself and to free himself from the bondage
of irrational passions. I must confess that during my analytic
work I have become increasingly impressed by the opposite
phenomenon: by the strength of the strivings for happiness
and health, which are part of the natural equipment of man.
'Curing' means removing the obstacles which prevent them
from becoming effective. Indeed there is less reason to be
puzzled by the fact that there are so many neurotic people
than by the phenomenon that most people are relatively healthy
in spite of the many adverse influences they are exposed to.
(1947:vii)

And Fromm the social critic:

I have always upheld the same point that man's capacity for
freedom, love etc., depends almost entirely on the given
socio-economic conditions, and that only exceptionally can
we find, . . . that there is love in a society whose principle
is the very opposite. (Quoted in Jay 1973:100, from personal
communication)

Fromm, unlike Reich, never retracted on his belief that the
realization of human potential requires a radical re-organization
of the social and economic system; yet, like Reich, his therapeutic endeavours led him to a rather optimistic position concerning the possibilities of health within this system. His confidence
in his therapeutic cures, like Reich's confidence in his contrasts
sharply with Freud's persistent reservations concerning the
therapeutic potential of psychoanalysis, even though the therapeutic goals that both Reich and Fromm set for themselves were
far more ambitious than Freud's. There can be little doubt that
both as a social critic and as a therapist Fromm underestimated
society's coercive influence on the individual by overemphasizing
social control through internalized structures. He thus failed to
see that society will punish spontaneous activity because such
activity poses a threat to the principle of cohesion of a society
based on a bureaucratic ethos of blind obedience to impersonal
rules, just as uninhibited orgasms pose a threat to a society
based on sexual renunciation.[15] The punishment usually takes the
form of isolation, either direct (in mental asylums and prisons)
or indirect. Eccentricity may be encouraged only insofar as it
does not threaten the reality principle - the long tradition of
British eccentricity may show that the exceptions do occasionally
re-inforce the rule; yet, when eccentricity threatens the reality
principle, the social bond or conventional 'rationality', by refusing to accept itself as eccentricity, it is classified as psychosis.
This important insight, which we find in embryo in Freud's works
on 'the distortion of the sense of reality', was developed by the

Frankfurt School and eventually provided the foundation stone
of R.D. Laing's 'anti-psychiatry' - yet, it seems to have
escaped Fromm. By identifying mental health with rationality,
he fails to see that a society based on the blocking of self-
realization, and which establishes this blockage as its reality
principle, will consider 'strivings for health and self-realization'
as deeply irrational, even if they are propelled by the 'sciences'
of Fromm's humanistic ethics or Reich's bio-energetics.

CONCLUSIONS

This brief review of the works of Reich and Fromm has revealed
extensive similarities in practically every aspect of their theories,
with the important exception of the psychologies. In postulating
what I referred to as a 'personality core', they each moved in
opposite directions from Freud, setting out the two extreme positions of the body-mind problematic. Reich and Fromm probed
underneath what they saw as a character-structure; Reich discovered a sensuous being, dominated by biological forces,
striving towards bodily pleasure through sexual discharge,
while Fromm discovered a deeply symbolic being, in constant
pursuit of meaning, identity and freedom. While Reich reduced
Freud's complex unity of 'psycho-sexuality' (1910k:11) to a
simple unity of undifferentiated genitality, Fromm saw sexuality
as an animal instinct not worthy of the human individual (1966:
48), and substituted it with a complex of a priori existential
strivings and constraints which motivate life. Yet, there are
considerable similarities, even in their psychologies. They both
rejected the death instinct, which they sought to reduce to
some variant of the frustration/aggression automatism.[16] They
both interpreted the period of early socialization in terms of
actual, visible interpersonal relations between the parents and
the child, involving actual threats, punishments, rewards, etc.,
while minimizing the importance of phantasies, desires and primary processes. By focusing on character and by developing
theories of 'personality', both Reich and Fromm stressed the
essential unity of the human psyche, contrary to Freud's
emphasis on the different mental institutions and their diverse
interests, conflicts and compromises. Freud had explicitly criticized the view of the individual as personality in a letter to
Abraham:

> Personality . . . is a loosely defined term from surface psy-
> chology that does nothing in particular to increase under-
> standing of the real processes, that is to say, metapsycho-
> logically it says nothing. But it is easy to believe that one is
> saying something meaningful in using it. (Quoted in Jacoby
> 1975:30-1)

Freud had looked at the ego's sense of self as an illusion, an

imago, a mirage; the ego, caught among numerous pressures
and subject to endless determinations, imagines itself to be all-
powerful and free; it imagines itself to be a transcendental
subject. In reality, the ego is torn and fragmented; its constitution involves a social component as well as a biological one,
a conscious component as well as an unconscious one, a narcissistic component as well as an altruistic one, a libidinal component
as well as a destructive one.

In contrast to Freud's fragmented view of the individual,
Reich's and Fromm's theories of character entail a view of the
individual over-integrated in his/her alienation, just as their
imageries of a personality core entail a view of the individual
over-integrated in his/her freedom. The same harmonistic perspective characterizes Reich's and Fromm's views on the relationship between the individual and society, in that they underplay
the depth and strength of present conflicts. Having discarded
the possibility of instinctual antinomy within the individual, they
both envisage a utopian society within reach of the present
civilization. While they both insist (though they often seem to
forget) that this society requires radical re-organization, they
remain optimistic, for in spite of their different understanding
of the way in which character emerges, they both regard
character as part of the psychic superstructure - human emancipation requires only a revolution in the social base and superstructure and in the psychic superstructure, it need not touch
the psychic base. Indeed, it is the psychic base, the essential
goodness in human nature, that stages the revolution against the
oppressive orders imposed from above (psychic superstructure)
and from outside (the social system). For Reich and Fromm, the
psychic base is not part of society; it is its victim and needs to
become its master.

It is quite ironic that Reich and Fromm, who criticized Freud
for not paying enough attention to the 'social factor', end up by
discovering a human core in each individual, which is totally
unpolluted by society; human nature is discovered in the profound depths of the individual's soul which are untouched by
society (in spite of Fromm's 'existential' argument that man is a
'social animal'). This is something that Freud in his later work
never does; nor does Freud have, properly speaking, an image
of human nature as an underlying constant looming behind all
his writings - his theory can account for kindness as well as
for aggression, for strivings after meaning as well as for
strivings after bodily pleasure, for egoism as well as for altruism,
for 'normal' as well as for 'abnormal' sexuality, etc., without
recourse to an invariant human nature. It is not accidental that
in a period when the concept of human nature has become deeply
suspect, Fromm and Reich have been among its most vigorous
defendants, using it quite liberally in their writings. They
defend it epistemologically as a valid scientific concept, and
morally as a deeply good entity. For Reich, the human nature's
goodness is located in biology; his is a religion of energy. For

Fromm, it is located in the inexorable capacity to engage in the
spontaneous activities of love and creative work and to strive
towards health and self-realization; his religion is humanistic
virtue.

Even at the peak of Nazi 'hysteria', both men were determined
to argue that the pathology of mankind is limited to the superstructure of the psyche, to a sick character-structure. Underneath it, there exists in every individual and at all times the
potential and objective possibility of health, freedom and
happiness. Happiness is, if not at hand, just around the corner.
It is not accidental that having discovered the goodness of human
nature in the individual, they proceed to develop utopias based
on the model of the analyst – analysand relationship. Human
emancipation is a recapitulation of the patient's cure through
therapy, it is a therapeutic emancipation writ large. Harmony
among orgastically potent individuals (for Reich) or among
spontaneously creative individuals (for Fromm) is taken for
granted at every stage; therapy (which both Fromm and Reich
fail to explain as a historical force) becomes the real revolutionary
agent in history.

Reich's and Fromm's harmonistic pre-occupations were not
limited to their view of the individual and his/her relationship to
society; they extended to their approaches towards theory.
They both accomplished the uncomfortable marriage of Freud and
Marx at the level of psychic and social superstructures. At this
level, they discovered an interpenetration of the ideological and
psychic structures of oppression – an interpenetration which
allowed for a certain degree of autonomy. Yet, the relation
between the social base and psychic base remains obscure in
their work, or, to be exact, is dissolved. Psyche and society, at
the level of their bases, remain unrelated and independent, each
sui generis. It is by keeping these two entities separate that
both Reich and Fromm tried to reconcile their twin roles as
psychotherapists dealing with the sickness of the individual and
as social critics dealing with the sickness of society. By keeping
the sicknesses separate, they underestimated the depth and
pervasiveness of them both, and hoped that there were direct
cures for both of them, in a way which would have shocked not
only Freud, but Marx himself.

Chapter 9
The discovery of the radical Freud:
Marcuse and Brown, the pessimistic utopians

The two thinkers I will discuss in this chapter differ in
this way from Reich and Fromm: they take seriously Freud's
idea that harmony between the individual and society is deeply
problematic and, certainly, not a simple matter of undoing
social and psychic superstructures. Like Freud, they believe
that the individual and society cannot be treated as independent
entities having a single common interface. They constantly
define each other at every analytical level, in a multi-faceted
relationship which involves both concordance and contradiction.
Moreover, like Freud, Marcuse and Brown believe that both
the individual and society are deeply sick without there being
an obvious solution in sight.

It comes as no surprise that both men moved towards Freud's
work as their personal pessimism about the possibility of a cure
for the human disease grew. Marcuse's and Brown's pessimism
did not evolve in response to fascism, nor did they identify the
human disease in terms of the contorted inhumanity of authoritarian personalities. Instead, they were deeply disturbed by
the total quiescence of the masses in the industrialized countries
of the 1950s, the apparent ability of the ruling class to buy
worker militancy off by offering higher material standards of
living, the increasing invisibility of power relations within
corporate structures and the accompanying paralysis of social
criticism in favour of a monopoly of technocratic reason, the
ease with which the mass media seemed to generate artificial
needs and induce political apathy, and the cynical inhumanity
with which capitalism seemed to exploit the Third World both at
home and abroad. The privatized manipulated world of suburbia
in its blissful coexistence with the big bureaucratic and military
machines which were deciding the fate of humanity seemed to
herald for Marcuse and Brown the arrival of a new era of alienation, whose parameters had already been sketched in 'Brave
New World' and '1984'. What is paradoxical perhaps is that,
although Brown and Marcuse were led to Freud by their pessimism
about the future of humanity, they each emerged with a utopian
vision of the future. Although these utopias hardly mitigated
their pessimism, they seemed to point at the possibility of a 'way
out' of the apparently unstoppable path towards mankind's self-
destruction.

Unlike Reich and Fromm, Marcuse and Brown see the sickness
of mankind as reaching deeper than the psychic superstructure
- they see it as having become part of the psychic base, part of

'human nature' itself. Consciousness is systematically distorted, needs are systematically manipulated, criticism is systematically thwarted; but, on top of all that, people have lost all power of imagining a better and indeed a different future, and are happy in their present state of alienation. So, the utopias offered by Marcuse and Brown cannot be seen as advocating the removal of an infected organ or a tumour, for the entire individual and his/her social and psychological worlds are infected. A change of political system or economic relations, a 'new attitude' towards life or a revolution in 'consciousness', is unlikely to cure the sick individual or the sick civilization; what is required is a new 'human nature', a new psyche, a new civilization:

> This qualitative change must occur in the needs, in the infrastructure of man (itself a dimension of the infrastructure of society): the new direction, the new institutions and relations of production, must express the ascent of needs and satisfactions very different from and even antagonistic to those prevalent in exploitative societies. (Marcuse 1969:14)

The two utopias developed by Marcuse and Brown do, in fact, involve a new vision of the individual, a new vision of society and a new vision of the relationship between individual and society. But, it will be asked, what are the claims to validity that these visions have, what is their meaning? How can pessimism be made compatible with utopia? How can the gloom of the end of humanity which constantly hangs over the work of these writers, a gloom as pervasive as the mushrooming silence of Hiroshima, become the motive force towards conceptualizing a new human nature? And how can psychoanalysis with its insistence that the present is not pregnant with the future (there is no Aristotelian teleology in Freud), but irredeemably burdened by the past,[1] become the instrument towards a complete annihilation of the present, the vehicle for a future that has no past?

It is possible to begin answering these questions by comparing the outlook of these thinkers with that of Reich and Fromm, and especially with their respective utopias. Earlier, I criticized the latter two writers for presenting such an integrated picture of the present that it is hard to visualize what the motive force will be which will bridge the gap between the present and the future, the reality and the utopia. Yet, their hopeful tone implies that there are strong forces within the reality that point in the direction of the future. The two writers I am presently considering make no such pretences. Their greatest achievement is in the area of social criticism - a kind of social criticism which lacks the strategic outlook of Reich and the moralistic attitude of Fromm; it is a criticism which gains its power from its shocking ability to show that the present civilization, the present reality principle, does not merely result in the multitude of Freudian discontents and disenchantments, but it is putting in jeopardy the very survival of humanity.[2] Within this reality principle

there can be no solution, since even the most 'progressive'
elements are symptoms of the overall disease. In the face of
imminent death, Marcuse and Brown propose a solution which
defies the reality principle; a solution, which, unlike the
solutions of Reich and Fromm, seems intangible and phantastic,
and as a phantasy it is unreasonable, untestable and unfounded.[3]
   The claims of Marcuse's and Brown's solutions to validity
(unlike Engels' 'scientific socialism') do not derive from having
shown that the 'natural laws' of the present point inexorably
to the future - quite on the contrary, the 'natural laws' of the
present can only point to death as humanity's future. As Marcuse
has argued:

> The critical theory of society possesses no concepts which
> could bridge the gap between the present and its future;
> holding no promise and showing no success, it remains
> negative. Thus it wants to remain loyal to those who, without
> hope, have given and give their life to the Great Refusal.
> (1964:257)

The utopias of Brown and Marcuse can rely on no proletariat,
no overman, no orgasm and no will to freedom to bring them to
fruition; they have no other vehicle but despair. And yet they
involve a stubborn refusal to translate despair into resignation.
   But what then is the meaning of these utopias which cannot
rely on reality-testing, or on a theory of historical transition
which links the present with the future, which do not articulate
historical project, do not generate hope and do not even claim
to constitute a consistent moral philosophy? Do such utopias
have any claims to validity?
   I think that ultimately the claims of these utopias stem from
their attempt to show that there could be a reality principle
different from the present reality principle, that there is an
alternative to death; their power stems from their ability to
shock:

> Catastrophe . . . appears not only in the constant menace of
> atomic war, in play with annihilation, but also in the social
> logic of technology, in play with ever-growing productivity
> which falls into ever-clearer contradiction to the system in
> which it is caught. Nothing justifies the assumption that the
> new form of the classic contradiction can be manipulated per-
> manently. It is just as unjustifiable, nevertheless, to assume
> that it cannot lead once more to new forms of oppression.
> More than ever before, breaking through the administered
> consciousness is a precondition of liberation. Thought in con-
> tradiction must be capable of surpassing the force of tech-
> nological repression and of incorporating into its concepts the
> elements of gratification that are perverted and suppressed in
> this repression. In other words, thought in contradiction
> must become more negative and more utopian in opposition to

> the status quo. . . . Totalitarian society brings the realm of
> freedom beyond the realm of necessity under its administra-
> tion and fashions it after its own image. In complete contra-
> diction to this future, autonomy over the technological
> apparatus is freedom *in* the realm of necessity. This means,
> however, that freedom is only possible as the realization of
> what today is called utopia. (1968:xix-xx)

If the purpose of these utopias is to shock our reality-oriented
intellects, if the purpose of phantasy is to challenge the
domination of the present reality principle, then we can see
where Freud's appeal comes from. At the time of its conception,
Freud's work appeared as a phantasy, at least to most of his
contemporaries.[4] Its purpose was not the bending of visible
realities, but the shaking of the repressed: 'Flectere si nequeo
Superos, Acheronta movebo', the motto on the title page of
'The Interpretation of Dreams' (which we encountered in Part I),
reveals the same activist spirit which characterizes much of the
work of Brown and Marcuse, an activism which is inextricably
related to a critique of the visible, the phenomenal, the
apparent. It is this critical edge of psychoanalysis, its ability
to see through things which originally appear opaque, its
capacity to shock, fascinate and raise questions, and its
dedication to the bringing into light the unpleasant (and
repressed) facts of civilization, that make it profoundly appealing to the desperate activism of the two thinkers we are presently discussing.

As we saw in Chapter 8, both Reich and Fromm derived their
utopias from psychotherapeutic prototypes writ large. The
orgasm and the spontaneous creative activity are seen by Reich
and Fromm respectively as providing both a cure for individual
problems, and an avenue for the liberation of mankind; they
are the bases of therapeutic utopias. Not so Marcuse's and
Brown's. Both of these authors draw a rigid line between the
critical and therapeutic functions of psychoanalysis and its twin
conception of normality. As a therapy, psychoanalysis can only
be assessed pragmatically, in terms of the rate at which it can
restore broken-down individuals to a useful (or at least non-
harmful) role in society, its ability to comfort, encourage and
'help' patients, in short, its positivity.[5] But as social criticism,
its validity and power rest on its negativity, its ability to break
things down (including the most precious achievements of civilization), to destroy, to shock, to reveal contradictions below the
surface of the reality principle, by stirring the hidden depths
concealed under an evasive reflexivity. For these writers, the
more shocking the psychoanalysis, the greater its negativity,
the greater its proximity to truth; in Adorno's famous words,
'in psychoanalysis only exaggerations are true'.

HERBERT MARCUSE

Perhaps the supreme achievement of Marcuse in his discussions
of Freud is the discovery of a revolutionary message without
engaging in the facile rejection of the most disturbing and
pessimistic parts of his theory. In a strange way, Herbert
Marcuse managed to draw his revolutionary message precisely
from these disturbing and pessimistic parts of the Freudian
discourse, such as the death instinct, the chronic conflict
between individual and society, the complex reading of sexuality.
In a well-known epilogue to his main treatise of Freud, Marcuse
criticized the cautious and moralistic approach to psychoanalysis
followed by his former colleague and friend Erich Fromm, and his
fellow Neo-Freudian revisionists Horney and Sullivan. Marcuse
criticized the 'yes . . . but' approach of these theorists with
their emphasis on mental hygiene, the spiritualization of love,
the proclamation of utopias based on models of individual adjustment and the mutilation of Freud's metapsychology.[6] In these
most 'bourgeois' and 'reified' aspects of Freud's thought is contained a revolutionary seed and a powerful utopian imagery,
which Marcuse sought to vindicate and develop.[7]

In the first part of 'Eros and Civilization', entitled 'Under the
Reality Principle', Marcuse develops many of the critical aspects
of psychoanalysis, discussed in Part I. The reality principle
describes a relationship between the individual and society, which
has characterized all civilizations, present and past; it is a
relationship in which society exercises a repressive influence on
human instincts. While civilizations may have taken different
forms, the conflict between individual and society described by
the reality principle has remained unchanged. Freud's great
achievement, according to Marcuse, is his discovery that, under
the rule of the reality principle, human civilization and human
beings have been chronically sick, that mankind has been suffering from a universal neurosis, whose essentials are laid out
in the hitherto unknown process of repression.

Both Marcuse and Brown begin their books on Freud with the
same theme:

> According to Freud, the history of man is the history of his
> repression. (Marcuse 1955:11)

> The essence of society is the repression of the individual and
> the essence of the individual is the repression of himself.
> (Brown 1959:4)

It is perhaps helpful to remind ourselves of the section towards
the end of 'Civilization and Its Discontents' in which Freud re-
affirmed his belief that the same pathogenic factor which is
responsible for the visible illness of neurotics, i.e. repression,
is in fact part of the constitution of all human beings living in
society and concludes:

> If the development of civilization has such far-reaching
> similarity to the development of the individual and if it employs
> the same methods, may we not be justified in reaching the
> diagnosis that, under the influence of cultural urges, some
> civilizations, or some epochs of civilization - possibly the
> whole of mankind - has become 'neurotic'. (1930a:21:144)

This extract, discussed extensively in Part I, contains in embryo
the central message of psychoanalysis as social critique and
forms the basis of Freud's pessimism.[8]

Yet, Marcuse (and Brown, as we shall see shortly) refuses to
draw the same pessimistic conclusions as Freud. Moreover, he
argues that Freud's formulations, those same formulations which
demonstrate that mankind may be 'neurotic', justify the conceptualization of a new society which has moved beyond the reality
principle, and whose relationship to the individual has been so
drastically modified that it no longer presupposes the repression
of desire. So, Marcuse devotes the second part of his book to
the discovery of a new principle which governs this relationship,
a new form of the pleasure principle that corresponds not to the
blind, mutilated, manipulated and repressed libido of all known
civilizations, but to a whole, liberated and powerful Eros.

Let us now examine how Marcuse re-interprets Freud's formulations concerning the instincts and the relationship between
individual and society. The original Freudian argument was discussed in detail in Chapter 2; its central theme can be summed
up as follows: the basis of all social and group bonds is libido.

> Collections of men are . . . libidinally bound to one another.
> Necessity alone, the advantages of work in common, will not
> hold them together. (1930a:21:122)

So, to put it as generally as possible:

> a group is clearly held together by a power of some kind: and
> to what power could this feat be better ascribed than to Eros,
> which holds together everything in the world? (1921c:18:92)

But the relation between Eros and civilization is not simple, for
many of the forms Eros assumes, such as the majority of direct
sexual experiences as well as the blissful self-sufficiency of the
couple, have anti-social consequences - uninhibited sensuousness, Cythera, cannot provide the basis of social cohesion;
instead, social relations are based on sublimated, de-sexualized
libidinal ties of a particular kind, which enhance the identification of group members with each other and with those individuals
and symbols which represent social or group unity. The weakening of Eros, however, which results from sublimation and de-
sexualization has a negative consequence, in that it gives the
upper hand to the death instinct, which strives to destroy
social as well as living units and return them to a state of inor-

ganic inertia.[9] Large amounts of destructive energy are unleashed, which can only be controlled by turning them inwards,
so that from the position of the super-ego they attack the ego.
Thus, the individual does not only experience the frustrations
of having to repress sexual impulses so that their energy can be
re-channelled along socially useful paths, but also experiences
an irrational, unconscious and undeserved sense of guilt; the
ego finds itself in an ambivalent and highly unpleasant position.

> Through its work of identification and sublimation it gives
> the death instinct in the id assistance in gaining control over
> the libido, but in so doing it runs the risk of becoming the
> object of the death instinct and of itself perishing. In order to
> be able to help in this way, it has had itself to become filled
> with libido; it thus itself becomes the representative of Eros
> and thenceforward desires to live and to be loved. But since
> the ego's work of sublimation results in defusion of the
> instincts and a liberation of the aggressive instincts in the
> super-ego, its struggle against the libido exposes it to the
> danger of maltreatment and death. (1923b:19:56)

In short, the stronger the social ties, the greater the sublimation
and de-sexualization of libido and, therefore, the lower its ability
to bind the destructive instincts successfully. As a result, these
instincts are either turned inwards and attack the ego causing
a deep malaise, or are turned outwards in diverse forms, ranging
from the collective violence of wars to the symbolic aggression
of sports and to the total collapse of the social bonds in a war of
all against all.

The contradiction in this argument is not a logical one, but
represents a deep-seated conflict. In Part I, we saw that depending on what paradigm of Eros we adopt (Eros as principle of
pleasure vs Eros as principle of union), the conflict can ultimately
be seen either as a conflict between Eros and the death instinct,
or as a conflict between the individual and society. In either
case, the instincts and civilization are trapped in a vicious
circle, in which both society and the individual are the dramatis
personae.

Both Marcuse and Brown accept this vicious circle as the
essence of all known civilizations, but they each try to discover
a way of breaking it. They both try to show that Freud's argument is an argument of existence, not an argument of essence,
that it represents the contradictions of known civilizations, not
of all civilizations; the present relation between the instincts
and civilization is a historical one, not a logical one. But while
Marcuse's attempt to break the Gordian knot hinges on his
argument that civilization is not in principle incompatible with
unsublimated, strong and free Eros, Brown's attempt is based
on the argument that underneath the historical dualism of Eros
and Thanatos there is a dialectic possibility of their re-
harmonization.

Marcuse's intervention in the Freudian discourse can, perhaps, be seen as an elaboration of the argument that, in the struggle of Eros and the death instinct, the defeat of the latter can only be achieved through the liberation of Eros. 'It is the failure of Eros, lack of fulfilment in life, which enhances the instinctual value of death' (1955:98). Within the present civilization, the destructive strivings of the death instinct

> testify to the destructiveness of what they try to destroy: repression. They aim not only against the reality principle, at non-being, but also beyond the reality principle – at another mode of being. They betoken the historical character of the reality principle, the limits of its validity and necessity. (99)

With this characteristic dialectic twist in the theory of instincts, Marcuse seeks to demonstrate the real possibility of re-directing Thanatos against its proper foundation, the reality principle, which has condemned Eros to life in the underworld.

At the same time, Marcuse discovers new possible vicissitudes for Eros – he suggests that not all sublimations need be repressive, and proposes the concept of non-repressive subli- mation as a possible re-organization of libido, which transcends the 'genital tyranny' in a re-activation of polymorphous and narcissistic sexuality, after the models of Orpheus and Narcissus. Marcuse emphasizes that the restriction of non-repressed sexu- ality to the genital (within the more-or-less strict constraints of institutional marriage) has served to transform the body, from an object of generalized pleasure into an instrument of alienated labour. Sexuality must be sublimated from the genital region, fill all parts of the body, which will then be able to yield the unmediated pleasure experienced by the new-born infant and re-captured in the Greek myths. But far from weaken- ing sexuality, this kind of sublimation strengthens Eros and enables him to contain his great adversary. Life ceases being a long struggle for achievement (captured in the Promethean prototype), characterized by an ascetic attitude towards enjoy- ment, and a new reality principle emerges. Under the old reality principle, Eros was a trouble-maker, under the new he becomes the supreme ruler:

> In the world symbolized by the culture-hero Prometheus, [Eros] is the negation of *all* order; but in this negation Orpheus and Narcissus reveal a new reality, with an order of its own, governed by different principles. The Orphic Eros transforms being: he masters cruelty and death through liberation. His language is *song*, and his work is *play*. Narcissus' life is that of *beauty*, and his existence is *contem- plation*. (156)

Marcuse's re-interpretation of the Freudian theory of instincts

and their relation to civilization has a rather paradoxical consequence. Both of the instincts lose their conservative and regressive character, so frequently emphasized by Freud; on the
contrary, both instincts become forces propelling humanity
forward, towards civilization without repression, civilization
where desire is met with satisfaction, where the lack of tension
does not co-incide with inorganic inertia but with organic well-
being. The equations of tension with life with pain on the one
hand, and inertia with pleasure and death on the other, are
broken or, at least, they become mere descriptions of the
present oppressive reality principle. Freud himself had not been
perfectly happy with these equations, and it may be remembered
that in The Economic Problem of Masochism (1924c) he had felt
compelled to introduce a 'qualitative factor' related to the
energies whose release leads to pleasure. Marcuse is now adding,
in effect, a qualitative factor to the strivings of the death
instinct: just as Eros strives after the release of those excitations
which entail pleasure, the death instinct tries to abolish those
tensions which build up as a result of frustrated sexuality. But
in so doing, both instincts in their very essence do not operate
towards a final inertia of death, but towards a final inertia of
pleasure; instead of the 'terrifying convergence of pleasure and
death' encapsulated in the nirvana principle (24), they are now
firmly pointed towards the Utopia of Eros.

Marcuse's utopia involves a different reality principle and a
different logic from the present civilization - a culture of pro-
ductivity, asceticism and domination gives way to a culture of
fulfilment, playfulness and receptivity. Such culture need not
concern itself with the intricacies of re-orienting, sublimating
and de-sexualizing Eros, for the sublimation of libido and the
creation of social bonds proceeds from Eros himself, the supreme
master.

> Libido can take the road of self-sublimation only as a *social*
> phenomenon: as an unrepressed force, it can promote the
> formation of culture only under conditions which relate
> associated individuals to each other in the cultivation of the
> environment for their developing needs and faculties. Reac-
> tivation of polymorphous and narcissistic sexuality ceases to
> be a threat to culture and can itself lead to culture-building
> if the organism exists not as an instrument of alienated labour
> but as a subject of self-realization - in other words, if
> socially useful work is at the same time the transparent satis-
> faction of an individual need. (192)

In this way Marcuse tries to show that his Utopia of Eros does
not fail the test of social cohesion, like the therapeutic utopias
of Reich and Fromm do by being individual utopias writ large.
He can support his argument that self-sublimated sexuality can
become the basis of lasting social bonds by quoting the following
passage from Freud:

> The social instincts belong to a class of instincts which need
> not be described as sublimated, though they are closely
> related to these. They have not abandoned their directly
> sexual aims, but are held back by internal resistances from
> attaining them; they rest content with certain approximations
> to satisfaction and for that very reason lead to especially firm
> and permanent attachments between human beings. (1923a:18:
> 258)

The word that Marcuse emphasizes is 'unsublimated' (1955:189),
i.e. that de-sexualization is not an essential ingredient for
social cohesion.[10] Yet, what Marcuse seems to disregard is the
fact that, whether Freud saw social instincts as sublimated or
not, he consistently maintained that they are re-channelled
instincts, and that the energy which corresponds to them cannot
simultaneously be made available for other purposes; in short,
what matters is not whether the social instincts are sublimated
or not (and there can be social instincts of both kinds), but the
fact that lasting social bonds correspond to a general sexual
impoverishment of a person's emotional life. It is possible that
Marcuse would invoke his concept of surplus repression to respond to this criticism - i.e. some repressions may be necessary
for civilization but not all. Yet, I feel that by emphasizing the
self-sublimating potential of Eros, Marcuse ends up in the position
that Freud had combated repeatedly, namely the herd instinct.

> In the light of the idea of non-repressive sublimation, Freud's
> definition of Eros as striving to 'form living substance into
> ever greater unities, so that life may be prolonged and brought
> to higher development' takes on an added significance. The
> biological drive becomes a cultural drive. (193)

In this way, Marcuse's conception of Eros comes close to a
resurrection of Trotter's concept of the herd instinct, under a
new guise.

As a result not only does Marcuse believe that self-sublimating
Eros is compatible with strong and lasting social bonds, but
he also sees it as the end of the antagonistic relation between
the two major forces, Eros and Thanatos. To be sure, the two
do not collapse into a single unity, as they do in Brown's
utopia, but achieve fulfilment simultaneously in the utopian
present. Through Marcuse's reading, Freud becomes the prophet
of subject-object identity, of reconciliation of sensuousness with
reason, of being and becoming - all of which suddenly become
conceivable if not visible in some distant future.

As we saw, although Marcuse tries to show that Freud's
analyses of the instincts and their relation to civilization have a
historical character and concern known civilizations, not all
civilizations, he is not in a position to elucidate either how the
present situation came into being or how it may be transcended
through the Utopia of Eros. To account for the genesis of the

repressive reality principle, Marcuse, like the Greeks, like
Freud, resorts to myth, and in particular the myth of the
primal murder and the setting up of the taboo. His interpretation
of Freud's myth, however, departs in several places from
Freud's own account; perhaps the most significant is his account
of how the death instinct assumed its historical form as a sense
of guilt. This happened, not as in Freud's account, because the
sons experienced guilt over the murder of the father they
both loved and hated, but because, so to speak, they betrayed
the revolution, by substituting one tyrannical law by another;
the failure of all subsequent revolutions to alter the established
reality principle, the established order through which man
exploits man, is but a recapitulation of the failure of the
original murder (60f).

If to account for the genesis of the reality principle Marcuse
invoked a myth (which may provide a successful metaphor but
no explanation), in order to assess the chances of transcending
the reality principle he uses a technological argument, which has
been widely criticized. In brief, present technology has progressed sufficiently to ensure that, under its rational administration, it is capable of liberating mankind from its historical
dependence on work. This creates the precondition for a resexualization of the body and the return to polymorphous
sexuality. 'No longer used as a full-time instrument of labour,
the body would be resexualized. . . . The body in its entirety
would become an object of cathexis, a thing to be enjoyed - an
instrument of pleasure' (184). Marcuse suggests that, in the
past, scarcity had provided rationalizations for the domination
of man by man, the 'automatization' of social relations in the
interests of 'efficiency' and totalitarian political systems. But
if technology is capable of eliminating scarcity, such rationalizations lose their power - the reality principle in its present
form is unable to justify itself. This argument, which is characteristic of the optimism about technology in the 1950s, was
repudiated by Marcuse in 'One Dimensional Man', in which he
argues that technology can create artifical scarcity by generating new needs (1964:xvi, 11ff, 158). In this book, Marcuse
argues that technology is not a neutral instrument subject to
good or bad administration, and saw it as political force contributing to the legitimation of the system, the paralysis of
social criticism and the increasing power of the technocrats.

Marcuse's technological argument was seen by many as an
implicit attempt to bridge Freud's theory of neurosis with Marx's
theory of alienated labour; in using the term 'performance
principle' to denote the particular form that the reality principle
assumes under capitalism, it is argued, Marcuse bridges the gap
between alienation and neurosis. On the side of alienation, the
performance principle represents not merely a system of ideologies emphasizing technical rationality over human fulfilment, but
an objective technical and social organization of production, of
which Taylorism is an important component. On the side of

neurosis, the performance principle, it is argued, represents the
particular demands made upon sexuality by capitalism. On the
basis of such arguments, Robinson (1979) has suggested that
Marx is the unacknowledged inspiration and overwhelming
influence behind 'Eros and Civilization'. But this cannot be so
for two reasons: on the side of neurosis, the performance
principle is of no consequence - Marcuse argues that all reality
principles since the primal murder have been repressive and
criticizes all of them.[11] On the side of alienation, the performance
principle represents a kind of old-fashioned technological determinism. There is only one way in which the performance
principle is set aside from earlier reality principles, and this is
in Marcuse's argument that, perhaps, it has created the preconditions of its own abolition, i.e. control over the forces of
nature and elimination of scarcity. But does this kind of argument not seek to reduce the complex process of history to a
'dialectic of the forces of production', which even the most
economistically oriented Marxists would reject today? The entire
complex network of social class relations, social conflict and
material interests, politics and ideologies, has been dissolved
into the single category of the 'performance principle', which
somehow seeks to capture the 'true essence of capitalism'. If
one gives this emphasis on the performance principle, the
criticism of technological determinism must inevitably be raised.[12]
But it seems to me that far too much emphasis is given to the
performance principle, which admittedly is introduced by
Marcuse with a great deal of fanfare, but is subsequently rarely
used, except as loosely synonymous to *all* historical forms of
repressive reality principle. I think that it is ultimately naive
to think that Marcuse believed that technology would prove the
ultimate saviour of mankind; the argument that he would have
supported, just like Marx, is that technology is one of the preconditions which will enable man to become his own saviour, at
some point in history, just as it may enable man to become his
own genocide. But unlike Marx, Marcuse has no real theory of
transition to offer, only a few hopeful hints.[13]

The overwhelming inspiration and influence behind 'Eros and
Civilization' is not Marx, but beyond all doubt Freud. Of course,
it is not the Freud familiar to the practitioners of therapy -
and it is possible to sympathize with the desperation of the
reviewer who wrote that Marcuse's 'Freud is not the analyst we
know but a dummy dressed in a red gown' ('Times Literary Supple-
ment', 8 January 1971). Marcuse's Freud is inextricably linked
to his Utopia of Eros. It is the pathos of this utopia, the power
of its imagination, the brilliance of its articulation, which motivate and justify his interpretation of Freud. Of course, the
Utopia of Eros can be criticized on 'rational' grounds since in its
very essence it is everything that the reality principle, in the
form of theories or good common sense, teaches us. Yet, this
misses the basic significance of the work, which lies in its
activist character. The Utopia of Eros represents a double inter-

vention by Marcuse; an intervention on the academic front,
through which he tries to break the monopoly over the work of
Freud held by therapeutic institutions and practitioners. On
this front, Marcuse tries to vindicate Freud from his epigoni,
whose obsession with therapeutic success and social respect-
ability led them to repress the more disturbing and critical
aspects of his work. There can be hardly any doubt that
Marcuse did inspire a broad interest into the work of Freud,
which would have been unthinkable as long as his work and its
interpretation and use was left to the psychoanalytic establishment. Second, and more important, Marcuse intervenes on a
wider social front; on this front, he tries to stir desire out of
the diverse social forms that contain it, shape it and mis-direct
it. Following the motto on the title page of 'The Interpretation
of Dreams', Marcuse seeks to shake the underworld, in the hope
that Eros may be liberated; he tries to excite his reader's
imagination and indeed his reader's desire, and for a few fleeting moments he succeeds in arousing deadened sensitivities and
in kindling visions of the future which grow from a critique of
the present. In this sense, the Utopia of Eros stands as a
symbol of hope and resistance and can only be judged as such.
But if this is so, Marcuse leaves the ranks of the theoreticians
of revolution in which so many of his critics have placed him,
and joins the ranks of revolutionary activists, revolutionary
artists. The one criterion which 'Eros and Civilization' never
fails to meet is Marcuse's own criterion of art:

> Insofar as philosophy accepted the rules and values of the
> reality principle, the claim of sensuousness free from the
> domination of reason found no place in philosophy; greatly
> modified, it obtained refuge in the theory of art. The truth
> of art is the liberation of sensuousness through its reconcili-
> ation with reason. . . . Art challenges the prevailing principle
> of reason: in representing the order of sensuousness, it
> invokes a tabooed logic - the logic of gratification as against
> that of repression. (1955:168)[14]

NORMAN O. BROWN

Like Marcuse, Brown begins his study of Freud with the diagnosis of the 'disease called man'; only psychoanalysis can elucidate
the causes and character of this disease, because it is the only
discipline which addresses the issue of repression head-on.
Freud's great discovery was that 'the essence of society is the
repression of the individual and the essence of the individual is
the repression of himself' (1959:3). Like Marcuse, Brown believes
that Freud's theory of Eros, Thanatos and civilization represents
the most advanced understanding of human alienation, and, like
Marcuse, he insists that Freud's analysis represents a historical
state, not a theoretical necessity. Yet, Brown's interpretation of

Freud is far more pessimistic than Marcuse's, his diagnosis of
the disease of humanity goes into the repressive organization
of the death instinct as well as into the repressive organization
of sexuality and his revision of Freud's ideas is more explicit
and more drastic than Marcuse's. Finally, his solution is more
radical, less tangible than Marcuse's, and he makes no attempt
at all to suggest that there is a ground for hope in the future
or that his utopia will appear to us as anything more than a
phantasy or a mirage.

Brown's interpretation of Eros shares Marcuse's emphasis on
polymorphous sexuality, but moves further from Freud's
original conception in arguing that both object-cathexis and
identification aim at the same thing - a union with the object of
desire. In fact, in the earliest oral phase of sexual differentiation, the two are indistinguishable.

> The distinction between object-choice and identification breaks
> down, both of them meeting in a project of incorporation or
> being-one-with-the-world, modeled on the primal relation of
> the child to the mother's breast. (42)

It is the project of being-one-with-the-world which defines the
pleasure-ego for good; pleasure is not its final aim, but accom-
panies the recreation of the primal oneness.

> The collapse of the distinction between identification and object-
> choice leaves love with one essential aim over and above
> pleasure, which is to become one with the objects of the world.
> (43-4)

As we saw in Chapter 1, Brown regards the pleasure-ego as a
body-ego, and there is nothing spiritual in the union towards
which it is striving. Yet, its project is constantly frustrated by
the reality-ego. It is here that Brown departs most drastically
from both Freud and Marcuse; the reality-ego is not the representative of an oppressive external order (a reality or 'performance' principle), but the product of an incapacity of accepting
reality, by a soul which has set itself apart from the body
through the work of sublimation (159f). Culture is nothing but
an enormous superstructure, it is the consequence of the
'disease called man', not its cause, as we shall see shortly.

Unlike Marcuse, Brown argues that all sublimations, like all
repressions, are pathological, they are part of the human disease.
But if culture is not the cause of this disease what is?

> The question is: What had to happen to an animal in order to
> make him into a man-animal? And a psychoanalysis which
> remains psychoanalysis must keep the duality of instincts. The
> essence of the man-animal is neurosis, and the essence of
> neurosis is mental conflict. The human neurosis must be traced
> to an instinctual ambivalence, a conflict between forces inherent

> in all organic life. . . . If, on the other hand, psychoanalysis
> is to retain hope . . . it must find a way to avoid Freud's
> metaphysical vision of all life sick with the struggle between
> Life and Death. It must hold fast to the vision that man is
> distinguished from other animals by the privilege of being
> sick; that there is an essential connection between being sick
> and being civilized; in other words, that neurosis is the
> privilege of the uniquely social animal. (82-3)

We must not be misled by this extract into believing that Brown
suggests that it is man's sociability which is responsible for
his disease, but rather that what makes man sick also makes
him social. What Brown is after is an instinctual meta-theory,
according to which the forces of life and death are in harmony
throughout the animal world, but have come in opposition in
man, in short, an instinctual dialectic. He continues:

> It must therefore maintain that instinctual ambivalence is a
> human prerogative. We need, in fine, a metaphysic which
> recognizes both the continuity between man and animals and
> also the discontinuity. We need, instead of an instinctual
> dualism, an instinctual dialectic. (83)

It is to the articulation of this instinctual dialectic that Brown
devotes his efforts in much of 'Life Against Death', and in
particular to the discovery of why the dialectic has assumed an
antagonistic character in man; in short, why man, of all animals,
has set life against death.

In the chapter entitled 'Death, Time and Eternity', possibly
the most brilliant of the whole work, Brown sets out to show how
the three groups of phenomena in which Freud identified the
death instinct, nirvana, the compulsion to repeat and masochism,
do not represent an opposition of life and death at the biological
level. At this level, life and death are parts of the same unity,
as Freud recognized in his formula 'the goal of all life is death'
(100). It is only when the pleasure principle is set apart from
the nirvana principle as a 'search of instinctual satisfaction
under conditions of instinctual repression' (90), when the compulsion to repeat has degenerated into an obsessive fixation to
the past, endlessly seeking to recreate this past in an unattainable future, and when the desire for rest is translated into a
morbid infliction of pain and death, only then is the dialectic
unity of life and death destroyed; but these are human, historical phenomena, not organic ones:

> We thus arrive at the idea that life and death are in some sort
> of unity at the organic level, and that at the human level the
> extroversion of the death instinct is the mode of resolving a
> conflict that does not exist at the organic level. The neurosis
> remains, as it should be a human privilege; life-and-death
> does not make nature sick. (100)

Brown has finally reached the central point of his argument:

> It is not the consciousness of death but the flight from death
> that distinguishes man from animals. . . . Pyramids and sky-
> scrapers - monuments more lasting than bronze - suggest how
> the world's 'economic' activity also is really a flight from death.
> If death is a part of life, if there is a death instinct as well as
> a life (or sexual) instinct, man is in flight from his own death
> just as he is in flight from his own sexuality. If death is a
> part of life, man represses his own death just as he represses
> his own life. (101)

It is this flight from death which lies at the heart of what is a
peculiarly human disease, and at the same time the launching
platform of what we call culture.

> Man is the animal which has separated into conflicting opposites
> the biological unity of life and death, and has then subjected
> the conflicting opposites to repression. The destruction of the
> biological unity of life and death transforms the Nirvana-
> principle into the pleasure-principle, transforms the repetition-
> compulsion into a fixation to the infantile past and transforms
> the death instinct into an aggressive principle of negativity.
> And all three of these specifically human characteristics - the
> pleasure-principle, the fixation to the past, and the aggressive
> negativism - are aspects of the characteristically human mode
> of being, historical time. (104)

Beyond the primal fact of the instinctual separation, no further
questions can be asked. It is a fact that Brown takes for what it
is, its causes remain unknown, but this is immaterial - an evolu-
tionary accident perhaps, a chromosomal disturbance, it is quite
immaterial; before this primal event, man was not man. But once
this primal event can be grasped, we can understand the genesis
of culture.

Being afraid of death, man sets himself up as an eternal soul
apart from the body. Sublimation is nothing but the bodily energy
which has been appropriated by the soul, to 'dilute life', to
enrich it with symbolic consolations, in order to make it bearable.
It is this process which brings the reality-ego into existence in
opposition to the body-ego - as we saw earlier, this reality-ego
comes into existence not as a result of adaptation to reality, but
out of an inability to accept reality. And the reality that the ego
is incapable of accepting is the reality of the unity of life and
death. But an ego which is not strong enough to die, is not
strong enough to live, for death is an inescapable Doppelgänger
of life. Thus the reality ego lives in phantasy; it seeks to re-
discover the objects of the world which it sets outside it in
imagination - and in so doing, it creates culture.

The reality which the ego thus constructs and perceives is

culture; and culture, like sublimation (or neurosis) has the
essential quality of being a 'substitute-gratification', a pale
imitation of past pleasure substituting for present pleasure,
and thus essentially desexualized. (163)

When Brown talks about culture he does not limit himself to what
we may call the symbolic sphere; everything is symbolic, not
only religion and art, but technology, politics, economics, science,
war, everything. Every material and spiritual creation is
symbolic, substitutive, consolatory. The whole of culture is an
immense symbolic superstructure that man has created; man
becomes an animal symbolicum, which compensates for its inability
to live and die with phantasies, which glorifies Apollo due to its
inability to celebrate Dionysus: 'everything is symbolic, everything including the sexual act' (1966:131).
   Man has created this immense symbolic matrix around himself
to save him, in Roheim's words, from 'being left alone in the
dark'. But although he seems incapable of living outside this
symbolic matrix, he is also threatened of being drowned by it
into extinction. Aggression against the other human beings and
against the world becomes man's distorted way of fighting death,
or rather of fleeing from death.

> Fear and be slain - no worse can come to fight;
> And fight and die is death destroying death.
> ('Richard II'; 2, II, 183-4)

   Brown envisages one single point where the symbolic matrix is
broken - psychoanalysis. It is the only thing that can lead us to
an understanding of the human disease, and by substitution of
Freud's antinomies of despair by Brown's 'dialectic of hope' can
lead us to a way out.

> The path of sublimation, which mankind has religiously followed
> at least since the foundation of the first cities, is no way out
> of the human neurosis, but, on the contrary, leads to its
> aggravation. Psychoanalytical theory and the bitter facts of
> contemporary history suggest that mankind is reaching the end
> of the road. (1959:307)

Psychoanalysis can lead mankind out of this fatal path, if instead
of siding with the ego and the reality principle, it becomes a
source of social criticism and self-understanding; its ultimate
goal can only be the total reconstitution of instinctual unity, the
acceptance of death and the resurrection of the body. Instead of
siding with the ego against the id, the psychoanalyst must seek
to reconcile the ego with the id and turn them both against
reality (153ff); psychoanalysis must become alloplastic, not auto-
plastic, it must change the world rather than the patient. It may
appear that Brown is about to become an advocate of Sex-Pol;
not at all. What appears as alloplasis to the psychoanalyst is, in

fact, nothing but autoplasis, for as we saw Brown categorically rejects the view that the human disease originates in society as distinct from the individual; it is not the reality of death that Brown seeks to modify, but our experience of this reality; it is not the reality of the body that Brown seeks to resurrect, but our experience of the body. Both Eros and Thanatos must be liberated, because they can only be liberated together in a reconstituted unity. And their liberation does not lie in the overthrow of a 'performance principle', the overthrow of external tyranny, but the internal resurrection of what has been destroyed – the radical emergence of a Dionysian consciousness. No transformation of external reality is possible, since all external reality is in the head – 'what we call reality Brown calls illusion, lie, dream' (Marcuse 1968:228). For Brown, therefore, the way out of the suicidal path of our civilization is not, as for Marcuse, the liberation of Eros, but the re-discovery of the original union of the instincts, of the nirvana and the pleasure principles, the ego and the id, the total destruction of the symbolic matrix of culture, and the dissolution of illusory distinctions like male-female, you-me, object-subject, nature-society. Brown's argument is unambiguous: if alienation arose from the breach of the original union and the setting up of all these antinomies, redemption must lie in the reconstitution of the union. His utopia could perhaps be called a 'Utopia of Fusion': 'Fusion: the distinction between inner self and outside world, between subject and object, overcome' (1966:253). Like Freud's 'oceanic feeling' from which Brown undoubtedly draws his inspiration, the Utopia of Fusion grows out of a primordial desire for union with the world and represents a relic of the early auto-erotic phase, before the splitting of the ego from the id.[15]

Undoubtedly, Brown's utopia goes beyond Marcuse's in certain ways: he accepts no compromise sublimations since all sublimations are negations of the body and of life and represent flights from death. He does not accept the idea that the death instinct can be silenced by the liberation of Eros. If the human disease started with the original division and the setting of one instinct against the other, the redemption can only be found in the fusion and re-unification accomplished by the resurrection of the body. It is this theme of unification and fusion which dominates Brown's next major work, 'Love's Body'. Unlike Marcuse, Brown makes no attempt to show that his utopia is compatible with the requirement for social cohesion, nor does he give any hints as to the possibilities of its realization. His theory of the instincts quite simply dissolves the problem of social cohesion; if Eros is in its very essence a force towards union with the other and with the world, and if Thanatos is not in its very essence a force towards destruction, then social cohesion is not a problem, except for a civilization in which the instincts have been distorted in their aims, by being turned against each other (i.e. all known civilizations). While social cohesion is unproblematic in Brown's Utopia of Fusion (since it follows almost *ex hypothesi*), it is a problematic in sick cultures, in which it is precariously established on the very same flight from death upon which these cultures are based. Politics is but the sublimated re-enactment of the sons' rebellion against the father, all political philosophy is but an endless sequence of footnotes on the twin themes of brotherhood and fatherhood, Plato and Aristotle, Sparta and Athens (1966: Ch. 1). Psychoanalysis sees through politics and technology, just as it sees through religion; it is not mystified by the emperor's new clothes and reveals them for what they are – phantoms, products of the imagination, which arise from a morbid fixation. Utopian speculation cannot be grounded in a technological, political or religious superstructure, for such superstructures are but symptoms of the disease; they are parts of the immense symbolic matrix, phantastic recapturings of frustrated desires:

> Heraldic devices: airplanes as penis symbols rather than 'modern conveniences'. One of the eternal verities is the human body as a measure of all things, including technology. The businessman does not have the last word; the real meaning of technology is its hidden relation to the human body; a symbolic or mystical relation. (1968:245)

> Political power is a web woven, a political well-wrought veil; a veil of deceit, the veil of Maya. It is non-existent cloth, the Emperor's new clothes. (1966:76)

Utopian speculation must, therefore, break from these political and technological pseudo-solutions, which simply re-inforce the human disease. It must be accepted in its own right:

> Utopian speculations . . . must come back into fashion. They are a way of affirming faith in the possibility of solving problems that seem insoluble at the moment. Today even the survival of humanity is a utopian hope. (1959:305)

There is only one level in the present society at which such speculations can exist without being compromised or ridiculed, poetry.

> Poetry, art, is not an epiphenomenal reflection of some other real (political, economic) realm which is the 'real thing'; nor a contemplation of something else which is the 'real action'; nor a sublimation of something else which is the 'real' carnal 'act'. Poetry, art, imagination, the creator spirit is life itself; the real revolutionary power to change the world; and to change the human body. To change the human body: here is the crisis, *hic Rhodus, his salta;* which, as Hegel said, is to be translated 'here is the Rose, here begin to dance.' To begin to dance; who can tell the dancer from the dance; it is the impossible unity and union of everything. (1968:246)

Brown's provocative analysis which seeks to reverse all the
assumptions that we normally make about what is real and what
is phantastic can, at times, lead his reader to despair. On the
one hand he exalts the 'creator spirit' and advocates a new
attitude towards life and death, and yet, on the other, he
seeks to re-establish the body, in full independence from the
elaborate meanings that we attach to it. A deeply spiritual
quality runs through his works, the very works which see
spirituality as the symptom of the human disease. He scorns
politics and technology, and yet, he is afraid of their consequences:

> History has brought mankind to the pinnacle on which the
> total obliteration of mankind is at least a possibility. At this
> moment of history the friends of the life instinct must warn
> that the victory of death is by no means impossible; the
> malignant death instinct can unleash those hydrogen bombs.
> (1959:307)

But here the supreme irony of Brown's argument emerges
clearly. Within the present system, utopias as he recognizes
can only exist as poetics, poetics which are 'the real thing',
the non-alienated essence of man. Hydrogen bombs may simply
represent sublimated re-enactments of renounced orgasms, but
they cannot be stopped through poetics, through the preaching
of the resurrection of the real body over the symbolic caricature
which has replaced it, the return of real orgasms in place of
the fake and sublimated, but deadly, ones. Granted that politics,
technology, armies, banks and corporations are institutions
established upon the flight from death, granted that they are
not the 'real thing', they have nevertheless acquired an existence
of their own and cannot be brought down by human will alone;
surely, this is the essence of man's alienation; his inability to
control his own creations and their systematic power to control
not only his actions but his will and his consciousness as well.
There is, unfortunately, nothing in Brown's theory to suggest
that a new poetic could dissolve atom bombs, corporate giants,
skyscrapers or religious doctrines. Marx showed how 'the object
which labour produces - labour's product - confronts it as
something alien, as a *power independent* of the producer' (1844:
57), even though this power is based on the fetish character of
commodities. Marx uses the term 'illusory' to refer to the mone-
tary system, just as Freud uses the same term to refer to
religious beliefs - yet, neither would deny that they are objective and real forces in the society in which we live. The reality
principle may indeed be phantastic, we may indeed all be living
in the dark cave; yet, it does not cease to function as a reality
principle. It may have arisen out of an inability to face reality,
yet it does not cease to confront people as the reality. To point
out that the reality principle leads to death will, unfortunately,
make death appear reasonable (as the great human enterprises

of self-destruction in the interest of 'religion', 'fatherland',
'our way of living', etc. amply demonstrate); it will not reveal
the phantastic character of the reality principle. It is not without justification that Marcuse reminds Brown, what the above
extract (1959:307) suggests that Brown already knew:

> Unfortunately, the emperor does [have clothes]: they are
> visible and tangible; they make history. In terms of the latent
> content the kingdoms of the earth may be shadows; but unfor-
> tunately they move real men and things, they kill, they persist
> and prevail in the sunlight as well as in the dark of the night.
> The king may be an erected penis, and his relation to the
> community may be intercourse; but unfortunately, it is also
> something different and less pleasant and more real. Brown
> skips the mediations that transform the latent into overt con-
> tent, sex into politics, the sub-rational into the rational.
> (1968:235)

But even if, suspending all disbelief, we were to accept that
utopian poetics have the power to stop bombs, that meta-politics
can displace politics, we are left with a deep ambiguity in
Brown's theory, which stems from his 'hyper-radicalist' argument that all reality is illusion and that only the Dionysian
utopia is real. Where does this utopia find its explosive potential, the potential which Brown seeks to trigger? As Freud has
shown, in his important studies on art, religious beliefs and
myths, the power of such phantasies lies in their capacity to
trigger off and fulfil symbolically real repressed desires.
'Oedipus Rex', as Brown well knows (1966:119), owes its emotional sweep to the invisible Oedipus not only in every single
member of the chorus but in every one of us - the hero is seen
as enacting what is repressed in all of us; the repressed is
shaken, the emotions overflow from every side. For repression,
far from annihilating desire, immortalizes it, by keeping it
sealed in that area of the soul in which time is frozen, in which
nothing gets old; the Apollonian spirit of civilization, far from
dissolving the Dionysiac, has merely forced it to the underworld
- the transparence of the Delphic Games does not destroy the
Mysteries of Eleusis, but accepts them as an equal. As a result,
Brown's efforts to 'construct a Dionysiac ego' seems as futile as
his wish to dissolve the Apollonian ego into nothingness.

CONCLUSIONS

Like the works of Reich and Fromm, the works of Marcuse and
Brown are infused with utopian imageries, inspired by Freud.
While, however, the utopias of Reich and Fromm emanated from
their psychotherapeutic experiences having as their starting
point the individual's potential to revolutionize his/her life, the
utopias of Brown and Marcuse are sweeping visions of a radical

transformation not only of society but of human nature itself.
Criticizing a society of blind communal subordination to the
Fuehrer, Reich and Fromm emphasized the individual's potential
to stand up against mass hysteria, to overcome social conditioning and to allow the essential goodness of his/her human nature
to find expression in his/her life. Brown and Marcuse, on the
other hand, criticize the privatized society of the 1950s, in
which impersonal machines, running amuck, gamble with the
future of humanity, and try to discover the possibility of a
complete overthrow of the reality principle and a radical re-
shaping of human nature. Their utopias grow out of a deep
pessimism, which contrasts sharply with the cheerful optimism
of Reich and Fromm, and they are infinitely more far-reaching
than those of Reich and Fromm, not only because they do not
have a basic model of good human nature to build upon, but
also because the enemy they are fighting is both more omni-
present and more intangible. Their objective is neither to
convince us nor to educate us (since we are all beyond such
strategies), but to shock us and shake us out of a complacent
individualism which grows out of impotence. Their utopias are
profoundly destructive ones, destructive of a society which
they see as leading humanity to its final death, destructive of
souls which experience their alienation in suburban comfort.

For these reasons it is very difficult to assess the utopias of
Brown and Marcuse in terms other than their activist effectiveness – unlike the utopias of Reich and Fromm, it is difficult to
criticize those of Brown and Marcuse for the assumptions upon
which they are built, since these assumptions are deliberately
unrealistic. Their utopias *are* unrealistic, and this constitutes
praise, since only unrealistic utopias, poetic phantasies, can
achieve the total destruction of past and present. At the same
time, they present us with a vision of a new possible reality,
one however, which unlike visions based on orgasms and
spontaneous activity, has no direct reference to the present. It
is a vision constructed through highly abstract speculations
revolving around Freud's theory of instincts, and which is
inaccessible to the broader public; this abstractness and complexity however does not detract from the value of their works,
since even if the precise nature of their utopias may be unclear
to most people, the utopian spirit in an undiluted and uncom-
promised form shines through. Could it be perhaps that these
utopias of Marcuse and Brown were the heralds of the resurrection of utopian imagination in the 1960s?

There is one aspect of Marcuse's and Brown's work which we
can undoubtedly assess – the strength of their social criticism.
But in order to do this, it is necessary to enrich our cultural
discussion of the post-Second World War period. This will be
done in the next two chapters – in Chapter 10, I will introduce
the work of the third great philosophical commentator of Freud
in the 1950s, Philip Rieff, and will compare his cultural theory
with that developed by Marcuse in 'One Dimensional Man'; and

in Chapter 11, I will introduce the work of Ernest Becker, which
has very little relevance for our discussion of Freud's social
theory, but forms an interesting counter-part to Reiff's cultural
analysis, which hinges, of course, on psychoanalytic insights.

Chapter 10
Psychoanalysis and contemporary American culture: the present as utopia in the work of Rieff

In this chapter, we will not only try to see in greater detail how Freud's work can be used to elucidate contemporary American culture, but our study will inevitably lead us to consider psychoanalysis itself as one of its important and rather intriguing components. There is a growing awareness that the impact of psychoanalysis on American culture is not limited to the important middle-class minority for whom the analyst has become an indispensable appendage, but has affected in a more general and pervasive way people's thinking; as a source of ideas concerning sexuality, inner conflicts and possible solutions through therapy, psychoanalysis can be said to have become part of the fabric of American society. This presents us with the apparent paradox of the United States, the forward-looking land of incurable optimists, adopting a pessimistic doctrine of humanity, which destroys many of its highest ideals and emphasizes the overwhelming weight of the past over the present. This adoption could not have materialized without psychoanalysis paying a heavy due. Like other exotic immigrants, it had to be acculturated before it was accepted; many of its key ideas were distorted or 'corrected' to generate an optimistic clinical psychology focusing on 'growth', 'self-realization' and, ultimately, adjustment of the individual to the demands of society. Freudian concepts with a critical edge, like desire, repression, renunciation and conflict, were smoothed over or eased out to allow for the domination of a new vocabulary of authenticity. The self-realization of authentic individuals was seen as perfectly compatible with the demands made by the social order. Some of these tendencies can be observed already in the work of Freud's pupils who emigrated to America; we have already seen how Reich and Fromm moved towards harmonistic, therapy-dominated positions - Freud himself had complained earlier at Rank's attempts to adapt the psychotherapeutic sessions to the American tempo of life.[1]

During the 1960s, when American society was dominated by the great political and cultural movements which furnished most of the novel elements of its culture, the psychotherapeutic perspective saw a relative decline. It is now widely recognized that if the 1960s were the decade of the political, the 1970s have been the decade of the personal. There is talk of privatization and the 'new narcissism', a return to a pre-occupation with the 'real self', 'feelings' and 'authenticity', and a proliferation of new therapeutic techniques claiming to bring people 'closer to their feelings' and their inner potential.

The right, after an uncomfortable, almost embarrassing decade, has returned to the old warhorses - end of ideology, future shock, generation gap, social engineering and so on. The left, for its part, has tried to show that the 'return of the personal' and the entire movement towards authenticity through therapeutic and mystical growth are futile paths of escape, which only re-inforce the dominant and oppressive ideologies of individualism and consumerism, and generate new domains of capitalist exploitation in the industry of 'personal growth'. Some left theorists have gone back to Freud as the source of the current trends, either to vindicate him by revealing the distortions suffered by his doctrines, or to criticize him and dismiss him, as the ideologue par excellence of bourgeois hegemony. However, the left, in its eagerness to reveal the reactionary character of the inward-looking ideology of the 1970s, has failed to provide any satisfactory analysis of why it is that this ideology has been embraced so intimately by post-Vietnam America. Ironically, even those theorists who have tried to save Freud from conservative distortions have failed to use psychoanalysis to shed light on contemporary American culture. With the possible exception of Christopher Lasch, most theorists have considered psychoanalysis as the science of the individual; by seeing psychoanalysis simply as a branch of psychology, they have ignored the fact that psychoanalysis is not only part of the cultural fabric of American society, but also a powerful theoretical instrument for understanding it.

This chapter is a critique of a theorist who did appreciate the strength of Freud's doctrine as a theory of culture and who used many of its insights to develop what may be the strongest version of privatization/end-of-ideology theory. Philip Rieff's analysis of contemporary America gains enormously from his understanding and elaboration of Freud's ideas concerning the relationship between the various requirements of society and the needs of the individual. Rieff takes seriously Freud's view that society and the individual are fundamentally in conflict and that their inter-relation is complex and ambivalent. Culture is not merely a constraint on the individual's instinctual demands but also a source of objects for instinctual investments (cathexes), of symbolic and substitutive satisfactions; society is a source of consolation. In studying the main features of modern American culture, therefore, Rieff looks at the subtle interplay of social and technological developments and their attendant psychological components. The assimilation of psychoanalysis and the subsequent proliferation of therapeutic ideologies are seen by Rieff as far too important developments to be reduced to the interests of a social class or to the expansion of commodity relations. He therefore tries to discover what it was in Freud's message that appealed to the needs of American people in the twentieth century; to this end, he proposes both a new interpretation of Freud and a new interpretation of American society. Freud emerges from Rieff's reading as a figure of supreme importance

in two ways. As a theorist, he grasped the essence of humanity's
malaise, frustration and anxiety which accompanied the crisis
of religious and political beliefs. As a therapist, he became the
prophet of this disillusioned and uncertain humanity, by offering
in the 'analytic attitude' a new orientation towards life - this
orientation does not look for consolation and salvation in some
dream of a better future, political or religious, but in a reconciliation with and a quiet enjoyment of the present.

Rieff's reading of Freud is a profoundly conservative one;
unlike Marcuse and Norman O. Brown, he finds no hidden revolutionary message in Freud. 'Freud is the least confused of modern
minds because he has no message; he accepts contradictions and
builds his psychology on it' (1959:xx). Unlike Ricoeur, however,
Rieff does not see the role of psychoanalysis in culture as
centred on the interpretation and demystification of humanity's
illusions; the great interest of his analysis lies in his effort to
show that Freud, 'the statesman of inner life, aiming at shrewd
compromises of the human condition, not its transformation', was
not only a seer of a new cultural era and a catalyst who acceler-
ated its arrival, but also its major prophet and ideologue:

> Freud is a prophet nonetheless. Smashing up the past, denying
> any meaningful future and yet leaving that question reasonably
> open, Freud concentrated entirely on the present. Posterity
> will revere him as the first prophet of a time that is simply each
> man's own, a visionary that looked neither backward nor for-
> ward except to stare down projections and to penetrate fix-
> ations. (1959:xxi)

Having uncovered many of mankind's age-old illusions, religious
beliefs, political panaceas, cultural ideals like art and love, having celebrated with Nietzsche the twilight of the idols, Freud
proceeds to equip the new era with its dominant ideology - what
Rieff terms the ideology of the 'psychological man'.

> The 'fundamental problems' to which Nietzsche alludes . . .
> are personal - even intimate - problems. They are pre-
> occupations of psychological man, who in our time has
> succeeded economic man as the dominant moral type of Western
> culture. Once again history has produced a type specially
> adapted to endure his own period: the trained egoist, the
> private man, who turns away from the arenas of public failure
> to re-examine himself and his own emotions. A new discipline
> was needed to fit this introversion of interest, and Freudian
> psychology, with its ingenious interpretation of politics,
> religion and culture in terms of the inner life of the individual
> and his immediate family experience, exactly filled the bill.
> (1959:3)

It now becomes clear that Rieff's interpretation of Freud is of
great importance in this decade, when we are experiencing a new

retreat to the personal following the allegedly futile excursions
into politics, during the 1960s. The ideology of the private man
is once again reigning supreme, and Rieff's interpretation of
Freud would suggest that this is the only ideology capable of
meeting man's present anxieties, based on a scientific understanding of our situation. 'The psychological man takes on the
attitude of a scientist, with himself as the ultimate object of his
science' (1963:13). Thus, Freud by developing and teaching us
to adopt the 'analytic attitude', emerges both as the scientific
interpreter of our era and as its leading ideologue.

RIEFF'S READING OF FREUD

Rieff reads Freud as a profoundly sociological writer. Unlike
Reich and Fromm, he sees no reason to add a sociological
dimension to psychoanalysis, for its central problematic is the
individual in society.

> [Freud] conceives of the self not as an abstract entity,
> uniting experience and cognition, but as the subject of a
> struggle between two objective forces - unregenerate
> instincts and overbearing culture. Between these two forces
> there may be compromise but no resolution. (1959:29)

The self is nothing but the sum total of compromises between
nature and culture. 'As nature, in Freud's conception, is separate from the conscious purposes of man, so Freud assigned to
man a nature apart from the purposes and meaning of society'
(279). Nature is, of course, instinct as far as man is concerned,
and Rieff sees the need to salvage this concept from the assault
of the Neo-Freudian revisionists as clearly as Marcuse and
Brown.

> Far from being a residual idea left over from his biological
> training, as the Neo-Freudians have maintained, Freud's
> theory of instinct is the basis for his insight into the painful
> snare of contradiction in which nature and culture, individual
> and society, are for ever fixed. (35)

Both in his reading of Freud as a sociological writer, and in
his insistence on the centrality of instinct and conflict, Rieff
follows the same path as Marcuse and Brown. Yet, at this point
both his direction and his emphasis change; his discussion of
instincts does not centre on their organic character, as material
forces from which mental and social life proceeds; instead,
Rieff's discussion focuses on the 'wish', the ideational component
of instincts.

> The message of bodily drives and sensations is never received
> directly but comes as an instinctual idea, and in this form it is

more or less imperfectly transmitted. All messages from inner as well as from outer reality, become obscure and need decoding. (74)

So, 'it is the mind - by means of its basic unit, the "wish" - which first defines the body's needs' (73). Freud's theory of instincts finds its way into Rieff's reading mainly through the hermeneutics of desire rather than through the vicissitudes of libido.[2]

If the emphasis in Rieff's interpretation of instincts is the opposite to that of Brown and Marcuse, the direction of his analysis of society - the other major determinant of the individual's predicament - is quite different. Rieff has no patience for Freud's view that civilization is an arena where the struggle between Eros and Thanatos, the two 'heavenly powers', unfolds. Freud's explanation of social cohesion as the product of Eros and Thanatos 'overestimates the community of groups' (257) and 'misses the function of apathy' (260). The key problematic, according to Rieff, is not society's struggle towards social cohesion, but the conflict between its demands and those of the individual. The instincts are firmly embedded in the individual and Rieff opposes their 'sublimation' by Freud to the social and cosmic spheres, for ultimately his interest lies with the individual.

> Freud never articulated a truly social psychology. . . .
> [H]is concern remains the individual and his instincts. . . .
> His interest in the social consistently mirrors his concern with the individual. It is because he is first of all a student of the individual that Freud could entertain the notion of individual and society in active and prolonged conflict with each other, in a theory that supports at different analytical points the claims of both. Notice that he asks not only how the individual endures the social order, but how the social order endures the individual. In our time the first question is imperative; but for the second question many of us have lost sympathy. (276)

Society, therefore, concerns Rieff insofar as it confronts the individual, as a source of instinctual renunciation and compromise. Does Rieff in this way revert to Freud's early and simplistic view of society as merely a constraint upon the instincts? What distinguishes Rieff's concern with society from Freud's earliest views is society's second key function, that of consoling the individual and justifying the suppression of desire. The twin aspects of culture, prohibition and consolation, emerge clearly, as we have seen already, in the psychoanalytic theory of religion. Freud's much-abused formula of religion as the 'universal obsessional neurosis of mankind' is aimed at demonstrating that religion, like neurotic symptoms, affords a substitutive satisfaction, in lieu of the desire which the individual has been forced

to relinquish. Just as symptoms seek to fulfil symbolically a
frustrated desire, religion is the socially sponsored fulfilment of
such desires - the individual turns to the divine in an attempt
to experience the protection and comfort desired from the father.
From Freud's paradigm of religion, Rieff generalizes that culture
is not solely an agency of regulation of the instincts but offers
what he calls a 'therapeutic', a mode of consolation for the
misery of life. It is through the use of such therapeutics that
cultures answer mankind's 'religious question', 'How are we to
be consoled for the misery of living?' (1966:29). Furthermore,
these therapeutics legitimate the controls imposed on the individual and infuse his/her life with meaning. Traditional
therapeutics can be seen as 'some compelling symbolic of self-
integrating communal purpose' (5), which project a character-
ideal as the model of the social behaviour and as standards
around which people organize their lives.

Rieff has argued that until the onset of the twentieth century
three such ideals have dominated Western culture; the political
man, handed down to us from classical antiquity, is embodied
in Plato's postulation of the citizen as the virtuous man; the
economic man, described by Tocqueville as the 'individual',
with his fear and suspiciousness of public life seeks to assert
the importance of his private needs in classical liberalism;
finally and most importantly, religious man, the product of
Christian tradition, asserts his ideal of faith 'in two opposing
ways, either mystic or ascetic' (1963:10). All three therapeutics
have been 'commitment therapeutics' (1966:68f) as individual
motivation stems from identification with and commitment to
the purposes of a political, economic or religious community. In
this way society re-asserts its domination over the individual;
not only does it demand the renunciation of the instincts' original
aims, but it also directs them 'outward, towards those communal
purposes in which alone the self can be realized and satisfied' (4).

Freud, in Rieff's interpretation, is the main critic of this state
of affairs; this is the heart of his argument and where Rieff's
originality lies. Now, reading Freud as a social critic is not new
to us. Since Reich's work, Freud has been considered a critic
of Victorian or indeed bourgeois morality, and in previous
chapters we have examined deeper threads of social critique
woven in his discourse. The special interest in Rieff's view is
that Freud criticizes society's therapeutics, i.e. commitment
therapeutics, and proposes a sphere of existence, a whole new
possibility of living, in which the individual can realize him/
herself without becoming dependent on communal symbolics.
Freud, following Nietzsche, realized that religion (as well as
the other two therapeutics) offers only hallucinatory satisfaction,
which interferes with reality and with truth - it is a therapeutic
which perpetuates humanity's sickness, by increasing the
individual's dependence on the very source of his/her misery.
What both Freud and Rieff find disturbing is that although
religion has nearly monopolized the function of consolation, it

has failed, in spite of the many illusions which it has introduced, to reconcile humanity to its predicament - it has failed to make men and women happy.[3]

> Religion has ruled human society for many thousands of years, and has had time to show what it can achieve. If it had succeeded in making the majority of mankind happy, in comforting them, in reconciling them to life and in making them vehicles of civilization, no one would dream of attempting to alter the existing conditions. (1927c:21:37)

Freud sensed that time was ripe for a new therapeutic, drastically different from those of the past: a therapeutic emanating from his 'god Logos'. Unlike previous therapeutics, his therapeutic did not attempt to console and motivate the individual by immersing him/her in a communal faith, but by informing him/her of humanity's condition and enabling him/her to pursue a path of optimizing private satisfaction.

> Commitment therapies can be distinguished from analytic therapies. The latter arise in an historical period concomitant with the rise of democratic individualism. Commitment therapies, however, operate by returning the individual to the cosset of his natal community or by retraining him for membership in a new community with a more effective pattern of symbolic integration; the therapeutic effort is transformative; the therapist is characteristically either a sacral or an exemplary figure. Analytic therapies, on the other hand, are uniquely modern and depend largely on Freudian presuppositions. The therapeutic effort is not primarily transformative but informative. The assumption of analytic theory is that there is no positive community standing behind the therapist. (1966:76)

Culture in Freud's therapeutic ceases to function as a positive community; it is a negative community, and its characterological ideal, the psychological man, reflects the needs, problems and emotions of the private individual.

Before we examine the special features of psychological man and the community within which he operates, it is worth noting a similarity in Rieff's and Marcuse's readings of Freud as a critic of society. Both theorists maintain that while Freud admitted the unavoidability of certain social restrictions on the instincts, he believed that society is also causing a great deal of unnecessary suffering. In addition, both Rieff and Marcuse detect a distinct possibility of the abolition of these extra sources of suffering, as technology leads humanity away from lives of squalor dominated by scarcity and material deprivation.[4] This is, however, where the similarities end; for Marcuse, the surplus instinctual renunciations are necessitated by a reality principle (a 'performance principle') which requires the total de-sexualization of the body and its transformation into an instrument of

toil and a generator of surplus value. In an era when scarcity
might have been overcome outside capitalist social relations,
the de-sexualization of the body and the restriction of sexuality
to the genital region are no longer a requisite of the necessity
to confront the forces of nature but serve the interest of
domination of man by man. Rieff, on the other hand, sees the
surplus suffering as the product of the illusions through which
commitment therapeutics, like religion, seek to console the
individual by increasing his/her dependence on society. So,
while Marcuse sees Freud's revolutionary message as the necessity
to move to a new reality principle, Rieff argues that Freud's
revolutionary mission was to reconcile the individual with the
reality principle and to re-educate him/her into a new therapeutic.
This re-education consists in unmasking the illusions of his
time through the interpretation of double meanings, for instance
religious symbols, which underneath their sacral appearance conceal frustrated instinctual strivings.[5] Moreover, Freud, according
to Rieff, tries to inform the individual that there is a state of
well-being once we give up the hope of discovering 'large and
general meanings for small and highly particular lives' (1963:21).

> The therapy of all therapies is not to attach oneself exclusively
> to any particular therapy, so that no illusion may survive of
> some end beyond an intensely private sense of well-being to
> be generated in the living of life itself. (1966:261)

Instead of seeking refuge and consolation from the miseries of
life in healing doctrines and identification with communal goals,
psychological man, 'adopting the attitude of the scientist with
himself as the object of his science', learns to live with his conflicts and contradictions and seeks to maximise pleasure through
the careful management of his inner life; by understanding his
desires, the psychological man can manage his libido. While
commitment therapeutics sought to legitimate renunciation
through symbolics of control, Freud's analytic therapeutic
introduces a symbolic of release and private well-being.

> That a sense of well-being has become the end, rather than a
> by-product of striving after some superior communal end,
> announces a fundamental change of focus in the entire cast
> of our culture - toward a human condition about which there
> will be nothing further to say in terms of the old style of
> hope and despair. (ibid.)

The new society, the negative community, is organized as an
archipelago of private units, of nuclear families striving after
private well-being, unknowns in the midst of unknowns, happily
lost and forgotten on the desert islands of their suburban
homes, discovering the 'gorgeous variety of satisfactions'
(241) that technology and self-knowledge have made available to
them. Their reconciliation with their conflicts is the foundation

of their aloneness, their freedom and their happiness.

RIEFF'S INTERPRETATION OF CONTEMPORARY AMERICAN CULTURE

Western culture, argues Rieff, has been going through a deep crisis in the twentieth century. Its two major therapeutics, the polity and religion, have failed to fulfil their twin functions of controlling and consoling; culture is unable to answer through these therapeutics the fundamental problems of our times - the personal, intimate problems of the individual; culture, therefore, is in risk of losing its control over the individual:

> By mid-century, the controls and remissions from those con-
> trols have grown so nearly equal that the one works no better
> than the other. More precisely, the old established controls
> are enunciated so vacuously, and in such hollow voices, that
> they sound like remissions; and remissions have become so
> elaborately stated, by some of the most charming voices in
> our culture, that they seem rather like controls. Such are the
> contrarieties of a revolutionary epoch. (1966:238)

As the moral fibre of the traditional therapeutics weakens, psycho-logical man has crept quietly into the cultural arena and is in the process of replacing his predecessors, driving them out of the arena in shame, rather than competing against them. His spectators are neither the anonymous citizenry of the agora nor the overawed flock of the church, and his promoter is neither the over-powering ruler nor the self-sacrificing prophet. The emergence of the psychological man dissolves the crowds and locks the arena; from now on, the individuals will discover him and celebrate him at home, emerging slowly through their numer-ous inter-personal contacts, not through the loss of self in communal festivals. The Greek chorus is replaced by the theatre of the absurd.

We have now entered the era of the individual, although the old therapeutics have not been driven altogether out of the cultural arena yet. 'In the United States, the rich have already adopted the character structure of the therapeutic' (253). The opposition encountered by the psychological man, in Rieff's reading, does not come from any new cultural prototypes, but from new versions of old ones; underneath the flamboyant, permissive release-oriented communalism of the youth movement lies the religious man, in his pathetic and barely concealed strivings towards a communal symbolic. The same futile strivings towards social justice loom behind the civil rights movement (18, 23). The counter-culture of the 1960s, seen by many sociologists as the backlash of the mass society of the 1950s, is largely for Rieff a futile attempt to resurrect the idols of the past. Neither Dylan nor Martin Luther King could provide the

roots of a new symbolic of commitment, because the youth as
well as the minorities were infected by the attitude of the psychological man, the private individual who strives for release, not
for faith; they were soon tired of communal outpourings of
emotion and started longing for intimacy . . .

Rieff's central pre-occupation, however, is not the challenge
to psychological man which comes from the relics of the past,
but the challenge which comes from within its own ranks; his
major effort in 'The Triumph of the Therapeutic' is to show that
those 'humanistic' critics of Freud who tried to convert psychoanalysis into a cure of souls seek to re-introduce commitment
therapeutics in new guises.

> No one has succeeded in converting *psychoanalytic* doctrine
> into a cure of souls, although many have tried it. What Adler
> and Jung did – what Reich, Horney, Fromm et al., and the
> existentialist writers did after them – is patently not psycho-
> analysis. Freud insisted on keeping the differences intact.
> He did not deny that cures others might develop may be
> efficacious modes of therapy. Many agencies have been shown
> to mitigate suffering, and the chief of these is faith. (89-90)

Faith and psychoanalysis are in contradiction; the success of
the latter depends first and foremost on abandoning the belief
that there can be salvation through faith – the only salvation
man has known. The strengthening of the ego, the increased
capacity to choose, the freeing of the individual from the com-
pulsiveness of unmediated instincts presuppose a reconciliation,
through scientific knowledge of ourselves, with our fate – a fate
of conflict from which there is no cure.

> To be religious is to be sick, by definition: it is the effort to
> find a cure where none can possibly exist. For Freud, religion
> can only be a symptom of what it seeks to cure. Psychoanalysis
> does not cure; it merely reconciles. Therefore it works best
> for the healthy men who are willing to sacrifice their precious
> first sons of thought on the altar of reality. . . . Psycho-
> analysis is a therapy for the healthy, not a solution for the
> sick – except so far as the sick themselves become analysis,
> and find in this therapeutic their personal solution, as Freud
> did. (1959:xiii)

Those who seek through analysis to discover 'the meaning of life'
will be bitterly disappointed, for all they can learn is that there
is none.

The 'return to the personal' of the 1970s, insofar as it is guided
by the humanist therapists or the blissful faces of West Coast
gurus, would be the continuation of the futile struggles of the
1960s, in Rieff's view. They both try in vain to confront personal
problems through a regression to faith – although they may provide
a temporary relief for some, they have nothing new to offer culture.

Yet, every failure of communal faiths, every new disillusionment which they bring about, educates humanity to the fact that
such faiths are incapable of providing the individual with the
release outlets he/she so badly needs. The solution lies in align-
ing oneself to the 'revolution of the rich, by which they have
lowered the pressure of inherited communal purpose upon themselves' (1966:240). So, the black movement, for instance, moves
slowly in the direction of the psychological man:

> The American Negro is himself limited in his demands by the
> successful revolution of the rich. Being American, the poor
> Negro believes that he too can live by bread alone. What the
> Negro asks, essentially, is a place at the American trough.
> But to gain his place he is constrained to ask for something
> more than his share of places. His moralizings become embar-
> rassment, for they hint at something greater than a place in
> a vaşter suburbia. (240-1)

The psychological man and his culture slowly establish themselves
on an ever firmer footing in our society. . . .
   As an analyst, Freud emerges from Rieff's reading both as the
most insightful student of the new culture and its most instruc-
tive educator. As a scientist, he liberates society from the old
daemons, and legitimates the new order of the private man.

> The alternatives with which Freud leaves us are grim only if
> we view them from the perspective of some past possibility,
> as though we were either political or religious men. Assuming
> that these character ideals are, in Freud's terms, regressive,
> the grimness is relieved by the gaiety of being free from the
> historic Western compulsion of seeking large and general mean-
> ings for small and highly particular lives. (59)

Rieff provides not only a coherent and convincing account of
Freud's views on the individual and society, therapy and faith,
character and culture, but his analysis of the cultural crisis of
the twentieth century is provocative and stimulating. His perspective represents the greatest challenge to the radical interpreters of Freud, like Brown and Marcuse. Their attempts are
ultimately reduced by Rieff to futile strivings of sick men, who
in their efforts to escape from the vicious circle of culture follow
the very paths which aggravate their sickness.
   Rieff's argument gains its momentum from what appears a
simple, novel and central fact of twentieth-century culture -
while the public domain has been reduced for the individual to an
impersonal bureaucratic machine, the home has become the source
of warmth, intimacy and meaning. Neither participation in the
political community through the ritual of voting, nor involvement
in the religious community provide the kind of satisfaction that
increasing numbers of individuals seem to experience in their
private lives at home. Gossip yields more pleasure than big

communal ceremonials, watching more than participation. One's
hobby re-affirms one's ability to make certain choices, while
involvement in public affairs emphasizes one's impotence to effect
change.

Public apathy and privatized well-being seem to focus each
individual's attention upon him/herself; Rieff attempts not only
to explain this pre-occupation with the self but to vindicate and
defend it. In this critique I will argue that both of these features,
novel though they may be, are not the outcomes of a cultural
revolution through which the individual has become educated
about his/her life-fate, but the result of a social process which
has immersed the individual even deeper in the oceans of self-
delusion, from which critics of prevailing consciousness like
Marx, Nietzsche and Freud tried to emancipate him/her. In my
critique, I will invoke some of Freud's original formulations not
because I regard them as immutable standards against which
theories of culture must be assessed, but to vindicate them from
Rieff's penetrating but ultimately distorting reading.[6] I also
wish to show how we can begin to use psychoanalysis in understanding and evaluating modern culture, a theme which will
return in later chapters.

Many difficulties in Rieff's argument stem from what may be a
deliberate ambiguity in his use of the term 'character'. Rieff's
character is neither Freud's particular organizations and sublimations of libido, nor Reich's armour of social conventions.
Rather, it is a myth which represents each culture's ideal and
standard of normality. For this reason, Rieff often uses the
term 'character-ideal'.[7] Character-ideals, however, have a
formative impact on individuals, by organizing their self-
interpretations, infusing their lives with meaning and furnishing
them with a motivating idea. Political men are guided and motivated by the Platonic ideal of the responsible citizen, while
religious men are guided and motivated by the Christian ideals
of the ascetic and the mystic. In his discussions of politics and
religion, the character-structures of political and religious men
are kept distinct from their respective ideals - while the ideals
purport to be the embodiment of virtue, happiness and truth,
the character-structures corresponding to them are those of
unhappy, self-deluded and sick men. In his discussion of psychological man, however, the character-structure and the character-
ideal are from the beginning merged into one. Soon after asserting
that 'psychological man is, of course, a myth' (1966:39) Rieff
encounters in flesh and bones the very same man, tucked away
in his private suburban kingdom.

> Nevertheless, psychological man can already be approached
> with the confidence that he is alive and prospering among us,
> nurturing his sense of well-being, the healthy hypochondriac
> who rightly expects to survive all interpretation. (40)

Now, I will not dispute that the ideology of the psychological

man has entered American culture, nor Rieff's contention that
such ideology may be derived from Freud. I will argue, however,
that this ideology can exist only in concert with various other
ideologies, with elements of communal symbolics; in and of
itself the concept of the psychological man is a wish-fulfulling
fiction which could never materialize, within the given socio-
political conditions or any conditions that would allow society
to function as a cohesive whole. Rieff's negative community cannot meet any of the criteria of social cohesion. I will then argue
that even if, in spite of all my previous objections, psychological man was to emerge as a character-structure rather than
merely as a character-ideal, he would be a deeply unhappy one.
Any satisfaction that contemporary Americans derive from
assuming the ideology of privatization requires a complementary
contribution from a communal symbolic, and islands of two or
three individuals cannot generate such symbolics. I will then
show that privatization far from representing the informed complacence and well-being of a new character-structure (the
psychological man), is but a new aggravated form of the old
sickness. All that will remain after we have stripped psychological man from his wish-fulfilling illusions will be a character
closely resembling Marcuse's one-dimensional man; hence the
uncanny similarity in the human archetypes provided by Freud's
most conservative and most radical interpreters.

We can gain an interesting perspective on Rieff's analysis of
contemporary American culture if we compare it with that of
Ernest Becker; while Becker's argument is far weaker than
Rieff's and his proposed solution to the sickness of humanity
much less convincing, his picture of the ideologies and contradictions of many American lives seems more accurate. Becker,
like Rieff, believes that since the decline of religious symbolics,
culture has failed to generate compelling, new 'universal systems
of meaning'. Yet, the individual does not for a minute abandon
his/her quest for meaning in life in favour of the delights of
the psychological man. His quest becomes one for mini-symbolics,
which will allow him to identify himself as 'an object of primary
value' (1962:84). Becker gives us the following telling example:

> Anthony Quinn in his great role in *Requiem for a Heavyweight*
> earned his inner sense of self-value by constantly reminding
> himself and others that he was *'fifth*-ranking contender for
> the heavyweight crown'. This made him somebody. (1962:84)

For Becker, the tragic fate of the twentieth-century individual
is that his meaning-systems are relative, shorn of absolute
character-ideals; but they still remain meaning-systems and they
permeate even the hermetic enclaves of suburban homes. Far from
having adopted the happy complacence of psychological men, the
American middle classes remind us of Becker's 'homo heroica',
even if their uncelebrated hero is Don Quixote. The suburban
American spends as much of his time grooming his image as he

does 'nurturing his sense of well-being'; he tries to entertain
his ennui, Baudelaire's delicate monster, striving for a sense of
inner value through the highly parochial and banal ideologies
of career, consumerism, sport, masculinity, success, etc.

Contrary to what Rieff argues, no group in American society
has adopted the character-structure of the analytic therapeutic,
neither 'the rich', nor the others. What evidence can be more
telling than the successes of the very schools of therapy which
have converted the Freudian therapeutic into a self-advertised
vehicle of salvation? The current vogue of Reichian, Jungian
and gestalt therapies is not an attempt to corrupt psychological
man through tantalizing reminders of his predecessors, but
reflects the unabated needs of the individual for consolation,
identity and meaning. Likewise, privatization cannot be seen as
signalling the arrival of psychological man. The emphasis on the
intimacy of interpersonal relations and family warmth must not
be confused with the character of the psychological men, who
'crowded more and more together, . . . are beginning to live
more and more distantly from one another, in strategically varied
and numerous contacts, rather than in the oppressive warmth
of family and a few friends' (1966:243).

So, the strivings of contemporary Americans towards well-
being are inextricably linked to their strivings towards meaning
and identity. What is more important, however, is that the
psychological man will never arrive, and certainly not if we
expect the 'technological Eden' to deliver him to us. Rieff sees
technology as the source of comfort and affluence; by relieving
humanity from the anxieties of immediate survival and by opening
the way towards a whole new range of satisfactions, technology
emerges as the great social tranquillizer. This proposition fails
to see that affluence is neither permanent nor uniform, because
Rieff fails to locate technology in the socio-political context
which drives it and directs it. The same technology which fills
suburban houses with diverse objects of delight is a source of
the misery of assembly lines and technological unemployment and
the cause of considerable discomfort of polluted cities. Moreover,
affluence itself, by being a relative condition rather than a
permanent and absolute state, acts as an apple of discord more
often than as a social tranquillizer.

But if we cannot count on technology to deliver modern man
from the manifold hardships of reality, neither can we hope that
Freudian therapy will reconcile him to his inner conflicts. Early
on in his career, Freud was quite optimistic about the possibilities of his therapeutic technique, but increasingly came to
recognize its limitations; not only was neurosis a much deeper
condition than he had thought, but the resistances working
against the therapist proved to be much more stubborn. The
work of transference towards reconciliation through self-
knowledge was opposed by the powerful mechanisms of defence;
in 'Beyond the Pleasure Principle', Freud recognized that the
resistances to treatment may have an instinctual foundation –

they often emanate from the death instinct which opposes the
work of the therapist, a fact that subsequent generations of
analysts chose not to advertise as an aspect of their profession.
Under certain circumstances, the analyst may be successful
in lifting the neurotic symptoms, but in the majority of cases
analysis is interminable - the individual may temporarily reconcile himself to a psychic conflict but the conflict may return
later, or may be substituted by another conflict triggered by
the person of the therapist himself. Moreover, the strength of
the instinct which precipitates the pathogenic conflict may be
such that no therapeutic effort by the analyst can bring about
a reconciliation. This is often the case in psychotic and narcissistic conditions.

Reconciliation with one's inner conflicts, under the present
reality principle, can be neither complete nor permanent, as
we saw in Chapter 3. Although Freud believed that his own
therapeutic, based on the education of the ego rather than its
abandonment in faith, was more effective than therapeutic seeking
to restore faith, he did not for a minute consider it an adequate
force to reconcile the conflicts of the vast majority of humanity.
Even in 'The Future of an Illusion', which as we saw is probably his one optimistic book, where he proclaims the ideal of
science as a means of taming the instincts, Freud is cautious to
concede:

> Perhaps it will turn out that human nature remains the same
> even if education is not abused in order to subject people to
> religion. (1927c:21:48)

But the most important argument against Rieff's announcement
of the arrival of psychological man as a novel character-structure,
is given by Freud in his next major work, 'Civilization and Its
Discontents'. A society composed of psychological men could not
hold together as a community. Rieff criticizes Freud for over-
estimating the importance of community in groups (1959:257)
and for missing the integrative function of informed mass apathy
(260). He himself simply wishes the problem of social cohesion
away; he admits that he has lost sympathy for the question of
how (i.e. under what conditions) the social order endures the
individual. For this reason, he misses, like all methodological
individualists, the fact that the individual is not simply confronted by the whole, but is part of the whole, and incorporates
the demands of the whole. The whole itself is not an external
given, but is itself deeply problematic; society cannot exist if
each individual is allowed to carry out his little private revolution and become a psychological man - it will, therefore, oppose
vehemently such attempts, from both within the individual
(through, for instance, the demands of the super-ego) and
outside. Let us see now why an imaginary society composed
entirely of psychological men, however apathetic and contented,
could not function as a society.

As we saw in Part I, before the First World War, Freud like
Rieff took society as a given, and indicted it for repressing
instinct, without really studying why this happened. Society
confronted the individual as an external reality imposing constraints. This view was to be modified considerably as Freud
developed his theory of the super-ego, which represents nothing
but the presence of society within the mental organization of
the individual, like a real fifth column of the mind. During the
same period Freud expanded and reformulated his theory of
instincts. While in his earlier view sexuality was a force within
the individual frustrated to a greater or lesser extent by
society, in the later theory the instincts are re-discovered at
the level of social organization, promoting as well as inhibiting
society's task - Eros may be sublimated to create strong bonds
of lasting duration, while Thanatos seeks to dissolve such bonds,
provided he is not channelled elsewhere. According to this
theory, society is neither given nor permanent; it is built on
libidinal ties between individuals, for 'necessity alone will not
hold them together' (1930a:21:122).

It is society's task to create these libidinal ties out of the
individuals' libido, by (i) turning it outwards, i.e. away from
narcissism, (ii) de-sexualizing it and sublimating it and (iii)
using it to create strong identifications between the members of
the collectivity, under the umbrella of their separate identifications with their leader and the collectivity's ideals and
symbols.

> [Civilization] aims at binding the members of the community
> together in a libidinal way . . . and employs every means to
> that end. It favours every path by which strong identifications
> can be established between the members of the community,
> and it summons up aim-inhibited libido on the largest scale
> so as to strengthen the communal bond by relations to friend-
> ship. In order for these aims to be fulfilled, a restriction
> upon sexual life is unavoidable. (1930a:21:108-9)

As we saw, Freud in a manner not dissimilar to Durkheim's
approaches social cohesion as the product of commitment to compelling ideas, powerful and emotionally appealing leadership,
regulation by a communal symbolic and strong but de-sexualized
emotional bonds. Rieff's negative community (i) has absolutely
no communal goals, (ii) has no moral leaders, for even analysts
(i.e. the people who function as a cultural élite, in his view)
are not exemplars, (iii) is not regulated by any communal
symbolic.

Freud's insistence on society's efforts to utilize Eros in creating social bonds is fuelled by his discovery of a force which is
working against these bonds - the death instinct. Even religion
is acceptable to him, insofar as it functions to appease it, to
prevent a general war of all against all:

> Religion has clearly performed great services for human
> civilization. It has contributed much towards the taming of
> the asocial instincts. (1927c:21:37)

Unlike Durkheim, Freud sees disintegration not simply as the
result of an absence of norms, but as the work of a concrete
force, which society seeks to control.

> Civilization has to use its utmost efforts in order to set
> limits to man's aggressive instincts and to hold the mani-
> festation of them in check by psychical reaction formations.
> (1930a:21:112)

The main avenue for the control of these instincts is their being
turned inwards – from the position of the super-ego, they attack
the ego which experiences a deep and incomprehensible sense
of guilt. This is the second source of the malaise of civilization,
and it is more important than the restriction on sexuality discussed earlier. Now Rieff, along with many other contemporary
American social commentators, like Lasch and Sennett, sees the
days of guilt and of the harsh super-ego as numbered; in American culture the commands of the super-ego have begun to
sound like the moralisms of a person from an older generation,
and the educated youth, the ego, can afford to defy them.
Aggression can, therefore, not be introjected by the psychological man. But neither can it turn outwards, for negative
communities, in their informed apathy, have no enemies. Even
the little path of the 'narcissism of small differences', that
malicious but symbolic form of antagonism, is blocked as the
psychological man's private well-being dissolves identifications
with even minor symbolics, like those of a football crowd.
Finally, Rieff (unlike my own argument in Chapter 13) can
suggest no alternative path along which the death instinct may
be channelled. But then, there is only one outlet for aggression
– to attack the already weak social ties between individuals;
exit negative communities.[8]
Freud's argument, apart from the impossibility of negative
communities to function as communities, reveals a depth in the
discontents created by civilization in its efforts to maintain
social cohesion far deeper than Rieff suspects, when he argues
that, under the reign of the psychological man, 'civilization
could be, for the first time in history, the expression of human
contents rather than the consolatory control of discontents'
(1966:27). Rieff's optimism concerning the well-being of the
hypothetical psychological man stems from his belief that once
the individual reconciles himself with the renunciation of 'crude
and primary' impulses and ceases to look for consolation in
doctrines which increase the range of prohibitions, then he can
orient himself towards *release,* guided by a 'polytheism of
values' (240); but what are these values which derive from no
communal symbolic, which lack moral power? Unlike Becker's

mini-symbolics which aim at giving the individual a sense of self-
esteem, Rieff's polytheism of values is nothing but a glorified
supermarket. The well-being of the psychological man is
founded on our old-familiar ideology of consumption - consumption of material commodities and consumption of each other.

> In Freud's opinion, [the isolation of the psychological man]
> is liberating. At last, in the assurance and control of his
> consciousness, the Western individual can live alone because
> he likes it. Left to ourselves, we will use each other; that is,
> in Freud's mind, the best that can be said about the value
> of love. All other relations except those of use, are pretenses
> with which the psychological man, in the sophisticated calm
> of his detachment, can do without. (1963:22)

The quality of life, according to Rieff, becomes synonymous to
the quantities of goods and people available for use and consumption:

> The reformer asks only for more of everything - more goods,
> more housing, more leisure; in short, more life. This trans-
> lation of quantity into quality states the algebra of our
> cultural revolution (1966:243).

That Rieff should discover the liberation of psychological man
in the ideology of the most banal consumerism is not surprising
- it is the logical conclusion of an argument built on the identification of the character-structure of this man with his ego-ideal;
liberation is identified with the present ex hypothesi. That this
conclusion should be attributed to Freud can only be understood
as a serious misreading of his work. Two observations: Freud
never related happiness with material weath; although he
frequently asserted that material deprivation added to humanity's
discontents, he never saw the choices afforded by wealth as a
road to happiness. As early as 1898, he entertained that 'happiness is the fulfilment of a prehistoric wish. That is why wealth
brings so little happiness: money was not a wish of childhood'
(1954: Letter 82). Second, Freud never suggested that the
value or indeed the pleasure of love dwells in using the other,
in dominating the other. Love 'aims of course at making the
subject independent of Fate. . . . It clings to the objects belonging to [the external world] and obtains happiness from an
emotional relationship to them' (1930a:21:81-2). Use of the other
is seen by Freud not as the quintessence of happiness and love,
but as an expression of humanity's innate aggression:

> Men . . . are . . . creatures among whose instinctual endow-
> ments is to be reckoned a powerful share of aggressiveness.
> As a result, their neighbour is for them not only a potential
> helper or sexual object, but also someone who tempts them to
> satisfy their aggressiveness on him, to exploit his capacity

for work without compensation, to use him sexually without his consent. (112)

It is only in this devious and destructive way that psychological man can be seen as happy man. Apart from it, it seems that there are few avenues of happiness for Rieff's poor psychological man. In his use of the other, he accepts that only the death instinct can find satisfaction in his society.

NARCISSISM AND CONTEMPORARY AMERICA: A FIRST CONSIDERATION

It may, however, be objected that individuals do, in fact, strive for happiness through material possessions and through 'using' their fellow human beings in 'love' relationships without emotional attachments and obligations. Don't they know best what gives them satisfaction? Is my entire argument going to collapse under the weight of everyday evidence? In this review, I have not for a minute disputed Rieff's 'factual observations' - there can be little doubt that many of the features of the psychological man are elements of contemporary American culture. What I have argued so far has been (i) that there are aspects of the contemporary individual, notably those pointed out by Becker, which do not comply with those of the psychological man or any of his predecessors, (ii) that neither technology nor Freudian analysis can bring about the character-structure of the psychological man, under the present socio-political system or under any system that can allow society to function as an integrated whole and (iii) that the strivings of the psychological man do not lead to happiness. These strivings have been discerned from contemporary American culture, slightly before Rieff, by another outstanding interpreter of Freud, whose work we are already familiar with. Marcuse's one-dimensional man, like Rieff's psychological man (and like the 'man' of the 'end of ideology' theorists), stands for political apathy and seeks to relieve his ennui through material well-being, easy sexual fulfilment and the 'instrumental treatment of love'. Both men have given up social criticism - they take society for granted in its present form, Marcuse's as a result of resignation, Rieff's as a result of reconciliation. Marcuse's and Rieff's analyses are similar; their uses of Freud and their interpretations of culture firmly differ. Marcuse uses Freud to criticize the present society, Rieff uses Freud to vindicate it. What for Rieff is the realization of a utopia, is for Marcuse the climax of a nightmare. The one-dimensional man has lost nearly all control over his condition, while the psychological man is in total control of his. The one-dimensional man is confronted with a total absence of real choices, while the psychological man confronts a veritable embarras du choix. Rieff celebrates what he sees as the liberation of humanity from age-old compulsions, by arguing that the

strivings of the psychological man lead to a definite happiness.
Marcuse, on the other hand, sees these strivings as the result
of the complete loss of control, as a symptom of deeper alienation. Use of the other as an object, sexually or status-wise,
is seen as a special case of reification; the psychoanalytic fee,
regarded by Rieff as the medium through which the individual
detaches himself from any emotional obligation towards the
therapist, is for Marcuse but a special case in the cash nexus,
the dehumanization of human relations. While Rieff studies
psychological man and his culture as the products of a cultural
revolution, more-or-less independent of socio-political developments, Marcuse sees his one-dimensional man as the outstanding
product of mature bureaucratic capitalism and the consummation
of its alienation. And this is perhaps the final and outstanding
difference between the psychological and the one-dimensional
men, those unrecognizable identical twins: while the former is
presented by Rieff as the embodiment of 'scientific' self-
knowledge, the latter emerges from Marcuse's discussion as the
personification of self-delusion.

What is perhaps more interesting than whether contemporary
man is alienated, in the context of this critique, is whether he
is neurotic. It is my belief that the strivings of the psychological
man, like those of his predecessors, are themselves the symptoms of an incomplete resolution of neurotic conflict. Rieff
provides a key to the answer himself, by ambiguously referring
to psychological man as the 'healthy hypochondriac' (1966:40).
Hypochondria, as Freud discovered in his important study of
narcissism, is the condition of excessive egoism:

> The hypochondriac withdraws both interest and libido . . .
> from the objects of the outer world. (1914c:14:83)

> A strong egoism is a protection against disease, but in the
> last resort we must begin to fall in love in order that we may
> not fall ill, and we are bound to fall ill if, in consequence of
> frustration, we are unable to love. (85)

Freud's hypochondria is the individual condition which corresponds to Durkheim's social state of egoism. The hypochondriac
finds it hard to love objects of the external world, and when he
does, his object choice is governed by the 'narcissistic type',
i.e. he/she chooses objects like him/herself, obtaining thus
narcissistic satisfaction. This would account for both of the
central features of the psychological man that we noted earlier;
material as well as human objects become sources of satisfaction,
in so far as they enrich his image; they afford a certain narcissistic satisfaction - it is, however, a substitute satisfaction,
for the hypochondriac's aim is ultimately unattainable. The
harder the hypochondriac tries, the more he finds to worry
about; unlike Narcissus, the more he looks at his image, the
more he finds to blame.

The relevance of Freud's notion of narcissism for contemporary American culture goes deeper, as the works of Christopher Lasch and others indicate, and will be re-examined in the chapters which follow. Narcissism can account not only for the frustrated strivings of middle-American suburbia, but also for their direct counter-cultural negatives - the fear of being used, the constant search for intimacy and warmth in polygamous relations, the desire for authenticity, and also the deep aversion for ageing and death. Characteristically, the popularity of psychoanalysis as a therapy may not rest so much in its ability to reconcile and reveal but in the celebration of 'self-discovery'. The importance of transference during the analytic session has receded in favour of the intimacy and closeness of the contact - analysis, by all criteria, has regressed towards catharsis. Above all 'being in analysis' has become the trademark of any person who can seriously claim to 'know himself' and wants to let others know it. Analysis has become one more element of a narcissistic self-image.[9]

What distinguishes the modern hypochondriac from the classical Narcissus is the former's constant need for re-inforcement from the outside and his incorporation of external objects as part of the self-image which he tries to celebrate. This element is so alien to the myth of Narcissus that it is highly doubtful that the term 'narcissism' provides an apt codeword for the phenomena grouped under 'new narcissism'. It does, nevertheless, reveal two features of the new narcissism - that it is both unfulfilled and forced. The hypochondriac's lack of fulfilment differs from that of Narcissus, who needs no encouragement in his playful (though ultimately frustrating) contemplation of love in his own image; moreover, the mythical Narcissus does not know that the image he admires is his own, but mistakes it for that of a beautiful water-nymph (according to some variants of the myth). His drama is his inability to understand why his love must remain ultimately incomplete.[10] The modern Narcissus faces a different drama. He is deeply self-conscious; he looks at his image, but even with the help of others can find little to admire. The more he looks at his image, the more make-up he puts on.

The new narcissism is not only unfulfilled narcissism - it is also forced narcissism. Under his/her narcissistic illusions, the individual may think that he/she is reconciled with him/herself. This applies especially to people who believe that they have discovered their authentic innerself, unpolluted by the pressures of society. Whether the vehicle for this 'self-discovery' is analysis or faith the experience of reconciliation is the same. Yet, as Lasch argues, new narcissism 'is the world view of the resigned'. While reconciliation proceeds from within, resignation is forced from outside. Reconciliation proceeds from the recognition of a friend in what was erroneously regarded as an enemy and dissolves the previous conflict. Resignation comes from the recognition of the enemy as superior, and leads to submission, complemented by resentment - the conflict remains, even if in a latent state.

We have rejoined a main Freudian theme; the modern individual's narcissistic condition is nothing but a variant (a distinct variant. but a variant nonetheless) of the malaise,
the individual's discontents, which stem from his subjection to
the superior forces of civilization - forces which, in today's
society, demand not only instinctual renunciations, but mould
the individual into a functionary of a big, bureaucratic machine
and deny him/her all chances to love the world in which he/she
lives and operates. Whether civilization will forever be a system
of consolatory controls by providing endless justifications and
small narcissistic tickles must remain an open question, Rieff's
resigned optimism can provide no more definite answer than
Freud's ambivalent pessimism.

CONCLUSION

For a moment we may be compelled to think that in Rieff we
encounter the first social commentator of Freud, who did not
succumb to the temptation of stretching psychoanalysis into a
utopian vision. Yet, on closer reflection this is not so; once we
have stripped the psychological man of his illusions, his narcissism, his false pretences, we are left with the psychological
man purely as a character-ideal, a characterological prototype
which seems desirable to Rieff and to a psychoanalytically-
oriented section of the population. Negative community fails to
convince us of its possibility, let alone of its actual presence -
it remains purely a utopian vision. Rieff, of course, would deny
this, since he believes that we are standing at the threshold of
a new cultural epoch, an epoch which is no longer dominated
by faith in the ghosts of the past, an epoch which permits and
actually encourages personal well-being along lines described
by the character-ideal of the psychological man.
  Yet, it is only as a utopia that Rieff's vision preserves its
power, once it has been critically analysed. As a utopia, it
stands perhaps closer to Freud's single utopian work than any
of the utopias discussed earlier. The guiding principle of Rieff's
Utopia of Logos is the familiar ruler of the concluding pages in
'The Future of an Illusion'. Like Freud, Rieff develops his
Utopia of Logos by temporarily blinding himself and ignoring
those very forces that psychoanalytic investigations had helped
to bring to light. Like Freud in the above work, Rieff believes
that the shaking of Acheron, the liberation of desire effected by
analysis, can be followed by its permanent taming by the
forces of Superos.
  Unlike the utopias of Marcuse and Brown, Rieff's utopia does
not emerge out of a detailed and critical discussion of Freud's
metapsychology, but arises from a generalization of the therapeutic paradigm, as a process of self-knowledge. In this way,
Rieff's utopia is closer to the therapeutic utopias of Reich and
Fromm. Yet, in Rieff's view, only Freud's own therapeutic,

promising no general salvation and entertaining no grandoise
hopes, the therapy of all therapies (one could almost say the
'therapy from all therapies'), can effect a genuine social transformation. No orgasms, no spontaneous activity, no spiritual
message, no political revolution can save mankind - only a
detached and clinical knowledge by each individual of his/her
desires, of the necessary restrictions on these desires, and on
the possibilities of their fulfilment.

Rieff's Utopia of Logos is a particularly conservative utopia;
contrary to Marcuse's and Brown's utopias which are based on
the negation of everything related to the present civilization,
Rieff's utopia arises by abstracting the 'positive' elements from
this civilization, and quite deliberately relegating all other
elements to relics of older and bankrupt civilizations, and,
then, arguing that the unstoppable march of psychological men
dissolves them. I hope that this chapter has shown that we are
unlikely to encounter any psychological men in the streets, and
that even in our imagination, psychological men and their culture
will appear as a nightmare rather than a utopia; for, underneath
the narcissistic strivings of contemporary individuals lie similar
psychical contortions as among the over-repressed puritans of
Vienna circa 1900.

Chapter 11
Ernest Becker's 'homo heroica': Narcissus as the cosmic hero without followers

Ernest Becker is an intriguing thinker. Rather like Reich, his work combines a rare feeling and brilliant insights into the cultural climate of his time with a tendency to generalize and project grandiose theories of human nature from such insights. These theories are, at times, disturbingly naive, and on the whole will not concern us here. Nor does his work have any special interest for our discussion of Freud, a thinker who influenced Becker only indirectly, via Fromm and Adler. What does interest us is his cultural analysis of American society, which complements the works of Brown, Marcuse and especially Rieff as well as those more recent theorists of 'new narcissism'. Becker reminds us that therapeutics of commitment are alive and well, in spite of the decline of political activism and religious faiths. Although the twentieth century, in Becker's view, has seen the decline and 'death of meaning', the contemporary individual always strives to infuse his/her life with meaning, in terms of some symbolic of values which stands above him, even if he can find no other followers of this symbolic. It is for this reason that I will introduce some of Becker's ideas, in the context of a broadening of my discussion of contemporary American culture, with special reference to the phenomenon of new narcissism.

Unlike the perspectives of Marcuse, Brown, Rieff and, of course, Freud, Becker recognizes no underlying antagonism between the individual and society.

> The most impressive thing about the study of culture and personality is how neatly the two elements dovetail into one coherent picture. When anthropologists and sociologists had succeeded in formulating this picture, they were struck by the genius of man's ordering of his world. (1962:92)

The concept of the 'genius of man' recurs ad nauseam in 'The Birth and Death of Meaning', to denote what Becker sees as humanity's unique ability to create a world, a culture, aimed at satisfying the individual's deepest needs. This harmonistic view goes far beyond the views of Fromm and Reich - while these two theorists envisage a possibility of final reconciliation between human nature and a certain kind of society, Becker believes that harmony prevails in all kinds of society, starting from the earliest human collectivities in Eastern and Southern Africa.

Moreover, Becker's harmonistic views extend to the relation
between man and nature; unlike Marcuse and Rieff who argue
that a reconciliation between humans and nature becomes possible
when technology curbs the terrifying 'arbitrariness' of nature,
Becker insists that harmony has always existed between the two.

> [The following] has been one of the happier circumstances of
> life on this planet. It seems that mankind has been fortunate
> largely because the earth has been so bounteous. There has
> been plenty to eat, delightful climates for the most part, lots
> of materials for clothing and shelter, lots of offspring. The
> result has been that man seems to have been permitted by
> natural bounty to live largely in a world of playful fantasy.
> (1962:132)

For Becker, man never fell from paradise. The realm of the
body, of need, of pain and struggle never appeared; fantasy
has always been the major element of civilization. Man did not
tame nature through his labour and industry but was always
free to abandon himself in playful fantasy. This view of fantasy
must be clearly distinguished from Freud's theory of phantasy
as a symptom of frustrated desires, as a mini-psychosis afford-
ing substitute gratification. For Becker, fantasy is a way of
acting and of interpreting one's acts in terms of a communal
symbolic, whose social function is the creation and maintenance
of socially cohesive groups, and whose psychological function
is the satisfaction of the most fundamental need of every individual. On the first function, Becker has little to add to the
formulations of such thinkers as Durkheim, Marx, Rieff and the
modern sociological schools of thought; he focuses on the second
function, the contribution of the symbolic to the well-being of
the individual.

The contours of Becker's anthropology begin to emerge. The
human being is for him, as for Cassirer, an animal symbolicum,
in the first instance. This, of course, reminds us of Brown,
who saw the whole of culture as a massive symbolic superstructure, created by man in his twin escape from love and death.
For Brown too, all things are symbolic: 'Everything is symbolic,
including the sexual act' (1966:131). Yet, for Brown the animal
symbolicum does not represent the essence of mankind, but
rather the sickness of mankind, the negation of the essence:

> The *animal symbolicum* . . . is *animal sublimans*, committed to
> substitute gratification of instincts for real gratification, the
> desexualized animal. By the same token the *animal symbolicum*
> is the animal which has lost its world and life, and which pre-
> serves in its symbol systems a map of lost reality, guiding the
> search to recover it. . . . The *animal symbolicum* is man
> enacting instinctual gratification, and therefore still caught in
> the dream solution discovered in infancy. (1959:167, 168)

Not so for Becker, who insists that the creation of elaborate
meaning systems, the erection of all-encompassing symbolics,
represents the fulfilment of humans' deepest need and the
expression of the 'dominant motive in Man.' The way in which
he derives this dominant motive shows the heavy influence of
Fromm's anthopology and Adler's psychology:

> In a word, Freud failed to explain satisfactorily human
> *motives. . . .* But if Freud was wrong about motives, it
> was because he was wrong about biological instincts. And if
> instincts do not drive man, what then does? The main reason
> that the great Alfred Adler is still contemporary is that he
> broke with Freud very early on this problem when he very
> clearly saw and strongly proclaimed that the basic law of
> human life is the urge to self-esteem. Once you make this
> break with Freud, stand up for it openly and build your
> theory and clinical interpretations around it, a whole new
> world of understanding opens up to you. (1962:74-5)

We need not examine whether Freud failed to explain motives
and, if so, what it was that he did explain. Becker's own
account of the process of 'socialization' is structured around
two dominant themes, the original confusion of the child and
his need to organize his experiences around a frame of reference
(similar to Fromm's 'frame of orientation'), so that he can optimize his sense of worth. Through socialization, the child learns
to be a metteur en scène, by discovering scenarios according to
which he can derive self-esteem. People have different characters, insofar as the modes of earning self-esteem vary, but the
pursuit of self-esteem is an underlying invariant - it characterizes all human beings and all cultures.
While the need for self-esteem cannot be reduced to any other
need, Becker sees this need as the response of human nature to
the enormous existential problems which confront it.

> The main anxieties of the child are frankly existential from the
> beginning, and his sexual pre-occupations reflect deep and
> vital questions about the mystery of life and death: 'What is
> my body, what do these appendages *mean*, why do I have
> them, who am I, why am I here?' and so on. (60)

Becker's way of projecting adult anxieties onto childhood experiences is truly amazing; the struggle for meaning comes long
before the struggle for pleasure, the child is more concerned
about the meaning of appendages than making them feel good.
One wonders what kind of meaning the child may be after.
It is easy now to see why Becker (like Brown, but for entirely
different reasons) endorses Roheim's famous definition of culture
as the sum total of defence mechanisms of an infant 'afraid of
being alone in the dark' (148). First, because for Becker the
fear of the dark is common to children and adults and it amounts

to an existential fear of being unable to locate oneself in a
symbolic matrix, it is a fear of anomie. Second, because the
mechanisms of defence are achieved through the construction of
symbolic scenarios, through which every individual can derive
a sense of self-worth. And third, because culture is nothing but
the standardization of these scenarios within each society, in
what Becker calls 'hero systems', without which the individual's
quest for socially approved self-esteem would be futile (83ff).

We can also understand the reasons for Becker's insistence
on the 'genius of man'; for in his theoretical system, the correspondence between the individual's need for symbolics and
culture's ability to provide precisely such symbolics has no
justification - it is truly the accomplishment of deus ex machina,
it is a miracle. As a result, Becker would seem incapable of
accounting for those cultures which, at certain times, fail to
provide their members with compelling symbolics, leading them to
mental break-downs or individual deviance. Is this due to the
ungenius of man?[1]

We now come to the significant part of Becker's contribution,
to his account of what he sees as the tragic fate of the contemporary individual. Coming from a background in ethnography,
Becker was impressed by the incredible variety of the symbolics
that different cultures mobilize in order to invest the lives of
their members with meaning. The heroes of one culture were
often found to be identical with the social outcasts of other
cultures, the gods of one were often the devils of other; moreover, Becker was impressed by the shattering effect that contact between cultures with different hero-systems had on each
other, for such contact undermines the absolute character of
each culture's hero-systems.[2] Like many anthropologists, Becker
is led to a position of cultural relativism: in spite of each
symbolic's need to appear to its adherents as absolute, symbolics
possess no truth value - hero-systems are relative (142).
The cultural absolutism of the ancient Greeks and Romans, of
the Spanish conquistadores and British colonialists, of every
self-respecting religious or political culture, has been displaced
today by a profound relativism of values; the twentieth-century
individual has become deeply aware that meaning systems are
relative and this is the drama that he/she faces. The relativism
of values, far from presenting the individual with a welcome
choice and the possibility of making up his/her own mind, according to the old liberal tradition and Rieff, creates a rather
intolerable situation for each individual. Becker arrives at the
same conclusion as Brown, albeit by a shorter and more empirical
path - there is no true meaning to life, death and love, people's
condition and actions have no ultimate purpose. Meaning is
fictitious, hero-systems are fictitious, the content of culture
itself is fictitious - the whole culture is an illusion. *But*

> if you reveal the fictional nature of culture, you deprive life
> of its heroic meaning because the only way one can function

as a hero is within the symbolic fiction. If you strip away the fiction, man is reduced to his basic physical existence - he becomes an animal like any other animal. (143)

Yet, the death of meaning does not correspond to humanity's return to what Becker considers the level of animals - the reason is that the big existential questions, which do not seem to bother our relatives in the animal kingdom, not only remain but they press more urgently than ever for a solution. The death of meaning makes the prospect of death intolerable and the need for new brands of heroism urgent. At this point, Becker's argument seems to collapse, both in 'The Birth and Death of Meaning' and in his last work 'The Denial of Death'. Having reached the point of suggesting that a radically new human being is in the process of emerging, he falls back on the old solution, cosmic heroism, which the death of meaning has rendered ineffective. The new form of heroism is 'the power to support contradictions, no matter how glaring or hopeless they may seem' (1962:196). Unlike Rieff, Becker is unwilling to give up his belief that the next therapeutic will be yet another therapeutic of commitment. What he argues is that this commitment, unlike the commitment of past therapeutics, must recognize and tolerate the fictitious nature of the symbolic which feeds it - commitment is knowingly attached onto a fiction. Rieff saw reconciliation with contra- diction (the contradiction between individual and society) as the beginning of a new culture - one which dissolves the meaning of the old religious question 'How are we to be consoled for the misery of life?' Becker, on the other hand, thinks that recon- ciliation with contradiction (the existential contradictions) means a renewed commitment to a symbolic which is recognized as fic- titious. The human being must learn to structure his/her life around a meaning system that is not rooted in reason, one which in fact contradicts reason.

> There is a driving force behind a mystery that we cannot understand, and it includes more than reason alone. The urge to cosmic heroism . . . is sacred and mysterious and not to be neatly ordered and rationalized by science and secularism. (1973:284)

It seems that it is, for Becker, a sign of cosmic heroism for the twentieth-century individual to erect his own golden calf and worship it.

Now, there are many weaknesses in Becker's argument which hardly need to be pointed out; by far the most striking weakness is his irritating tendency to project cultural objectives, anxieties and needs of contemporary middle-class America onto the whole of mankind. I find this tendency irritating because I believe that his observations are both accurate and insightful when applied to the contemporary American middle-class culture; in this way his arguments provide a good critique of Rieff, because they remind us that (i) a large number of people are indeed motivated by an apparent need to promote their self-esteem, and (ii) the symbolic fragmentation of this society makes social re-inforcement of self-esteem very much more difficult than before.

If we pursue a little further the comparison of the views of Becker with those of Rieff we notice an interesting antithesis in their concepts of social cohesion; while Rieff's formulations correspond to Durkheim's mechanical solidarity, where the source of social cohesion and individual health and happiness is the common faith and its corresponding symbolic, Becker's views correspond to Durkheim's organic solidarity - the individual is not content in sharing a common symbolic, but needs to identify himself as 'an object of primary value' (1962:84) in terms of this common symbolic. As the extract from 'The Birth and Death of Meaning' quoted in the previous chapter suggested, Anthony Quinn, in 'Requiem for a Heavyweight', felt that he was somebody by reminding everyone that he was the 'fifth-ranking contender'. In short, for Becker, the individual is not integrated in the community through sharing a common symbolic, common exemplars and common norms, for example that boxing is a game for real men, that Marciano was a great boxer, but the individual must derive a sense of personal self-value through this symbolic; he must be able to distinguish himself from others, he must be unique, in however small a way. The primary function of culture is to provide individuals with such symbolics against which they can all measure themselves and derive their self-esteem. In the past, cultures relied on relatively few symbolics, deriving mostly from religion and politics, but as the relative character of symbolics becomes evident, more and more symbolics become available, so that most people can attach themselves to some symbolic or other and thus obtain self-esteem.

Becker, by projecting what he sees in human beings of today to all human cultures, ignores the very long stretch of history when individuals derived their solidarity in a community by not being themselves objects of primary value, by not being individuals, but by sharing the same identification with the leader. In a culture dominated by a single symbolic, each individual, far from being an object of unique value, shares the same or similar positions with many other individuals, in terms of the symbolic. It is as cultures become more organized, as a result of the increasing complexity of the division of labour, that solidarity acquires an organic character. Rieff, on the other hand, seems to commit the opposite error, namely, of thinking that as soon as mechanical solidarity, based on communal faith, disintegrates, all community-based symbolics dissolve, Becker and Durkheim remind us that even in the twentieth century there can be powerful symbolics which function to integrate society, even if these symbolics are neither universal nor absolute.

Although one may feel tempted to be ironic towards Becker's equation of each individual's adoration of his/her golden calf

with 'cosmic heroism', as well as towards several others of his
arguments, it seems to be that his fundamental insight into
culture was not mistaken; ultimately, the compulsive search for
mini-symbolics, in terms of which every person can be a hero,
when followed to its natural conclusion can only lead to the
phenomenon we introduced in the previous chapter - narcissism.
Each mini-symbolic is reduced to a purely personal symbolic,
the golden calf ends up by being each person's self-image. But
is this 'purely personal symbolic' not exactly what a neurotic
symptom is defined as by Freud? Have we not once again been
led, via a circuitous path, to the very same conclusion that
was reached at the conclusion of the previous chapter?

This comparison of the views of Becker with those of Rieff brings
out sharply the strengths and weaknesses of their respective
arguments. At the same time, however, it is important not to
underestimate the important similarity in their views of the problems which confront contemporary culture - the absence of a
communal symbolic with the power of the old symbolics of religion
and politics, which can infuse people's lives with meaning and
relieve the discontents of civilization. For both Rieff and Becker,
culture has lost its ability to generate meaning systems which
regulate and integrate the community; meaning is all but dead.

In the works of Brown and Marcuse, we studied a rather
different view. Culture has far from exhausted its capacity of
generating systems of meaning, even if those of contemporary
culture may lack the sweepingly compelling force of the grand
symbolics of the past. Narcissism may indeed represent a fragmentation of traditional meaning systems, but this, far from
representing a break-down of all communal symbolics, coincides
with the rise of a new symbolic gestalt. This gestalt, comprising
the values of consumerism, status and careerism, individualism,
conformity (and all the values that critics of narcssism, like
Lasch, Wolfe and Sennett, have perceptively depicted -
authenticity, intimacy, no commitment, etc.), has been generated
by the modern culture, with its vast appareil of mass media; it
is a gestalt which has dissolved all visions of alternative social
and cultural modes, a gestalt which emphasizes freedom of
choices without permitting any real choices. In the view of
Brown and Marcuse, the mini symbolics which people develop in
order to derive their narcissistic feeling of self-esteem are all
contained within one mass impersonal symbolic - the symbolic of
consumer society, with its myriads of televisual symbols, constantly re-inforced through ritual reproduction. One has an
infinite choice of standardized things, standardized products,
standardized life-scenarios, standardized adventures. Narcissism,
far from existing in a communal vacuum, in a world depleted of
symbolics, is the product of a new symbolic, a new culture,
which motivates individuals in carrying out the most cheerless
functions with the zeal of compulsive neurotics. Even in their
profoundly personal mini-symbolics, the narcissists are unwittingly choosing among standardized models of neuroses.

Chapter 12
Narcissism and contemporary culture

Few labels appear to have captured the spirit of an era better
than that of narcissism when applied to post-Vietnam America.
Through this concept an increasing number of American social
commentators and critics seek to express and analyse some of
the phenomena encountered in the discussions of Marcuse,
Brown, Rieff and Becker; in particular, the break-down of traditional communities and their integrating symbolics, the fragmentation of values, a general disillusionment with politics, the
pursuit of pleasure for its own sake mostly through consumption
of commodities and images, the avoidance of responsibilities
generated by lasting emotional commitments and the simultaneous
need for intimacy and approval, the turn towards therapy as a
means of resolving personal problems and the general privatization of what has been described as the 'me-generation'.
Some of the cultural analyses centring on the concept of
narcissism were prompted by psychiatric research into narcissism by clinical writers like Kohut and Kernberg. Since the
Second World War, it has been suggested, transference neuroses,
so prevalent in Freud's time, have been eclipsed in Western
societies by character disorders associated with feelings of
emptiness and meaninglessness, diffuse ego boundaries, hypochondria and a lack of cohesive sense of self. Since the 1960s
these disorders have led to a re-awakening of interest in
narcissism as the key to their aetiology. The significance of this
shift in psychiatric interest lies in its implication that mental
disorders are nowadays associated not with the over-regulation
of libido and the resolution of the Oedipal trauma, but rather
with the individuals' inability to relate with the world in deep
and meaningful ways - in short, with the individuals' unwillingness to invest their libido in satisfactory ways.
The symptoms of these narcissistic disorders appeared to the
cultural commentators and critics to reflect the traits of a
prevalent social character and of a cultural set-up, just as the
symptoms of the over-repressed neurotic had appeared a generation earlier to match the character traits of the authoritarian
personality and the cultural parameters of fascism. Narcissism
emerged, therefore, as the central psychoanalytic concept from
which an analysis and critique of contemporary culture could be
undertaken. The consequences of the introduction of this concept into cultural discussions have been mixed; on the one hand,
many features of our culture have been identified and their
proper psychological standing has been established; on the other

hand, however, there has been a tendency to regard every
cultural phenomenon as a manifestation of the new narcissism
or ignore it altogether when it cannot be assimilated in the
discussion of narcissism. This reductionism has led to monochromatic and excessively integrated pictures of contemporary
societies and has also obscured some of the ambiguities inherent
in the concept of narcissism. The principal concern of this
chapter is neither the precise characterological account of the
narcissistic personality nor the detailed discussion of those
cultural features which make up the culture of narcissism;
both of these tasks have been carried out in detail and with
considerable success by writers like Christopher Lasch, Richard
Sennett, Tom Wolfe, Simon Sobo, Jim Hougan and many others.
Instead, we will examine the factors which have led to the
prominence of narcissistic traits, the extent of this prominence
and its implications.

Like Rieff's psychological man, the narcissist (especially in
Lasch's arguments) emerges from the ashes of the economic man
and in particular of the organization man. But the forces which
bring him into the world are neither the new technological
Eden nor the liberating potential of psychoanalysis; instead, the
modern narcissist is the product of the lovelessness of the
modern world, its cultural and spiritual impoverishment and the
domination of the economy, politics and culture by large-scale,
impersonal organizations. Life within such organizations involves
for the majority a blind following of bureaucratic rules and
routines with a minimum of initiative, originality or creativity.
The success, growth and power of large-scale bureaucracies are
the result of their ability to co-ordinate the activities of vast
numbers of individuals in entirely impersonal, stable and predictable patterns, in which relations between individuals approximate
those between components of a machine. Neither emotional bonds
between individuals nor overall identification with the organizations and its goals are required; in the impersonal world of
bureaucracy there is little room for Eros in any of its embodiments as studied by Freud and as analysed in Part I. Unlike
primary groups, it is not Eros which holds them together, but
the virtual certainty that individuals will behave according to
their predetermined routines. Although some highly placed
executives may in fact develop a corporate identity, as bureaucratization expands 'the "organization man" gives way to the
bureaucratic "gamesman" - the "loyalty era" of American
business to the age of the "executive success game"' (Lasch
1979:92).[1]
But if the bureaucratic order of our culture represents a
world without feeling or passion, the two old bastions of feeling
and passion, politics and religion, are also, at least in much of
the Anglo-Saxon world, losing their grip over individuals and
their ability to generate strong libidinal bonds amongst them.
Massive political and religious apathy reflects the general dis-

illusionment with large-scale ideals, which we encountered in
our discussion of Rieff, and the break-down of these traditional
communities marks the decline of the necessity for social regulation through moral constraint. Politics, as Lasch and others
have succinctly shown, has turned into a spectacle, in which
policies are overshadowed by public images, conflicts of
interests are eclipsed by televisual duels, and tragic blunders
of policy are obscured by innocuous public slips. Politicians
become experts in public relations - politics, the production of
grand spectaculars at the right time.

Spectacle itself has lost its communal ritual or orgiastic
character[2] and has become a commodity for privatized consumption. Television has completed a process which not only excluded
the audience from being part of the spectacle, but transformed
spectacle from a communal celebration to an item of voyeuristic
'entertainment'. The delirious lamentations of ancient Greek
theatre-goers (which so scared Plato), the wild paroxysms of
the Roman arenas have been replaced by the venerating silence
of modern concert halls and theatres and the forced silence of
privatized consumption of entertainment. In this way, spectacle
has lost its ability to provide not only a cathartic outlet for
emotional tension, but also a basis of emotional bonds and a
sense of identity among the audience. Like bureaucratic staffs,
the contemporary audience can hardly be said to be cemented by
love bonds, like the ones which Freud analysed.[3]

These brief arguments, following the arguments of Marcuse and
Rieff examined earlier, begin to suggest a fundamental difference
between the Freudian model of society, held together by libidinal
bonds, and contemporary society, in which such bonds have
receded in importance. It would seem, in other words, that contemporary culture has progressed beyond the point where it
has to rely on sublimated love bonds, cemented by compelling
communal symbolics and strong leadership, to ensure social
cohesion. In the regimented public spaces of modern cities, in
office blocks and factories, in shops and halls of entertainment,
in churches and political meetings, in streets and on pavements,
in bars and restaurants, one will encounter individuals who go
about their business, unknown in the midst of unknowns, parts
of a crowd but not parts of a community. While it would be premature to argue with Rieff that Eros has been effectively banned
from public life, it must be recognized that his public appearances are becoming increasingly rare; but then two direct
questions are raised. First, how does our culture establish and
preserve social cohesion, and second, what forms does Eros
assume within this culture? The first question will be left for
the following chapter, but the second question will pre-occupy
us for the rest of this one.

Finding it difficult to discover Eros in public life, we may
turn to private life and to the famous sexual revolution, which
replaced the old Victorian taboos with a healthy attitude towards
sexual enjoyment. It would seem that in our permissive society

Eros has finally discovered his natural habitat, in uncomplicated,
free sexual relationships, unburdened by the old-fashioned
impediments of possessiveness, procreation, morality and love.
There is a compelling simplicity in this view - our culture has
relieved us of the hideous libidinal contortions imposed on
past generations, has surrendered all claim to sexuality (since
it no longer needs to sublimate it in the interest of social
cohesion), and has enabled us to maximize our pleasure by
investing our libido in attractive sexual propositions with
minimal liabilities (a view, incidentally, which reverberates in
Rieff's 'managerial ego'). Sheltered from the complications of
public life, private life has become the ghetto of the pleasure
principle, a kind of Cythera of permutating twosomes, in which
the old-fashioned vicissitudes of sexuality become redundant -
sublimation, regression, phantasy, repression, identification
and, perhaps, love are replaced by freely flowing libido, dis-
charged regularly on a succession of sex objects. From the
point of view of the individual's libido, this ghetto appears as
a veritable supermarket of sex objects to be chosen, used,
consumed and even returned, in exchange for presenting him/
herself as an attractive sex object.

I wonder whether such misinterpretation of culture based on
a misinterpretation of his theory would have amused Freud.
While relaxation of sexual morals is, from a Freudian point of
view, welcome, unrestricted sexual relationships, to the extent
that they may be possible, in no way guarantee the consummation
of Eros, happiness or even pleasure in the narrow sense. By
using the theoretical concept of 'love-object' on which libido
is cathected, Freud exposed himself to very serious misunder-
standings and misinterpretations. For Freud, love-objects, far
from being 'quite literally objects' (Parsons 1952:24) selected on
the basis of external appearance, are 'symbolic images or unconscious presentations made up of innumerable single impressions'
(1917e:14) and their attractiveness lies in different associations
with persons loved in the past, incidents which occurred earlier
in life, anaclitic and narcissistic orientations, libidinal regressions
and so on.[4] In short, the love-object is selected not on the
basis of its external characteristics as an object, but rather on
the basis of the meaning attributed to it through unconscious
associations; libido is not invested in a thing but in an imago.
Second, Freud never suggested that the love-object is purely an
instrument of pleasure; on the contrary, he persistently casti-
gated the Victorian divorce of the object of 'tender feeling',
affection and respect (the wife), from the object of sexual desire
(the mistress, the prostitute), and argued that relations limited
to the one or the other dimension of sexuality are incomplete and,
ultimately, frustrating.[5] Freud never envisaged sexual satisfaction as a matter of 'scientific management of libido' (to use
Marcuse's apt expression), a matter of the technics of orgasm;
on the contrary, the preconditions of erotic fulfilment lie in the
mind, in the qualities with which the love-object is invested, the

idealization and the feeling of reciprocation and being loved.

> [Love] aims of course at making the subject independent of
> Fate. . . . It clings to the objects belonging to [the external
> world] and obtains happiness from an emotional relationship
> to them. (1930a:21:18-2)

Phantasy, illusion and ideal are all integral ingredients of erotic
satisfaction, and the sense of being independent of fate may
indeed be the principal illusion of Eros. The state of being in
love, as analysed by Freud (1921c:18:111ff, 140ff; 1930a:21:66),
according to which there is a certain loss of the sense of self,
an impoverishment of the ego and an idealization of the loved
person, has nothing in common with the consumption of love-
objects which prevails in the Cythera of permutating twosomes.
On the contrary, treating people as 'sex objects' for ephemeral
sexual satisfaction inhibits the consummation of Eros, and, by
necessity, creates various libidinal complications which we have
already encountered in our discussion of Rieff's psychological
man, to whom we shall return shortly.

It is easy, I think, to see how a culture which transforms
human beings into objects in their public lives, promotes treatment of human beings as sex objects in their private lives. Just
as public lives are governed by bureaucratic routines, private
lives become structured along routines repetitively aired by the
media, which dictate the attributes of an attractive man or
woman. Object-selection loses its personal character, moulded
through memory, phantasy and experience, and acquires the
compulsive automatism of a Pavlovian response; sexual behaviour
loses its playful spontaneity to become governed by a precisely
regulated ritual of consumption, from which commitment, responsibility or indeed feeling are excluded, since after all the
magic of consumption is the total absence of obligation towards
that which is being consumed. It is this total depersonalization
of sexuality, the images of bodies as objects of sexual consumption, that provides one of the two clues for the success of pornography, and yet at the same time it provides us with the clue
to why sexual consumption does not equal erotic fulfilment – for
sex, among carnal objects, as portrayed in pornography, is sex
in the realm of phantasy, the realm of unrealized and often
prohibited desires, a realm which undermines the very thinghood of the bodies which are portrayed.[6]

In trying to answer our original question 'What has happened
to Eros, the "invincible in battle", who promises to make man
independent of fate?' we are confronted with a situation in
which Eros finds no objects to attach himself, with a world
lacking objects of love and an individual unable to construct
them. Nevertheless, it would be fair to say that in the lovelessness of modern cities, modern organizations, modern homes,
people still strive to infuse objects with emotional significance,
they strive to create imaginary love-objects out of automobiles,

pet animals, hobbies and different material possessions. In a
world so empty of feeling, emotion and affection, it is often
disturbing to observe the amounts of displaced love directed
towards things which can be manipulated physically and
symbolically, without raising objections and without actively
reciprocating this love, things that, to use Freud's expression,
do not deserve our love. The idealization of the loved object
which Freud observed in the state of being in love has been
displaced towards things; but instead of an impoverishment of
the ego, idealization of material objects seems to strengthen
the ego temporarily. It is this factor which suggests that such
objects are not cathected libidinally, but rather absorbed as
part of the ego's self-image. But this situation is already
familiar to us, from our discussion of Rieff's psychological
man – it is the trademark of the modern narcissist, who does
not love objects but assimilates them into his/her ego (after
the early oral experience) in order to enrich his/her self-image
with the idealized properties of these objects. Just as material
commodities are consumed to enrich man's physical constitution,
material *and* human commodities are consumed to enrich the ego's
self-image, the imago which it carefully grooms and loves.

At this stage it may be objected that there is nothing new
about this 'new narcissism', which has attracted so much attention in recent years. After all, as early as 1914, Freud had
argued that every ego is also an imago, a precipitate of past
identifications, which is subsequently enriched through further
identifications with one's treasured possessions, including one's
children,[7] as well as with cultural artifacts. Later, Freud gave
culture a more general narcissistic function,[8] as part of the
great cultural project to console individuals for the miseries of
life. What then is the novelty of the new narcissism?

It will be remembered that in our critique of Rieff's psychological man, it was pointed out that this man's narcissism, far
from being spontaneous and emancipatory, is forced and unfulfilled – forced, because it is caused by an inability to find
lovable objects, and unfulfilled because, as Freud points out,

> the realization of impotence, of one's own inability to love in
> consequence of mental or physical disorder, has an exceed-
> ingly lowering effect upon self-regard. (1914c:14:98)

Contrary, however, to Freud's assessment, the new narcissist's
inability to love is not the result of a personal disorder, but
rather of the fact that he/she lives in a loveless world, in a
double sense – a private world devoid of love-objects and a
public world shorn of institutions and ideals with which he/she
can identify. The consumption of material as well as human
objects, seen from the point of view of libidinal economics, does
not direct the libido outwards towards the objects of the world,
but inwards towards a temporarily gorged ego. But this ego,
instead of re-directing libido outwards by establishing emotional

relationships or upwards towards sublimated cultural ideals,
keeps it all to itself; what then happens to all this libido appropriated by the ego? It will be recalled that Freud envisaged part
of it as forming the ego's anti-cathexes which keep the content
of the unconscious safely repressed and part of it as equipping
the ego with a constant amount of self-love which protects it
from the attacks of the super-ego; but with the general reduction in the power of the super-ego which we noted earlier,
the necessity of these two libidinal investments is seriously
diminished, and as a result there arises a libidinal inflation in the
ego, leading to a regression to a stage of auto-erotic megalomania,
the stage when all the libido was concentrated in the undifferentiated ego/id in early infancy. This is a phenomenon characteristic of what Freud referred to as 'paraphrenias':

> The difference between paraphrenic affections and trans-
> ference neuroses appears to me to lie in the circumstance that,
> in the former, the libido that is liberated by frustration does
> not remain attached to objects of phantasy, but returns to the
> ego; the megalomania then represents the mastery of this
> volume of libido, and thus corresponds with the introversion
> onto the phantasy-creations that is found in the transference
> neuroses; the hypochondria of paraphrenia, which is homo-
> logous to the anxiety of the transference neuroses, arises from
> a failure of this effort in the mental apparatus. (1914c:14:86)

Thus, paraphrenia with its attendant illusions of omnipotence,
its inability to cathect objects of the world and cultural artifacts,
and its underlying hypochondria, seems to provide the clinical
paradigm for the condition of the new narcissism. Yet, the
underlying difference between the new narcissism, as described
by Lasch, Sennett, Wolfe and others, and Freud's clinical account
lies in the new narcissist's dependence 'on others to validate his
self-esteem. He cannot live without an admiring audience'
(Lasch 1979:38). This contrasts sharply with the pronounced
autism of narcissistic conditions, which makes them unsuitable
for psychoanalytic treatment, 'la belle indifférence' in Charcot's
expression. Contrary to the indifference of the clinical paradigm,
the modern narcissist is totally pre-occupied with the others'
opinions of him; he carefully cultivates his 'public' image, keeping thousands of little secrets to himself (demanding respect for
his 'privacy'), thinking carefully before disclosing information
about himself and yet constantly seeking the approval of intimacy
in his social encounters.

This paradox can be resolved by considering Lasch's crucial
and controversial argument on the changing character of the
super-ego in contemporary societies. This argument furnishes
perhaps what is the seminal psychological criterion distinguishing the moral, integrated, authoritarian, guilt-ridden individual
of yesteryears which pre-occupied Freud and also Fromm and
Reich, and the narcissist of today who has captured the attention

of Marcuse, Rieff, Lasch and others. Lasch, following a long
line of American research into the 'socialization of reproduction'
by state and professional agencies, into the weakening of the
patriarchal family as the original nucleus of authority relations
and into changing parental attitudes and permissive child-
rearing, argues that 'the decline of parental authority reflects
the "decline of the super-ego" in American society as a whole'
(305), or, more precisely,

> to an alteration of its contents. The parents' failure to serve
> as models of disciplined self-restraint or to restrain the child
> does not mean that the child grows up without a super-ego.
> On the contrary it encourages the development of a harsh and
> punitive super-ego based largely on archaic images of the
> parents, fused with grandiose self-images. (ibid.)

In short, the decline of conscience and of moral authority does
not coincide with a lessening of the authoritarianism of the
super-ego but rather with an increase of its arbitrariness. The
process is compounded by the growth of bureaucracy which
undermines not only parental authority but all moral authority,
by replacing obedience to leaders with obedience to office-
holders. The growth of bureaucracy

> erodes all forms of patriarchal authority and thus weakens the
> social super-ego, formerly represented by fathers, teachers
> and preachers. The decline of institutionalized authority in an
> ostensibly permissive society does not, however, lead to a
> 'decline of the super-ego' in individuals. It encourages instead
> the development of a harsh, punitive super-ego that derives
> most of its psychic energy, in the absence of authoritarian
> social prohibitions, from the destructive, aggressive impulses
> within the id. (41)

This situation contrasts sharply with Freud's account of the
narcissist who uses the surplus ego-libido to erect an ego ideal
and maintain it:

> That which prompted the person to form an ego ideal, over
> which his conscience keeps guard, was the influence of paren-
> tal criticism (conveyed to him by the medium of the voice),
> reinforced as time went on, by those who trained and taught
> the child and by all other persons of his environment - an
> indefinite host, too numerous to reckon (fellow-men, public
> opinion). Large quantities of libido which is essentially homo-
> sexual are in this way drawn into the formation of the nar-
> cissistic ego-ideal and find outlet and gratification in
> maintaining it. (1914c:14:76)

In 'Moses and Monotheism', Freud argues that when instinctual
renunciation proceeds from a strong identification with authority,

far from leading to frustration, it produces a 'feeling of security and satisfaction'.

> This good feeling could acquire the peculiar narcissistic character of pride only after the authority itself had become part of the ego. (1939a:23:117)

In situations like this, the authority embodied in the super-ego requires no re-inforcement from social sources - narcissism of this type is indifferent to praise by other people.

The case of the modern narcissist, however, as outlined by Lasch, is drastically different. His super-ego having failed to establish itself on the basis of internalized moral authority, in short, having lost its function as conscience, is unable to provide and sustain an ego-ideal but at the same time remains as a generalized principle of self-aggression. Unlike the Freudian model where the distance between ego and ego-ideal resulted in guilt while their coincidence resulted in narcissistic satisfaction (1921c:18:63), the narcissist is burdened with a constant source of self-aggression which can under no circumstances be quietened. His ego is left in a fundamentally weak position as a target of this aggression, in spite of its libidinal surplus. It is for this reason that the modern narcissi finds himself in the paradoxical position of needing an audience in an era of disappearing audiences - his failure to establish an ego-ideal which he can emulate and admire marks him apart from both Freudian and mythological prototypes of his condition.

Lasch's discussion of the super-ego has attracted a fair amount of criticism, often from people who accuse him of looking back nostalgically at the days of the authoritarian conscience based on strict parental and social discipline. Yet, the weakness of his argument appears to be more fundamental and quite separate from the issue of whether an authoritarian patriarchal family is more desirable than socialization of child-rearing functions by professional and bureaucratic agencies. For although Lasch's arguments on the decline of the super-ego resemble those of Rieff, Marcuse and others and carry considerable weight, he offers no convincing evidence for the existence of a 'sadistic super-ego' which develops 'at the expense of the severe but solicitous inner voice we call conscience . . . as it so often happens in a society that has radically devalued all forms of authority' (1979:41fn). Nowhere in his brilliant characterology of the modern narcissist do we see this sadistic super-ego at work; his one attempt to describe its operations is patently reminiscent of the old-fashioned super-ego/conscience described by Freud. 'It holds to the ego and exalted standard of fame and success and condemns it with savage ferocity when it falls short of this standard' (305).

The modern narcissist's discontents as they are described by Lasch and other commentators have little to do with the 'unreasonableness' or 'arbitrariness' of the super-ego. It is perfectly clear

from Lasch's own arguments that the cause of the narcissist's
frustration lies not in the demands of the super-ego but in those
of society. Having found few lovable objects in the world, the
narcissist's libido returns to his/her ego. Yet, the ego, lacking
the guiding influence of the super-ego, finds it impossible to
erect an ego-ideal, which it can seek to emulate. Its megalo-
maniac delusions of omnipotence, beauty, freedom and independence can find no expression in a desirable image or a course
of action to be followed. More importantly, these delusions are
painfully tested every day in experiences which underline his/
her powerlessness, depersonalization, alienation. Finally, the
narcissist's need for special recognition and re-inforcement is
constantly frustrated through his/her constant humiliation as
a functionary of impersonal machines and through his/her own
inability to develop emotional bonds with the narcissists who
surround him/her.

The modern narcissist finds himself in a most unpleasant situation: faced with a libidinal surplus, he seeks to attach it to an
imago which he thinks he may still manipulate, enrich and
embellish, that of his ego. Yet, this ego, lacking a strong super-
ego, cannot be sheltered from the ravages of daily life, which
reduces every narcissist to a product of a homogenizing culture,
depriving him of all individuality. As Horkheimer and Adorno
put it in their memorable lament of lost individuality:

> What is individual is no more than the generalities' power to
> stamp so firmly that it is accepted as such. The defiant reserve
> or elegant appearance of the individual on show is mass-
> produced like Yale locks, whose only difference can be
> measured in fractions of millimeters. The peculiarity of the
> self is a monopoly commodity determined by society. (1972:154)

The narcissist's libidinal surplus, far from resulting in Rieff's
strong managerial ego, leads to a weakened ego, chronically
unable to channel this surplus to a worthy cause. Thus the
narcissist's discontents are not those of an ego torn by contrasting demands on its meagre resources and subjected to constant
abuse by its super-ego, but those of an ego which is unwilling
to love and unable to be loved.

Of course, one avenue is always open to the narcissist -
consumption. Having failed to establish an ego-ideal on the basis
of identification with moral exemplars, the narcissist regresses
to a pre-genital oral organization of the libido, in which the
'sexual *aim* consists in the incorporation of the object' (1905d:7:
117). He temporarily invests his libido in commodities, images,
places or people and he then reclaims it by incorporating them,
either by consuming them orally or by appropriating them into
the organization of his ego. It is only through the incorporation
of commodities, images, places and people that the narcissist
can hope to enlarge his ego and temporarily fulfil his megalo-
maniac delusions. In his/her compulsion to consume, the modern

narcissist is assisted by contemporary capitalism and its massive
cultural agencies which daily re-affirm consumption as the way
to the good life, as the means for satisfying all material and
spiritual needs. Sadly, however, for the narcissist, consumption
while temporarily gorging his/her ego, far from filling his/her
inner vacuum deepens it; no amount of status symbols can
relieve his/her status anxiety, no power symbols can obscure
his/her impotence to effect real change, no beauty aids can
overcome his/her fear of ageing and dying. As we saw in our
discussion of Rieff, by espousing consumption as the dominant
mode of satisfying his/her needs, the narcissist buries him/
herself deeper in the order which denies him/her all individuality and all uniqueness. While he/she develops a total dependence on his/her diverse beautifying accoutrements, his need
for more is constantly re-inforced.

The characterological account of the new narcissism, which
combines megalomania and hypochondria, an ethic of hedonism
as well as an ethic of survival, a recognition anxiety and a
profound fear of ageing and death, a constant pre-occupation
with appearances and a tendency to look at life as a sequence
of photographic snaps, a superficial division of the world into
the herd and the glamorous, and so on, has been provided so
successfully by theorists like Lasch, Sennett, Hougan and others,
that it will not concern us here. Nor is it necessary to establish
the banality and fatuousness of the various 'ideologies' which
have sprung in opposition to the discontents of social life,
like intimacy, authenticity, survival, success and so on; these
constitute the chief illusions and ideals of narcissist society.
For we must not, like Rieff, regard the decline of the great
illusions and ideals of the past as the end of all such phenomena.
Of course, contrary to the ideals and illusions of earlier eras
which were shared by individuals and led to particular courses
of action, these modern variants are far from shared. And contrary to the grand integrating symbolics of the past, the
symbols of the culture of narcissism are parochial and fragmented.
Thus, one narcissist's authenticity is another's epitome of hypo-
crisy, one narcissist's experience of intimacy is easily ridiculed
by another narcissist as the embodiment of interpersonal hell,
one narcissist's survival appears to another as emotional suicide.
Likewise, although each narcissist depends emotionally on his
diverse symbols of power, beauty, status, authenticity and so
on, he can find few with whom to share them.

Like the sublimated Eros of emotional communities, the introjected Eros of the culture of narcissism remains a foundation of
illusions and ideals; yet, the nature of these illusions and ideals
is highly personal and their appeal supremely precarious. The
courses of action in which they result tend to appear to others
as 'trips', whose motive seems to escape the subject but is transparent to everyone else. Trips are expressions of the extreme
fragmentation of ideals and of the gradual de-anchoring of
personal illusions from the grand unifying illusions of the past;

they are private mini-Odysseys guided by their mini-symbolics,
or scenarios to use Becker's expression, through which every
narcissist seeks to emerge as a super-hero, to join the ranks
of the glamorous and to escape the anonymity of the herd, in
his/her own eyes. The narcissist, aided by an ever-increasing
appareil of gadgets and a constantly changing set of standards,
sails in an ocean of half-truths which purport to define his
course and guide his actions. The reason why I refer to such
privatized beliefs as half-truths is not that they are half-lie
and half-truth, but rather that the narcissist himself does not
treat them constantly as total truths, but invokes them conveniently in order to enrich his ego or rationalize his actions.
These half-truths are frequently in contradiction with each
other, like old proverbs, but there is one for practically every
contingency. Beliefs such as 'fast cars are the sign of success',
'fast cars are the sign of the nouveaux riches', 'I am beautiful',
'people love me', 'you need friends to survive', 'you can only
count on yourself to help you', to name some particularly trite
ones, are not strictly illusions, since the narcissist is unlikely
to defend them with particular fervour unless his ego, at that
precise moment, is being threatened. In this sense, they do not
constitute self-deception, since the narcissist will rarely admit
that he adheres to them and will gladly change them when it is
convenient. As Kernberg has argued, 'the value systems of
narcissistic personalities are generally corruptible, in contrast
to the rigid morality of the obsessive personality' (1975:238).
   Although the half-truths adhered to by the narcissist are the
modern equivalent of the old illusions and ideals, they have
neither the tragic pathos of mauvaise foi, nor the disarming
playfulness of phantasy. They do not bring new visions within
the realm of the possible, by liberating the imagination and
inspiring new desires, nor do they mark a symbolic triumph of
the pleasure principle over the reality principle. The narcissist
develops them carefully, grooms them and protects them, without however putting undue reliance on just a few of them; as
they are neither consistent nor verisimilar, contact amongst
them or between them and reality must be prevented at all costs.
Their function is to provide the narcissist with an unlimited
and reliable set of rationalizations for his trips and re-inforce
his narcissistic illusions of beauty and omnipotence.
   The fragmentation of the great ideals of the past into myriads
of operational half-truths presents us with a direct analogue of
a phenomenon which will be examined at length in the next
chapter - the fragmentation of traditional norms into operational
rules devoid of moral content; such rules will be found to provide the backbone of bureaucratic administration. One particularly disturbing feature of the narcissist's half-truths is that,
lacking the integrating influence of a communal ideal and a
generally accepted symbolic, they threaten to collapse every
minute, with the narcissist's every social encounter. It is not
surprising that at every moment the narcissist looks carefully

after his particular constellation of half-truths, avoiding narcissists who subscribe to constellations different from his own. This creates an additional tension in him, for while the enrichment of his self-image is dependent upon his ability to accumulate constantly new experiences, these experiences must never jeopardize the precarious equilibrium of half-truths but only reinforce it. The narcissist's experiences therefore must fulfil one basic condition - while enriching the narcissist's ego, they must never change it. The modern narcissist is the perpetual tourist, who constantly seeks new places, consumes new images, comes into contact with new objects and, yet, never changes by developing an emotional relationship with things which cross his path; the common denominator of his experiences is that they mix unobstrusively with the metabolism of his ego - his experiences constantly change, they have to change, but they never change him.

Modern technology has brought an extraordinary range of experiences within the individual's reach - strange places and cultures are brought to within a few hours of travel, music at the pressing of a button, the greatest accomplishments of culture at the flicking of a page. Yet the modern narcissist never changes; he visits foreign places in order to recreate his alienation at work and at home in caravan-sites and hotels, absorbing next to nothing from the different cultures that unfold in front of his eyes; Mozart as well as Bob Dylan become 'background music', reproductions of Van Gogh and the Impressionists find their places (often next to symbols of a sexist mass culture) in domestic interiors. At times, the narcissist may test himself to the extreme - he may experiment with psychedelic drugs, he may seek the sensations of surfing and gliding, he may witness the pathos of a bullfight; he is trying to show to himself that he 'can take it', he can survive it, unaffected, unchanged, with a bolstered ego. It is in this way that all these experiences are muted and emasculated; they lose their shock power, their ability to shake and liberate sensitivities, and become an integral part of a painless, joyless, colourless world which provides the narcissist's escape from the greyness of his daily routine. A tranquillized world, a riskless world, as if life had become modelled on the method of birth without tears of Docteur Leboyer.

The preceding discussion of the phenomenon of narcissism in contemporary culture indicates that a substantial change is taking place in the configuration of Eros in modern societies. It would appear that today's culture is gradually dispensing with the need to sublimate Eros and to construct social bonds by de-sexualizing the individuals' libido and turning it outwards. Of course, it would be premature to argue that all communal manifestations of Eros have disappeared - the rebirth of religious fundamentalism, the stubborn persistence of nationalism and the periodic resurgence of class politics, the environmental, the feminist and other social movements have all been sufficiently prominent features of capitalist societies over the past thirty

years to regard the narcissist as the unchallenged hero of our
culture. It would also be unwise to seek to reduce these features
into attributes of a narcissistic culture, because we may then
lose what is most useful in the discussion of narcissism - the
possibility or indeed the gradual arrival of a culture in which
Eros, far from being sublimated, is introjected.

A culture of narcissism marks a definite overcoming of the
traditional pair of discontents generated by past cultures,
repression of sexuality and guilt. Sexual energies, no longer
necessary for communal bonds, are freed and re-appropriated
by the individual; moreover, the inevitable ensuing relaxation
of moral and social constraints on sexuality permits the cathexis
of libido outside the parameters of monogamous heterosexual
relationships. At the same time, the decline of the super-ego,
which proceeds from the same weakening of sublimated love
bonds through identification, allows for a relaxation of the
sense of guilt, which represented the introjection of the death
instinct from the super-ego. Yet, this by no means implies that
a culture of narcissism is without its own discontents. As the
preceding discussion has indicated, the narcissist's discontents
are not the product of the frustration of desire but of forced
libidinal wastage, and inability to find satisfactory objects to
love and relate to in meaningful ways.

Nor, as we saw, is the culture of narcissism free from
illusions; although its illusions lack the universal character of
earlier ones, their consequences are no less serious. One of the
most important aspects of Freud's critique of religion lies in his
demonstration that religion owes its great emotional grip to the
fact that, while creating formidable social discontents, it presents itself as the only possible consolation for the miseries of
life. Far from threatening the religious regime, the discontents
bolster it. A similar vicious circle is observed in many clinical
conditions, in which relief from neurotic symptoms and suffering
is accompanied by a 'negative therapeutic response', as the
patient derives a secondary gain from both symptoms (as substitutive satisfactions) and from his suffering (as an appease
ment of the unconscious sense of guilt). It is now possible to
offer the parallel argument that modern capitalism not only
tolerates but thrives on the neurotic cripples it creates in a
similar way; for it presents itself, through the narcissist's
illusions, as ideally suited for the relief of the very insecurities
and anxieties which it generates. Having turned the contemporary
individual into an infinitely gullible and malleable consumer,
unable to tolerate pain or generate joy, constantly pre-occupied
with the protection of his precarious self and in constant need
of having his individuality and identity affirmed, capitalism
consoles him by offering him what he needs - a world saturated
with commodities and devoid of risk. Meaninglessness and
insecurity may have replaced sexual frustration and guilt as the
dominant modes of human discontents, yet the underlying situation has not changed - culture remains both the cause and the

consolatory treatment of the disease called man.

This chapter leaves us with at least three unanswered questions.
First, our earlier question of how a culture of narcissism holds
together without the need of creating emotional communities.
How is it possible for the activities of huge numbers of individuals to be co-ordinated on an ever-increasing scale to generate
the complex social fabric of modern bureaucratic societies?
Directly related to this is the question of the psychic foundation
of bureaucracy. Lasch's discussion undoubtedly places bureaucracy at the root of the culture of narcissism - yet, his
discussions fail to study bureaucracy itself as a psychic as well
as a social phenomenon; it is, so to speak, as if bureaucracy
was forced on modern societies by a divine hand and caused a
radical change in the configuration of Eros in these societies.
This view of bureaucracy as a metaphysical externality, which
brings to mind some of Weber's discussions, disregards the
Freudian tenet which underlines most of Lasch's work, namely
that social phenomena have their psychical counterparts and that
society and individual cannot be regarded as independent entities.
Finally our discussion of the decline of the super-ego and our
rejection of Lasch's view of a generalized principle of self-
aggression having replaced conscience raise the issue of what
has become of the death instinct in a culture of narcissism; for
as we argued in criticizing Rieff one may expect that in a situation like this the death instinct, having been denied its
customary outlets, will attack the already weak communal bonds
and destroy the very possibility of a cohesive society.
In the next chapter, I will propose a new form that the death
instinct has assumed in modern societies which goes some way
towards answering the other two questions as well.

Chapter 13
The death instinct and the age of the machine

Our earlier discussions have suggested that although the contemporary individual continues to strive to infuse his life with
meaning, his culture, having failed to provide him with large-
scale symbolics, makes this struggle futile. As the powerful
symbolics of politics and religion decline, the individual, at
least in his private life, withdraws into himself, looking inwards
both for the understanding and for the resolution of his distress,
and also for the fulfilment of his desires. This much is common in
Rieff's psychological man, Marcuse's one-dimensional man, Lasch's
narcissist and the 'Oedipalized individual' of Deleuze. In his
relations with other people, the new Narcissus is obsessed
with appearances; and yet, the more authenticity is hailed as
his cultural ideal, the more artificial his appearance.

The anomic character of much of contemporary culture is a
central theme in most of the authors we have discussed, as well
as many other American social scientists of all political persua-
sions.[1] The prospect of a society disintegrating not through
external dangers but through its own inability to bind individuals
together has haunted twentieth-century thought and has,
ironically, guaranteed the immortality of Durkheim's conception.
Yet, in spite of the work of authors like Beckett and Solzhenitsyn,
moral disintegration has not been the most persistent nightmare
of the twentieth century about the future. It would not be
inaccurate to suggest that it is in the 'dystopias' of '1984' and
'Brave New World' that the most pervasive anxieties about the
future of humanity meet; they represent a vision in which the
individual's life is not under-regulated but over-regulated. To
be sure the regulation does not take place through normative
or moral constraints but by an arsenal of technical and social
machines; like the Charlie Chaplin of 'Modern Times' or the
citizens of 'Alphaville', the individual emerges from these visions
as the perfect 'extension' of different machines – a cheerful
robot, in Mills' chilling expression.[2]

In this chapter we will argue that moral disintegration and
social over-regulation do not necessarily represent opposites
but can become complementary conditions; it will be argued that
Durkheim's states of anomie and fatalism both represent central
features of the culture of narcissism and that if the former
describes the narcissist's predicament in his private experience
of meaninglessness and emptiness the latter characterizes his
public powerlessness and unfreedom.

Even in his earliest formulations, Marx saw the worker, under
capitalism, as the victim of a technical division of labour.

> Owing to the extensive use of machinery and to the division
> of labour, the work of the proletarians has lost all individual
> character, and consequently, all charm for the workman. He
> becomes an appendage of the machine, and it is only the most
> simple, the most monotonous, and the most easily acquired
> knack that is required of him. (1848:341)

Mechanization and automation have, of course, escalated to levels
that even Marx may have found hard to anticipate, forever reducing the physical effort required from the worker, forever
liquidating traditional skills, forever diminishing the amount of
control exercised by the individual over the work process, forever forcing the domination of the machine (dead labour) over
man (living labour). The loss of control which started with the
transition from cottage industry to the factory system reached its
apotheosis with the Taylorist principles of management and the
introduction of the assembly line, which to this day dominate the
world of production.[3] Full automation of process production tech-
nologies, which originally created hopes of restoring control over
the machinery by humans,[4] has, if anything, consolidated the
domination of the machine and, as the wave of innovation we are
currently witnessing suggests, is extending it to the office and
(horror!) to the professions. Thus, the work process, far from
marking man's mastery of nature and its adaptation to his needs,
is experienced as the worst form of subordination to machines.
  Even when machines are used outside the constraints of work,
their ability to stamp their character and logic on the user is
remarkable. Motor-cars, domestic appliances, entertainment
machines and so on have not so much made man a 'prosthetic god'
(to use Freud's doubly ironic expression) as turned him into the
human prosthesis of his mechanical creations.

> The relations between . . . *Homo psychologicus* and the
> machines he uses are very striking, and this is especially
> so in the case of the motor-car. We get the impression that
> his relation to this machine is so very intimate that it is almost
> as if the two were actually conjoined - its mechanical defects
> and breakdowns often parallel his neurotic symptoms. (Lacan
> 1953:17)

But of course it is not only the mechanical artifacts which
leave their regularity, defects and intelligence stamped on contemporary man, turning him into an operative, a passive extension. If in the technical division of labour man has become
increasingly the servant (tender) of the machine, in the social
division of labour he has become an extension of administrative
machines, a functionary of impersonal apparatuses. The relations
of production no longer appear as a form of domination of man

by man - within contemporary bureaucracies domination is
invisible, since the commands emanate not from persons but
from offices. As Marcuse has argued, 'domination is transfigured
into administration. The capitalist bosses and owners are losing
their identity as responsible agents; they are assuming the
function of bureaucrats in a corporate machine' (1964:32). Within the impersonal bureaucratic hierarchies, 'the performance of
each individual is mathematically measured, each man becomes a
little cog in the machine and, aware of this, his one preoccupation is whether he can become a bigger cog' (Weber in Mayer
1956:126-7). The common denominator of the domination of
humans by technical and administrative machines is the control
of human activity not directly by other persons, but by rules.
In the technical division of labour, technical rules, as those
perfected by Taylor himself, circumscribe the precise movements
and timing of the worker's activities, define the optimum division
of tasks which will allow a minimum of initiative to the worker,
and standardize the optimal instruments for each task without
regard for the individuality of each operator. Under the Taylorist regime, the worker is treated as an all-purpose machine,
just as under the Weberian theory of bureaucracy he is treated
as a functionary sine ira et studio.

This much is important in Weber - his realization that a central
secret of contemporary societies may lie in the extraordinary
domination of individual behaviour by impersonal rules and the
recognition that these rules are more than vague guidelines
within which individual creativity may be exercised. What Weber
failed to appreciate, due to his insistence on looking at these
rules and embodiments of 'rationality', was that these rules lack
a normative content; far from emanating from some moral conception of values, technical and administrative rules masquerade
behind ill-defined concepts of rationality in order to conceal
the fact that their existence merely consolidates the domination
of man by man. Like the Laws which visit Socrates in prison in
the course of his dialogue with Crito, the rules that Max Weber
referred to are laws of domination, but, unlike the former, they
lack a moral basis. Obedience does not rest on moral commitment
to the rules and the normative order from which they emanate,
nor does it rest on the rationality of that order.[5] By mid-
century, the idea that bureaucracy represented a genuine
rationality of means (let alone a rationality of ends) was
beginning to evaporate from Western culture.[6] In Robert Michels'
theory, we can find the perfect answer to Weber's view of
bureaucracy: the power and constant growth of the bureaucratic order do not rest on its technical efficiency (since even
inefficient bureaucracies are powerful and grow), but on the
control which they can exercise on individuals within them - the
power of bureaucracy rests on its ability to turn each individual
into its agent, it rests on bureaucracy itself, the domination of
man by office.

Nor should it be thought that this power of bureaucracy to

stamp its character on the individual is limited to situations
where the latter is contractually bound. For the individual's
behaviour is entirely predictable, not only when he/she acts
as a worker, a manager or an official, but also in areas of life
where the appearance of freedom still exists, as in the election
of industrial and political representatives, in choice of work
and indeed in the sphere of consumption. Marketing experts
have been making increasing use of what is known in learning
theory as the 'principle of exercise', according to which 'the
more a certain response to a situation is repeated, the more
likely the same response will occur in the same situation later'
(Brink 1963:133-4). The use of mass media by the 'depth boys'
of advertising, catching the consumers in their most vulnerable
and insecure state (normally after a tiring day at work), creates
'a state of dazed acceptance of whatever goods and services were
put before them'. It is surely telling that marketing experts
themselves are willing to concede that, under the techniques of
mass manipulation, the consumer, our culture's archetypical
definition of freedom, is 'turning into a virtual automaton'
(352-3). What we are arguing here is that people's lives as
shaped by modern bureaucratic organizations are governed not
by norms which command moral commitment, nor by a system of
laws implementing 'goals' in a technically optimal fashion, but by
a host of minute and highly specific rules which determine
behaviour down to every detail.[7] As consumers of goods and
services offered by such organizations, their behaviour is
reduced to an elaborate, but ultimately predictable, set of conditioned reflex responses to techniques of mass pressure and
manipulation, involving little originality and practically no freedom.

The theme of bureaucratization, as embodied in the proliferation of technical, administrative and other bureaucratic rules
which are obeyed blindly and mechanically, is the central problem of this chapter. The absence of moral commitment as well as
the depersonalization of relations (including relations of domination and subordination) are fundamental features of bureaucratization, which has invaded most spheres of human life. But if
compliance with technical and administrative rules is based
neither on moral commitment nor on an acceptance of their
rationality, what is it based on? This is the question which will
bring us back to Freud.

Yet, at this point a clarification is necessary. In concentrating
on the proliferation of bureaucratic rules in all aspects of social
activity and the routinization of so much human behaviour, I
do not share the assumption that the observation of rules is
unproblematic or that these rules are inviolable. On the contrary,
the violation of technical rules by the worker, administrative
rules by the functionary, industrial relations rules by unions
and management, and so on, must surely be as essential for an
understanding of contemporary society as their observation.
Struggles to modify these rules, bend them or ignore them,

organized and spontaneous opposition to their operation and
confrontations over their interpretation take place daily within
the various machines which strive to dominate human life -
factories, schools, offices, government departments, courts,
prisons, research establishments, hospitals, armies, shops, etc.
Wherever we look, we see manifestations of people refusing to
act as 'factors of production', 'factors of administration',
'factors of accountancy', and so on, to the great distress of
economists, sociologists, accountants and all those professionals
who build their elaborate theories in realms uninhabited by
human beings.

In addition to internal opposition from individuals or groups,
every bureaucracy faces opposition from other bureaucracies,
including competitors, state agencies and employee organizations.

Yet, one of the truly remarkable features of a bureaucratic
society is that these challenges faced by different bureaucracies
do not amount to a challenge to bureaucratic relations themselves;
bureaucracies have an admirable capacity for transforming the
problems which they generate into bureaucratic problems to be
dealt with through bureaucratic procedures. Organized internal
opposition, in an attempt to be effective, leads to the formation
of a counter-bureaucracy with its own rules and impersonal
hierarchies, trade unions and staff associations. Relations
between bureaucracies are then regulated through agreements
which result in further bureaucratic rules and regulations
covering every conceivable issue affecting the employees' lives.
Similar agreements cover relations between interacting, interdependent or indeed competing bureaucracies.

What is more significant for the purposes of our discussion is
the individual's inability to escape the tight hold of bureaucratic
rule-following. Taking as an example an individual who suffers
a mental or physical break-down, his new condition marks
simply a transition of routines, from those of the factory, the
office, the school or the shop to those of the psychiatric, medical
or welfare establishments. It is not surprising, therefore, that
much of contemporary sociology has chosen to approach the
individual as a bearer of social structures, as a soulless, passion-
less, faceless figure, like the ones which decorate the covers of
many a sociology textbook. Men and women are players in a
game which has lost every element of uncertainty, in a society
with few tolerances, few openings and few margins, or more
exactly they are pawns of a game played way above their heads,
just as in Homer's account of the Trojan War, where victories and
defeats, bravery and cowardice in the war among men reflected
exactly the developments of the war among the Olympians. It is
important, however, for us to establish the psychic basis of
rule-following behaviour, rather than regard it as the outcome
of commitment or rationality, for only then is it possible to assess
the real costs of such behaviour and also the conditions under
which such behaviour breaks down. The two questions are in this
way inseparable. What is the basis of the contemporary indivi-

dual's compliance with the myriads of rules imposed by the bureaucratic society he/she inhabits and under what circumstances does this compliance break down?

The depersonalization of modern life, the result of bureaucratic domination of contemporary societies, is a prominent feature in the writings of several pessimistic social commentators, who argue that as social norms are replaced by bureaucratic rules man becomes an automaton (Fromm 1966:208), a robot (Mills 1970:189), a thing (Marcuse 1964:32). It is this 'thingification' or 'self-reification', the turning of the individual into an object or a thing and the treatment of others as things (after the fashion in which the bank-teller is treated), that lies in the heart of Eliot's *The Cocktail Party*. At the most basic level, one is reduced to a thing in the hands of the professionals:

> . . '. take a surgical operation.
> In consultation with the doctor and the surgeon,
> In going to bed in the nursing home,
> In talking to the matron, you are still the subject,
> The centre of reality. But, stretched on the table,
> You are a piece of furniture in a repair shop
> For those who surround you, the masked actors;
> All there is of you is your body
> And the 'you' is withdrawn. (1969:362-3)

Would it not be a banality to comment that in the modern hospital you are a thing the moment you sign on the in-patient register, and that you soon learn that the matron, these days, is referred to as the 'divisional nursing officer'? Once your life becomes entangled with the workings of an impersonal order, as manager, official, worker, patient, member, client, consumer, prisoner, motorist, voter, student or whatever, your behaviour becomes an extension of its logic.

> There's a loss of personality;
> Or rather, you've lost touch with the person
> You thought you were. You no longer feel quite human.
> You are suddenly reduced to the status of an object –
> A living object, but no longer a person.
> It's always happening, because one is an object
> As well as a person. But we forget about it
> As quickly as we can. When you've dressed for a party
> And are going downstairs, with everything about you
> Arranged to support you in the role you have chosen,
> Then sometimes, when you come to the bottom step
> There is one step more than your feet expected
> And you come down with a jolt. Just for a moment
> You have the experience of being an object
> At the mercy of a malevolent staircase. (362)

The example offers no consolation; for, as Eliot's characters gradually realize, it is not only when you are at the mercy of the unyielding logic of the unexpected bottom step that you are reduced to a thing. Like a self-conscious marionette, Edward confides 'I have ceased to believe in my own personality' and receives the physician's reply: 'Oh, dear yes; this is serious. A common malady. Very prevalent indeed' (402). Few people have appreciated as well as Eliot how individuals, in public life as much as in their personal relations,

> Maintain themselves by the common routine,
> Learn to avoid excessive expectation,
> Become tolerant of themselves and others,
> Giving and taking, in the usual actions
> What there is to give and take. (417)

A sobering vision indeed! Society, institutions, social and interpersonal life sustained through routine alone - no justification, no rationale, nothing. No collective consciousness, no norms or values, no Eros to hold society together, merely routine. It seems to be that if we undertake a serious consideration of this picture of social reality we cannot, like Rieff, argue that apathy becomes the basis of the social bond. Rather, we must look at the psychic foundations of routinized behaviour which complement its social foundations in the bureaucratic fabric, and investigate the circumstances under which unquestioned adherence to rules occurs.

Freud was not unfamiliar with phenomena which seemed to proceed neither from a vicissitude of sexual desire nor from the dictates of the super-ego and conscience; moreover, the phenomena which caught his attention in this way possess a considerable similarity to the phenomena that we are discussing here. They had a compulsive and mechanical character and seemed to proceed quite independently from the person's will as if he/she were possessed by an alien spirit; above all, as in Chaplin's behaviour in the opening sequences of 'Modern Times', all of these phenomena were compulsively repeated, independently of whether they were pleasurable or painful in themselves. It was such phenomena which led Freud to postulate a compulsion to repeat as a primary psychic force, independent of both pleasure and reality principles of mental functioning. For the purposes of this discussion a fundamental insight can be gained by approaching the individual's compulsive adherence to his/her different routines as a by-product of this compulsion to repeat. The compulsion was observed by Freud in a variety of situations in which a daemonic element was prominent - war-dreams and other repeated nightmares, the femme fatale and Don Juan syndromes, the patient's resistance to psychoanalytic treatment, and above all in transference phenomena (where a patient is seen to 're-experience or repeat an earlier experience') and in children's play and stories. On several occasions Freud noted the experiences of individuals who seem to undergo the same traumatic event (an 'accident', the death of a loved one, the break-down of a relationship or of a business venture) time and again, with uncanny regularity, and it was such experiences which brought out most clearly the 'daemonical character' of the compulsion to repeat (1920g:18:15, 29f and 1933a:22:107). Phenomena of such repetitive nature seemed to possess an individuality all of their own, in that they could not be understood in terms of the two great principles of mental functioning which dominated Freud's psychology before 1920, the pleasure principle and the reality principle. Such phenomena, as we saw, showed no concern as to whether the repeated action was in itself pleasurable or unpleasurable, nor as to whether they contributed towards self-preservation.

Although Freud did not underestimate the importance of the compulsion to repeat,[8] neither he nor his successors seemed to appreciate adequately its scope. It seems to me that this compulsion and its psychic foundations are central not only in religious rituals (which Freud had noted as early as 1907), but in literature (and not only in poetry or in children's stories),[9] in music (where, as in poetry, the rhythmic component is related quite obviously to this compulsion) and in many other cultural phenomena. Moreover, in relation to the phenomena discussed earlier in this chapter, it is rather strange that the idea of connecting routinized behaviour with the compulsion to repeat and its psychic foundation has not been studied before; the cheerful robot, in this sense, would represent the latest version of the invisible neurotic – he is the compulsive neurotic in a social guise (insofar as he shares the same symptoms with many others), just as religious man was the socially invisible neurotic of the past. The daemonic character of the compulsion to repeat fits perfectly with the self-reification of life discussed earlier, since in both cases man is reduced to an extension of powers over which he has no control – the bottom step of the staircase, the assembly line, the feeding machine, the office, the weekly accident, the hourly washing of hands.

There is an intriguing but rarely noticed passage in 'Civilization and Its Discontents', in which Freud momentarily grasps the relationship between order and routine in human life and the compulsion to repeat:

> Man's observation of the great astronomical regularities not only furnished him with a model for introducing order into his life, but gave him the first points of departure for doing so. Order is a kind of compulsion to repeat which, when a regulation has been laid down once and for all, decides when, where and how a thing shall be done, so that in every similar circumstance one is spared hesitation and indecision. (1930a: 2:40)

Had Freud lived in our times he may well have been tempted to

study the implications of this statement; of all the Freudian
commentators, the only one who has touched on this theme
seems to be Habermas, who draws

> a comparison of the world-historical process of social organ-
> ization with the socialization process of the individual. As long
> as the pressure of reality is overpowering and the ego organ-
> ization weak, so that instinctual renunciation can only be
> brought about by the forces of affect, the species finds
> collective solutions to the problem of defense, which resemble
> neurotic solutions at the individual. The same configurations
> that drive the individual to neurosis move society to establish
> institutions. What characterizes institutions is at the same time
> what constitutes their similarity with pathological forms. Like
> the repetition compulsion from within, institutional compulsion
> from without brings about a relatively rigid reproduction of
> uniform behaviour that is removed from criticism. (1972:276)

The importance of Habermas' argument lies in the fact that when
he talks about institutions he does not refer to primitive religious
rituals; Freud, in his brilliant essay 'Obsessive Actions and
Religious Practices' (1907b), had drawn attention to the compulsion to repeat as the common feature between the two sets of
phenomena. But what Habermas suggests is a parallel between
the neurotic individual and contemporary social institutions;
bureaucracy (and I would add 'rationalization of productive
techniques', 'rationalization' of industrial relations and so on),
far from being the embodiment of administrative rationality,
represents a 'pre-rational' configuration analogous to the
individual neurotic's symptoms, which grow out of his/her
inability to confront reality rationally. As an institution, bureaucracy deals through a uniform system of rules with all external
contingencies, as if incapable of accepting the social reality in
its infinite colour and variety; at the same time it furnishes the
individual with routines of regimented behaviour through which
he/she will become a socially invisible neurotic.
Habermas' argument can be found in embryo in Marcuse's
critique of technocratic reason, as the main form of ideological
domination in contemporary societies. Technocratic consciousness,
embodied in bureaucratic administrations, functions to eclipse
seminal moral and political questions involved in decision-
making, by reducing them merely to technical problems. The
modern bureaucrat is carefully shielded from having to make
choices with a self-consciously moral or political character; he
is trained to keep his morals and his politics to himself, and
either to dominate situations 'intellectually' or simply 'to carry
out orders',[10] keeping his emotions to himself. He is capable of
pressing a button which annihilates lives with the same alacrity
as he may switch on his electric shaver; he fires and asks
questions later, if at all. This type of bureaucratic decision-
making requires a general and complete paralysis of the super-

ego and the general subordination of moral, political and human
feelings to the apparent rationality of technical expedience. But
this paralysis of the super-ego is already familiar to us from
our discussion of the modern narcissist and the decline of the
authoritarian patriarchal family as the major agency of socialization. According to Marcuse (1970:45ff), socialization in
advanced capitalism does not take place through the internalization of the paternal imago and subsequently of social norms
in the super-ego, but instead through a passive, mechanical
mimesis of set forms of individuality. Assuming a bureaucratic
role is nothing but an extension of the assumption of stereo-
typical forms of appearance and action earlier in life.

In spite of these considerations, there is no reason why
bureaucracy, through its chief political and theroetical spokes-
persons, should not seek to present itself as the 'instrument'
of administrative and technical rationality, forever obscuring
the nature of the goals served by such an instrument. Nor is
there any reason why the individual may not seek to justify his/
her compulsive adherence to rules and orders as rational - the
pursuit of a career would provide an acceptable, if rather
banal, post hoc rationalization, while an almost religious commitment to the rule in its letter has provided a convincing motive
for the character of Police Inspector Javert in 'Les Misérables'
and an almost plausible defence for the scientific exterminators
of the Third Reich. While it would be rash to deny that there
may be some 'organization men' for whom the bureaucratic rule-
book assumes the significance of a moral code, I think that in
the vast majority of cases such rationalizations are rationalizations in the Freudian not the Weberian sense - they are retro-
active attempts to justify routinized, uncritical forms of
behaviour by invoking a convenient goal for such behaviour.

Let us recapitulate. Advanced industrial societies are characterized by a proliferation of rules which regulate most aspects of
life, including the technical division of labour, administration
and industrial relations. These rules cannot in any meaningful
way be said to emanate from any superior principle of rationality
nor from any compelling system of moral values. With few
exceptions, their observation does not depend on any sort of
moral commitment, nor is it conditional on their serving a useful
purpose. On the contrary, the uncritical and often unconscious
observation of these rules and the repetitive routinized behaviour
which results seem to be rooted in a compulsion to repeat, which
characterizes neurotic behaviour, religious ritual and behaviour
in modern institutions alike. Under the compulsion to repeat, the
regulation of behaviour takes place without the individual being
necessarily aware of the rules which govern his/her existence.
Repetition of small rituals is accompanied by an undoubted sense
of comfort, and departures from people's daily routines are
experienced as uncomfortable; a vast number of interactions,
with colleagues at work, with shop-assistants and tellers, with

the diverse agents of the state and so on, become totally depersonalized - the person inside the uniform, behind the counter,
in the office, etc., is never seen as a person but merely as an
agent. All such interactions are routinized, ritualized and
depersonalized - they are regulated by very precise rules aimed
at removing any personal element. In short, in vast numbers of
social transactions individuals do, in fact, treat each other as
extensions of machines, and in so doing present themselves as
extensions of machines.

But if the compulsion to repeat is the psychic foundation of
much of routinized behaviour in our society, we can begin to
understand how 'positive science' may begin to negotiate human
behaviour; if indeed human behaviour has become an extension
of the various impersonal machines we have encountered in this
chapter, then positive science can predict human behaviour by
analysing the machines from which it emanates. In short, human
behaviour is understood by being seen as thing-behaviour. Now,
there has, undoubtedly, been one important group of people
whom their society relegated firmly to the status of things -
slaves.[11] But if modern man, like slaves, has his behaviour
regulated down to every detail by myriads of rules, then
Durkheim's condition of fatalism, which was seen as the cause of
suicides of over-regulated slaves, may be far more relevant for
an understanding of contemporary societies than Durkheim suspected. Fatalism would, in this case, represent the condition of
modern man's uncritical submission to all these rules which exist
in our society, not through moral commitment or respect for the
rules' rationality but through resignation. This resignation is
already familiar to us, as an outstanding feature of contemporary
societies from our discussion of Rieff's psychological man and
the concept of new narcissism - as we observed earlier narcissistic self-obsession in private life grows out of resentful resignation to the superior forces of society in public life.

But if the rules of modern societies, the compulsion to repeat
and fatalism form a complex establishing the predicament of
modern man, as this discussion suggests, we are faced with some
intriguing possibilities. First, fatalism and anomie, far from
constituting polar opposites as Durkheim thought, can coexist as
complementary elements of the same gestalt - the collapse of
the powerful all-inclusive symbolics of the past is accompanied
by the oppressive regulation and regimentation of human
behaviour by scores of small and highly specific rules, devoid
of all moral content. Regulation of human behaviour through rules,
which become part of the individual by virtue of the compulsion
to repeat, replaces normative regulation of human expectations
through the moral constraints which become internalized in the
super-ego. Internalization of norms is thus substituted by a
repetitive application of rules. Modern societies can then be said
to be regulated both excessively and inadequately - anomie and
fatalism being present at the same time.

In order to understand the circumstances which have led to

this paradox (paradox, at least in Durkheim's formulations), we
must pursue the argument which sees the compulsion to repeat
as the psychic foundation of rule-guided behaviour within contemporary institutions. Where does this compulsion come from?
If it cannot be reduced to an expression of rationality (reality
principle) or of the impulse towards pleasure (pleasure principle),
what is its position in mental life? Where does it gain its strength
and persistence?

As with so many other concepts central to his work, although
the compulsion to repeat came to the forefront of Freud's theory
in 'Beyond the Pleasure Principle', it can be traced to some
early works, like Obsessive Actions and Religious Practices
(1907b), The Theme of the Three Caskets (1913f) and Remembering, Repeating and Working-Through (1914g). Undoubtedly,
the precursor of the compulsion to repeat was Fliess' concept of
periodicity, employed by Freud in one of his very earliest writings, A Reply to Criticism of my Paper on Anxiety Neurosis
(1895f).[12] Periodicity is from the outset connected with a law
above human power, with fate and, eventually, with death. In
the regular and immutable succession of the seasons, early cultures recognized a superior form of regularity, a superior law,
which was immediately embodied in the various deities of Seasons,
Horae or Hours. These deities, which recur in the mythologies
of many early civilizations, stand as representatives of an
unyielding 'law of Nature, and of the divine order of things
whereby the constant recurrence of the same things in unalter-
able succession in the natural world takes place' (1913f:12:74).
From periodicity, regularity and superior law in nature, to
repetition, death and fate in human affairs, the symbolic step
is a small one:

> This knowledge of nature reacted on the conception of human
> life. The nature-myth changed into a myth of human life; the
> weather-goddesses became goddesses of destiny. But this
> aspect of the Hours only found expression in the Moerae, who
> watch over the needful ordering of human life as inexorably
> as do the Hours over the regular order of nature. The
> implacable severity of this law, the affinity of it with death
> and ruin, avoided in the winsome figures of the Hours, was
> now stamped upon the Moerae, as though mankind had only
> perceived the full solemnity of natural law when he had to
> submit his own personality to its working. (298)

Thus, the Moerae or Fates arise from a recognition that man too
is a part of nature, and become the symbolic representatives of
the superior laws of destiny over human beings; among the
Fates, the third one always stands for that which no mortal can
hope to avoid, death.

But as always, Freud's study of the phenomenon of periodicity does not terminate with the hermeneutic examination of
regularity and repetition as symbols of death, recurring in

mythology and cultural artifacts of different historical periods.[13] For his theory must, at some point, confront the question: from where does this symbolism draw its great and apparently universal power? What desire lies at its root? Freud's investigations naturally led him to consider not only periodicity as a cultural *symbol*, but also repetition as a psychic function of outstanding significance. He became acquainted with this function in a wide variety of phenomena, such as children's play, neurotic symptoms, accident proneness, recurring nightmares, and the 'daemonic' misadventures mentioned earlier. Above all, Freud confronted repetition as a transference phenomenon – a phenomenon which is both an ally and an enemy of the analyst,[14] since it both leads to a re-enactment of a pathogenic conflict and prevents the recognition of the conflict on the part of the patient. Freud's attempts to explain this compulsion to repeat through his pre-1920 psychology failed him in 'Beyond the Pleasure Principle', and it would be no exaggeration to suggest that it was the lever which forced the major re-working of his meta-theory signalled by that book. The most prominent feature of the compulsion to repeat seemed to be that it defied both the pleasure principle and the reality principle, the two major regulatory principles of the mental apparatus; it seemed to represent an altogether different class of mental phenomena, which can ultimately not be reduced either to pleasure or to self-preservation. This residual character of the compulsion led Freud to postulate that it can only be an attribute of the instincts, i.e. that it must be seen as a direct representative of instinctual forces, just as the various guises of desire had been identified as the psychic representatives of libido, some fifteen years earlier. This step, however, necessitated a major overhaul of the instinctual theory, because in the light of the compulsion to repeat, the instincts, or at least some of them, must have an essentially conservative character, seeking to restore an earlier state of things:

> But how is the predicate of being 'instinctual' related to the compulsion to repeat? At this point we cannot escape a suspicion that we may have come upon the track of a universal attribute of instincts and perhaps of organic life in general which has not hitherto been clearly recognized, or at least not sufficiently stressed. *It seems, then, that an instinct is an urge inherent in organic life to restore an earlier state of things* which the living entity has been obliged to abandon under the pressure of external disturbing forces; that is, it is a kind of organic elasticity, or, to put in another way, the expression of the inertia inherent in organic life. (1920g:18:36)

By pursuing this speculative line, which involves the questionable leap from the 'conservative' character of the instincts to their 'regressive' character, Freud reached his famous conclusion that 'everything living dies for *internal* reasons. . . .

The aim of all life is death' (38).

In this way, the death instinct represents the forces which
inevitably lead life to inorganic inertia. But Freud never fell
into a naive instinctual monism of death, such as the one
described by Kalin (1975:171). On the contrary, the discovery
of the death instinct led Freud to a greater appreciation of Eros,
as the true life instinct, for Eros is the 'great exception in
life's march towards death' (Ricoeur 1970:291), he is the power
who introduces fresh tensions into life, prolonging it, who perpetuates life inter-generationally and creates new 'syntheses'
of life.

Having entered the Freudian discourse in this admittedly precarious and speculative way, the death instinct soon found a
firm place in it, resolving many earlier riddles, including
masochism, narcissism and homeostasis. Still, serious questions
could be raised at the birth of the idea of the death instinct
from what appears to be an arbitrary leap from conservatism
to regression if it were not for one extraordinary contribution
made by this idea: the 'unconscious sense of guilt', so central
for an understanding of both neurosis and culture, and until
then illustrated through the phylogenetic myth, could finally
be explained as an introjection of the death instinct. In this
way, as we saw earlier, the relationship between individual and
society was seen from a new and uniquely illuminating perspective, in which the super-ego became the protagonist through
which the death instinct was channelled towards sustained
culture, in a tenuous and tragic equilibrium - that of life
haunted by death. We are now forced to consider the possibility
that the organization and regimentation of life around roles
involving the repetition of standardized routines, when viewed
from a point of view of mental economics, represents a new
impersonation of the death instinct, in a form which completely
by-passes the super-ego. The death instinct remains at the
heart of the process of social regulation, no longer in the form
of a merciless sense of guilt, but rather in that of a psychic
incapacity to deviate from routines of prescribed behaviour.
What is more, once regulation becomes mechanical by by-passing
cultural norms and cultural super-ego, it is no longer contingent
upon the individual identifying with the cultural collectivity and
its moral ideals. Social integration, in this sense, becomes
redundant, for in a society of cheerful robots no love bonds are
required to hold individuals together.

The idea that the death instinct stands behind the regimentation of modern life should not shock us; the very real possibility of the death instinct becoming the only basis of social
cohesion should. If the death instinct represents a drive towards
inorganic inertia nothing can be seen as a more genuine realization of its aim than the transformation of men and women into
things, objects whose movements and behaviour are determined
solely by factors outside themselves, beyond their control. In

his paroxysms of movement, mirroring the movements of the
machine, Charlie Chaplin in 'Modern Times' represents the
quintessence of inertia, of thinghood. It is indeed a sobering
realization that capitalism does not merely tolerate neurotic
cripples, but thrives on them, depending on them to answer
its telephones, man its assembly lines, reproduce its ideologies,
fill its institutions.

The vision of a possible 'civilization' serving the death instinct
must certainly force us to re-examine Freud's view that civilization is the accomplishment of Eros, whose existence is jeopard-
ized by his great adversary. In the state of affairs which we
are presently examining, the death instinct need no longer fear
civilization, nor need it seek to destroy it. It has already undermined the accomplishment of its adversary and adapted it to its
own purposes. It has created a form of social organization in
which people are not just dead for eight hours a day, but which
can effectively be said to have institutionalized suicide. If it is
true that the organization of personality around social roles and
orderly, repetitive behaviour is in the last instance an expression
of the death instinct, then, from the economic point of view, the
institutions within which such behaviour takes place ensure the
overall reduction in the amount of aggression expressed as outward destructiveness; thus, there is less aggression to turn
inwards in the form of guilt and less aggression to turn outwards
against objects of the world. We have already seen how Erich
Fromm posited automaton conformity and destructiveness as
alternative mechanisms of escape (1966:Ch. 5); my suggestion
supports Fromm's view, but offers a psychological, not an
existential, explanation for the interchangeability of the two
phenomena.

The sociological importance of the hypothesis I have proposed
is almost self-evident. First, it gives a psychological basis to
the various arguments which we considered earlier. Thus,
behind the worker's submission to the Taylorist apparatus of
control and organization of production, behind the bureaucrat's
submission to administrative rules, behind the unionist's submission to the rules of industrial relations, lies the death
instinct, not rational or moral commitment. Institutionalization
of industrial conflict through collective bargaining, by involving
the parties of industrial relations in the observation of rules
and rituals, curbs the amount of destructive energy which is
available for direct hostilities. More generally, one can argue
that large amounts of aggressive energy, which until the
twentieth century were being utilized in controlling natural
forces, are now being channelled into the repetition of routinized
tasks and the adherence to fixed rules. Whenever an individual's
routine is broken, there is an immediate experience of dis-
orientation and discomfort, which has little to do with the
violation of deep-seated moral norms; in the former case, the
source of discomfort is not guilt unleashed by the super-ego
whose dictates have been violated, but rather a kind of unbound

aggressive energy which embarrasses and at times overwhelms the ego.

Before, however, accepting the argument that the death instinct has found a new form of expression (an expression which it may have known in the lives of slaves), in the form of fully routinized behaviour, it is important to consider one glaring instance where our hypothesis seems to be disconfirmed. Our hypothesis that contemporary social institutions provide an outlet for the death instinct, by absorbing it in the form of alienated rule-following and automaton conformity, implies that these types of 'institutional suicides' will limit the amount of overt aggression between people. Yet, there are certain cases of oppressive bureaucratic machines in which total conformity to the rules and overt exercise of violence seem to re-inforce each other. The secret police of authoritarian states along with extensive mechanisms of oppression and intimidation, fascist gangs of youths which roamed the European countryside during the period before the Second World War and, in general, formal ritualized violence would seem to run against my hypothesis. Above all, in military organizations, perhaps the oldest form of bureaucratic order, we have a case where strict adherence to rules and systematic violence have coexisted since years immemorial.

If we consider the army first, we will observe many of the features associated with automaton conformity; strict adherence to rules, total loss of individuality inside a uniform, complete absence of criticism and unquestioned obedience to all orders. The daily routine of the soldier is predetermined down to the minute details, more than that of the most meticulous bureaucrat. Yet, the soldier is also the embodiment of naked violence, the only agent in our society still enjoying the privilege of legitimate murder. Is it then possible to argue that automaton conformity and overt violence are alternative rather than mutually re-inforcing incarnations of the death instinct? If we look at the army as a social organization, rather than as a collection of automata, we observe that adherence to rules (especially during the course of overt hostilities) is far from a compulsive repetition of routinized behaviour. On the contrary, as Freud's own dis-cussion suggests (1921c:18), it derives from a profound identi-fication with the leader and a profound commitment to the collectivity, its values, ideals and illusions. The total deper-sonalization of the soldier inside the uniform, blind obedience and all the features mentioned above help to promote this moral commitment to a supra-individual order, a mythical entity, a grand illusion; it is in this way that strong social bonds are created which ensure a most uncommon degree of cohesion in the army. In Durkheim's discussions of the army, we are presented with the prototype of a highly integrated and regulated collec-tivity, in which discipline and obedience rest not on habit or unconscious repetition but on a deep respect for the authority from which they emanate.[15]

So, it should not be thought that all adherence to rules proceeds from the compulsion to repeat and the death instinct; on the contrary, as both Freud and Durkheim appreciated, strong normative regulation may well be built upon strong social bonds and internalized group values.[16] But the two manifestations of the death instinct, that which expresses itself through the super-ego and guilt and that which we encounter in the compulsion to repeat, should under no circumstances be confused. Nor should we assume automatically that a strong super-ego equals internalized aggression, for it can just as well lead to external aggression. Of course, in what Freud called the 'saintlihood syndrome' we have a classic case where self-control and self-discipline re-inforce internal aggression. In contrast, the strong super-ego of fighting men and women results in aggression against an external adversary, since violence comes in response to some moral command. As scores of religious wars suggest, outward aggression can be as important a means of placating one's super-ego as loving one's neighbour, and this, surely, must be the case with the military.

Thus, the army does not disconfirm our original hypothesis, since allegiance to its rules is based on an altogether different principle to the adherence of the bureaucrat to the impersonal rules of his organization. This does not mean that the army cannot turn into a bureaucracy pure and simple, with no moral commitment; but this would happen either during a protracted period of peacetime (when no 'hot violence' takes place), when no ideals can be found to cement the social bond, or when the means of violence reach such a level of technical sophistication that the elimination of large numbers of people or indeed the total destruction of part of the planet becomes merely a function of administrative decision-making.[17]

A similar argument to the one presented above can be made apropos of paramilitary organizations, youth gangs and all groupings in which ritualized violence is accompanied by strict rule-following. Once again, I suggest that rule-following in such organizations has little to do with bureaucratic automaton-conformity, and indeed may spring as a reaction to the latter. The only major difference from the army organization must surely be the prominence of the various little rituals of identity adhered to by these groups, which Freud interpreted so brilliantly through his notion of the narcissism of minor differences. Once again the important point is that the principle of rule-following lacks the mechanical regularity of the bureaucrat's and arises from a felt commitment, a commitment which is bolstered by further rules and rituals aimed at establishing the group's identity.

It is interesting that contrary to popular stereotypes, which tend to see the agents of surveillance, control and intimidation in countries under dictatorial regimes as impersonal Kafkaesque administrators, recent evidence of the organization of the military police in Greece, during the period of the military dictatorship,

reveals it as a highly cohesive organization, drawing intense
moral commitment from its members, strengthening their sense of
identity through a multiplicity of 'small differences' from other
military units. Extensive 'hot' violence was accompanied by a
profound identification with the values of the military rulers and
a quasi-religious anti-communism, so that it could in no way be
seen as a blind following of orders and rules or as 'automatized'
behaviour; in fact, torture involving personal and physical
contact was used almost exclusively, at the expense of imported,
sophisticated methods.[18]

The type of organization which we are discussing as our model
of automaton-conformity has little to do with the ones outlined
above. Violence may indeed form part of its operations, but it
stems neither from moral convictions nor from personal enmity
and hatred; it is almost always routinized, impersonal, 'cold'.
It is here that the death instinct assumes the form of a strict
mechanical adherence to rules and repetitive behaviour. This
apparatus, which, in my opinion, is far more important for an
understanding of contemporary society, dominates people's lives,
not by drawing all their energies and commitment, but by subtly
controlling their behaviour, structuring their daily routines and
inscribing its banal rules and regulations in their lives; men
and women become its extensions and its victims. Eros has no
place within its territory, since its operations involve neither
love nor hate, neither passion nor belonging.

One of the clearest discussions of the transition from hot
violence to cold, bureaucratic violence is presented by Michel
Foucault in his study of penal regimes through the ages. Foucault
begins his work by counter-posing two modes of punishment; in
the first place, he considers the fate of Robert Damiens, who in
1757 slightly injured Louis XV with a knife, and was subsequently
tortured to death in public, by having among other things his
flesh torn from him with red-hot pincers, his wounds burnt with
sulphur, his right hand cut off and his body drawn and quar-
tered by four particularly inept horses. He then examines the
rule-book of a corrective institution, whose rationale is not to
punish the body but to reform the soul through regulations which
control every minute of the prisoners' lives, with provisions
covering mental and bodily hygiene, work, recreation, meals,
education and so on. Only eighty years separate the two modes
of punishment and yet the relationship between crime and
punishment has totally changed, so as to suggest an entirely new
conception of the nature of crime and of the purpose of punishment. 'Physical pain, the pain of the body itself, is no longer
the constituent element of the penalty. From being an art of
unbearable sensations punishment has become an economy of
suspended rights' (1975:11). Foucault deciphers this transformation of penal regimes in great and illuminating detail and
relates it to a general transition in Western knowledge following
the French Revolution, from an age of a classifying conception
of reality to one which looks for causes and effects.

From our perspective we can understand the replacement of
physical public torture with impersonal suspension and control
of rights as a transition from hot violence to cold violence, from
a regime which unleashes massive amounts of aggressive energy
on a sinner to one which rehabilitates an offender by immersing
him/her in its order. The former corresponds to Durkheim's
conception of crime and the social function of punitive justice;
the latter corresponds to one of the all too many instances where
a bureaucracy resolves the problems it creates (deviance) by
extending its routines in ways which will absorb the deviant
into a new form of regimentation from which he/she cannot
escape; the industrial trouble-maker is accommodated within the
institutions of collective bargaining, the social deviant within
penal institutions, the mentally deranged in psychiatric institutions.

This discussion of the counter-hypothesis which regards violence
and rule-following as mutually re-inforcing rather than as alternative expressions of the death instinct has strengthened our
earlier hypothesis; at the same time, it has enabled us to articulate both of these phenomena in a more precise way. It is
not all forms of rule-following behaviour which concern us
here, but specifically those we encounter within many contemporary social institutions (including those of administration and
technical division of labour), which do not rely on personal
commitment and loyalty but on a blind execution of specific
functions. Our hypothesis enables us to propose a rudimentary
form of the economics of Thanatos, analogous to Freud's propositions on cultural erotics, discussed in Chapter 2. In short,
we propose that the death instinct may assume one of the following forms:

(a)   external aggression, including domination over the
      forces of nature and domination over other people,
(b)   internalized self-aggression or guilt,
(c)   repetitive behaviour.

External aggression, as Freud repeatedly argued, is the
primary threat to social cohesion. At the same time, however,
outgroup violence may strengthen the identity of the group and
promote social integration, as Durkheim's analysis of political
crisis indicates. Both internalized self-aggression and repetitive
behaviour, likewise, contribute to social cohesion - the former
through the internalization of morality and social norms, the
latter through the elimination of all critical content from people's
lives and their complete subjugation to impersonal machines.
Thus, just as certain forms of Eros are more conducive to the
formation of stable social bonds, it does not surprise us that
certain forms of the death instinct can, likewise, contribute to
society holding together. A central theme of this chapter is that
there has been a distinct and pronounced shift in the expressions

of the death instinct from the first and second forms to the third
form over the twentieth century. Direct 'hot' violence, associated
with an authoritarian super-ego, has been curbed and has tended
to disappear from people's lives, as the super-ego has lost some
of the terrifying strength and arbitrariness with which Freud
presented it to us. Routinized, repetitive and rigid behaviour,
on the other hand, has expanded beyond all recognition. This,
of course, does not imply that the death instinct in its traditional
forms of aggression and guilt has disappeared, but rather that
these two forms have assumed a secondary significance for the
time being. To some extent, these forms of direct violence have
been replaced by 'spectator-violence' in the ritualized violence
of sport and television shows – this can, perhaps, be seen as
our culture's attempt to 'sublimate' the death instinct, to strip it
of its potency and to find symbolic ways of satisfying it. More
importantly, however, our culture seems to channel the death
instinct in erecting social institutions established on a quasi-
neurotic compulsion to repeat uniform and rigid forms of
behaviour. In this way, it uses the death instinct as the psychic
foundation of the order captured by Orwell in '1984' and by
Kafka in his great novels, inhabited by Marcuse's one-dimensional
men and Mills' cheerful robots. It is for this reason that we can
voice our support for Himmelstein's view that 'Thanatos permeates
the whole structure of civilization' (1979:112), and not because
(as he suggests) the death instinct is the source of all renunciation of love.

The view which has been developed in this chapter is not in
complete disagreement to Freud's arguments that primary groups
are held together by libido, that social and group ties are de-
sexualized love bonds; in his discussion of such ties, Freud was
careful to limit such arguments to groups without 'too much
organization' (1921c:18:116) in which conceivably cohesion is
not the product of Eros. It is precisely in this type of society,
one with 'too much organization', that the compulsion to repeat
and the death instinct have displaced Eros and sublimation of
libido as the principles of social cohesion. In this situation,
cohesion is the result of the virtual certainty that, under the
compulsion to repeat, every part will behave in accordance to
its predetermined programme, or, to put it simply, that the
human factor becomes an extension of technical and social
machines.

It is rather indicative of man's baffled sense of impotence in
his encounters with machines of all kinds that they are almost
invariably portrayed as fallible, unreliable or indeed stupid.
Computer experts ritually re-assert that 'the machine is stupid',
bureaucracies are invariably presented as inefficient or irrational
and every comedian who knows his/her trade knows that his best
ally is the 'daemon in the machine'. It is significant that both
in 'Modern Times' and in Kafka's 'In the Penal Settlement' the
machines ultimately fail. Through demeaning the machine or
laughing at it, contemporary man seeks to comfort his profound

insecurity and his fear that he may already have become the slave of his own creations. It is perhaps the final irony that in both his mechanical and social artifacts which dominate him, man has projected the automaton in himself, for their inhumanity is no less human that the humanity of the most intimate and tender feeling.[19]

Chapter 14
Conclusions

Of course, the cheerful robot of the previous chapter and the modern narcissist are one and the same person. The same factors which account for the depersonalized regimentation of public life create the preconditions of modern narcissism, its fragmented illusions and ideals, its anxieties and insecurities, its limitless stock of half-truths and its own particular brand of despair. It is by turning inwards and investing his ego with the imaginary qualities of the objects he consumes that the modern narcissist seeks to escape from the zombie-like existence of public life. But as we saw earlier, narcissism, like the other great consolatory illusions of the past, far from cancelling the discontents of civilization, adds to them. The modern narcissist has to deal constantly with the contradictions between the illusions of power and beauty that sustain him and his need for personal approval on the one hand, and the daily experience of powerlessness, ugliness and impersonality on the other. Anxiety and insecurity permeate his existence, while his inability to organize his ego as a consistent and attractive imago creates a permanent problem of identity and meaning. Thus, although Western culture may have moved away from the traditional pair of discontents, arising from guilt and sexual frustration, it is highly dubious whether it has lightened the burden of the individual - just as religion created a set of discontents and proceeded to present itself as the only possible consolation for these discontents, our culture creates a new set of discontents and then proceeds to offer as consolations the very causes of these discontents, a risk-free, narcotized and regimented existence.

In spite of the profound discontents that it creates, our culture ensures the total dependence of the individual on it. The narcissist may resort to a variety of therapies in desperate efforts to relieve his suffering and infuse his life with meaning, but this does not prevent him from carrying out his bureaucratic duties; in fact, as Lasch has pointed out, 'the narcissist has many traits that make for success in bureaucratic institutions, which put a premium on the manipulation of interpersonal relations, [and] discourage the formation of deep personal attachments' (1979: 91). Lasch believes that the narcissist's discontents, his chronic inability to satisfy his need for self-esteem and find meaning in life, his profound mistrust of politicians and authority, his general apathy towards public affairs and so on indicate that the present system is in profound crisis and permit the hope that 'western civilization may yet

generate the moral resources to transcend its present crisis'
(20). This, however, is a view with which we strongly disagree.
Far from representing a threat to the system, the narcissist's
discontents are part of the system, ensuring his continuing
dependence on it; nothing is more abhorrent to the narcissist
than the prospect of a system (he may call it 'socialism') which
would interfere with his private life, seek to dissolve his
individuality by involving him in collective decision-taking,
restrict his freedom of choice of commodities in the interest of
rational utilization of resources, force him to participate in
public affairs and make claims upon his free time.

Capitalism is not in crisis and, even if it were, the responsibility of the crisis could not be found in the narcissist's
discontents; capitalism is possibly in decay or even in crises;
there may be a crisis in politics, an economic crisis, a crisis
in the institutions of the family, education and so on. But these
crises have become endemic to the system and present few
problems to its continuing existence; on the contrary, such
crises, very frequently, hit hardest the forces which may have
threatened the system, while indirectly strengthening the system
itself.

If the bipolarity of tranquillized robot and resigned narcissist
defines the underlying relationship of the contemporary individual to a social world dominated by impersonal machines and by
consumption as the principal mode of social exchange, then we
may observe something of a reversal in the traditional configuration of instincts in Western culture. According to this
configuration, analysed extensively in Part I, Eros provided the
basis of social bonds while the death instinct was forced inwards,
re-inforcing the individual's commitment to culture, her constraints and artifacts. The discontents arising from this
configuration consisted of an unstoppable sense of guilt (internalized aggression) and sexual frustration (as culture appropriated libidinal energies and sublimated them to create social
bonds), and in two senses these discontents were self-
reinforcing; first, the greater the individual's self-control of
outward aggression under the dictates of the super-ego, the
greater the amounts of internalized self-aggression and guilt,
and, second, the greater the sublimation of libido, the lesser
its ability to defuse the destructive impulses, which sooner or
later find their natural target, the individual ego. In the new
configuration, social integration and regulation are attained without the need of libidinal bonds or internalized aggression, on
the basis of repetitive observation of myriads of rules; these
rules are observed without moral commitment to the order from
which they emanate (one may accurately say that they are
observed 'unconsciously', on the whole) under the mental
principle of the compulsion to repeat, which is one of the dominant manifestations of the death instinct. In this sense, we
suggested that the death instinct is sublimated, its goal being

deflected from complete inorganic inertia to a state of institutional inertia, based on mechanical adherence to routine, free of risk and contradictions. According to this second configuration, it is Eros which is turned inwards, as the ego becomes hyper-cathected, leading to the familiar symptoms of megalomania and hypochondria and the psychological make-up of the modern narcissist. While in the first configuration Eros is sublimated and the death instinct is introjected, in the second configuration the death instinct is sublimated and libido is introjected. Far from demanding libidinal sacrifices from individuals in order to channel energy along the sublimated paths of work and community, culture leaves individuals with a libidinal surplus, which, being unable to direct outwards to the 'objects of the world', they seek to attach to their ego. In order to do so successfully, the ego strives to conceal its impoverishment (in terms of relations, identifications, achievements and so on) by incorporating what culture does offer - experiences and commodities which can be readily consumed. This second configuration is itself neither free from contradictions nor without its discontents; the narcissist's strivings are ultimately doomed to frustration. Yet, as in the earlier configuration, culture can take advantage of the discontents it creates to increase the individual's dependence on its offerings, its mutating panem et circenses.

The picture that has emerged from our analysis of this configuration of instinctual drives and derivative desires in contemporary culture seems remarkably stable, insofar as the system develops mechanisms for defusing contradictions and indeed for growing on them. Yet, it would be premature to conclude that we have moved to a self-perpetuating 'meta-historical' dystopia, like the one embodied in the visions of Orwell, Huxley and others. Even superficial cultural analysis reveals many significant phenomena which quite simply defy the argument presented here. The first pole of the robot-narcissism axis is challenged by the systematic manipulation of bureaucratic rules; most bureaucracies face periodic or constant attempts by individuals or groups to modify their rules or have such rules systematically violated or ignored, so that to represent all behaviour in them as being governed by the compulsion to repeat is to overemphasize order at the expense of conflict. The domination of bureaucracy may be challenged not only by workers throwing spanners in the works, but by parents seeking alternative education for their children, communities struggling for increased self-determination, women discovering alternatives to gynaecology, different types of groups seeking expressions outside the parameters of the media, people learning to live in arrangements different from those of nuclear family and creating recreation in spaces unoccupied by mass entertainment. Of course, it is true that bureaucracies constantly seek to extend their domination into these alternatives, alternative food, alternative energy, alternative childbirth and

medicine, alternative transport and so on, forever looking for
new possibilities of profit and growth; yet, their ability to
accommodate and defuse alternatives is by no means guaranteed.

It is equally true, however, that the second pole of the axis,
narcissism, is challenged by a variety of cultural phenomena,
such as the recent cultural and political movements, the resurgence of nationalist and fascist ideologies, the ever-increasing
emphasis on leadership and the search for charismatic figures,
persistent incidents involving 'hot' violence (including much-
publicized incidents of 'crowd violence') and a stubborn counter-
culture based on quasi-religious or psychotherapeutic commitment.
While it may be tempting to reduce these and other phenomena
which defy our arguments to residues of the earlier configuration,
it would be unwise to do so, since they frequently derive their
emotional appeal precisely from the contradictions of the robot-
narcissism axis. The regeneration of feminist activism and
thinking does not represent merely the resurrection of earlier
feminist arguments, but much more importantly the emergence of
an emphatic challenge to the configuration which we have been
discussing. Rejecting the dichotomies of private and public,
personal and political, staging a massive assault on stereotypes
of consumption (and thus refusing to play the narcissistic game
open to the housewives of the 1950s), developing new myths
and phantasies, articulating new emotions and passions, awakening new sensitivities, feminism cannot be reduced to a 'flight
from feeling', a manifestation of the New Narcisssism or a new
social tranquillizer (as Lasch seems to be doing); nor are the
energies which it has mobilized and the passions which it has
triggered those of our archetypical narcissist. As a challenge to
the culture based on the robot-narcissism axis, the women's
movement reveals how discontents effectively blocked by culture
for many years (through the isolation of women in the home, the
medical and psychiatric institutions and their respective myths
of femininity, etc.) can be liberated, how consciousness distorted systematically can seek new forms and expressions.

Nor should we forget that our analysis has taken for granted
culture's continuing ability to offer, or at least to promise, an
abundance of commodities on an ever-increasing scale, with
which the narcissist of our time can temporarily enrich his ego.
It is doubtful that a society dominated by mass unemployment,
widening social inequality and increasing deprivation will not
generate some challenge to its own rule; in spite of its remarkable ability to turn the narcissist's discontents into a stabilizing
factor, our culture may still face a massive challenge if the vast
amounts of introjected (and frequently wasted) libido are re-
aligned outwards, towards a project of social transformation.
In this sense, a resurgence of public passions, a collapse of
bureaucratic routines on a massive scale and even the re-
discovery of charisma cannot be ruled out. It is one of the
great assets of Freudian theory that in its analyses, whatever
the success of a culture in muting libidinal energies and in

manipulating them, Eros may always introduce fresh tensions, inspire new phantasies and fuel new movements. The creative ambiguity in Freud's twin paradigms of Eros (discussed in Part I) does not permit the reduction of culture to a simple expression of Eros or alternatively of Eros as a passive servant of culture. Although culture involves relatively stable configurations of Eros (as well as of the death instinct), these configurations, with all their contradictions and disharmonies, cannot be taken for granted – their continuing existence remains problematic. If in the old configuration it was repressed libido which constantly threatened to surge forward precipitating change, in the new configuration it is unutilized libido which introduces the factor of instability.

Now, most thinkers studied in Part II, as well as large numbers of other social theorists, have been pre-occupied with discovering a single principle of motion inherent in the social system. They have sought to articulate a mechanism of transition which would reveal to us the future of Western culture; this project has been dominated by two monumental perspectives and their respective utopias. For Marx, the motive force of history is the class struggle which embodies the contradictions of the mode of production as well as related ideological and political contradictions. For Freud, on the other hand, the motive force of history is the endless return of unfulfilled desire forever demanding total satisfaction. Class struggle and the return of desire, as we saw in our discussion of utopias, have become the predominant myths of salvation of contemporary man, and between them they have inspired more utopian imagination than any other. At the same time, these two concepts represent the two most incompatible, or indeed incommensurable, faces of historical materialism and psychoanalysis. Class struggle and the return of the repressed desire do not so much represent competing motive forces of history as alternative ways of explaining history – the proletariat and libido are not so much alternative revolutionizing agents as alternative ways of envisaging the possibility of revolution. It is at this precise point that attempts to 'reconcile' or 'synthesize' the two perspectives come inevitably to grief. Consider, for instance, their interpretations of fascism as a historical phenomenon. While historical materialism understands fascism as a particular political configuration, a special episode in the class struggle corresponding to a specific level of economic development under appropriate political and ideological circumstances, psychoanalysis approaches it as a psycho-cultural phenomenon resulting from a unique type of social vicissitudes of libidinal and aggressive energies, corresponding to a particular need for community and a particular orientation to authority. Their very conceptualization of that which is to be interpreted is fundamentally different.

The incommensurability of historical materialism and psychoanalysis on the issue of the motive force contrasts with the emphasis they both attribute to systematically distorted con-

sciousness as a central feature of the alienation of contemporary
man. In the views of both Marx and Freud the alienation of
consciousness is not an independent existential fact, but it is
the product of specific types of lived experience; likewise, the
emancipation of consciousness, although an indispensable factor
in general liberation, cannot be simply a process of education
but must be a genuine process of demystification. Yet, once
again, while for Marx the demystification of consciousness can
only take place in the course of the proletariat's revolutionary
political practice, for Freud demystification is the product of a
radically new instinctual configuration, a configuration which
does not banish large regions of human desire into the unconscious and seek to compensate the situation through substitutive,
illusory, phenomena. It is not accidental that Marxists, like
those of the Frankfurt School, who lost their faith in the
proletariat as the revolutionizing agent of society turned to
psychoanalysis as an alternative system of thought which provided such an agent (as well as to other systems of thought
which made similar provisions, such as Hegel's). Yet, it seems
to me that the attempt to attribute the movement of history to a
single unifying principle is unjustified; as I argued earlier the
natural world is too complex, too capricious and too interesting
to submit itself to the unifying laws of positivism - equally,
history may be too inventive to accept a unifying principle of
motion. It is significant that when Marx and Freud approached
particular historical situations, their arguments departed considerably from any monistic (or indeed 'dialectic') principle of
motion. Although class struggle and the connection between class
and material conditions of existence are central in Marx's discussion in 'The Eighteenth Brumaire', we are struck by two
features. First, the class struggle far from being a direct conflict
between the two major social classes involves an extremely intricate conflict of manifold interests, traditions and prejudices.
Indeed, in much of the period covered by Marx, the proletariat
is reduced to a spectator through an early defeat (1852:23, 71),
the bourgeoisie is split into different groups with conflicting
material interests and is unable to rule, while the lumpenprole-
tariat led by a 'grotesque mediocrity' ends up playing 'the role
of the hero', in the interest of a group whose class consciousness
is no more than that of a sack of potatoes, the small-holding
peasantry. Second, the text is littered with expressions like
'national bond', 'community', 'historical tradition', 'fears',
'memories', 'prejudices', 'illusions' and even 'instinct', all of
which are woven into the class analysis without strictly forming
concepts in the Marxist discourse.

Likewise, Freud repeatedly invokes the concept of class as
well as the economic system of production and distribution and
social inequality in his discussions without in any way seeking to
reduce them to the vocabulary of libido. Both thinkers are
willing to investigate what they regard as the principle of movement of history in a wide variety of vicissitudes and configurations,

so that both class struggle and libido are genuinely protean in
the hands of their creators. Moreover, they are both willing to
allow elements which they cannot subsume in the vicissitudes of
their central principles. It would then seem to me that both men
were far more sensitive and flexible in their concrete analyses
than a narrow reading of their theoretical texts may suggest.
Many of their followers, in their keenness to discover the secret
of history, may have assumed unwisely that history has always
got one and the same secret, or that the secret can be learned
in one way only. A slightly greater respect for history may
justify trying to solve its many riddles in as many ways as
possible, just as a greater respect for nature encourages toler-
ance of alternative approaches. Far from being embarrassing,
the existence of alternative approaches and traditions, their
mutual respect and interaction can only deepen our understanding. Demystification of consciousness may have to proceed
from many directions simultaneously. Trying to resolve the riddle
of history, however, through one inspired gesture not only
displays a naive contempt for history, but also inevitably leads
to a rather pathetic pessimism, a suppression of imagination and
a chauvinistic dogmatism. While displaying great arrogance and
self-confidence in grasping the meaning of history through one
unifying principle, this attitude precludes the possibility of
historical movements which will depart from this principle. The
realization that a given culture has muted or indeed halted this
unifying principle appears as history having reached a halt.

The keen reductionism of many contemporary social thinkers
(including many Marxists) when they address history clashes
spectacularly with the historical sensitivity of those Marxists
who left their mark not on historical scholarship but on history
itself. In a striking passage, anticipating much subsequent
theoretical debate, Lenin argues that

> History as a whole, and the history of revolutions in particu-
> lar, is always richer in content, more varied, more multiform,
> more lively and ingenious than is imagined by even the best
> parties, the most conscious vanguards of the most advanced
> classes. (1967:401)

To such people history teaches the importance of unexpected
or 'accidental' factors which sometimes prove more seminal than
the movements which accord with the 'laws of motion'; a few
critical days can sometimes achieve more in the way of change
than whole centuries of 'development'. What is not accidental
is that history so frequently catches by surprise not only the
most perceptive social commentators but also the most ardent
revolutionaries.

Psychoanalysis, its concepts, its discoveries, its hypotheses
and even its myths have served us well in trying to resolve
some of the riddles of contemporary culture and in providing
interpretations for some of its central features. It has shed

some light into the nature of humanity's present discontents
and illusions, its anxieties and insecurities, and has revealed
some of the central contradictions, which may or may not
become the source of future change. Finally, it has inspired
imagination and supported different visions of a better future,
opening new possibilities for thought and action. To ask for
more would be asking it to fulfil the wishes it has generated –
it would indeed be looking at it as the illusion of the future,
a predicament which Freud's work deserves even less than the
crude mistreatment accorded to him by his enemies.

An attempt at integration – Talcott Parsons

The writer to whom we turn now shares the view of Marcuse and
Brown in their implicit opposition to Rieff and Becker; he agrees,
in other words, that contemporary society, like all societies, is
characterized by a symbolic system of expectations, rewards,
meaning and norms. Yet, he disagrees with Marcuse and Brown
on nearly everything else. Instead of using Freud's speculations
on instincts, life and death, to engage in a vigorous line of
social criticism of the present system, he uses psychoanalytic
insights in order to articulate the relation between the individual
and society – the personality and the social systems. Unlike
Becker who took the 'dovetailing' of the two systems for granted,
as the product of the 'natural genius of Man', Parsons sees it as
problematic – more precisely, he sees the minimization of the
discrepancy between the two systems as one of the important
functions of every society. In this, he tends to underplay
Freud's emphasis on the systematic conflict between the interests
of society and the demands of the individual, in favour of a view
which stresses the more or less successful interpenetration of
the two, i.e. the individual is the bearer of society, just as
society is the bearer of the individual.

Parsons makes extensive use of Freud's formulations on object-
relations formed during infancy, in order to study the process
of socialization, i.e. the process through which social reality
becomes constitutive of the personality structure. The success
of this process determines to a large extent the success with
which society minimizes the discrepancy between its own demands
and those of the individual during his/her maturity. This type
of enterprise is not altogether novel; as we saw earlier, it was
undertaken by Reich and Fromm in the development of their
theories of character-formation. As we shall see, in spite of
some important differences, Parsons shares their views on many
issues – the function of the family, the process of socialization,
the structure of personality or character, etc. Moreover, they
share the conviction that Freud was basically a theorist of the
psyche, whose ideas can and must be integrated with a theory
of society, in order to yield a complete view of social reality – a
conviction which contrasts with the views of Marcuse and Brown
that psychoanalysis is in and of itself social theory.

One rather central feature of Parsons' work, which stands
out when compared with the works of those thinkers we have
examined this far, is the total absence of negative criticism and
utopian imagery. As the chief representative of the modern

sociological tradition, Parsons believes that social phenomena can
be described, analysed and, to a lesser extent, causally
explained, without involving value or normative considerations.
This, as we shall see, is intimately related to the general
emphasis of his work on order and cohesion, in contrast to the
outlooks of the thinkers considered earlier with their emphasis
on personal and social disorder and conflict or at least the
potential for change residing within the present.

It may reasonably be asked how a theorist, so pre-occupied
with order, could be interested in the work of Freud, who
always searched underneath apparent order for conflicts,
dualisms and oppositions. But as we have seen already, Freud's
work seems to be so rich in its potential and in its ideas that it
can appeal to thinkers with diverse theoretical and political
position, from political and sexual radicals, to enlightenment
liberals, to piecemeal reformists and to orthodox conservatives.
It would, therefore, be misleading to suggest that all theorists
who have been inspired by his work have also been fascinated
by the utopian elements, which all the theorists examined so
far (with the exception of Becker) have developed. Parsons'
work is representative of those theorists who have used Freud's
insights in a purely analytical way, to articulate the relationship
between the individual and society and to elucidate the 'personality' system.

In this review of those of Parsons' works which have been
influenced by psychoanalytic thinking, I will first deal with his
views on the possibility, feasibility and desirability of an integration of the theories of personality and social systems and
then I will discuss a few key regions of his theory, like the
formation and structure of personality, the functions of the
family in contemporary societies, the process of socialization and
the significance of love and eroticism in this process.

Parsons' 'general theory of social action' studies human action
as a system, i.e. as a structured ensemble of interdependent
and interacting units. A change of state in any one of the units
corresponds to a determinate change of state in all other units
belonging to the system - it follows that a system has a boundary
which discriminates it from its environment, which includes all
units that are unaffected by changes within the system. However,
changes in the environment are followed by adaptive responses
on the part of the system, insofar as they affect the system's
equilibrium. An act is determined in terms of its effect on the
system (and the system's relation to its environment) along four
principal co-ordinates of action space - gratification of the units
in the system, designated as goal-attainment, manipulation of
the environment in the interest of goal-attainment, designated as
adaptation, the attachment of member-units to each other in
their distinction from the system's environment, designated as
integration and, finally, the integration of the member-units
themselves as systems; the last co-ordinate corresponds to the

degree of tension within the system and is designated as
tension-management or latency.

For the purposes of empirical measurement, Parsons groups
the four co-ordinates in two broad indices; these indices correspond to the findings of Bales' study of leadership and interaction in small groups, under experimental conditions. Bales
observed that activity in such groups can have either an
instrumental or an expressive character and Parsons associates
goal-attainment and adaptation with the first and integration
and latency with the second type of activity.[1]

Analytically, Parsons breaks down his general theory of action
into the study of four independent but interpenetrating sub-
systems, the organism, the personality, the social system and
the cultural system (1958:50). Parsons maintains that there is
a neglected thread in Freud's thought, which deals, on the one
hand, with the organization of the personality as a system, and
on the other with the relation between the social system and the
process of personality development (48). This thread can
provide not only the theoretical tools necessary for the study of
personality as a distinct entity, but also the means through
which a theoretical bridge can be built between sociology and
psychology; the two disciplines, like their subject matters,
interpenetrate. Nevertheless, Parsons does not seek to liquidate
the theoretical distinctness of the two disciplines, or the independence of their subject-matter: the social system is viewed 'as a
distinct and independent entity which must be studied and
analysed on its own level, not as composite of the actions of
component individuals' (1950:337). The fabric of this entity is
structured patterns of expectations concerning the behaviour of
individuals who occupy particular statuses. These expectations
are defined and regulated by specific roles; institutions are
defined as stable clusters of expectations and roles.

Now, roles do not only regulate expectations - they also
become essential parts of individuals' personalities, through the
process of internalization. However, there is no one-to-one
correspondence between personality structure and institutional
position for the simple reason that personality constitutes an
independent system with its own relational needs (1958:50); in
spite of the fact that personality is formed through a process
of internalization of roles, it remains a separate system and does
not become a subsystem of the social system, involving both
learned and instinctual components (68).

Parsons' account of the two systems avoids Becker's error of
presupposing a harmonious co-existence between the two as well
as the shortcomings of Rieff's methodological individualism (in
respect of present culture). The alignment of institutional
position and motivation on the one hand, and personality
structure and motivation on the other, is neither the achievement of the 'genius of Man' nor a theoretical given; it is the
product of what Parsons calls the 'structural generalization of
goals', which may be more or less successful. The profit motive,

for example, is an institutional motivation which may or may not have a direct psychological equivalent.

In order, however, to assess the success with which a society achieves the generalization of goals, it is necessary to study the mechanisms through which these goals become part of the personality structures of individuals. Parsons criticizes the long sociological tradition of positing *ad hoc* assumptions about human psychology and individual motivation whenever such assumptions are required. Parsons does not claim that sociologists should become psychologists every time their theories require assumptions about the psychological make-up of individuals, as this would imply a total integration of the two disciplines; instead, he suggests that psychology can provide the assumptions required by sociology (concerning, for instance, motivation) and vice versa (1950: 342ff). Parsons' castigation of ad hoc assumptions about psychology by sociologists are identical with Freud's criticisms against psychologists who tended to improvise any number of convenient biological instincts, in order to 'explain' psychological behaviour. Moreover, just as Freud is not very precise about the relation between biological forces and the psychic 'representatives', Parsons is not too clear about the relation between institutional and individual motivation.[2]

SOCIALIZATION

The process of personality development takes place in the family, which as we shall see is not a microcosm of society, but a differentiated part of a larger system (1955: 32-3). Personality develops through a process of differentiation of a very simple internalized object-system into progressively more complex systems (54). It is interesting that while Parsons and Fromm (and Becker) provide similar substantive accounts of the process of early socialization, Parsons stresses the internal system differentiation, while Fromm stresses the child's dynamic adaptation to extra-systemic conditions, such as changing parents' expectations - Parsons stresses more the autonomy of the personality system, Fromm stresses its dynamic inter-relation with the environment.

This in no way implies that Parsons neglects the importance of social interaction in socialization. On the contrary, he explicitly criticizes Freud for his tendency to underplay the interactive element of object-relations and symbolism, in favour of the cathectic element of object-relations and the expressive (instead of the communicative) element of symbolism (1952: 25f). But social interaction between mother and child does not introduce new elements from the environment (social system) into the personality of the child; it simply precipitates a sequence of internal system differentiation.

The question now arises of what the raw material is, upon which the process of structural differentiation operates, the

seed which gives birth to the tree of personality. Parsons
categorically denies that the original and relatively simple
organization of personality is constituted by the instincts
residing in an undifferentiated unity of ego/id; the instincts
in themselves do not constitute a form of personality, not even
in a primitive form. Instead, Parsons posits certain elemental
object-relations, as the core of personality. In this, he has the
support of Freud's theory of the super-ego as the precipitate
of the original object-relation of the child to his (and, to a
lesser extent, her) father (1958:49). One of Parsons' major
efforts is his attempt to show that all parts of the personality
(i.e. the ego and the id as well as the super-ego) are involved
in the original core of object-relations, which constitutes the
raw material for the subsequent development of personality
through structural differentiation. In order to demonstrate this
point, Parsons considers in detail the process of interaction
between the mother and the child and, then, the triadic interaction of the Oedipal situation. From the point of view of the
child, three elemental object-relations are involved: (i) identification with the mother in the oral stage, (ii) the first object-
choice, usually with the mother and (iii) internalization or
introjection of the father, at the resolution of the Oedipal episode.
All three are phases of interaction of the child with an active
part of his environment, but also phases through which the
child's personality system is shaped. They are learning processes,
and at the end of each phase the personality has incorporated
a feature of the social system into its organization.

Thus, the super-ego is not the only agency of the personality
that possesses a learned and an instinctual component. The ego
too is the precipitate of the early object-relations on the psyche.
Specifically, the ego represents the organization that is set up
in the psyche through the early interaction between the mother
and the child; the latter's behaviour is organized according to
the behaviour of the mother and the learning of the courses of
action which lead to reward. In this way, Parsons concludes, the
ego must be seen as a system of cybernetic control over the
instincts, and as such it represents the demands of the social
system within the personality system. Elsewhere, Parsons had
developed theoretically an analogous process which gives rise
to the second major institution of the personality system, the
super-ego; this too represents an organization of the personality
precipitated by social interaction - the main difference between
the processes which give rise to the ego and those which give
rise to the super-ego is that in the former the lever for learning
is the loss of pleasure (especially oral gratification) while in the
latter the lever is the loss of love (and the accompanying)
anxiety) (1952:27ff).

Finally, Parsons makes an attempt to show that the third major
agency of personality, the id, has also both learned and instinctual components; he is least successful here, as he fails to
articulate the specific object-relations that give rise to the id -

he simply asserts that they are among the oldest object-relations,
and as at this stage neither reality testing nor the ego have been
established, the id retains a more intimate orientation towards
the person him/herself (1958:69).

In this introduction, I have not outlined the analyses that
Parsons has provided concerning the early phases of socialization. I will simply mention two important processes which take
place during these early phases; first, during the early identification with the mother (during the infant's complete oral
dependence), the child learns the fact that it constitutes a
member of a social relationship and, by implication, a social
collectivity. 'Being like' his/her mother means that he/she forms
part of the same collectivity as the mother (57).[3] This corresponds to the third kind of identification outlined by Freud in
'Group Psychology and the Analysis of the Ego' (1921c:18:105ff).
Second, these early phases are accompanied by a gradual
diffusion of sexuality: 'Eroticism . . . is a mechanism of internal
rewards by which fixation on the more specific instinctual
gratifications is overcome in favour of pleasure in the diffuse
and generalized relation to a nurturing social object' (1958:56).
Thus, Parsons does not fall into the same error as Becker, who
(arbitrarily) asserted that the child's primary need is the
'generalized need for closeness and support' (1962:58). This
need is not primary but develops as the child goes through the
early phases of socialization, in a society where the incest taboo
prevails (for reasons which we will examine shortly) and primary
gratification has to give way to secondary ones (1958:68).

THE EGO, THE ID AND THE SUPER-EGO

One of Parsons' major efforts in the realm of psychology has
been to provide a systematic account of the process of structural
differentiation through which the personality develops out of
the original core of relatively simply object-relations and internalizations into a complex system of action, which interpenetrates
with the social system. The underlying principle of this process
is what Parsons calls 'binary fission', according to which each
internalized object generates two such objects at each successive
stage of differentiation. As the child becomes integrated in
progressively larger social systems (first with the mother, then
within the family, then within the school, etc.) the roles which
he/she internalizes become more numerous and more complex -
the original four-fold structure of the nuclear family along the
dimensions of power and expressive/instrumental priorities
undergoes fission and gives rise to an eight-fold differentiation
of role-types.[4] Parsons also develops a 'genealogy of need-
dispositions', an account of the differentiation undergone by the
child's motivational complex; as the personality structure
becomes increasingly differentiated, need-dispositions become
increasingly complex, themselves subject to binary fission.[5]

Parsons tries to analyse the social interactions that precipitate the development of personality through the various stages and to show that the same basic conceptual components can be used for an analysis of the personality and the social system. My assessment of this attempt within the present context will be limited to those aspects of Parsons' theory of personality which are drawn from psychoanalytic theory, and in particular to his views on the ego, id and super-ego configuration.

The super-ego is the point where Parsons observes a convergence of the theories of Freud and Durkheim. It represents the process of internalization of moral values and this is the missing bridge between two extremely important problematics: the central problematic of psychology, motivation, and the cultural problematic of sociology, order. The second important missing bridge between the two problematics is the concept of a system of interaction between two or more persons.

> On the one hand, Freud and his followers, by concentrating on the single personality, have failed to consider systematically the implications of the individual's interaction with other personalities *to form a system*. On the other hand, Durkheim and the other sociologists have failed, in their concentration on the social system as a system to consider systematically the implications of the fact that it is the *interaction of personalities* which constitutes the social system with which they have been dealing, and that, therefore, adequate analysis of motivational process in such a system must reckon with the problems of personality. (1952:20)

Thus, Parsons attempts to build the two bridges, by examining the function of the super-ego within the interactive system, and for this purpose he chooses a simple two-person interaction, each participant in such an interaction constitutes an object to the other in three basic respects, (i) cognitively, (ii) emotively and (iii) morally. In other words, each person (i) knows who the other person is, (ii) relates to the other person through a common system of expressive symbolism and (iii) evalutes the other person according to a system of moral standards (ibid.). Now, all three orientations of action occur within a common culture, whose various elements have been internalized by both participants. Freud's visualization of the super-ego limits the internalization to the third orientation, the moral one, but Parsons objects that the other two are equally based on different elements of the common culture that have become internalized. Considering the cognitive orientation first, Parsons observes that cognition of another person, unlike cognition of inanimate objects, involves the cognition of the status of the alter in the interactive system, and such cognition depends on generalized expectations. These expectations, in turn, represent the ego's internalization of cultural elements. Likewise, the emotive orientation of action involves the internalization of cultural elements

such as language, facial expressions, gestures, etc. It is only
in this way that each participant can understand the meaning of
the other's actions and respond through his own. In sum,

> Freud's insight was profoundly correct when he focused on
> the element of moral standards. This is indeed central and
> crucial but it does seem that Freud's view was too narrow. The
> inescapable conclusion is that not only moral standards, but
> *all the components of the common culture* are internalized as
> parts of the personality structure. (23)

The result of this modification is that Freud's distinction between
the ego and the super-ego vanishes, at least insofar as the
former was seen as the organization of responses to external
reality and the latter the product of internalization of authority
through identification; Parsons argues that the ego too is the
product of internalizations of cultural patterns. Moreover, given
that cognitive recognition of the object and moral evaluation
'are part and parcel of the same fundamental cultural patterns'
(24), the boundary between the ego and the super-ego more or
less dissolves. While, however, Parsons asserts that the ego and
the super-ego are products of internalization of similar cultural
elements, he does not abolish the distinction between them, as
some theorists tend to do. For Parson, the super-ego remains the
seat of morality, while the major characteristic of the ego is
organization (30). This corresponds to what Anna Freud had
termed 'the ego's need for synthesis' (1966:60). But in order
for the ego to exercise this function it requires 'cybernetic
control' over the crude inputs of the id. It is in this way that
Parsons reads Freud's celebrated analogy of the rider and the
horse. His view of the horse, however, differs somewhat from
Freud's; Parsons suggests that it too has both instinctual and
learned components and its main difference from the other two
subsystems are (i) the general orientation towards the person's
own organism as an object, and (ii) the regressive nature of
this orientation, which arises from its origin in the very earliest
object-relations.

Why is Parsons interested in the work of Freud, a theorist so
pre-occupied with conflicts, dualisms and antinomies, with a
different overall perspective from his own? There are two elements of Freudian theory which obviously appeal to Parsons;
the first, as Parsons acknowledges, is the concept of the
super-ego as the product within the personality of internalized
moral values. The second is a certain functionalist element that
characterizes the Freudian view of the ego; as we saw in Chapter
5, the ego may be seen as the agency which promotes the
integration of the self as a whole. This element was prominent
in Freud's first major theoretical break-through, his theory of
psycho-neuroses as defences. Arguing against Janet's genetic
theory of hysteria and, implicitly, against Breuer's hypnoid

theory, Freud suggested that the 'splitting of consciousness'
should be seen as an 'act of will', aimed at defending the individual against an intolerable idea.

It is this functionalist thread of Freud's argument that Parsons
develops, at the expense of the threads which highlight psychic
conflict.[6] In his rejection of the libido theory, Parsons resembles
the 'ego-psychologists', of whom Erich Fromm was examined in
detail earlier. Like Fromm, Parsons is pre-occupied with the
ways in which early interaction (within the family system)
generates the personality system. However, as we saw, unlike
Fromm and Becker, Parsons does not see personality as the
outcome of adaptive responses, but as an internal process of
structural differentiation, once the personality core has been
formed through the earliest object-relations. Moreover, unlike
Becker and Fromm, Parsons does not invoke ad hoc motives and
existential needs. Yet, his formulation of the 'instinctual content'
of personality is exceedingly vague and it is particularly hard
to discover an imagery of 'human nature' which, in conjunction
with the early object-relations, will give rise to the original
personality core. Ultimately, Parsons does not explain what the
human 'raw material' is which becomes the subject of the various
early object-relations. The only assumption that he seems to make
about the mass of flesh that establishes and experiences the
primary identification with the mother is that this mass of flesh
is orally dependent; all subsequent needs arise from binary
fission of this original organic need.

Correspondingly, eroticism which is originally specific in its
aim becomes generalized and diffused as a sense of well-being.
It might be thought that Parsons postulates the exact opposite
view concerning the development of sexuality to the views of
Brown and Marcuse, where the original polymorphously perverse
Eros gives way to increasingly specific organizations of libido
around erogenous zones, culminating in the 'genital tyranny'.
But in fact, the importance attributed by Parsons to eroticism
is much smaller than that attributed by Brown and Marcuse.
For Parsons, eroticism is not so much 'the psychic representative
of an invariant force of excitation whose origin is bodily', but a
generalized interest which involves a very large component
which is learned. In this way, both sublimated and unsublimated
sexuality become part of what Parsons calls eroticism; what
becomes lost is the instinct's aim, the possibility of this aim
being deflected, and the cost involved in this deflection. It may
be true that some gratifications result from successful sublimations, like creative writing, successful career, etc. Yet, this in
no way marks the victory of the pleasure principle – the sense
of well-being which rises from diffuse eroticism is never related
by Parsons to libidinal economics, so that it is difficult to assess
either its value or the cost were such gratification to be forfeited.

Parsons' rejection of the libido theory undoubtedly conceals
any systematic conflict that may exist between individual personalities and the social system. But it also results to a rather

misleading picture of the components of personality. Parsons'
view of the id strikes one as the most immediately vulnerable,
because of his reluctance to accept the reality of any instincts
and his inability to specify the object-relations that generate
its organization. The id, in this way, becomes an extremely
abstract and esoteric entity, having been stripped of both its
economic content (as the ultimate reservoir of psychic energy)
and its topographic specificity (as the locus of repressed
impulses). However, I must underline that Freud himself did
not maintain that the id has no 'learned' components, although
he did argue that it is immune to being educated; on the contrary, the ideational content of the unconscious (i.e. repressed
ideas or representations) as well as the 'phylogenetic' content
derive from the social reality. What Freud did maintain is that
primary processes do not obey the criteria of reality testing and
the laws of logic; it seems to me that to deny this is tantamount
to a rejection of the concept of the unconscious.[7]

Furthermore, Parsons' cybernetic conceptualization of the
relation between the ego and the id underestimates seriously the
conflict involved in this relation. In Freud's metaphor of the
rider and the horse, not only must the rider control and direct
the superior forces of the animal, but the animal has very strong
ideas of its own, as to where it wishes to go, and these ideas
show no respect for reality, as embodied in ditches, fences and
cliffs. The horse constantly resists the rider, so that the final
direction that it will follow will depend on the relative strengths
of the two. Freud never abandoned this economic aspect of
repression, and, in fact, extended it by arguing that the ego
must carry out its repressions and organize its anti-cathexes
with energies borrowed through the device of narcissism. Unless
we have a proper appreciation of these economic factors, we will
remain unable to explain the rider's frequent failures to control
his horse, his occasional falls, his constant exhaustion and his
permanent state of alert.

Of course, Parsons' cybernetic view is not mistaken; Freud
himself argued that the signal of anxiety as well as the experimental action of normal thinking (1911b:12:221), carried out with
very small amounts of mental energy, are such cybernetic
devices, which set in motion indispensable psychic processes.
The ego is both a cybernetic and an energic system, and these
two aspects complement each other.

> We have just said what the ego does: it makes use of an
> experimental cathexis and starts up the pleasure-unpleasure
> automatism by means of a signal of anxiety. After that, several
> reactions are possible or a combination of them in varying
> proportions. Either the anxiety attack is fully generated and
> the ego withdraws entirely from the objectionable excitation;
> or, in place of the experimental cathexis it opposes the excita-
> tion with an anti-cathexis, and this combines with the energy
> of the repressed impulse to form a symptom; or the anti-cathexis

> is taken up into the ego as a reaction-formation, as an identi-
> fication of certain of the ego's dispositions, as a permanent
> alteration of it. (1933a:22:90)

Parsons' emphasis on the cybernetic at the expense of the energic
aspect of the ego emphasizes the ego's control over the id and
conceals the conflict between the two. His imagery of the horse
and the rider becomes a relaxed dressage exercise, not the desperate effort of the rider to maintain control over and hang
onto the impetuous animal.

I find that the same imagery of harmony prevails in Parsons'
account of the relation of the ego to its second 'harsh master',
the super-ego. Parsons has criticized Freud for confining the
process of internalization to moral standards and for taking cognition as a given, and has suggested that both the ego and the
super-ego are products of internalization of different cultural
elements:

> The essential point seems to be that Freud's view seems to
> imply that the object, as cognitively significant, is given
> independently of the actor's internalized culture, and that the
> super-ego standards are then applied to it. This fails to take
> into account the extent to which the constitution of the object
> and its moral appraisal are part and parcel of the *same* funda-
> mental cultural patterns; it gives the super-ego an appearance
> of arbitrariness and dissociation from the rest of the per-
> sonality - particularly from the ego - which is not wholly in
> accord with the facts. (1952:24)

But it seems to me that Freud's conceptualization of the super-
ego hinges precisely upon these two features, its arbitrariness
and its dissociation from the rest of the personality. He repeatedly talks about man's moral character, whereby an individual's
every act is guided by his/her moral standards without, however, mitigating an unyielding sense of guilt. In fact, Freud
suggests that the greater the compliance with moral standards
aimed at inhibiting aggressiveness, the greater the harshness
and arbitrariness of the super-ego, the greater the suffering
of the ego. Parsons' failure to appreciate this point (arising,
no doubt, from his neglect of the economic factor) leads to a
fundamental misinterpretation of the super-ego as an integrated
part of the personality instead of as a genuine fifth column
within an individual's mental apparatus.

But even if the super-ego were not in possession of the powerful heritage of guilt, even if it were not the seat of the aggressive instincts when they turn inwards, the prospects of a
harmonious symbiosis between the ego and the super-ego would
be slim for two reasons. First, the standards of morality are
themselves not free from contradictions and are not arranged
in tidy hierarchies of value; a person is frequently expected to
abide by contradictory moral standards, as the great tragedians

have shown us. These contradictory demands can exist side by
side in the super-ego, large parts of which are unconscious and
subject to primary processes. In situations like this, whichever
course of action the ego opts for will attract the wrath of the
super-ego. Second, the demands of the super-ego are frequently
incompatible with the desires which arise from the id. Caught
between contradictory demands, the ego experiences intense
discomfort; if it tries to meet the demands of one institution it
finds itself in great conflict with the other, and if it endeavours
to please both of them simultaneously it runs the risk of complete rupture within its own constitution.[8]
But the situation, in Freud's account, is even more complex and
even more difficult for the ego due to the demands of the third
harsh master, external reality. And here I must raise certain
objections to Parsons' argument that Freud tends to see the
objects of cathexes as quite literally objects, with no capacity
for communication and response (24ff). Parsons takes a line
strongly reminiscent of the 'ego-psychologists', namely that
object-cathexis is not a one-sided affair but involves interaction
and positive and negative re-inforcement. 'It may be regarded
as almost a truism that it is difficult if not impossible in the long
run to love without being loved in return' (22). Although Freud
towards the end of his life gave increasing emphasis to the
phenomenon of masochism (which involves non-reciprocal love)
and although many of his patients seemed to be fixated with
persons who could not fully reciprocate their love, Freud might
have agreed with Parsons; but what he would add is that when
reality frustrates our desires, when, for example, a loved
person refuses to reciprocate our love, the ego is required to
repress our love for this person to the unconscious space of our
mind. So, although at the conscious level it may be rare for a
person to love without being loved, in our unconscious we all
love persons who have not reciprocated our love. So, it is hard
to agree with Parsons' statement that to Freud 'the object tends,
even if human, to be an inert something on which a "charge" of
cathectic significance has been placed'(24). On the contrary,
the object's response is really decisive as to whether the ego
can proceed with the cathexis or whether it is forced to set in
motion the process of repression. Both parents' responses are
absolutely vital in the context of the resolution of the Oedipus
Complex and may well determine a person's entire future orientation to authority as well as to love.
It is now possible to examine a related aspect of the ego, its
'need for synthesis', and indeed its general pre-occupation
with organization and integration. Parsons, after arguing convincingly that not only emotive/communicative but also cognitive
elements of culture are internalized, suggests that

> the element of *organization*, which is the essential property
> of the ego, would then not be derived from the 'reality
> principle' - that is from adaptive responses to the external

> world alone. Instead it would be derived from two fundamental
> sources: the external world as an environment; and the common
> culture which is acquired from objects of identification. Both
> are, to be sure, acquired from the outside, but the latter
> component of the ego is, in origin and character, more like
> the super-ego than it is like the lessons of experience. (31)

Yet, it seems to me that this does not explain why it is that the
ego acquires its 'obsession' for organization and control, from
where the need for synthesis originates. In other words, Parsons
does not explain why it is that the ego extends itself in different
directions, internalizes a variety of cultural objects, modifies
itself and tries to subsume every new input from the reality
within its organization. Freud did not argue that the reality
principle was responsible for this need, for the reality in and of
itself cannot motivate the ego in its epic efforts to remain in
control. In his early theory, Freud could answer this question
by appealing to the ego as representative of the ego instincts,
i.e. self-preservation. In his later theory, Freud's answer is
much more complex, as we saw in Chapter 2, but no less ambiguous: the main motive of the ego in its synthetic function is its
fear of the super-ego. As long as the ego can keep its organization free from contradiction, the intensity of criticism from the
super-ego and the possibility of conflict are minimized. It is in
response to this situation that the ego acquires the character
that Parsons attributes to it; it is because of the continuous
pressure from the super-ego that the ego builds up its organization. If, as Freud insists, 'to the ego . . . living means being
loved - being loved by the super-ego' (1923b:19:58), then the
ego's life becomes dependent upon its ability to maintain its
organization as free as possible from contradiction.

In spite of these shortcomings, Parsons' view of the ego gives
us several important new insights; in particular, his account of
communicative symbolism (through which emotions, feelings and
attitudes are communicated to the objects of cathexes) complements Freud's views on expressive symbolism. Likewise, his
articulations of the mechanisms through which the ego internalizes its various roles are important, even though, as I mentioned, they tend to obscure the costs at which internalization
takes place. His identification of the super-ego as the point where
institutional and individual motivation converge has been justly
influential, for it represents a point of contact of the grand
problematics of Freud and Durkheim. However, I think that had
Parsons been prepared to do greater justice to the libidinal
situation which corresponds to the process of identification, he
would have identified a further point of convergence in the
theories of Freud and Durkheim. Just as internalization of common normative values in the super-ego provided the psychological complement to Durkheim's theory of social regulation,
Freud's theory of the de-sexualization of libido and the sublimation of love provides an indispensable psychological complement

to Durkheim's theory of social integration. What Freud points
out is that the social bonds, when viewed from the individuals'
points of view, are nothing but de-sexualized libidinal ties.
Nowhere is this clearer than in Freud's account of the Church
as a religious group, where, in the best Durkheimian tradition,
he examines the integrative function of religion and its implications for the libidinal economics of the individual (1921c:18:93ff).
In particular, Freud is concerned to show that the religious
bond minimizes each member's narcissism, transforms egoism
into altruism and controls intra-group aggression, all of which
are central to Durkheim's problematic.

An examination of instinctual economics reveals a further
similarity in Freud's and Durkheim's considerations of aggression
directed against other social groups, whether it is manifested
as direct hostilities or in the symbolic form of the narcissism of
small differences. In their discussions of the persecution of Jews
in Europe, Freud and Durkheim give complementary accounts of
the same basic phenomenon. Freud, with bitter irony, observes
the contribution that Jews have made to Western civilization by
becoming the recipients of generalized out-group aggression
(1930a:21:114), while Durkheim stresses the integration of
the Jewish community itself which arises 'from the hostility
surrounding them' (1951:160).

Needless to say that these parallels between Freud and Durkheim should not obscure their one fundamental difference –
while for Durkheim, morality integrates the individual and society
and in so doing liberates the individual and infuses his/her
existence with life,[9] for Freud, the internalization of morality
results in a turning of aggression inwards and strengthens self-
dstructive tendencies. While Durkheim in 'Suicide' sees self-
destruction as the result of insufficient (or, in rare cases,
excessive) integration, Freud views self-destructive tendencies
as the product of normal morality itself, which turns man's
instinctual aggressiveness against himself. The two views are
not necessarily incompatible, for Freud does not argue that self-
destructiveness corresponds necessarily to a higher propensity
towards suicide, but rather to a higher degree of discomfort
and guilt.

At the same time, the contrast in Freud's and Durkheim's
views reveals the greater depth of Freud's thought; unlike
Durkheim (and Parsons) Freud is not satisfied with merely
showing how morality promotes social order, but seeks to reveal
the cost in illusions and discontents at which order is achieved
and the conditions under which it may persist. It is this critical
aspect of Freud's insights into the social order that Parsons
seems to have missed – although he skilfully uses psychoanalytic
insights to analyse the mechanisms through which society
becomes part of every individual, his account represents, I
think, an 'oversocialized conception of man', a conception in
which the conflict between the requirements of the social order
and the demands of the individual has been dissolved. Moreover,

Parsons' analysis of the personality system, like other theories of personality, tends to present it as a cohesive and integrated system with minimal internal conflicts - and this is certainly a far cry from Freud's picture of the individual as a fragmented, and conflict-ridden soul torn away from a frustrated and subordinated body.

Notes

CHAPTER 1 BODY AND MIND

1   See also 1905d:7:168ff. As many commentators have pointed out, Freud
    avoided using the word 'Instinkt', opting instead for the word 'Trieb',
    which may be translated more accurately as 'instinctual impulse' or 'drive'
    to differentiate it from the animal instinct. See, for instance, Mitchell
    1974:21 and Hartmann 1964:79. In this work, we will nevertheless use the
    word 'instinct', in accordance to the psychoanalytic tradition.
2   This does not mean that Freud is a naive empiricist – the mental apparatus
    is not a passive recipient of stimuli, but, as we shall see, interprets them,
    manipulates them and shapes them.
3   See also 1920g:18:7.

> In the theory of psychoanalysis we have no hesitation in assuming that
> the course of mental events is automatically regulated by the pleasure
> principle. We believe, that is to say, that the course of those events is
> invariably set in motion by an unpleasurable tension, and that it takes a
> direction such that the final outcome coincides with a lowering of that
> tension – that is, with an avoidance of unpleasure or a production of
> pleasure.

4   See, for example, Hartmann 1964: 72, who having drawn the distinction
    between the 'drives which we actually encounter in clinical psychology' and
    the 'biologically oriented set of hypotheses of the "life" and "death"
    instincts' which 'have not added much to our understanding of the specific
    functions of the drives', proceeds to focus exclusively on the former
    group.
5   See, for example, Himmelstein 1979.
6   See, for example, Reich 1972:15. 'The libido is reflected in consciousness
    as a psychical and psychic urge for sexual gratification.'
7   For the most convincing argument in this area, see Solomon 1974:33ff.
8   See especially Wollheim 1971:44ff.
9   I use this term in opposition to the 'materialist' interpretation, and not in
    the sense associated with Noam Chomsky, i.e. in opposition to behavioural
    views of the mind.
10 See Wollheim 1974: xiii for such a view.
11 See, for instance, Mannoni 1971:138. My inclusion of Ricoeur in the
    mentalist camp must be qualified; Ricoeur, unlike Habermas, argues that
    energetic quantities are, in fact, directly manifested in affects (1970:142ff),
    and towards the end of his long book he concludes that transference is the
    apex in the Freudian discourse, where energetics and hermeneutics finally
    meet – the point where energy is transferred to the ego, in assisting it to
    overcome its resistances and achieve demystification, through the accurate
    interpretation of meanings. So, Ricoeur, unlike Habermas, does not reduce
    to hermeneutics the entire discourse on mental economics, which he regards
    as indispensable for the explanation of affective events and especially
    transference. Note also how the second view respects Freud's insistence
    that an instinctual impulse cannot be repressed, unless it is verbalized, or
    at least capable of being verbalized. See Lacan 1953:11 and, of course,

Freud 1915e:14:196ff.
12 At the same time, Freud is adamant that in spite of its quantitative
    dimension, repression is precipitated purely by psychological factors:

> Fliess was inclined to regard the difference between the sexes as the
> true cause and motive of repression. I can only repeat that I do not
> accept this view: I do not think that we were justified in sexualizing
> repression in this way - that is to say, in explaining it on a biological
> instead of a purely psychological basis. (1937c:23:251)

13 See note 12 above.
14 Ibid. Note also that here Brown differs considerably from Marcuse's view
    of the ego, studied earlier.
15 This analysis gains considerably from Freud's theory of the consolatory
    function of religion; see, for instance, 1927c:21:35, 1933a:22:161f and
    Ricoeur 1970:545ff.
16 See, for instance, Lacan 1953:12. 'Our view is that the essential function
    of the ego is very nearly that systematic refusal to acknowledge reality'
    ('méconnaissance systématique de la réalité'), i.e. the refusal we find in
    'Negation' 1925h. Mannoni 1971:177 echoes Brown's view:

> The absence of the object is the very condition necessary for the
> development of symbolic thought, and even though Freud did not in
> those words add it to his study on negation, where it rightly belonged,
> one nevertheless finds its scattered elements throughout his entire works.

17 See Freud 1921c:18:108f, 129ff.
18 Note that the infantile ego in this extract is the undifferentiated ego-id of
    the auto-erotic phase, before the ego has properly set itself up as a
    separate entity.
19 See, for example, Mitchell 1974:71, 80f.
20 Heinz Maus, 'Materialismus', quoted in Alfred Schmidt 1971:40.

CHAPTER 2 INDIVIDUAL AND SOCIETY

1 Reich addresses the relation between psychology and sociology and their
   common interface in an imaginative way; see 1972:59ff.
2 See 1950:337ff. Parsons' arguments concerning the relations between the
   two disciplines echoes some of the views expressed earlier by Heinz Hartmann;
   see 1964:Ch. 2. Parsons' argument that sociology can draw some of its key
   assumptions from psychoanalysis is reminiscent of Freud's own view that
   psychoanalysis could not escape making some biological assumptions and
   hope that biology will one day justify them.
3 See, for instance, Hartmann 1964.
4 'Incommensurable' is a term popularized in the philosophy of science by
   Kuhn and Feyerabend to denote theories or paradigms which use different
   methods, concepts and assumptions, and although they may address
   similar questions their claims cannot directly be compared. See Lakatos
   1970:226ff, Feyerabend 1975:Ch. 17.
5 Gender is seen as an element in 'the imaginary misrecognition of the "ego"';
   see Althusser 1971:219.
6 See also Wrong 1976:45.
7 The post-Freudians' reaction to what they saw as Freud's methodological
   individualism was to commit the opposite sin, in providing an 'oversocialized view of man' (Wrong 1976:45). The individual is thus seen as the
   product of adaptation to social forces - any tension in the relation between
   the individual and society is due to maladjustment.
8 For a still earlier formulation, see Letter 71 to Fliess.
9 See, for instance, 1921c:18:101 and 1930a:21:114.
10 See Himmelstein 1979.

11 This is a point of crucial significance for Chapter 13.
12 See, for instance, 1930a:21:133.
13 See 1930a:21:Ch. 2.
14 See 1927c:21:32, 35, 49ff and 1933a:22:161–2; also Rieff 1966:27 and
    Ricoeur 1970:249ff.
15 For a discussion of the functions of culture, see 1933a:22:161ff.
16 Apart from Rieff, this view is taken in different variants by Herberg 1957:
    Ch. 10 and Wollheim 1971:Ch. 8.
17 Reich's theory of the clash between biological and cultural factors is an
    earlier version of the relation between individual and society as a real
    opposition.
18 See Kaufmann 1956:Chs 7 and 8, and especially 204ff.
19 Brown sees the alienation of the individual from society as co-incidental
    of an alienation of Eros from Thanatos. Man alone of all animals breaks
    apart 'the undifferentiated or dialectical unity of the instincts' (1959:84),
    and man alone sets up the aims of the individual in opposition to the aims
    of the species.

CHAPTER 3 NORMALITY, NEUROSIS AND THERAPY

1   This phenomenon is discussed by Born (1979), Levine (1978) and Foucault
    (1961) apropos of lepers, alcoholics and dementeds respectively.
2   It is also clear that normality is not a statistical mean either, in Freud's
    view: a society may hold a criterion of normality which the majority of its
    members fail to meet.
3   1924b:19:152, 1937c:23:226 and 1940a:23:182–3.
4   See 1923b:19:49 and 1940a:23:179f.
5   See 1937c:23:244ff and Wollheim 1971:140.
6   See Brown 1959:155.
7   See also Hartmann 1960:20: 'The aim of [psychoanalytic therapy] is the
    aim of every therapy, and the value of this therapeutic aim is not ques-
    tioned; moral considerations are kept from interfering with it.'
8   'We . . . succeed in establishing a complete intellectual acceptance of what
    is repressed – but the repression itself is still not removed' (1925h:19:236).
9   See also 1933a:22:108f and 1940a:23:177ff.
10 See Chapter 5.
11 See 1916–17:16:451ff, 1904a:7, etc.
12 Although this connection between knowledge and interest is a key feature
    of both Marxist and pragmatist philosophies, Habermas uses the concept
    'anthropologically' (1974:8), which in a way robs the term both of the
    political character that it has for Marx, and the practical immediacy that it
    has for the pragmatists.
13 By far the most eminent exponents of this view have been Arlow and
    Brenner, since their famous monograph of 1964.
14 Contrary to Rieff who argues that the twentieth century creates the con-
    ditions for therapy through understanding, Freud's later works grow
    increasingly pessimistic about the prospect of educating the patient,
    although, perhaps surprisingly, in 'The Future of an Illusion', he expresses
    some optimism for the possibility of educating humanity out of collective
    illusions, like religion.

CHAPTER 4 CULTURE, NORMALITY AND MORALITY

1   Compare Freud's view of pleasure with Aristotle's, who, while starting with
    a psychological concept of pleasure like Freud, proposes the universal
    rule of the mean as the means of achieving pleasure.
2   See 1927c:21:11ff and 1930a:21:80.
3   I will not call this criterion rationality, as de Sousa does, since Freud fre-
    quently referred to rationalization as a mechanism of defence, preventing

true knowledge of oneself. See, for example, 1925h:19 and Anna Freud 1966:21.
4   'The whole thing is so patently infantile, so foreign to reality, that to any-one with a friendly attitude to humanity it is painful to think that the great majority of mortals will never never be able to rise above this view of the world.' (1930a:21:74)
5   See 1933a:22:159 and 1940a:23:199.
6   See Chapter 1.
7   'There is something to be deplored in this suppression of all but the genital aim of sexuality' (Rieff 1959:173).
8   Yet, in his earlier essay 'Observations on "Wild" Psychoanalysis' (1910k) Freud had argued that although 'expressions of tender feeling' are an integral part of sexuality, they do, in fact, represent vicissitudes of libido; they 'have become inhibited in regard to their original sexual aim or have exchanged this aim for another which is no longer sexual' (1910k: 11:222). The same view of affection as sublimated sexuality prevails in Freud's later works, after the idea of self-preservation instincts had been dropped.
9   Hartmann, as a representative of analytic orthodoxy, restricts himself to the first view of normality and looks at mental health as successful adapta-tion. What may be confusing is that pleasure and truth are constituents of both standards of normality; thus, Hartmann is quite willing to argue that both 'rational man' and 'instinctual man' must be present in the healthy man – but his healthy man is nothing but the well-adapted individual. See 1964:8-9.
10   For a similar view, see Kazin 1957.
11   See page 83.
12   Indeed, Brown goes as far as suggesting that all sublimations are also repressive (1959:138ff), while Marcuse differentiates between repressive and non-repressive sublimations (1955:154, 190ff).
13   See Brown 1959:5 and Marcuse 1955:224ff.
14   See also Brown 1959:141ff, and especially 143-4.

CHAPTER 5 SCIENCE AND PHILOSOPHY

1   For epistemological critiques of psychoanalysis and a cross-section of attempts to fit it in the tight shoes of positivism, see the collections edited by Wollheim (1974) and Hook (1959). Of course, philosophers of science have been joined by those devoted to pure and hard scientific psychology, like Hans Eysenck, who are obviously not having much trouble convincing their readers.
2   See Feyerabend 1975, especially p. 295. It was rather refreshing to watch A. J. Ayer in a 1978 television interview declare that the main unfortunate thing about logical positivism is that it 'is almost entirely false'.
3   Freud suggests, for instance, that there is nothing surprising in that Schopenhauer had anticipated his views on the death instinct – 'why should not a bold thinker have guessed something that is afterwards confirmed by sober and painstaking research?' (1933a:22:107).
4   'The contribution of psychoanalysis to science lies precisely in having extended research to the mental field' (1933a:22:159).
5   See 1940a:23:182.
6   See Wollheim 1971:141 and Fingarette 1974.
7   Anna Freud 1966:60f and Parsons 1952.
8   Although Hartmann's view of the ego is essentially a functionalist one (1964:Chs 7 and 14), he is cautious to acknowledge that some of the ego functions may be antagonistic to others, i.e. that there may be contra-dictions in the operation of the ego. Yet, his account tends to de-emphasize conflict much like Parsons'.
9   See his letter to Wilhelm Fliess, dated 21.9.1897, in which he confides 'the great secret which has slowly been dawning upon [him] in recent months'.

10 Strictly speaking the unconscious cannot love and hate, or be the seat
     of emotional experiences. 'There are no unconscious affects in the sense
     in which there are unconscious ideas' (1915e:14:178). But the unconscious
     may contain ideas which, were they to become conscious, would produce
     contradictory affects.
11 See, for example, 1923b:19:17ff, 25-7, and 1933a:22:69ff.
12 Freud preferred the term 'construction' to 'interpretation', emphasizing the
     necessary inter-connections among individual interpretations. See 1937d.
13 This chapter will not consider the numerous practical applications of
     psychoanalytic theory outside therapy which testify to its direct relevance
     and, indeed, validity. It is very interesting and ironic that Freudian
     concepts and postulates have been most widely appropriated by those
     disciplines which are least about the scientificity of a theory and most about
     whether it works or not, media studies, marketing and consumer behaviour,
     public relations and social work. Ideas like subliminal perception, 'sub-
     conscious' associations, motivations and symbols, oral and phallic fixations,
     narcissism and the like are commonplace in most contemporary marketing
     manuals; without a doubt, they form a major weapon in the arsenal of the
     'hidden persuaders' and manipulators, those known in the trade as 'the
     depth boys'. In Packard's words,

> the use of mass psychoanalysis to guide campaigns of persuasion has
> become the basis of a multimillion-dollar industry. Professional per-
> suaders have seized upon it in their groping for more effective ways to
> sell us their wares - whether products, ideas, attitudes, candidates,
> goals or states of mind. (1962:11)

Thus Freud's scientific discoveries, far from being related to esoteric
areas in the theory of mind, have been put to immediate practical uses in
various areas of consciousness manipulation. It seems that even if psychoanalysis has failed the tests of scientificity devised by Popper and Co.,
it has passed with flying colours the tests of 'social engineering'. What
people want is not what they say they want or what they think that they
want - this is the admen's via regia to the unconscious.

CHAPTER 6 UTOPIA AND ILLUSION

1 Existential thinking and the re-discovery of Marx's 1844 Paris Manuscripts
     were perhaps the only other sources of utopian inspiration to match
     psychoanalysis.
2 See Chapters 3 and 4.
3 A rather different Utopia of Logos emerges from the reading of Habermas,
     who, nevertheless, starts from the same emancipatory point.
4 See Chapters 4 and 5.
5 See, for example, 1927c:21:42, 51ff.
6 This is not the case with Rieff, who, as we saw, developed a similar Utopia
     of Logos, but considers the psychoanalytic community to be a cultural
     élite, undertaking what may be described as a task of 'social transference'.
7 In the final analysis, both the utopian and the tragic aspects of Freud's
     theory are critical, as Gouldner's earlier quote suggests; they underline
     the distance between the actual and the desirable. It is interesting how
     even the titles of some of Freud's works entail this critical dimension.
     Consider, for instance, 'Civilized' Sexual Morality and Modern Nervous
     Illness (1908d), A Child is Being Beaten (1919e), The Future of an
     Illusion (1927c), Civilization and Its Discontents (1930a), Why War?
     (1933b).

CHAPTER 7 PSYCHOANALYSIS AND CULTURE

1 Compare, for instance, Freud's abstract definitions with Russell's definition
   of matter as 'a convenient formula for describing what happens where it
   isn't' (quoted in Koestler 1972), or Eddington's 'that which is, is a shell
   floating in the infinitude of that which is not' (1935). It is as though modern
   physics after centuries of proceeding without precise definitions of some of
   its central terms has, during the twentieth century, decided to look at the
   pre-Socratics for its definitions. After all, Popper may indeed be paying
   Freud a compliment by drawing his parallel between Freud's concepts and
   the Homeric gods.
2 We must not forget that ancient audiences regularly joined in the
   lamentations of the chorus.
3 See 1900a:2-2:Ch. VI, Part D.
4 See, for example, Mannoni 1971:148.
5 This argument in no way implies that the agencies are articulated or defined
   solely through their relations to the external.
6 Thus, for example, the fear of the father becomes fear of horses.
7 The basic forms of such displacement may be found in the famous early
   paper The Neuro-Psychoses of Defence (1894a).
8 See, for instance, Rieff 1959:VI, VII, and Billig 1976:26-43.
9 See Jahoda 1977:78-9.
10 For a similar argument see 1937c:23:240-1.
11 For a good account of Freud's Lamarckism, see Clark 1980:379ff, 437.
12 Malinowski's remains the clearest critique of Freud's anthropological
   speculations, when seen as literal accounts of real events. Malinowski
   reveals not only cases where his field research falsified Freud's account,
   but also several inconsistencies in this account; above all, he seeks to
   show that even if there was a primal murder, culture preceded it (1927:
   152ff).
13 My emphasis on the distinction between theory and myth does not clash
   with Feyerabend's splendid arguments on the similarity and inter-relation
   between myth and science; both intellectual integrity and common sense
   require that we should not defend psychoanalytic myths as science, but
   accept them for what they are. See 1975:295ff.

CHAPTER 8 THE FIRST RADICALIZATION OF FREUD:
REICH AND FROMM, THE OPTIMISTIC UTOPIANS

1 The art of ad hominem criticisms of psychoanalysis by other psychoanalysts
   (in which Freud was the undisputed master) should not be rejected as
   logically fallacious given the nature and subject of psychoanalysis -
   scientific investigations are inextricably linked to the overcoming of inner
   resistances by the analyst himself. For Reich's interesting analysis of the
   ways in which Freud's own circumstances and superstitions entered his
   metapsychology, see 'Reich Speaks of Freud'; Fromm expresses similar
   views throughout his works; see, for instance, 1966:24ff, 294fn.
2 See 1905d:7:238 and 1908b.
3 See Thompson 1957:63ff.
4 Reich, of course, came to renounce political transformation altogether.
5 It should be pointed out that, unlike Anna Freud (1966:58, etc.), Reich saw
   this fear of instincts as a pathological condition, instilled through the
   patriarchal family, not as part of the ego's normal defences.
6 See 1968:Ch. 1.
7 The following extract suggests that Reich misunderstood Freud's concept
   of the unconscious, rather than modified it: 'It is altogether logical that
   the instinct itself cannot be conscious, because it is what governs us. We
   are its object' (1968:51). Reich, instead of looking at the instinct as the
   amount of energy attached to conscious and unconscious (repressed) ideas
   and desires, looks at the instinct as the unconscious force which is mani-

fested in conscious ideas and desires.
8   See Mitchell 1974, Robinson 1969, Rieff 1966, etc.
9   Robinson 1969:20 and Thompson 1957:189.
10 Reich's discovery of the intimate relationship between the harsh super-ego
    and morality with fascism and the atrocities of mass violence seems to have
    escaped as perceptive a social critic as Christopher Lasch, who has rightly
    been accused of looking nostalgically back at the pre-narcissistic days of
    the strong super-ego.
11 See 1966:24ff.
12 The second aspect of relatedness is 'assimilation', discussed in 'Man for
    Himself'. The five orientations towards assimilation are defined as receptive,
    exploitative, hoarding, marketing and productive.
13 It is very interesting that Fromm himself uses this same argument to show
    that destructiveness is not a 'natural' human characteristic, and to reduce
    Freud's death instinct to a variant of the frustration/aggression syndrome:
    'The more the drive toward life is thwarted, the stronger is the drive
    towards destruction; the more life is realized, the less is the strength of
    destructiveness. *Destructiveness is the outcome of unlived life*' (1966:207).
    Does this argument not anticipate Marcuse's 'historicization' of the death
    instinct in 'Eros and Civilization'?
14 As we saw in Chapters 3 and 4, Freud always rejected distinctions of
    natural and unnatural manifestations of sexuality.
15 This theme will form the centre of my discussion in Chapter 8.
16 Fromm's attempt to account for aggressive behaviour is, as in most cases,
    far more thorough than Reich's - see 1964:24-61.

CHAPTER 9 THE DISCOVERY OF THE RADICAL FREUD:
MARCUSE AND BROWN, THE PESSIMISTIC UTOPIANS

1   See Rieff 1959:237-9.
2   See, for instance, Brown 1959:307.
3   See Freud 1911b:12:225.
4   See Jones 1963:229f, for an account of the reception of 'The Interpretation
    of Dreams'.
5   Marcuse 1955:224, Brown 1959:155 and especially Freud 1933a:22:152.
6   Marcuse's critique shares many elements with a critique of Fromm's work
    raised by another of his Frankfurt School colleagues, Adorno. For a
    summary of this unpublished critique, see Jay 1973:103ff.
7   The Fromm-Marcuse debate did become something of a lengthy and sterile
    serial, which obscured both the differences and the common ground in
    their theories.
8   The quotation marks used by Freud around the word 'neurotic' remind us
    of the distinction of the two conceptions of neurosis, discussed in Part I.
9   See 1920g:18:50 and 1923b:19:54ff.
10 See also 1921c:18:115.
11 This sets Marcuse apart from Reich, Fromm, Brown and others who have
    provided detailed analyses of the particular kinds of repressions required
    by different reality principles, e.g. protestant, fascist, etc.
12 Mitchell's criticism of precisely this point is accurate (1974:410). I find it
    harder to understand and accept Therborn's (1970:89) praise of Marcuse's
    technological argument in 'Eros and Civilization'.
13 Marcuse has sometimes been accused, not altogether unfairly, of having
    lost faith in class struggle and the proletariat, and of prematurely heralding
    sexual perverts, black activists, the hippies and the women's movement as
    the vanguards of a new revolutionary agent.
14 In these sections Marcuse quotes approvingly classical idealist aesthetics,
    in an attempt to show that art is the only area in capitalist societies in
    which the pleasure principle prevails over the reality principle. In so far
    as good art arouses human sensuousness and excites the imagination, all
    good art is revolutionary. See 1955:Ch. 9.

15 But for a critique of this view, see Chapter 2.

CHAPTER 10 PSYCHOANALYSIS AND CONTEMPORARY AMERICAN CULTURE:
THE PRESENT AS UTOPIA IN THE WORK OF RIEFF

1 See 1937c:23:216.
2 Rieff's discussion of the 'wish' is analogous to Ricoeur's discussion of
   'desire'. Ricoeur's reading of Freud can be seen as an attempt to bridge
   the differences in emphasis between Rieff's interpretation of instinct and
   those of Marcuse and Brown.
3 Ricoeur makes a similar point (1970:539ff).
4 For the term 'surplus-repression' see Marcuse 1955:32; on the role of
   technology, see Rieff 1966:22 and Marcuse 1955:33, 121ff, 184 and 217.

5   Aware at last that he is chronically ill, psychological man may never-
       theless end the ancient quest of his predecessors for a healing doctrine.
       His experience with the latest [therapeutic], Freud's, may finally teach
       him that every cure must expose him to new illness. (Rieff 1959:392)

   See also Rieff 1963a:17. Although Ricoeur does not draw the same conclusions as Rieff concerning Freud's therapeutic, he too sees Freud's theoretical
   mission essentially as one of demystification. Ricoeur sees Marx and
   Nietzsche as the two theorists who, like Freud, struggled to redeem humanity from false consciousness. See Ricoeur 1970:32ff.
6 The relation between social and cultural change requires some clarification
   before I embark on a critique of Rieff's views. In a footnote, Rieff admits
   that 'this book is about one major aspect of cultural change; I cannot
   undertake to examine here the relation between cultural and social change'
   (1966:69fn). This gives his account a strongly idealist character, for the
   changes in culture are seen as more or less autonomous and are not studied
   in conjunction with attendant social and political developments. Thus, the
   emergence of psychological man is studied in vitro, with no reference to
   two world wars, economic crises, the increasing bureaucratization of society,
   strikes, Third World liberation movements, etc. As we shall see, technological change as 'progress' is the only extra-cultural factor in Rieff's
   account, and even technology is simply seen as a vehicle towards affluence.
7 See Rieff 1959:59, 391; 1963a:8; 1966:39-40.
8 Rieff might have used some other criterion of social cohesion (such as, for
   instance, the one I introduce in Chapter 13), but he uses none.
9 As Freud insisted, transference cannot be established in narcissistic or
   psychotic conditions (1933a:22:155); so, the character disorders which,
   according to most psychotherapists, prevail in our culture are not, in
   principle, available for treatment through a therapy based on transference.
10 See Marcuse 1955:152, Mitchell 1974:40, and Engel 1980:77f.

CHAPTER 11 ERNEST BECKER'S 'HOMO HEROICA':
NARCISSUS AS THE COSMIC HERO WITHOUT FOLLOWERS

1 I will not summarize Becker's attempt to systematize the types of existential
   problem which cultures address, since, like Fromm's, they seem to represent an impromptu basket of middle-class American anxieties.
2 Once again, Becker is confusing *our* culture's shock at other cultures' symbolics, whether they be 'savage behaviour' or Plato's 'orthos paiderastein'.
   Yet, this may represent a peculiarly Western compulsion for universalistic
   truths, which re-inforces cultural intolerance and arrogance. Certainly,
   in Malinowski's accounts, the Trobrianders had no difficulty at all in accepting the totally different sexual *mores* and after-death beliefs of their
   neighbouring Amphletts. See 1922:43.

CHAPTER 12   NARCISSISM AND CONTEMPORARY CULTURE

1   Lasch invokes some interesting empirical material to support a view similar
    to the one on which the arguments of the previous chapter were based,
    namely that in 'our overorganized society . . . large-scale organizations
    predominate but have lost their capacity to command allegiance' (1979:99).
2   This seems to me to be the key point apropos the relation between politics
    and spectacle; Lasch and others have perhaps overestimated the novelty
    of politics as spectacle - after all, from Pericles' famous wartime orations
    to the massive fascist rallies, history is littered with political spectaculars.
    The novelty of politics as spectacle lies in the privatization of the audience.
3   It is undoubtedly premature to declare the end of crowds, bonded
    emotionally along the traditional lines; pop concerts and sports activities
    provide glaring exceptions to the arguments which follow and suggest that
    public passions are alive, even in our culture.
4   See, for instance, 1914c.
5   See 1910h.
6   Erica Jong's 'zipless fuck', sex without material or symbolic extensions,
    exists after all purely in the world of phantasy.
7   'Parental love, which is so touching and at bottom so childish, is nothing
    but parental narcissism born again and, transformed though it be into
    object-love, it reveals its former character infallibly' (1914c:14:72).
8   See, for instance, 1927c:21:17-18.

CHAPTER 13   THE DEATH INSTINCT AND THE AGE OF THE MACHINE

1   For a characteristic discussion, see Horowitz 1974.
2   See Mills 1970.
3   See Braverman 1974:87.
4   See Blauner 1964.
5   An earlier variant of the same theme is found in Stephen Marglin's argu-
    ment that the power and growth of the factory system rested not on its
    technical superiority over handicraft production but on the superior control
    it afforded over the worker and the work process. The factory system
    systematized control of production, while bureaucracy completed the pro-
    cess by making control invisible.
6   The sociologist is often prone to forget how Weber's concept of bureaucracy
    seems to contradict everything that common sense teaches us about bureau-
    cratic organizations.
7   One function of modern education which has strangely been neglected by
    critics, from Illich to Bowles and Gintis, is the forced transition of the
    child from the personal authority of the parent to the impersonal authority
    of the school, and his/her subjugation to the regimented existence of rules
    and regulations, timetables and homework. It is the impersonal order of
    the school which introduces the child to the experience of being 'one of
    many', or of having a 'role'.
8   It is true that in 'Beyond the Pleasure Principle' Freud expresses some
    reservations concerning his emphasis on the compulsion to repeat.

> It is true that my assertion of the regressive character of instincts also
> rests upon observed material - namely the compulsion to repeat. It may
> be, however, that I have overestimated its significance. (1920g:18:59)

9   In 28,000 Homeric lines, there are 25,000 repeated phrases!
10 See Winter and Robert 1980 for an interesting characterology.
11 See, for instance, Aristotle's 'Politics', i and ii. Homer envisages the
    slaves of Vulcan as fully automated and self-propelled robots, which he had
    constructed himself. See 'Iliad', Σ, 373ff, 417ff and 469ff.
12 Freud may have been drawn to the symbolism of periodicity by his own
    morbid conviction, under the spell of Fliess' numerology, that he would die

in 1907. See Mannoni 1971:38 and Clark 1980:96, 220f.
13 It is perhaps in music that repetition as a symbolism of Fate has found its
    most emotionally compelling habitat. Notwithstanding the brilliant repetitious
    uses of short rhythmic motives by Beethoven, Mahler and Tchaikovsky in
    their 'Fate Symphonies', and by Verdi in 'The Force of Destiny', it is Wagner
    who perfected this technique to carry maximum emotional weight. Among
    countless cases, I note the thirteen-fold repetition of the brilliant Valhalla
    leitmotiv at the conclusion of Rheingold, which turns the gods' moment of
    supreme glory into the premonition of their inevitable doom.
14 See pp. 46 and 230ff above.
15 Following Durkheim, we may add that both adherence to rules and moral
    commitment are higher among officers than among enlisted men (1951:228ff).
16 Of course even in this situation the death instinct is not absent, for
    through the super-ego, it ensures conformity with these values.
17 See, for instance, Allison's intriguing analysis of the Cuban crisis, where
    according to one of his three theories, decisions were simply organizational
    outputs.
18 See Harrison 1976.
19 It is not accidental that in this chapter which has dealt with the vicissitudes
    of the death instinct not a word was said about the 'fear of death'. I am in
    agreement with Freud that this fear cannot be seen as a direct mental
    representative of the death instinct or as an immutable existential or
    psychological fact. Rather, the fear of death must be seen in conjunction
    with other fears, anxieties, insecurities and the type of malaise which
    characterize different cultures. In cultures founded on a ruthless super-
    ego, the fear of death was associated with the sense of guilt - defiance of
    death was the result of a total acceptance of the dictates of the super-ego.
    In our culture with much lesser reliance on the super-ego, the fear of
    death is related to the ego's narcissistic insecurities, which are discussed
    in Chapter 14.

APPENDIX

1 For details, see Parsons and Bales 1955:Ch. V.
2 Parsons' account of the relation between psychology and sociology is complemented on the side of psychoanalysis by Hartmann (1964), who refers
   approvingly to Parsons' work.
3 Parsons' account of the formation of the ego out of the original identification
   with the mother bears a great resemblence to Lacan's influential formulations
   concerning the formation of the 'je' out of what he calls 'the mirror phase',
   where the child identifies with himself in a mirror or in the image of his
   mother. The ego is thus formed through reference to the alter - the
   original identification gives rise to the ego. But, contrary to Parsons,
   Lacan regards the first recognition of the ego as a misrecognition, which
   derives from the contradiction between the child's felt helplessness and the
   image of an integrated gestalt. Instead of a cybernetic ego, Lacan views the
   ego as the product of a fundamental alienation; it is nothing but an imaginary imago invested with those desirable qualities which the ego would dearly
   love to possess but does not. See Lacan 1968.
4 See, for example, 1955:45ff.
5 See 1955:149.
6 For an extended critique of the view which concentrates on the functionist
   element at the expense of the economic, see Chapter 5.
7 Mitchell has criticized Reich on precisely the same point. See 1974:165f,
   185-6.
8 See Freud 1924b:19 and 1924e:19.
9 'The individual submits to society and this submission is the condition for
   his liberation' (Durkheim 1974:72).

Bibliography

References in the text to works by Freud are given in terms of the date of
publication and the letter-suffix, as they appear in the Standard Edition, and
the volume of the Standard Edition in which each work is included. All page
references refer to the Standard Edition, even in the few cases where other
translations were used. Most works by other authors are identified in the text
in terms of the date of the original publication, even where the original edition
is not used for page references. In the bibliography which follows, the date of
the first edition (where appropriate) is in parentheses after the title.

WORKS BY FREUD

(1894a) The Neuro-Psychoses of Defence
(1895c) Obsessions and Phobias
(1895d) 'Studies in Hysteria' (with J. Breuer)
(1895f) A Reply to Criticism on my Paper on Anxiety Neurosis
(1898a) Sexuality in the Aetiology of Neuroses
(1900a) 'The Interpretation of Dreams'
(1901b) 'The Psychopathology of Everyday Life'
(1904a) Freud's Psychoanalytic Procedure
(1905a) On Psychotherapy
(1905c) 'Jokes and their Relation to the Unconscious'
(1905d) 'Three Essays on the Theory of Sexuality'
(1907b) Obsessive Actions and Religious Practices
(1908b) Character and Anal Erotism
(1908d) 'Civilized' Sexual Morality and Modern Nervous Illness
(1910a) Five Lectures on Psychoanalysis
(1910c) 'Leonardo da Vinci and a Memory of his Childhood'
(1910e) The Antithetical Meaning of Primal Words
(1910h) A Special Type of Choice of Object Made by Men
(1910k) Observations on 'Wild' Psycho-analysis
(1911b) Formulations on the Two Principles of Mental Functioning
(1912d) On the Universal Tendency to Debasement in the Sphere of Love
(1912e) Recommendations to Physicians Practicing Psychoanalysis
(1912g) A Note on the Unconscious in Psychoanalysis
(1912-13) 'Totem and Taboo'
(1913c) On Beginning Treatment (Further Recommendations)
(1913f) The Theme of the Three Caskets
(1913j) The Claims of Psychoanalysis to Scientific Interest
(1914b) The Moses of Michelangelo
(1914c) 'On Narcissism: an Introduction'
(1914g) Remembering, Repeating and Working-Through (Further Recommend-
     ations)
(1915a) Observations on Transference-Love (Further Recommendations)
(1915c) Instincts and their Vicissitudes
(1915d) Repression
(1915e) The Unconscious
(1916-17) 'Introductory Lectures on Psychoanalysis'
(1917a) A Difficulty in the Path of Psychoanalysis
(1917e) Mourning and Melancholia

(1920g) 'Beyond the Pleasure Principle'
(1921c) 'Group Psychology and the Analysis of the Ego'
(1923a) Psychoanalysis and Libido Theory
(1923b) 'The Ego and the Id'
(1924b) Neurosis and Psychosis
(1924c) The Economic Problem of Masochism
(1924e) The Loss of Reality in Neurosis and Psychosis
(1925h) Negation
(1926d) 'Inhibitions, Symptoms and Anxiety'
(1926e) 'The Question of Lay Analysis'
(1927c) 'The Future of an Illusion'
(1930a) 'Civilization and Its Discontents'
(1933a) 'New Introductory Lectures on Psychoanalysis'
(1933b) 'Why War?'
(1937c) Analysis Terminable and Interminable
(1937d) Constructions in Analysis
(1939a) 'Moses and Monotheism'
(1940a) 'An Outline of Psychoanalysis'
(1950a) 'The Origins of Psychoanalysis', Basic Books, Doubleday, 1954
   (referred to in the text as Freud 1954)

WORKS BY OTHER AUTHORS

Allison, G.T. (1971), 'Essence of Decision', Little, Brown.
Althusser, L. (1971), Freud and Lacan, in 'Lenin and Philosophy', Monthly
   Review Press.
Aristotle, 'Politics' and 'Ethics'.
Arlow, J.A., and C. Brenner (1964), 'Psychoanalytic Concepts and the
   Structural Theory', International Universities Press.
Becker, E. (1962), 'The Birth and Death of Meaning', Penguin Books, 1972.
— (1973) 'The Denial of Death', Free Press.
Bibring, E. (1941), The Development and Problems of the Theory of Instincts,
   'International Journal of Psychoanalysis', XXI.
Billig, M. (1976), 'Social Psychology and Intergroup Relations', Academic Press.
Blauner, R. (1964), 'Alienation and Freedom', Phoenix Books, University of
   Chicago Press.
Bocock, R. (1976), 'Freud and Modern Society', Nelson.
Boden, M.A. (1974), Freudian Mechanisms of Defence: A Programming Per-
   spective, in Wollheim (ed.).
Born, M. (1979), 'L'Île aux Lépreux', Grasset.
Bowles S., and H. Gintis (1976), 'Schooling in Capitalist America', Routledge
   & Kegan Paul.
Braverman, H. (1974), 'Labour and Monopoly Capital', Monthly Review Press.
Brink, E.L., and W.T. Kelly (1963), 'The Management of Promotion', Prentice-
   Hall.
Brown, B. (1973), 'Marx, Freud and the Critique of Everyday Life', Monthly
   Review Press.
Brown, N.O. (1959), 'Life Against Death', Wesleyan University Press edn, 1970.
— (1966), 'Love's Body', Random House.
— (1968), A Reply to Herbert Marcuse, in Marcuse.
Buber, M. (1950), 'Paths of Utopia', New York.
Castel, R. (1976), 'Le Psychanalysme', Collection 10/18.
Chomsky, N. (1968), 'Language and Mind', Harcourt, Brace & Jovanovich.
Clark, R.W. (1980), 'Freud: The Man and the Cause', Jonathan Cape and
   Weidenfeld & Nicolson.
Culler, J. (1976), 'Saussure', Fontana.
de Sousa, R. (1979), Norms and the Normal, in Wollheim (ed.).
Durkheim, E. (1951), 'Suicide', Free Press.
— (1960), 'The Division of Labour in Society', New York.
— (1974), 'Sociology and Philosophy', Free Press.
Eddington, A.S. (1935), 'The Nature of the Physical World', Dent.

Edelson, M. (1976), Toward a Study of Interpretation in Psychoanalysis, in 'Explorations in General Theory in Social Science', ed. J.J. Loubser et al., Free Press.
Eliot, T.S. (1969), 'Collected Works', Faber & Faber.
Ellenberger, H.F. (1970), 'The Discovery of the Unconscious', Allen Lane.
Engel, S. (1980), Femininity as Tragedy: Re-examining the 'New Narcissism', 'Socialist Review', no. 53, September.
Feyerabend, P. (1975), 'Against Method', New Left Books.
— (1978), 'Science in a Free Society', New Left Books.
Fingarette, H. (1974), Self-Deception and the 'Splitting of the Ego', in Wollheim (ed.).
Flanders, A. (1969), Collective Bargaining: A Theoretical Analysis, in 'Collective Bargaining', Penguin.
Foucault, M. (1961), 'Madness and Civilization', Tavistock Publications, 1967.
— (1970), 'The Order of Things', Tavistock Publications.
— (1975), 'Discipline and Punish', Peregrine Books, 1977.
Freud, A. (1966), 'The Ego and the Mechanisms of Defence', International Universities Press.
Fromm, E. (1947), 'Man for Himself', Fawcett Premier Books (undated).
— (1966), 'Escape from Freedom' (1st edn. 1941), Avon Library.
— (1964), 'The Heart of Man', Harper & Row, Colophon, 1968.
Gabriel, Y. (1978), Collective Bargaining: A Critique of the Oxford School, 'Political Quarterly', vol. 49, no. 3.
Giddens, A. (ed.) (1974), 'Positivism and Sociology', Heinemann.
Glymour, C. (1974), Freud, Kepler and the Clinical Evidence, in Wollheim (ed.)
Goldthorpe, J.H. (1974), Industrial Relations in Great Britain: A Critique of Reformism, 'Politics and Society', vol. 4, no. 4.
Gordon, C. (1977), The Unconscious of Psychoanalysis, 'Ideology and Consciousness', no. 2, Autumn.
Gouldner, A. (1976), 'The Dialectic of Ideology and Technology', Macmillan.
Habermas, J. (1972), 'Knowledge and Human Interests', Heinemann.
— (1974), 'Theory and Practice', Heinemann.
Hacker, F.J. (1957), Freud, Marx and Kierkegaard, in Nelson (ed.).
Hampshire, S. (1974), Disposition and Memory, in Wollheim (ed.).
Harrison, P. (1976), The Sociology of Lower Hell, 'New Society', Dec. 2.
Hartmann, H. (1960), 'Psychoanalysis and Moral Values', International Universities Press.
— (1964), 'Essays on Ego Psychology', Hogarth Press.
Herberg, W. (1957), Freud, the Revisionists and Social Reality, in Nelson (ed.).
Himmelstein, J.L. (1979), The Pleasure Principle is not Enough, 'Psychoanalytic Review', vol. 66, no. 1.
Holland, R. (1977), 'Self and Social Context', Macmillan Press.
Hook, S. (ed) (1959), 'Psychoanalysis, Scientific Method and Philosophy', New York University Press.
Horkheimer, M., and T. Adorno (1972), 'Dialectic of Enlightenment', Herder.
Horowitz, I.L. (1974), Sociology and Futurology: The Contemporary Pursuit of the Millenium, 'Berkeley Journal of Sociology', vol. XIX.
Jacoby, R. (1975), 'Social Amnesia', Harvester Press.
Jahoda, M. (1977), 'Freud and the Dilemmas of Psychology', Hogarth Press.
Jay, M. (1973), 'Dialectical Imagination', Little, Brown.
Jones, E. (1963), 'The Life and Work of Sigmund Freud', ed. Trilling, Anchor.
Kalin, M.G. (1975), 'The Utopian Flight from Unhappiness', Littlefield, Adams.
Kaufmann, W. (1956), 'Nietzsche', Meridian Books.
Kazin, A. (1957), Freud and the 20th Century, in Nelson (ed.).
Kernberg, O. (1975), 'Borderline Conditions and Pathological Narcissism', Jason Aronson.
Koestler, A. (1972), 'The Roots of Coincidence', Hutchinson.
Lacan, J. (1953), Some Reflections on the Ego, 'International Journal of Psychoanalysis', vol. XXXIV.
— (1968a), 'The Language of the Self' (with Introduction by A. Wilden), Delta Books.

— (1968b), The Mirror-phase as Formative of the Function of the I, 'New Left Review', no. 51, September.
Lakatos, I., and A. Musgrave (eds) (1970), 'Criticism and the Growth of Knowledge', Cambridge University Press.
Lasch, C. (1976), The Narcissist Society, 'New York Review', September 30.
— (1979), 'The Culture of Narcissism', Abacus Press, 1980.
Lenin, V.I. (1967), Left-Wing Communism - An Infantile Disorder, in 'Selected Works', vol. 3, Lawrence & Wishart.
Levine, H.G. (1978), Discovery of Addiction - Changing Conceptions of Habitual Drunkenness in America, 'Journal of Studies on Alcohol', vol. 39, no. 1.
Lichtman, R. (1977), Marx and Freud, 'Socialist Revolution', vols 30,33 and 36.
Malinowski, B. (1922), 'Argonauts of the Western Pacific', Dutton, 1961.
— (1927), 'Sex and Repression in Savage Society', Routledge & Kegan Paul.
Mannoni, O. (1971), 'Freud', Random House.
Marcuse, H. (1955), 'Eros and Civilization', Vintage Books, 1962.
— (1964), 'One Dimensional Man', Beacon Press, 1966.
— (1967), Love Mystified: A Critique of Norman O. Brown, reprinted in Marcuse 1968.
— (1968), 'Negations', Beacon Press, 1969.
— (1969), 'An Essay on Liberation', Pelican Books, 1972.
— (1970), 'Five Lectures on Psychoanalysis', Beacon Press.
— (1972), 'Counter-Revolution and Revolt', Beacon Press.
Marx, K., Economic Political Manuscripts (1844), in 'The Marx-Engels Reader', ed. R.C. Tucker, Norton, 1972.
— (1846), 'The German Ideology', same as above.
— (1848), 'The Communist Manifesto', same as above.
— (1852), 'The Eighteenth Brumaire of Louis Bonaparte', International Publishers, New York, 1963.
— (1904), 'A Contribution to a Critique of Political Economy', Chicago.
Matte Blanco, I. (1975), 'The Unconscious as Infinite Sets', Duckworth.
Mayer, J.P. (1956), 'Max Weber and German Politics', Faber & Faber.
Mills, C.W. (1970), 'The Sociological Imagination', Penguin (1st pub. 1959).
Mischel, T. (1974), Concerning Rational Behaviour and Psychoanalytic Interpretation, in Wollheim (ed.).
Mitchell, J. (1974), 'Psychoanalysis and Feminism', Vintage Books, 1975.
Mullahy, P. (1955), 'Oedipus - Myth and Complex', Grove Press.
Nagel, T. (1974), Freud's Anthropomorphism, in Wollheim (ed.).
Nelson, B. (ed.) (1957), 'Freud and the 20th Century', Meridian Books.
O'Shaughnessy, B. (1974), The Id and the Thinking Process, in Wollheim (ed.).
Packard, V. (1962), 'The Hidden Persuaders', Penguin.
Parsons, T. (1950), 'Psychoanalysis and Social Structure', reprinted in 'Essays in Sociological Theory', Free Press 1954.
— (1952), 'The Super-Ego and the Theory of Social Systems', reprinted in 'Personality and Social Structure', Free Press, 1964.
— (1954), 'The Incest Taboo in Relation to Social Structure and the Socialization of the Child', reprinted in the above.
— (1955), (with R. Bales) 'Family, Socialization and Interaction Process', Free Press.
— (1958), Social Structure and the Development of Personality: Freud's Contribution to the Integration of Sociology and Psychology, reprinted in 'Personality and Social System', ed. N.J. Smelser and W.T. Smelser, John Wiley, 1970.
Pears, D. (1974), 'Freud, Sartre and Self-Deception', in Wollheim (ed.).
Reich, W. (1968), 'The Function of the Orgasm', Panther Books.
— (1970), 'The Mass Psychology of Fascism', Farrar, Straus & Giroux.
— (1972), 'Sex-Pol, Essays 1929-1934', Vintage Books.
Ricoeur, P. (1970), 'Freud and Philosophy', Yale University Press.
Rieff, P. (1959), 'Freud: The Mind of a Moralist', Doubleday.
— (ed.) (1963), 'Freud: Therapy and Technique', Collier Books.
— (1966), 'The Triumph of the Therapeutic', Chatto & Windus.

Robinson, P. (1969), 'The Freudian Left', Harper & Row.
Rosenthal, L.A., 'A Meta-Social Psychology: Some Sociological Implications of Freudian Theory', unpublished manuscript, University of California, Berkeley.
Salmon, W.C. (1974), 'Psychoanalytic Theory and Evidence', in Wollheim (ed.).
Sartre, J.-P. (1956) 'Being and Nothingness', Philosophical Library, New York.
Schmidt, A. (1971), 'The Concept of Nature in Marx', New Left Books.
Schneider, M. (1975), 'Neurosis and Civilization', The Seabury Press.
Sennett, R. (1977), 'The Fall of Public Man' (1974), Cambridge University Press.
Solomon R. C. (1974), Freud's Neurological Theory of Mind, in Wollheim (ed.).
Strauss, L. (1953) 'Natural Right and History', University of Chicago Press.
Thalberg, I. (1974), Freud's Anatomies of the Self, in Wollheim (ed.).
Therborn, G. (1970), The Frankfurt School, 'New Left Review', no. 63.
Thompson, C. (1957), 'Psychoanalysis: Evolution and Development', Grove Press.
Thompson, E.P. (1978), 'Poverty of Theory', Merlin Press.
Walker, N. (1957), A New Copernicus?, in Nelson (ed.).
Watts, A.W. (1973), 'Psychotherapy East and West' (1961), Penguin Books.
Whyte, L.L. (1962), 'The Unconscious Before Freud', Tavistock Publications.
Winter, M.F., and E.R. Robert, (1980), Male Dominance, Late Capitalism, and the Growth of Instrumental Reason, 'Berkeley Journal of Sociology', vol. XXV.
Wolfenstein, M., Fun Morality (1951), in M. Mead and M. Wolfenstein (eds), 'Childhood in Contemporary Culture', University of Chicago Press, 1955.
Wollheim, R. (1971), 'Freud', Fontana.
— (ed.) (1974), 'Freud: A Collection of Critical Essays', Anchor Books.
— (1975), Review of Mitchell's 'Feminism and Psychoanalysis', in 'New Left Review'.
Wrong, D. (1976), 'Skeptical Sociology', Heinemann, 1st edn. 1977.

Index of names

Index of subjects